Focus on GRAMMAR 3

FOURTH EDITION

 W9-ANM-368

Marjorie Fuchs
Margaret Bonner
Miriam Westheimer

ALWAYS LEARNING

PEARSON

**FOCUS ON GRAMMAR 3: An Integrated Skills Approach, Fourth Edition
Teacher's Resource Pack**

Pearson Education, 10 Bank Street, White Plains, NY 10606

Staff credits: The people who made up the ***Focus on Grammar Teacher's
Resource Pack*** team, representing editorial, production, design, and
manufacturing, are Iris Candelaria, Dave Dickey, Christine Edmonds,
Nancy Flaggman, Ann France, Shelley Gazes, Lester Holmes, Stacey
Hunter, Pamela Kohn, Theodore Lane, Christopher Leonowicz, Jennifer
McAliney, Lise Minovitz, Jennifer Raspiller, Mary Perrotta Rich, Debbie
Sistino, Ken Volcjak, Marian Wassner, and Adina Zoltan.

Contributing writers (Level 3): Carol Chapelle, Leslie Grant, Bethany Gray,
Elizabeth Henly, Joan Jamieson, Xiangying Jiang, Hsin-Min Liu, Ruth
Luman, Kathleen Smith, Raudy Lance Steele, Gabriele Steiner, Silvia
Tiberio, BJ Wells, and Kevin Zimmerman.

Cover image: Shutterstock.com
Text composition: ElectraGraphics, Inc.
Text font: New Aster

ISBN 10: 0-13-216971-1
ISBN 13: 978-0-13-216971-4

Printed in the United States of America

2 3 4 5 6 7 8 9 10—V001—16 15 14 13 12

CONTENTS

INTRODUCTION

ABOUT THE TEACHER'S RESOURCE PACK

This Teacher's Resource Pack offers a multitude of ideas for working with the material for the new edition of *Focus on Grammar 3: An Integrated Skills Approach*. The Teacher's Resource Pack includes:

- a **Teacher's Manual** (including General Teaching Notes, Unit Teaching Notes, Student Book Audioscript, and Student Book Answer Key)
- a **Teacher's Resource Disc** (including interactive PowerPoint® grammar presentations, placement test, photocopiable Unit and Part assessments, and test-generating software)

THE TEACHER'S MANUAL

The Teacher's Manual includes the following sections:

- **General Teaching Notes** (pages 1–13) provide general suggestions for teaching and assessing the activities in the Student Book. A Strategies for Teaching Grammar section offers a quick reference for some of the most common and useful grammar teaching techniques. A Frequently Asked Questions section answers some of the most common issues that teachers encounter.
- **Unit Teaching Notes** (pages 15–172) provide step-by-step instructions on how to teach each unit and supplementary "Out of the Box Activities." They also include suggestions on when to use activities and tests from **www.myfocusongrammarlab.com**, assignments from the workbook, and materials from the Teacher's Resource Disc.
- The **Student Book Audioscript** (pages 173–185) includes scripts for the Listening and Pronunciation exercises in the Student Book.
- The **Student Book Answer Key** (pages 186–227) includes answers or suggested answers for the exercises in the Student Book.

THE TEACHER'S RESOURCE DISC

The Teacher's Resource Disc includes additional teaching resources and a complete assessment program:

Teaching Resources

- **PowerPoint® Presentations** of all Grammar Charts for each unit in the Student Book offer an alternative teaching tool for introducing the grammar presentation in the classroom. For select units, animated theme-based grammar presentations provide interactive follow-up practice activities for the contextualized instruction of grammar.
- **Internet Activities** for each unit in the Student Book provide opportunities for students to expand on the content and interact with each other creatively and fluently.

Assessments

- **Placement Test** in PDF format can be printed and used to place students into the appropriate level. Along with this 40-minute test is an audioscript and an answer key in PDF format, and audio as MP3 files.
- **Part and Unit Tests** in PDF format can be printed and used in class. These include Part Pre-Tests, Part Post-Tests, and Unit Achievement Tests. Also included are assessment audioscripts and answer keys in PDF format, and audio as MP3 files.
- **Test-Generating Software** provides thousands of questions from which teachers can customize class-appropriate tests.

GENERAL TEACHING NOTES

These notes are designed to guide you in teaching and assessing the recurring sections of the Student Book. Experimenting with the various options will enliven your classroom and appeal to students' different learning styles.

In the following section and in the Unit Teaching Notes, the icon ⏱ indicates an optional step you may wish to include if time permits.

The **Part Overview** previews the grammar and themes covered in each unit.

⏱ Part Pre-Tests

Before beginning each part, you may want to have students complete a diagnostic test. There are two options.
1. You can use the provided Part Pre-Tests to help you determine how well students know the material they are about to study in the next part of the Student Book. Since the material is usually new, students often score low on these tests. Each test takes about 50 minutes and includes about 60 items. The test begins with a listening exercise, includes several contextualized grammar exercises, and ends with an editing exercise. The tests are offered in two formats:
   - automatically graded tests at **www.myfocusongrammarlab.com**
   - reproducible tests on the Teacher's Resource Disc in this manual
2. You can use the **Test-Generating Software** on the Teacher's Resource Disc to create customized part diagnostic tests of any length. The test items focus on grammar.

The **Grammar Overview** portion of the Unit Overview (offered in this Teacher's Manual) highlights the most important grammar points of each unit. It also points out common grammar trouble spots for students. You may also find it helpful to review the Grammar Charts and Grammar Notes in the Student Book before teaching each unit. The **Unit Overview** previews the unit theme.

Step 1: Grammar in Context

Each unit opens with a reading selection designed to raise students' interest and expose them to the target grammar in a realistic, natural context. The selections include newspaper and magazine excerpts, websites, advertisements, reviews, brochures, biographies, blogs, emails, and other formats that students may encounter in their day-to-day lives. All of the texts are recorded and available on the audio program or at **www.myfocusongrammarlab.com**.

Before You Read (5 minutes)
This prereading activity creates interest, elicits students' knowledge about the topic, and encourages students to make predictions about the reading.

Suggested Procedure
1. Have the class look at the illustrations.
2. Ask students to respond to the questions. Ask these questions in a conversational way, instead of reading them from the book.

Option A
- Have the class read the questions in pairs or small groups and discuss their answers.
- Call on pairs to share their ideas with the class.

Option B
- Ask students to prepare questions they have about the topic in pairs.
- Call on pairs to share their questions and write them on the board.

Read (15–20 minutes)

Depending on the needs of your class, have students complete the reading in class or at home. Encourage students to read with a purpose and to read the passage once or twice without stopping to look up new words.

Suggested Procedure

1. Write the comprehension questions from the Unit Teaching Notes on the board.
2. Play the audio and have students follow along in their books. Have them underline any new words.
3. Have students read the passage again silently, looking for answers to the questions.
4. (!) Have students discuss their answers with a partner or in small groups.
5. (!) Put students in pairs or small groups to discuss the reading. Invite them to respond to the reading in a way that is meaningful to them: What was most interesting? What did they learn? Refer to the discussion topics in the Unit Teaching Notes to help generate ideas for discussion.

Option A (At Home / In Class)

- Write the comprehension questions on the board for students to copy or prepare them as a handout for students to take home.
- Have students read the passage and answer the questions at home.
- Have students write a few additional questions about the reading.
- (!) Have students discuss their answers in pairs or small groups.
- (!) Have students take turns asking and answering the questions they prepared at home.
- Follow steps 3–5 in the Suggested Procedure for Read above.

Option B (In Class)

- Have students work in pairs. Divide the reading in half and have each student in the pair read one half.
- Have students summarize the information in their half of the reading for their partner.
- Follow steps 3–5 in the previous notes for Suggested Procedure for Read.

After You Read (10–20 minutes)

Depending on the needs of your class, have the students complete the exercises in class or at home. Following the Student Book practice, you may want your students to go to **www.myfocusongrammarlab.com** for automatically graded Vocabulary or Reading homework. The Vocabulary homework provides additional practice with the words in the Student Book; the Reading homework is on related topics.

A. Vocabulary (5 minutes)

These questions help students develop vocabulary skills by focusing on the meaning of targeted words in the opening text. The words are recycled throughout the unit.

Suggested Procedure

1. Have students find and circle the target words in the opening text.
2. Elicit or explain the meanings of any new words.
3. Have students complete the exercise individually or in pairs.
4. Call on volunteers to read their answers aloud.
5. (!) Have students record new words in a notebook or on vocabulary cards. Have them write the word, part of speech, meaning, and a sample sentence.

B. Comprehension (5 minutes)

These post-reading questions help students focus on the meaning of the opening text. In some cases, they may also focus on the target grammar without explicitly presenting the grammar point.

Suggested Procedure

1. Have students answer the questions individually.
2. Have students compare answers in pairs.
3. Call on volunteers to read their answers aloud.

Step 2: Grammar Presentation

There are many ways to teach the material in the Grammar Presentation. As a general rule, the more varied and lively the classroom activities, the more engaged students will be—and the more learning will occur. Approaching grammar from different angles and trying out different classroom management options can help increase student motivation. The Strategies for Teaching Grammar on page 10 provide some guidelines to keep in mind when presenting a new grammar point. In addition to these strategies and the procedures outlined below, you can find specific suggestions for presenting the unit's grammar in the Unit Teaching Notes.

Grammar Charts (5–10 minutes)

The Grammar Charts provide a clear reference of all the forms of the target grammar. Students also become familiar with grammatical terminology. The charts also enable you to pre-teach some of the Grammar Notes that follow. You may want to use the charts in the PowerPoint® presentations on the Teacher's Resource Disc to help direct all of your students' attention to the same focus point. Select presentations also include colorful graphics, animations, and interactive practice activities that reinforce the grammar point.

Suggested Procedure

1. Using the examples from the charts and/or the PowerPoint® presentations, draw students' attention to important features in the models by asking them questions or by pointing out the key features.
2. Confirm students' understanding by engaging them in some recognition activities. Try one or two activities from Strategies 3, 4, 5, or 6 (page 10).
3. Get students to manipulate the new structures through substitution or transformation drills. See Strategy 7 (page 10) for an example of a transformation drill.
4. Encourage students to make sentences that are personally meaningful using the new grammar.

Option A

- Have students study the Grammar Charts at home.
- In class, follow step 1 in the suggested procedure above.
- Move directly to the Grammar Notes section. Carry out steps 2, 3, and 4 in the suggested procedure above using the notes together with the charts.

Option B

- Assign individual students responsibility for presenting a topic to the class by combining the information in the charts and the relevant notes. You may want to give them large pieces of paper and markers to prepare posters.
- ⏱ Meet with students individually. Allow them to practice their presentations. Provide any coaching needed.
- Call on students to present their topics to the class. Encourage questions from the class.
- Choose appropriate practice activities from Strategies 4–8 (page 10) or move directly to the Grammar Notes section.

Grammar Notes (20–30 minutes)

These notes provide helpful information about meaning, use, and form of the grammatical structures that students have encountered in the opening text and Grammar Charts. They include the following features to help students understand and use the forms.

- Where appropriate, timelines illustrate the meaning of verb forms and their relationship to one another.
- *Be Careful!* notes alert students to common errors among English-language learners.
- Additional *Notes* provide guidelines for using and understanding different levels of formality and correctness.
- References to related structures are provided below the notes.

Suggested Procedure

1. Have students read each note at home and/or in class.
2. For each note, write examples on the board and elicit or point out the key features of the form (see Strategy 1, page 10).
3. If possible, demonstrate the meaning of the grammatical form(s) by performing actions (see Strategy 6, page 10).
4. Model the examples and have students repeat after you so that they become comfortable with the appropriate stress, intonation, and rhythm.
5. Engage students with the grammar point by choosing appropriate activities, for example:
   - Elicit examples of the target structure.
   - Confirm students' understanding by having them categorize examples or perform actions that illustrate the structure (see Strategies 5 and 6, page 10).
   - Provide controlled practice with quick substitution or transformation drills (see Strategy 7 on page 10).
   - Encourage students to make personally meaningful sentences using the new grammatical forms.
   - Use the Focused Practice exercises in the Student Book.
6. You may want to repeat steps 2–5 for each Grammar Note.

Option

- Photocopy one set of Grammar Notes for each group of three or four students in your class. Cut them up so that the notes and their corresponding examples are not attached.
- Divide the class into groups of three or four students and give a set of cut-up notes to each group.

- Give students their task:
  1. Match the examples with the correct notes.
  2. Attach the notes and corresponding examples to a sheet of newsprint (a large piece of paper).
  3. Have students create more examples for each note.
- Circulate to ensure that students are on the right track and provide help as needed.
- Have students post their results around the room and invite groups to look at each other's work.
- Regroup as a class to answer questions.

Identify the Grammar (5–10 minutes)

This optional activity helps students identify the target grammatical structures embedded in the context of the opening text. This helps students learn the form, meaning, and usage of the target grammar point and helps you make a smooth transition from the Grammar Presentation to Discover the Grammar in Focused Practice.

Step 3: Focused Practice

The exercises in this section provide practice for the structures in the Grammar Presentation. You may want to have students complete the corresponding exercise immediately after you have presented the relevant Grammar Note. Another option is for students to complete one or more of the exercises at home.

If you decide to have students complete the exercises in class, you can keep them motivated by varying the order of the exercises and/or the way you conduct them. Following are various ways of conducting the exercises.

Following the Student Book practice, you may want students to go to **www.myfocusongrammarlab.com** for automatically graded grammar homework or to the workbook for traditional grammar exercises. You may want to assign these to be completed in class or as homework.

Discover the Grammar (5–10 minutes)

This opening activity gets students to identify the target grammar structures in a realistic context. It also sometimes checks their understanding of meaning. This recognition activity raises awareness of the structures as it builds confidence.

Suggested Procedure
1. Go over the example with the class.
2. Have students complete the exercise individually or in pairs.
3. Elicit the correct answers from the class.

Controlled Practice Exercises (5–10 minutes each)

Following the Discover the Grammar activity are exercises that provide practice in a controlled but still contextualized environment. The exercises proceed from simpler to more complex and include a variety of exercise types such as fill in the blanks, matching, and multiple-choice. Students are exposed to many different written formats, including letters, electronic bulletin boards, résumés, charts, and graphs. Many exercises are art-based, providing a rich context for meaningful practice.

Options
- Have students complete the exercises in pairs.
- If the exercise is in the form of a conversation, have students practice the completed exercise in pairs and role-play it for the class.
- When going over answers with students, have them explain why each answer is correct.
- Whenever possible, relate exercises to students' lives. For example, if an exercise includes a timeline, elicit from students some important events that have happened in their own lives.

Editing (10 minutes)

All units have an editing exercise to build students' awareness of incorrect usage of the target grammar structures. Students identify and correct errors in a contextualized passage such as a student's composition, a journal entry, or an online message-board posting. The direction line indicates the number of errors in the passage.

Suggested Procedure
1. Have students read the passage quickly to understand its context and meaning.
2. Tell students to read the passage line by line, circling incorrect structures and writing in the corrections.
3. Have students take turns reading the passage line by line, saying the structures correctly. Alternatively, read the passage aloud to the class and have students interrupt you with their corrections.
4. There are also usually examples of the correct usage of the structures in each editing exercise. After students have identified the errors, point out the correct usages and ask why they are not errors.

Step 4: Communication Practice

These in-class exercises give students the opportunity to use the target structure in communicative activities. These activities help develop listening and speaking fluency and critical thinking skills, as well as provide opportunities for students to "own" the structures. As with the Focused Practice exercises, you may wish to vary the order of these activities to keep student motivation high.

Since there are many different exercise types in the Communication Practice section, specific ideas and guidelines are provided in the Unit Teaching Notes. Following are general suggestions for the three main types of exercises. (**Note:** See the FAQs on pages 11–13 for more information about setting up pair work and group work.)

Following the relevant Student Book practice, you may want your students to go to **www.myfocusongrammarlab.com** for automatically graded Listening, Pronunciation, Speaking, or Writing exercises and activities. The Pronunciation homework provides additional practice with the pronunciation feature from the Student Book; the Listening, Speaking, and Writing homework exercises and activities are on related topics.

Listening (10 minutes)

The first or second exercise in each Communication Practice section deals with listening comprehension. Students hear a variety of listening formats, including conversations, television scripts, weather forecasts, and interviews. After listening, students complete a task that focuses on the form or meaning of the target grammar structure. The recordings for the listening exercises are on the audio program and at **www.myfocusongrammarlab.com**, so students can complete the exercises outside of class.

Suggested Procedure

Before Listening

1. Explain the situation or context of the listening passage. Provide any necessary cultural information and pre-teach any vocabulary students may need to know. Since some of these words and phrases may appear in the listening, not in the exercise itself, refer to the audioscript at the back of this manual as necessary.
2. Ask students to read the exercise questions first so that they know what to listen for.

First Listening Task

1. Play the audio. Have students listen with their pencils down.
2. Play the audio again. Have students listen and complete the task.
3. You may want to let students listen as many times as necessary to complete the task.

Second Listening Task

1. See steps 2–3 from the first listening task for general instructions.
2. Have students compare their answers in pairs or small groups.

After Listening

1. Elicit answers for the exercise items and write them on the board. Answer any questions the students may have.
2. ⏱ Students listen a final time and review the passage.

Option A

- Rather than play the audio, read the audioscript aloud.
- Speak with a lot of expression and at a natural pace. Change positions and tone of voice to indicate who the speaker is.
- Draw stick figures on the board and label them with the characters' names. Then point to the appropriate character as you change roles.

Option B

- Make photocopies of the audioscript and hand it out to students.
- Play the audio recording and have students read along with it in chorus. Explain that this exercise will help them to hear and practice the rhythms, stresses, and clusters of English sounds.

Option C

Have students listen and complete the exercise at home or in a language lab.

Pronunciation (10 minutes)

The first or second exercise in each Communication Practice section deals with pronunciation. The pronunciation exercise generally focuses on the grammar presented in the unit or a difficult sound that appears in the opening text. It also prepares students for the speaking activities that follow. The recordings for the pronunciation exercises are on the audio program and at **www.myfocusongrammarlab.com**, so students can practice the exercises outside of class.

Suggested Procedure

First Task

1. Go over the instructions and point out the Pronunciation Note.
2. Play the audio.

Second Task

1. Play the audio. Have students close their eyes and notice the pronunciation feature.
2. ⏱ Play the audio again. Have students listen again and follow along in their books.

Third Task

1. Play the audio again.
2. Have students repeat in pairs or small groups. Circulate and monitor their pronunciation.
3. ⏱ Call on volunteers to practice in front of the class.

Information Gaps (10–20 minutes)

Information Gaps are designed to encourage communication between students. In these activities, each student has a different set of information. Students have to talk to their partners to solve a puzzle, draw a picture (describe and draw), put things in the right order (describe and arrange), or find similarities and differences between pictures.

Advantages of Information Gaps

- Information Gaps are motivating and fun.
- There is a real need for communication in order to combine the information to solve a problem and complete the task.
- Information sharing allows students to extend and personalize what they have learned in the unit.

Suggested Procedure

1. Explain how the Student A and Student B pages relate to each other (how they are different or similar).
2. Refer students to the examples and to any language provided.
3. Divide the class into pairs (Student A and Student B). Have them position themselves so that they cannot see the contents of each other's books.
4. Tell the Student Bs what page to turn to. Circulate to check that they are looking at the correct page.
5. Have students read their separate instructions. Check comprehension of the task by asking each group, "What are you going to do?"
6. Remind students not to show each other the contents of their pages.

7. As students are working, circulate to answer individual questions and to help students with the activity.

Games (10–20 minutes)

Games are designed to encourage communication among students. In these activities, students compete in pairs or small groups to complete a task such as guessing something or winning points.

Advantages of Games

- They can create a fun and stress-free environment.
- They involve friendly competition and keep students engaged.
- They can improve students' ability to speak in a communicative way.

Suggested Procedure

1. Go over the instructions to make sure students understand the task.
2. Have students model the example or provide one of your own.
3. Have students carry out the instructions. Circulate and help as needed.
4. Go over answers as a class or ask who won.
5. ⏱ Write on the board any sentences you noticed using incorrect grammar. Have the students correct them as a class.

Role Plays / Interviews (10–20 minutes)

In these classroom speaking activities, students role-play a real-life encounter, such as a business meeting or an interview.

Advantages of Role Plays / Interviews

- They are fun and motivating for most students.
- Role-playing characters often allows the more hesitant students to be more outgoing than if they are speaking as themselves.
- Interviews can help students build confidence in their ability to ask and answer extemporaneous questions.
- By broadening the world of the classroom to the world outside, role playing allows students to use a wider range of language than less open-ended activities.

Suggested Procedure

1. When possible, bring in props or costumes to add drama and fun.
2. Review the task so students understand what is required.
3. Perform a sample role play with a volunteer in front of the class.
4. Divide the class into the suggested groupings and give them a fixed time limit for completing the task.

5. Have students write a script for the role play. Then have them write key words on cards and perform the role play using the cards as prompts. (OR: Have students plan the action without a script and present it extemporaneously.)
6. While students are working, circulate among the pairs or groups to answer students' questions and help them with the activity.
7. Have various pairs or groups perform their role plays in front of the class. If possible, record the role plays for students' own listening or viewing.

Discussions (10–20 minutes)
In these classroom speaking activities, students express their ideas about a variety of topics. These activities include Quotable Quotes, Problem Solving, Picture Discussion, Cross-Cultural Comparison, Reaching Agreement, For and Against, and Compare and Contrast.

Advantages of Discussions
- They help students move from speaking accuracy to speaking fluency.
- They help students develop critical thinking skills as they explore the pros and cons of a given topic.
- They help students build confidence in their ability to express opinions on a variety of topics.

Suggested Procedure
1. Go over the instructions so that students understand the task.
2. Elicit or present useful language and write it on the board.
3. Have two or three students model the example discussion.
4. Divide the class into the suggested groupings and give them a fixed time limit for completing the task.
5. Circulate while the students discuss the topic. Help with language or monitor their grammar as needed.
6. Ask volunteers from each group to summarize the discussion or conclusions.
7. ⏱ Write on the board any sentences you noticed using incorrect grammar. Have the students correct them as a class.

Writing (15–25 minutes)
These activities give students the opportunity to develop their writing skills and provide additional practice using the target grammatical structures. There are a variety of realistic formats, including paragraphs, essays, emails, worksheets, fact sheets, and advertisements. The themes are related to material covered in the unit so that students already have some preparation for the writing task.

Suggested Procedure
Prewriting (in class)
1. Go over the instructions with the class.
2. Brainstorm ideas for the assignment with the class and write them on the board.
3. Encourage students to include grammar and vocabulary from the unit in their assignment.

Writing and Editing (at home)
1. Have students compose a draft of the writing assignment at home.
2. Have students use the Editing Checklist to correct their work.

Wrap-Up (in class)
1. Have students submit the draft to you or share it with a partner in class.
2. Give students a score on the draft. You can comment on the following features:
   - Content: Has the student responded appropriately to the task? Are the main points well supported?
   - Organization: Is the flow of ideas logical and effective?
   - Accuracy: Are there any major errors in the grammar points taught in the unit?
3. ⏱ Depending on your class's needs, you may want to have students complete a second draft at home. When you check these drafts, point out any further areas needing correction, concentrating especially on errors in the target grammar point or grammar points from a previous unit.

Option A

Have students share their final drafts in class. For example:

- Post students' work on the class bulletin board.
- Publish their work on a website or in a class magazine.
- Have students exchange papers with a partner.
- Have students read their papers aloud in small groups or to the class.

Option B

Have students put the final drafts of their written work in a folder, or portfolio, that you can review at the end of the course. This will allow your students and you to see the progress they have made.

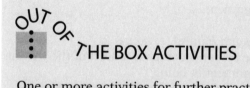

One or more activities for further practice (in the Teacher's Manual only) can be found at the end of every unit in the Unit Teaching Notes. These exercises offer additional communicative practice with the target structure of the unit. Many can be done in class with no before-class preparation. The activities often involve a combination of skills, such as grammar and speaking or grammar and writing.

Unit Review

The last section of each unit of the Student Book is a review feature that can be used as a self-test. These exercises test the form and use of the grammar content presented and practiced in that unit. They give students a chance to check their knowledge and to review any problematic areas before moving on to the next part. An answer key is provided at the back of the Student Book.

Suggested Procedure

1. Have students complete the exercises at home and check their answers in the Answer Key.
2. During the next class, go over any remaining questions students may have.

Option

- Have students complete the exercises in class. Give them a time limit of 10 minutes and circulate as they work.
- Have students use the Answer Key to check and correct their answers in pairs. Or you can go over the answers as a class.

Unit Achievement Tests

After the Unit Review, you may want to have students complete an achievement test. There are two assessment options.

1. You can use the provided **Unit Achievement Tests** to help you assess students' knowledge of the specific grammatical topics presented in the unit. If students have mastered the material presented in the unit, they should answer most of the questions correctly. Each test takes about 30 minutes and includes about 30 items. The test begins with a listening exercise, includes two or three contextualized grammar exercises, and ends with an editing exercise. The tests are offered in two formats:
   - automatically graded tests at **www.myfocusongrammarlab.com**
   - reproducible tests on the Teacher's Resource Disc in this manual
2. You can use the **Test-Generating Software** on the Teacher's Resource Disc to create customized unit achievement tests of any length. The test items focus on grammar.

Part Post-Tests

At the end of each part, you may want to have students complete an achievement test. There are three assessment options.

1. You can have students go to **www.myfocusongrammarlab.com** for an automatically graded review. Students can complete the review on a computer in class, at home, or in a language lab. Each review takes about 25 minutes and includes about 30 items. The test focuses on grammar.
2. You can have students take the provided **Part Post-Tests** to help you determine how well they have mastered the material they have studied in that part of the Student Book. If students have mastered the material presented in the part, they should answer most of the questions correctly. Each test takes 50 minutes and includes about 60 items. The tests begin with a listening exercise, include several contextualized grammar exercises, and end with an editing exercise. The tests are offered in two formats:
   - automatically graded tests at **www.myfocusongrammarlab.com**
   - reproducible tests on the Teacher's Resource Disc in this manual
3. You can also use the **Test-Generating Software** on the Teacher's Resource Disc to create customized part achievement tests of any length. The test items focus on grammar.

From Grammar to Writing

The From Grammar to Writing section at the end of each part of the Student Book integrates grammar presented in the units. It also goes beyond the grammar in the units and gives additional information about writing in English. This information may include cohesion (e.g., compound sentences, time clauses), coherence (e.g., pronouns), format (e.g., emails, personal statements), and exemplification (e.g., giving examples). Following these exercises, students practice prewriting strategies. These strategies may include the use of graphic organizers, such as charts, cluster diagrams, timelines, notes, and outlines. Finally, students apply the teaching point in a writing task. Text types include both formal and informal writing, such as notes, emails, and stories. The section concludes with peer review and editing.

Depending on your class's needs, you may want to have students go to an additional From Grammar to Writing exercise at **www.myfocusongrammarlab.com**.

Suggested Procedure

Prewriting
1. Have students complete the controlled practice exercises individually. Then have them exchange books and compare answers.
2. Go over the answers as a class and answer any questions.
3. Explain the prewriting task. Where appropriate, provide a model for students on the board or on an overhead.
4. Have students complete the prewriting task in pairs or small groups. Circulate and answer any questions.

Composing and Correcting
1. Go over the instructions to make sure students understand the task.
2. Have students complete the writing assignment at home.
3. In class, complete the peer review portion of the task. Circulate while students are working together to make sure they are on task and to provide appropriate feedback. (See Suggested Procedure for Writing on page 7 for examples.)
4. ⏱ Have students revise their writing and turn in the second draft to you.

Option
- Have students complete the controlled practice exercise(s) at home.
- In class, have students compare answers in pairs.
- Follow the suggested procedure for steps 3 and 4 in the prewriting phase.

STRATEGIES FOR TEACHING GRAMMAR

1. Develop awareness
- Ask questions that help students become aware of the form of the structure. For example, for *can* to talk about ability (Student Book, page 178), read the affirmative statements, "I can dance now; she can dance now," and ask: "How do you form affirmative statements with *can*?" (can + *base form of verb*) Ask students what *base form* means. *(the simple form without an ending)* Then ask: "Does *can* change when the pronoun changes?" *(no)* Point out that *can* is a modal and it is the same for all pronouns.
- Compare information in the Grammar Charts. For example, for the simple past (Student Book, pages 18–19) there are Grammar Charts for the past of *be* and for other verbs. Ask: "How many forms are there for the simple past of *be*?" *(two: was and were)* "How do you form the negative with *be* in the simple past?" *(wasn't, weren't)* "How many forms are there for the negative with other verbs?" *(one: didn't + base form)* Ask: "Do you use the base form for past *yes/no* questions with *be*?" *(no)* "Do you use the base form for past *yes/no* questions with other verbs?" *(yes)*

2. Present meaning
Show the meaning of a grammatical form through a classroom demonstration. For example, to illustrate the use of present perfect progressive, you could show a picture of a person carrying grocery bags full of food. *(He/She has been shopping.)*

3. Identify examples
Ask students to go back to the Grammar in Context section and label examples in the reading passage with the grammatical terms in the Grammar Charts.

4. Generate examples
Find examples from the reading or elsewhere that could fit into the Grammar Charts. An interesting way to do this is to photocopy and enlarge the Grammar Chart. White out the targeted structures and draw a blank line for each missing word. Make copies and distribute them to students in pairs or small groups. Have students fill in the blanks, using examples from the reading. Then generate more examples. Books can be open or closed, depending on the level of challenge desired.

5. Show understanding by categorizing
Check comprehension of a grammatical principle by asking students to label multiple examples appropriately. For example, students can label verbs "present" or "future," or they can label examples "correct" or "incorrect."

6. Show understanding by performing actions
Ask students to show their understanding of the meaning of a grammatical form by following instructions or devising a demonstration. Ask students, for example, to think of and perform a set of actions that they could describe using the present progressive.

7. Manipulate forms
Have students manipulate the examples in the Grammar Charts to practice the form. Drills such as substitution or transformation help students to build fluency. For example, in Unit 6 (Student Book, page 76) you might put one form on the board *(He is going to leave soon.)* and then elicit other forms by saying, "Negative" *(He isn't going to leave soon.)*, "Yes/no question" *(Is he going to leave soon?)*, "Short answer, affirmative" *(Yes, he is.)*, "Wh- question, when" *(When is he going to leave?)*, and so on to get students to produce the other forms rapidly.

8. Personalize
Ask students to provide personal examples. For example, on page 358 of the Student Book, students see the example, "Eva enjoys going to the park. Eva wants to go to the park." Ask students what they enjoy or want to do. *(I enjoy playing soccer. I want to join a soccer team.)*

9. Repeat, reinforce
Students need to be exposed to new grammar many times in order to internalize it completely. You can first present a new structure on the board, then point it out in the book, then have students use it in an informal oral exercise, then do a written exercise in pairs, and finally review the same structure in homework. Varying the content and focus of these activities will keep students interested, and the grammar will be reinforced almost automatically.

FREQUENTLY ASKED QUESTIONS (FAQs)

1. When should I have students work in pairs or groups rather than individually or as a whole class?

Varying your classroom organization to suit particular activity types will result in more effective and more interesting classes. Many students are not accustomed to working in pairs or groups, so it is important to use these groupings only when they are most beneficial.

- **Whole-class teaching** maximizes teacher control and is especially good for:
  — presenting information, giving explanations, and providing instructions
  — showing material in texts and pictures or on audio or video recordings
  — teacher-led drills (such as substitution or transformation) or dictations
  — reviewing answers or sharing ideas after students have completed an activity
  — enabling the whole class to benefit from teacher feedback to individuals

- **Students working individually** allows quiet, concentrated attention and is most effective for:
  — processing information or completing a task at students' own pace
  — performing writing tasks

For objective exercises such as fill-in-the-blank, matching, multiple-choice, and editing, vary your class organization to keep student motivation high. Students can sometimes complete these exercises individually, and sometimes they can work with a partner.

- **Students working in pairs** maximizes student speaking time, breaks up the routine and "teacher talk," and is ideal for:
  — information-gap activities
  — role plays
  — writing and/or reading dialogues
  — predicting the content of reading and listening texts
  — comparing notes on what students listen to or see
  — checking answers
  — peer assessment

Pair work can also be very effective for completing objective exercises such as fill-in-the-blank, matching, multiple-choice, and editing.

- **Students working in groups** creates ideal conditions for students to learn from each other and works well for:
  — generating ideas
  — pooling knowledge
  — writing group stories
  — preparing presentations
  — discussing an issue and reaching a group decision

2. How should I set up pair work and group work?

Here are a few different techniques:

- **Streaming.** Grouping students according to ability or participation has certain advantages.
  — **ability:** Grouping weaker and stronger students together allows more able students to help their less fluent classmates.
  — **participation:** If you see that some students participate less than others, you could make a pair or group of weak participators. By the same token, you can also put especially talkative students together.

- **Chance.** Grouping students by chance has many benefits, especially if it results in students working with varied partners. You can group students by chance according to:
  — **where they sit:** Students sitting next to or near one another work in pairs or groups. This is the easiest option, but if students always sit in the same place, you will want to find other ways of grouping them.
  — **the "wheels" system:** Half the class stands in a circle facing outward, and the other half stands in an outer circle facing inward. The outer circle revolves in a clockwise direction, and the inner circle revolves in a counterclockwise direction. When you tell them to stop, students work with the person facing them. This is an effective way to have students engage in meaningful repetition, such as asking the same question of many different partners.
  — **assigned letters:** Assign each student a letter from A to E. Then ask all the As to form a group, all the Bs to form a group, and so on.

— **birthdays:** Students stand in a line in the order of their birthdays (with January at one end and December at the other). The first five students form one group, the second five students another group, and so on.

— **native language:** If possible, put students in groups or pairs with others who don't share a native language. This helps create an "English-only" classroom.

3. How can I make activities more successful?
Before the activity:

• **Motivate students and explain the purpose.** Make it clear that something enjoyable or interesting is going to happen. Explain the rationale for the activity. Make sure students understand that the purpose of the activity is to help them practice what they learned and encourage them to participate.

• **Provide clear directions.** Explain what students should do in every step of the activity. Have students paraphrase or demonstrate the task to be sure they understand it.

• **Demonstrate.** Show the class what is supposed to happen in an activity. This might involve asking a student to demonstrate the activity with you or having two students role-play at the front of the room.

• **Provide a time frame.** It is helpful for students to know how much time they have and exactly when they should stop. Approximate times are given for all the activities in this Teacher's Manual.

For open-ended activities, such as the writing exercises, you will also want to:

• **Stimulate thinking.** When there are choices for students to make, it is often helpful to set up small-group and/or whole-class brainstorming sessions to define the focus and/or content of their task.

• **Prepare language.** Review grammar and vocabulary that students may need to complete the task. This can be done as a follow-up to a brainstorming activity where you elicit ideas and write key language on the board.

During the activity:

• **Observe students.** Walk around the room watching and listening to pairs or groups.

• **Provide assistance as needed.** (See FAQ 5 for suggestions on giving feedback and correcting errors.)

After the activity:

• **Elicit student responses.** For some activities, you may ask for volunteers or call on students to share some of their ideas with the class. For other types of activities, a few pairs or groups can be asked to role-play their discussions to demonstrate the language they have been using.

• **Provide feedback.** In many cases, this is most conveniently done in a whole-class setting. It may be preferable, however, for you to meet with individuals, pairs, or groups. While the principal focus in a grammar class is language use, it is also important to acknowledge the value of students' ideas. See FAQ 5 for suggestions on feedback and error correction.

4. What can I do to encourage students to use more English in the classroom?
It is perfectly natural for students to feel the need to use their first language in an English class. There are a number of actions that teachers can take to promote the use of English.

• **Set clear guidelines.** Some teachers in monolingual classes find that activities such as providing vocabulary definitions, presenting a grammar point, checking comprehension, giving instructions, and discussing classroom methodology are best done in the students' native language.

• **Use persuasion.** Walking among the students during speaking activities and saying things such as "Please speak English!" or "Try to use English as much as possible" helps to ensure that students will speak English most of the time.

5. What's the best approach to giving feedback and correcting errors?
Here are two considerations:

• **Be selective in offering correction.** Students can't focus on everything at once, so concentrate first on errors relating to the target grammar point and grammar points from units previously studied, as well as any errors that interfere with communication. Whether you respond to other errors depends on your judgment of students' readiness to take in the information. If you see a teachable moment, seize it. Rather than correct every error individual students make in the course of activities, it is generally preferable to note commonly occurring mistakes and give a short presentation for the whole class at the end of the activity.

- **Recasting.** If a student makes an error, for example, "I *didn't came* to class yesterday because I was sick," you can recast it as, "You *didn't come* to class yesterday because you were sick?" The student ideally notices the difference and restates the original sentence: "Right. I didn't come to class yesterday because I was sick." This process can be effective because the student has the opportunity to self-correct an error that is still in short-term memory. As a variation, you can restate but stop, with rising intonation, right before the potential error: "You didn't . . . ?"

6. What can I do to accommodate different learning styles?

Focus on Grammar recognizes different styles of learning and provides a variety of activities to accommodate these different styles. Some learners prefer an analytical, or rule-learning (deductive), approach. Others, especially younger learners, respond best to an inductive approach, or exposure to the language in meaningful contexts. Indeed, the same students may adopt different styles as they learn, or they may use different styles at different times.

As teachers, we want to help the students in our classes who prefer to follow rules become more able to take risks and to plunge into communicative activities. We also want to encourage the risk-takers to focus on accuracy. *Focus on Grammar* provides the variety to ensure that students achieve their goal: to learn to use the language confidently and appropriately.

UNIT TEACHING NOTES

PART I OVERVIEW

PRESENT AND PAST

UNIT	GRAMMAR FOCUS	THEME
1	Present Progressive and Simple Present	Different Cultures
2	Simple Past	Poets
3	Past Progressive and Simple Past	Accidents
4	*Used to* and *Would*	Memories
5	*Wh-* Questions	In Court

Go to **www.myfocusongrammarlab.com** for the Part and Unit Tests.

Note: PowerPoint® grammar presentations, test-generating software, and reproducible Part and Unit Tests are on the *Teacher's Resource Disc*.

UNIT 1 OVERVIEW

Grammar: PRESENT PROGRESSIVE AND SIMPLE PRESENT

Unit 1 focuses on the meanings and uses of the present progressive and the simple present and on the similarities and differences between them.

- The present progressive describes an action that is happening right now or in the extended present time.
- The simple present describes an action that happens regularly.

Theme: DIFFERENT CULTURES

Unit 1 focuses on language that describes cultural differences and temporary changes to routines.

A cross-cultural IQ measures how much a person knows about other cultures and his/her ability to recognize and accurately interpret cross-cultural misunderstandings.

Step 1: Grammar in Context (pages 2–3)

See the general suggestions for Grammar in Context on page 1.

Before You Read

- Have students look at the pictures and read the text in the bubbles.

- Have students discuss the questions in pairs. Then call on pairs to share their answers.
- ⏱ Ask: "Why do you think the people feel uncomfortable/embarrassed/confused?" (*because they don't belong to the same culture and their customs are different*)

Read

- To encourage students to read with a purpose, write these questions on the board:
  1. Why is Dan wearing shorts and a T-shirt? (*because he is not expecting people to arrive early*)
  2. Why is Jason standing at Dan's door? (*because he thinks the party starts at 8:00 sharp*)
  3. Why is Marty standing so close to Ina? (*because in her culture people stand quite close*)
  4. Why is Ina moving away from Marty? (*because in her culture people don't stand so close*)
- Have students read the text. (OR: Play the audio and have students follow along in their books.) Then call on students to share their answers to the questions on the board.
- To get students to share their ideas on the reading, have them discuss the following questions in pairs or small groups. Write the questions on the board if necessary.
  1. Is it important to learn about other cultures before traveling abroad? Why or why not?
  2. What other cultural differences do you know about that can cause misunderstandings?
  3. How do you think the people in the cartoons could resolve their misunderstandings?

After You Read

A. Vocabulary
- Have students complete the exercise individually. Encourage them to use context clues to help.
- Have students compare answers in pairs. Then call on pairs to give answers.

B. Comprehension
- Have students complete the exercise individually.
- Have students compare answers in pairs. Then call on pairs to give answers.

Go to **www.myfocusongrammarlab.com** for an additional reading, and for reading and vocabulary practice.

Step 2: Grammar Presentation (pages 4–6)

See the general suggestions for Grammar Presentation on page 2.

Grammar Charts

- To compare the present progressive and simple present, write two sets of contrasting sentences on the board:

Present Progressive | Simple Present
They <u>are visiting</u> their friends now. | They <u>visit</u> their friends every day.
She <u>is wearing</u> jeans. | She always <u>wears</u> jeans.

  — Point to the examples of the present progressive. Ask: "How many words are in the present progressive?" *(two)* "How do you form the present progressive?" *(form of be + -ing form of verb)*
  — Point to the examples of the simple present. Ask: "How many words are in the simple present?" *(one)* "How do you form the simple present?" *(base form of verb OR base form of verb + s)*
  — Point out that some verbs form the simple present by adding *-es*. Write on the board: kiss → kiss<u>es</u>   watch → watch<u>es</u>

- To explain negative present progressive statements, write these examples on the board:
They <u>are not feeling</u> comfortable.   People <u>do not arrive</u> at a party on time.

  — Ask: "How do you form the negative present progressive?" *(form of be + not + -ing form of verb)* "How do you form the negative simple present?" *(form of do + not + base form of verb)*
  — Write an example with *does not* on the board:
Marty <u>does not stand</u> too close to people.

- To explain contractions, restate the examples using negative forms. Say: "They <u>aren't</u> feeling comfortable. People <u>don't</u> arrive at a party on time. Marty <u>doesn't</u> stand too close to people."
  — Point to the first set of examples under Present Progressive on the board. Have a student make them negative, using contractions. *(aren't visiting / isn't wearing)*
  — Point to the first set of examples under Simple Present on the board. Have a student make them negative, using contractions. *(don't visit / doesn't always wear)*

- To explain *yes/no* questions and short answers, write on the board:
Is Dan giving a party?   Do people arrive early?
  — Ask: "How do you form *yes/no* questions in the present progressive?" *(form of be + subject + -ing form of verb)* "How do you form *yes/no* questions in the simple present?" *(form of do + subject + base form of verb)*
  — Have students provide affirmative and negative short answers for each question that is on the board. *(Yes, he is. / No, he isn't. Yes, they do. / No, they don't.)*

- To explain *wh-* questions, write on the board:
What is Jason doing?   What do people do in Marty's culture?
  — Ask: "How do you form *wh-* questions in the present progressive?" *(wh- word + form of be + subject + -ing form of verb)* "How do you form *wh-* questions in the simple present?" *(wh- word + form of do + subject + base form of verb)*

Grammar Notes

Note 1

- To explain the use of the present progressive to describe what is happening right now, stand up and say: "Right now I'm standing." Then ask a student: "What about you? Are you sitting or standing?"
- To explain the use of the present progressive to describe what is happening in a longer present time, write two contrasting sentences on the board:
Oliver is getting up early this week.   Oliver gets up early.
- Ask: "Which sentence expresses a routine—what Oliver always does?" *(Oliver gets up early.)* "Which sentence expresses a change in routine—what Oliver is doing these days?" *(Oliver is getting up early this week.)*
- If needed, refer students to Appendix 21 on page A-10 for spelling rules for the present progressive.

Note 2

- To review the simple present to describe what regularly happens, ask students to say what they—or the people in their family—usually do after school or work in the evening. *(Example: I watch TV. My sister walks the dog. My mother prepares dinner.)*
- If needed, refer students to Appendix 20 on page A-9 for spelling rules on forming the third-person singular of the simple present and Appendix 29 on page A-14 for pronunciation rules for the simple present.

Note 3

- To provide practice with simple present and adverbs of frequency to express how often something happens, write on the board:
  How often do you . . . ?

go to a movie	play sports
eat out	give parties
watch TV	other: _____

  How often are you . . . ?

late to school/work	late to parties

- Have students think of their own ideas for the last item on the first list. Have pairs take turns asking and answering the questions on the board. Have students use frequency adverbs in their answers.
- Draw attention to the *Be Careful!* note. To check comprehension, write on the board:
  I feel tired.   I am tired.
- Have a student come to the front and rewrite the sentences, inserting the adverb *always* in each:
  I always feel tired.   I am always tired.

Note 4

- To review simple present with action and non-action verbs, write on the board in two columns as shown:
  exercise   want
  buy   like
- Ask: "Which verbs express actions?" (exercise *and* buy) "Which verbs express states or situations?" (want *and* like) Point out that non-action verbs are not usually used in the present progressive.
- Write two examples on the board:
  Steve is <u>exercising</u> because he <u>wants</u> to lose weight.
  Maria <u>is buying</u> a CD because she <u>likes</u> music.
- Point out that although both the actions (*exercise* and *buy*) and the states (*want* and *like*) exist at the moment of speaking, only the action verbs (*exercise* and *buy*) are used in the present progressive.
- If needed, refer students to Appendix 2 on page A-2 for a list of non-action verbs.

Note 5

- To check comprehension, write two contrasting examples on the board:
  The food <u>smells</u>   She <u>is smelling</u>
    nice.   the roses.
- Ask: "What does *smells* mean in the first sentence?" (*has a particular smell*) "What does *is smelling* mean in the second sentence?" (*is putting her nose near the roses to discover what type of smell they have*)

- Write on the board:
  Sharon is in Florida. She has/is having a new apartment there. She has/is having a great time.
- Have students choose the correct form of *have* in each case. (*has; is having*)

🕐 **Identify the Grammar:** Have students identify the grammar in the opening reading on page 2. For example:
  Jason **is standing** at Dan's door.
  He **thinks** he's on time for the party . . .
  . . . he **doesn't see** any guests . . .

Go to **www.myfocusongrammarlab.com** for grammar charts and notes.

Step 3: Focused Practice (pages 7–11)

See the general suggestions for Focused Practice on page 4.

Exercise 1: Discover the Grammar
- Go over the example with the class. Ask: "What does *I'm sitting* describe—what is happening now or what regularly happens?" (*what is happening now*) "What does *have* in *have dinner* describe?" (*what usually happens*)
- Have students complete the exercise individually.
- Call on students to give answers.

Exercise 2: Present Progressive or Simple Present
- Go over the example with the class. Ask: "Why is *'s talking* the correct answer?" (*because the person is talking about what is happening now*)
- Have students complete the exercise in pairs and then role-play the conversations.
- Call on two pairs to read the conversations aloud.

Exercise 3: Questions and Statements
- Go over the example with the class.
- Have students complete the exercise individually and then compare answers in pairs.
- Call on two pairs to read the conversations aloud.

Exercise 4: Affirmative and Negative Statements
- Go over the example with the class. Be sure students understand that the second column lists the activities Brian normally does and the third column lists changes in his routine, that is, special activities he is doing today.
- Have students complete the exercise individually. Then call on students to give answers.

- 🕐 Call on students to share any of their regular activities that are different today. (Example: *I usually teach in the morning, but today I'm teaching in the afternoon.*)

Exercise 5: Present Progressive or Simple Present

- Go over the example with the class. Have students say why *make* is the correct answer. *(because new food, customs, and routines always make travel interesting, not just today)*
- If needed, clarify the meaning of *honeymoon* (a vacation taken by two people who have just gotten married), *rejection* (the act of not accepting something), *adjustment* (a change in the way you behave or think), and *adaptation* (the process of changing something so that it can be used in a different way or in different conditions).
- Have students complete the exercise individually. Then call on students to give answers.

Exercise 6: Affirmative and Negative Statements

- Go over the example with the class. Point out that the statements are part of a quiz to be taken by people who are living in a country that is not their own.
- Have students complete the exercise individually. Then call on students to give answers.
- Have students who are living in a culture that is not their own take the quiz, check their results, and then share them with the class.

Exercise 7: Editing

- Have students read the journal quickly to find out what it is about. Ask: "What city is the student in?" *(Toronto)* "Is the student in his/her own culture?" *(no)* "What does he/she miss?" *(speaking his/her language with friends and his/her old routine)*
- Go over the example with the class.
- Have students find and correct the mistakes individually. Then call on students to explain why the incorrect structures are wrong.
- 🕐 Have students point out examples of correct usage of the simple present and the present progressive.

Go to **www.myfocusongrammarlab.com** for additional grammar practice.

Step 4: Communication Practice (pages 11–14)

See the general suggestions for Communication Practice on page 5.

Exercise 8: Listening

A
- Have students try to complete the sentences individually.
- Play the audio and have students listen and check their answers. If necessary, stop the recording after each answer is given to allow students time to confirm/correct their answers.

B
- Have students listen again and complete the exercise.
- Have students make complete sentences using the simple present or the present progressive, as appropriate. *(She is speaking English right now. She usually speaks Spanish.)*

Exercise 9: Pronunciation

A
- Play the audio. Have students read along as they listen to the Pronunciation Note.

B
- Play the audio. Have students listen and repeat the questions. Be sure students pronounce both types of questions using *Whaddya*.

C
- Have pairs take turns reading and answering the questions in Part B.

Exercise 10: Find Someone Who . . .

A
- Go over the example with the class. As a class (before students walk around the classroom) elicit a question for each item. (Example: *Do you like visiting foreign countries? Do you speak more than two languages? Are you studying something in addition to English? Do you watch sports on TV? Are you planning to travel abroad this year?*)
- Have students write their own questions.
- Have students write notes as they interview their classmates. Encourage them to ask follow-up questions.

B
- 🕐 Have students use their notes to report back to the class something interesting they learned about a classmate.

Exercise 11: Picture Discussion

- To help students generate ideas, write the following questions on the board:
  Where are the people?
  Who are they talking to?
  What are they saying?
- Encourage students to use their imagination.
- Go over the example. Point out that *looks* is used to express what the man seems to be doing. Point out that *maybe* is used to express possibility. Write some useful language on the board for students:

He/She	looks . . . seems . . . appears to be . . .	Maybe Perhaps	he/she is . . .

- Call on students to express their opinion of what the people in the photographs are doing.

Exercise 12: Compare and Contrast

A

- Have students write *Yes* in front of appropriate questions and *No* in front of questions that they think are not appropriate to ask someone they just met. Have them write notes explaining why some of the questions are inappropriate.
- Encourage students to use their notes as they discuss in groups.

B

- Have students write one or two inappropriate questions individually and then discuss them in groups.
- To review, call on students to express their views about two of the questions from Part A.

Exercise 13: Writing

A

- Write these questions on the board to elicit vocabulary and help generate ideas:
  What new experience are you having this week/month/year?
  How is this experience different from what you usually do?
  How do you feel?
- Have students make notes for each question and then use them as a guide as they write.
  Note: If some students find it difficult to come up with personal new experiences, have them write about the new experience(s) of someone they know.

B

- Have students correct their work using the Editing Checklist.

OUT OF THE BOX ACTIVITIES

Writing and Speaking

- Have students work in pairs to write a short description (30 to 60 words) of what people usually do in a city or country of their choice. If the people in the chosen place are doing something special at this time of the year, students should include this information as well. Encourage them to use the simple present to describe what the people usually do and the present progressive to describe what the people are doing right now (or in the extended present time).
- Have pairs read their description aloud to another pair. The other pair should guess the place. (Example: *In this city, the people like music and dancing. They go to its wonderful beaches during the day and go out to restaurants and discos at night. At this time of the year, they are preparing spectacular costumes and parades.* [Rio de Janeiro, Brazil])

Reading and Speaking

- Form small groups and give each group a newspaper. Each group member should get a page of the newspaper.
- Give students three to four minutes to skim through the newspaper page they have.
- Have students use the present progressive (current events) and the simple present (habitual actions), as appropriate, to tell each other about the news they read. (Example: *In France, the police are looking for a man who robbed a bank just before closing time. In France, banks close at . . .*)

Go to **www.myfocusongrammarlab.com** for additional listening, pronunciation, speaking, and writing practice.

Note:
- See the *Focus on Grammar Workbook* for additional in-class or homework grammar practice.

Unit 1 Review (page 15)

Have students complete the Review and check their answers on Student Book page UR-1. Review or assign additional material as needed.

Go to **www.myfocusongrammarlab.com** for the Unit Achievement Test.

UNIT 2 OVERVIEW

Grammar: SIMPLE PAST

Unit 2 focuses on the meanings and uses of the simple past. It covers the simple past of *be* and regular and irregular verbs.

- The simple past describes finished actions, states, or situations.
- It can be used with time expressions that refer to the past.

Theme: POETS

Unit 2 focuses on famous poets, such as Matsuo Basho, Emily Dickinson, and Ana Castillo, and on important events in their lives.

Haiku is a traditional form of Japanese poetry, popular since the 17th century. It is a three-line poem of usually seventeen syllables in lines of five, seven, and five syllables each. It traditionally focuses on images of the natural world.

Step 1: Grammar in Context (pages 16–17)

See the general suggestions for Grammar in Context on page 1.

Before You Read

- Have students look at the picture and read the text above the picture.
- Have students discuss the questions in pairs. Then call on pairs to share their answers.

Read

- To encourage students to read with a purpose, write these questions on the board:
  1. Why was Basho famous? *(for the haiku/ three-line poems he wrote)*
  2. What other important things did he do? *(He taught poetry and traveled all over Japan.)*
- Have students read the text. (OR: Play the audio and have students follow along in their books.) Then call on students to share their answers to the questions on the board.
- To get students to share their ideas on the reading, have them discuss the following questions in pairs or small groups. Write the questions on the board if necessary.

1. Do you like the poem? Is it effective? Is it fun? Why?
2. Why do you think Basho's poems made him famous?

After You Read

A. Vocabulary

- Have students complete the exercise individually. Encourage them to use context clues to help.
- Have students compare answers in pairs. Then call on pairs to give answers.

B. Comprehension

- Have students complete the exercises individually. Be sure students understand that they may have to check more than one box in each case.
- Have students compare answers in pairs. Then call on pairs to say an answer each.

Go to **www.myfocusongrammarlab.com** for an additional reading, and for reading and vocabulary practice.

Step 2: Grammar Presentation (pages 18–20)

See the general suggestions for Grammar Presentation on page 2.

Grammar Charts

- To review the simple past of *be*, write on the board:
  Basho <u>was</u> restless.
  Basho's poems <u>were</u> famous.
  — Ask: "What are *was* and *were* the simple past of?" *(be)* "Which subject pronouns need *was*?" *(I, he, she, it)* "Which subject pronouns need *were*?" *(you, we, they)*
  — Erase *was* and *were* in the examples and ask a student to make the sentences negative. Then ask the class: "How do you form the negative simple past of *be*?" *(was not or wasn't; were not or weren't)*
  — Have another student turn the examples on the board into *yes/no* questions. Have the student write the questions on the board. Then ask the class: "How do you form *yes/no* questions with the simple past of *be*?" (was or were + *subject*)
- To review the simple past of regular and irregular verbs, write on the board:
  He <u>traveled</u> on foot.
  He <u>moved</u> to Edo.
  He <u>had</u> 2,000 students.

— Point to the examples and ask: "Which verbs are regular?" (traveled, moved) "How do you form the simple past of regular verbs?" (*base form + -ed or base form + -d*) "Is *had* regular or irregular?" (*irregular*) "How do you form the simple past of irregular verbs?" (*There is no rule.*)

— Erase *traveled* and *had* and ask a student to make the sentences negative. Then ask the class: "How do you form the negative simple past of regular and irregular verbs?" (didn't + *base form of verb*)

— Point to the last two examples. Have a student turn them into *yes/no* questions. Have the student write the questions on the board. Then ask the class: "How do you form *yes/no* questions with the simple past of regular or irregular verbs?" (did + *subject + base form of verb*)

• To review *wh-* questions, write on the board:
Who was Basho?
What did he do?

— Ask: "How do you form simple past *wh-* questions?" (wh- *word + was/were + subject*; wh- *word + did + subject + base form of the verb*)

• Call on different students to provide answers for the *yes/no* questions and *wh-* questions on the board.

Grammar Notes

Note 1

• Remind students that the simple past is used for finished actions, states, or situations. Say: "Basho was a poet. He's not a poet now."

• To review simple past questions and statements, have students talk in pairs about members of their family who lived in past times. Encourage students to ask follow-up questions. For example:
A: My great-grandfather was Spanish.
B: Was he from Madrid?
A: No. He lived in the south of Spain.

Note 2

• Elicit time expressions and write them on the board. For example:
yesterday   two weeks ago
last month   last summer
in June   three years ago

• Point out that when time expressions come first in a sentence, they are usually followed by a comma. Have students compare the first two examples in the Student Book.

Note 3

• To review regular verbs, write on the board:

Base Form	Simple Past
want	wanted
live	lived

• Point to the verbs on the board and ask: "What kind of verbs are these?" (*regular*) "How is the past of *want* formed?" (*by adding* -ed) "How is the past of *live* formed?" (*by adding* -d) If necessary, explain that when a verb ends in *-e*, you only need to add *-d*.

• To review spelling changes, write on the board:

Base Form	Simple Past
study	studied
play	played
hop	hopped
prefer	preferred
visit	visited

• Have students study the spelling changes in pairs. If needed, refer students to Appendix 22 on page A-10 for spelling rules of the simple past. To review as a class, have students explain a verb each. (y *changes to* i *in* studied *because it is preceded by a consonant;* y *does not change to* i *in* played *because it is preceded by a vowel.*)

Note 4

• To review irregular verbs, write on the board:

Base Form	Simple Past
do	did
eat	ate
cut	cut

• Point to the verbs on the board and ask: "What kind of verbs are these?" (*irregular*) "Why are they irregular?" (*because their past tense is not formed by adding* -d *or* -ed) "Can a past form of an irregular verb be the same as its base form?" (*yes*)

⏱ **Identify the Grammar:** Have students identify the grammar in the opening reading on page 16. For example:
Matsu Basho **wrote** more than 1,000 haiku . . .
He **chose** topics from nature . . .
He **did not want** to become a samurai . . .

Go to **www.myfocusongrammarlab.com** for grammar charts and notes.

Step 3: Focused Practice (pages 21–25)

See the general suggestions for Focused Practice on page 4.

Exercise 1: Discover the Grammar
- Go over the example with the class. Ask: "Is *grew up* a regular or an irregular past form?" *(irregular)* "What is it the past of?" (grow up)
- Have students underline the verbs and complete the timeline individually. Encourage students to write short, simple past sentences on the timeline.
- Have students compare answers in pairs. Then call on pairs to share their answers.

Exercise 2: Affirmative Statements
- Have students complete the biography individually. If needed, refer students to Appendix 1 on page A-1 for irregular verbs. Point out that if a verb is not included in the appendix, it is regular.
- Have students compare answers in pairs. Then call on a student to read the biography aloud.

Exercise 3: Affirmative and Negative Statements
- Have students complete the facts individually.
- Have students compare answers in pairs. Then call on students to each read a sentence aloud.
- Books closed. Have students share facts about Emily Dickinson that they found interesting. (Example: *She knew a lot of people, but she never went far from her home*.)

Exercise 4: Regular and Irregular Verbs
- Have students complete the poem in pairs. Encourage them to use the pictures to help them understand its meaning.
- If needed, clarify the meaning of *bite (to cut or crunch something with your teeth; in the poem the bird uses its beak), angle-worm (small tube-shaped creature with a soft body and no legs that lives in the ground), fellow (man; in the poem* fellow *refers to the worm), raw (not cooked), dew (the small drops of water that form on outdoor surfaces during the night),* and *beetle (an insect with a hard, round back).*
- Have pairs practice reading the poem. Then call on a student to read the poem aloud.

Exercise 5: Questions and Answers
- Go over the examples with the class. Be sure students understand that if a verb is underlined a *yes/no* question is needed and that if other words are underlined a *wh*-question is needed. Before students complete the exercise, remind them that the base form (not the past form) is used in questions with *did*.

- Have students complete the questions and answers individually.
- Have pairs role-play the questions and answers. Then call on pairs to read a question and answer each.

Exercise 6: Affirmative and Negative Statements
- Have students read the article and complete the exercise individually.
- Have students compare answers in pairs.
- To review answers, read the statements in the exercise aloud and have students say "That's right" or "That's wrong" and provide the correct information.

Exercise 7: Editing
- Have students read the journal quickly to find out what it is about. Then ask: "What did the student read in class?" *(a poem by Robert Frost)* "What decision did the person in the poem have to make?" *(to choose between two roads in a forest)* "Why was this an important decision?" *(because it changed the person's life)* "What important decision did the student make?" *(moving to a new country)*
- Go over the example with the class.
- Have students find and correct the mistakes individually. Then call on students to explain why the incorrect structures are wrong.
- ⏱ Have students point out examples of correct usage of the simple past.

Go to **www.myfocusongrammarlab.com** for additional grammar practice.

Step 4: Communication Practice (pages 26–28)
See the general suggestions for Communication Practice on page 5.

Exercise 8: Listening
A
- Have students listen once for general meaning. Then have them read the sentences, listen again, and circle the correct answers.

B
- Have students listen again to complete the timeline. If necessary, stop after each answer is given to allow students time to write. Call on students to say complete sentences. (Example: *Murat was born in 1970.*)

Exercise 9: Pronunciation
A
- Play the audio. Have students read along as they listen to the Pronunciation Note.

B

- Play the audio. Have students complete the sentences individually.

C

- Play the audio. Have students repeat the questions. Be sure students pronounce *did* as "d." Then have pairs take turns reading the questions and answers.

Exercise 10: Compare and Contrast

- Point out the use of *both* in the example to express a similarity. Have students work in small groups to write how the poets were different and similar. Encourage students to use *both* in their sentences for common information.
- Call on groups to read ideas aloud.
- As students say their ideas, put them on the board in note form. Then have students write a paragraph comparing the two poets, using the notes as a guide.

Exercise 11: Writing

A

- Write these questions on the board to help students generate ideas and elicit vocabulary:
  Where were you born?
  What were your favorite pastimes when you were a child?
  Where did you live?
  What school did you go to?
  What did you do when you finished school/ college?
  What memorable experiences did you have?
- Have students make notes for each question and then use them as a guide as they write their paragraph.

B

- Have students correct their work using the Editing Checklist.

C

- Give each student a classmate's paragraph. Have students read the paragraph and ask questions to try to find its writer.

Exercise 12: Information Gap: Celebrity Profile

- Have students (quickly) read the profile to decide what kind of information is missing.
- Elicit *wh-* words that students will need to ask the questions. *(what, where, when)* Write them on the board.
- As students compare their profiles, encourage them to use the negative simple past to talk about the differences, if any. *(Example: He didn't live in Belfast. He lived in Denmark.)*

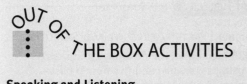

OUT OF THE BOX ACTIVITIES

Speaking and Listening

- Brainstorm some common verbs and their past forms with the class and write them on the board.
- Have the first student begin a story using one of the verbs on the board. (Example: *Yesterday I went to the store.*)
- Have the second student repeat the phrase and add a new one to it. (Example: *Yesterday I went to the store. I bought some strawberries.*) Continue until everyone has had a chance to add a sentence.

Reading and Speaking

- Bring in copies of a poem that uses the simple past.
- Have students read the poem individually.
- Have pairs underline the past form of the verbs and circle the rhyming words. Then call on pairs to take turns reading the poem aloud, reading a stanza each.

Go to **www.myfocusongrammarlab.com** for additional listening, pronunciation, speaking, and writing practice.

Note:
- See the *Focus on Grammar Workbook* for additional in-class or homework grammar practice.

Unit 2 Review (page 29)

- Have students complete the Review and check their answers on Student Book page UR-1. Review or assign additional material as needed.

Go to **www.myfocusongrammarlab.com** for the Unit Achievement Test.

Grammar: PAST PROGRESSIVE AND SIMPLE PAST

Unit 3 focuses on the meanings and uses of the past progressive and the simple past—specifically when these verb forms appear in sentences with two clauses.

- The past progressive describes an action that was in progress at a specific time in the past. It focuses on the duration of a past action.

- The simple past focuses on the completion of a past action.

- When the simple past and the past progressive appear together in a sentence, the simple past describes the action that interrupts the action in progress.

Theme: ACCIDENTS

Unit 3 focuses on language that describes past events and the relationship between them. It focuses on accidents such as the *Titanic* and a traffic accident.

Step 1: Grammar in Context (pages 31–32)

See the general suggestions for Grammar in Context on page 1.

Before You Read

- To get students to share prior knowledge, have them look at the picture and discuss the questions in pairs.

- Call on pairs to share their answers with the class. Encourage students to say simple sentences. (Example: *The* Titanic *was a very big ship. It sank in the Atlantic Ocean. A lot of people died.*)

Read

- To encourage students to read with a purpose, write these questions on the board:
  1. What was special about the *Titanic*? *(It was the largest luxury ship in the world. People thought it was unsinkable.)*
  2. Why did it sink? *(because it hit an iceberg)*
  3. What were people doing when the accident happened? *(sleeping, reading, playing cards)*
  4. How many passengers were on board? *(more than 2,200/2,224)*
  5. How many of them survived? *(more than 700)*

- Have students read the text. (OR: Play the audio and have students follow along in their books.) Then call on students to share their answers to the questions on the board.

- To get students to share their ideas on the reading, have them discuss the following questions in pairs or small groups. Write them on the board if necessary.
  1. The ship's band kept playing after the accident. Why do you think this happened? Was it a good idea?
  2. The *Titanic* did not have enough lifeboats. Why do you think it didn't?
  3. What did people learn after this accident?

After You Read

A. Vocabulary

- Have students complete the exercise individually. Encourage them to use context clues to help them.

- Have students compare answers in pairs. Then call on students to read their answers aloud.

- (⏱) Have students use the words in simple sentences about the reading. (Example: *There was a disaster at sea. The sinking of the* Titanic *was a disaster.*) Call on students to share their sentences with the class.

B. Comprehension

- Have students complete the exercise individually and then look back at the text to confirm their answers.

- Have students compare answers in pairs. Then call on a student to read the events in order aloud.

Go to **www.myfocusongrammarlab.com** for an additional reading, and for reading and vocabulary practice.

Step 2: Grammar Presentation (pages 33–35)

See the general suggestions for Grammar Presentation on page 2.

Grammar Charts

- To explain past progressive statements (both affirmative and negative), write on the board:
  The *Titanic* was sailing to New York.
  Some people were sleeping when it hit the iceberg.
  The *Titanic* was not carrying more than 3,000 passengers.
  — Ask: "How do you form the past progressive?" *(past form of* be [OR *was/were*] + -ing *form of verb)* "Which verb forms are in the past progressive in the first two examples on the board?" (was sailing, were sleeping) "Which pronouns need *was* plus an *-ing* form?" (I/he/she/it) "Which pronouns need *were* plus an *-ing* form?" (you/we/they)

— Ask: "How do you form the negative past progressive?" (was/were + not + -ing *form of verb*)
— Point to the first two examples on the board. Have a student make them negative, using full forms. *(The* Titanic *was not sailing to New York. Some people were not sleeping when it hit the iceberg.)*
— Have another student make the same examples negative, using contractions. *(The* Titanic *wasn't sailing to New York. Some people weren't sleeping when it hit the iceberg.)*
• To explain *yes/no* questions and short answers, write on the board:
Was water entering fast?
— Ask: "How do you form *yes/no* questions in the past progressive?" (was/were + *subject* + -ing *form of verb*)
— Write the following cues on the board: band / sank / was / when / playing / it
— Have a student use the cues to write a *yes/no* question on the board. *(Was the band playing when it sank?)*
— Call on a student to come to the board and write the two possible short answers to the question. *(Yes, it was. / No, it wasn't.)*
• To explain *wh-* questions, ask another student to turn the question on the board into a *wh*-question. *(What was the band doing when it sank?* OR *Why was the band playing when it sank?)*
— Ask: "How do you form *wh-* questions?" (wh- *word* + was/were + *subject* + -ing *form of verb*)

Grammar Notes

Notes 1 and 2
• To compare the past progressive and the simple past, write on the board:
1. He <u>was traveling</u> around the world.
2. He <u>traveled</u> around the world.
Ask: "In example 1, do we know if the man actually finished his trip?" *(no)* "Why?" *(because the past progressive focuses on the duration of a past action; it does not indicate completion of the action)* "In example 2, do we know if the man finished his trip?" *(yes)* "Why?" *(because the simple past focuses on completion of an action)*
• Write on the board:

In the afternoon At 7:00 P.M. yesterday Early this morning	I was doing some shopping.

• Point out that we often use the past progressive with a past time expression.

• Draw attention to the *Be Careful!* note. Then write on the board:
He seemed interested.
~~was seeming~~
• Point out that *seem* is a non-action verb, so it is not used in the past progressive. The past simple is used instead.
• Have students say other non-action verbs. If necessary, remind students of the verbs they saw in Unit 1 (page 6).

Note 3
• To explain the use of the past progressive with the simple past, say: "At 10:00 yesterday I was watching a movie." Draw a simple timeline on the board:

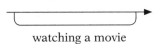
watching a movie

• Then say: "I was watching the movie when I heard a strange noise." Write *heard a noise* and then draw a cross on the line to indicate the interruption:
heard a noise

watching a movie

• Point out that there are two ways to express the same idea. Write two contrasting examples on the board:
I <u>was watching</u> a movie <u>when</u> I <u>heard</u> a strange noise.
<u>While</u> I <u>was watching</u> a movie, I <u>heard</u> a strange noise.
• Have the class study the examples. Then ask: "What verb form follows *when*?" *(simple past)* "What verb form follows *while*?" *(past progressive)*

Note 4
• Point out that if two actions were in progress at the same time in the past, both actions are expressed in the past progressive. (Example: *While I was reading, my brother was cooking*.)
• Draw a timeline on the board:
was reading

was cooking

Note 5

- Draw attention to the *Be Careful!* note. To check comprehension and to show the difference between a sentence with both clauses in the simple past compared to a sentence with one clause in the simple past and one in the past progressive, write the following examples on the board:

  He was doing his homework when his mother came home.

  He did his homework when his mother came home.

  She was writing her essay when the lights went on.

  She wrote her essay when the lights went on.

- Have students study the examples and restate them using *First . . .* and *Then . . . (First he started doing his homework. Then his mother came home.)*

Note 6

- To review the order and punctuation of time clauses with *when* and *while*, write two timelines on the board:

  she/came in

  ————————✕————————▶

  he/working in the garden

  she/taking a shower

  ————————————————▶

  he/answering his emails

- Have students use the first timeline to write a sentence with *when* and the second timeline to write a sentence with *while*. Point out they can use time clauses at the beginning or end of sentences.

- Call on students to say the sentences and write them on the board. *(When she came in, he was working in the garden. He was working in the garden when she came in. While she was taking a shower, he was answering his emails. She was taking a shower while he was answering his emails.)* Point out the comma at the end of the time clause that comes first in the sentence.

🕐 **Identify the Grammar:** Have students identify the grammar in the opening reading on page 31. For example:

  It **was** a clear night.

  The *RMS Titanic*, the largest luxury ship in the world, **was sailing** . . .

  . . . Frederick Fleet **was looking** at the sea when, suddenly, he **saw** a huge white form . . .

Go to **www.myfocusongrammarlab.com** for grammar charts and notes.

Step 3: Focused Practice (pages 35–39)

See the general suggestions for Focused Practice on page 4.

Exercise 1: Discover the Grammar

- Go over the example with the class. Ask: "In choice A, which action happened first—the passengers arrived or the ship left?" *(the ship left)* "And in choice B?" *(the passengers arrived)*

- Have students choose the correct answers individually.

- Have students compare answers in pairs. Then call on pairs to say the correct answers.

Exercise 2: Past Progressive Statements

- As a class, have students look at the schedule and use the cues to describe it. *(At 10:00 Douglas was having breakfast at Sea Breezes with Donna. At 11:00 he was exercising in the gym with Michel.)*

- Go over the example with the class. Point out that students have to choose between the past progressive affirmative and negative, as appropriate.

- Have students complete the exercise individually. Then call on students to read the sentences aloud.

Exercise 3: Past Progressive or Simple Past

- Explain that these eyewitness accounts are reports by people who were on the *Titanic* when it crashed.

- Have students read the accounts for meaning and then read them again to complete them individually. If needed, refer students to Appendix 1 on page A-1 for irregular verbs. Point out that if a verb is not included in the appendix, it is regular.

- 🕐 Have students play a memory game. Allow them one minute to look at the accounts again. Write the eyewitnesses' names— *Beesley, Dodge, Shutes, Bride*—on the board. Form small groups. Have students take turns saying what they remember about the accounts. Encourage them to use the past progressive and the simple past. (Example: *When Beesley looked out the window, he saw an iceberg.)*

Exercise 4: *Yes/No* and *Wh-* Questions

- Go over the example with the class.

- Have students complete the interview individually.

- Have students role-play the interview in pairs. Then call on two students to read the interview aloud.

Exercise 5: Statements with *When* and *While*

- Go over the example with the class. Remind students to use *when* plus the simple past and *while* plus the past progressive.
- Have students write the sentences individually.
- Have students compare answers in pairs. Then call on pairs to read their sentences aloud.

Exercise 6: Editing

- Have students read the journal entry quickly to find out what it is about. Then ask: "What movie were they showing at school?" (Titanic) "Why?" *(because it was the anniversary of the disaster)* "Who were the main characters in the movie?" *(Jack and Rose)* "Did they survive?" *(Rose did, but Jack didn't)* "Did the student like the movie?" *(Yes, but it was very sad.)* "What did the student witness on his/her way home?" *(an accident between two pedestrians and a car)* "What did the student do?" *(called the police because nobody else was in the area)*
- Go over the example with the class.
- Have students find and correct the mistakes individually. Then call on students to explain why the incorrect structures are wrong.
- ⏱ Have students point out examples of correct usage of the past progressive and the simple past.

Go to **www.myfocusongrammarlab.com** for additional grammar practice.

Step 4: Communication Practice (pages 40–43)

See the general suggestions for Communication Practice on page 5.

Exercise 7: Listening

A
- Write this useful vocabulary on the board:
  look both ways
  start to cross the street
  pay attention to the traffic
  talk to each other
  drive fast/slowly
  honk
  hit the pedestrians
- Have pairs describe the pictures using the three versions of the accident, the vocabulary on the board, and their own ideas.

B
- Play the audio. Have students choose the most accurate set of pictures. Review the correct answer.

C
- Play the audio. Have students complete the exercise individually.

Exercise 8: Pronunciation

A
- Play the audio. Have students read along as they listen to the Pronunciation Note.

B
- Play the audio. Have students listen and put the commas where they hear the pauses.

C
- Play the audio. Have students listen and repeat the sentences. Be sure students pause where necessary. Then call on pairs to take turns reading the sentences.

Exercise 9: Game: Are You a Good Witness?

- Encourage students to write as many sentences as they can about what was happening in the picture. Remind them to use the past progressive to describe what the people and animals were doing.
- Have students compare answers in pairs, discuss the differences, and see who remembered most. (Example: *You put that the cat was eating, and I put that the cat was drinking milk. The little boy wasn't holding a teddy bear. He was holding a monkey.*)
- ⏱ If students need further practice, say true and false statements about the picture. In pairs, have students consult their notes and each other before answering. Then have students check their answers by looking at the picture one last time.

Exercise 10: Role Play: Alibi

A
- Go over the examples by having pairs read them aloud.
- As a class, brainstorm more questions to ask a witness and a suspect. Write some of them on the board, for example:
  Questions to ask a witness:
  What were you doing when the robbers walked into the bank?
  What were you doing at the bank?
  What were the robbers doing when you first saw them?
  Were they carrying guns?
  Questions to ask a suspect:
  What were you doing at [time]?
  What were you doing there?
  Why were you going to [place]?
  Were you driving?
- Form groups of three to six students. Have students choose their roles and then role-play the interviews. Encourage them to be creative and invent what happened and what they were doing.

B

• Have students discuss the questions in groups.

C

• Call on groups to tell the class what happened at the bank, what alibis the suspects had, and whether they believe the alibis.

Exercise 11: Writing

A

• Write these questions on the board to elicit vocabulary and help students generate ideas:
What event did you witness?
Where were you?
What were you doing?
What were the people doing?
What happened?

• Have students make notes for each question and then use them as a guide as they write.

B

• Have students correct their work using the Editing Checklist.

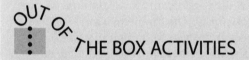
OUT OF THE BOX ACTIVITIES

Speaking and Listening

• Brainstorm major events of world significance and write them on the board. (Example: *the death of a public figure, the beginning of the new millennium, a natural disaster, a plane crash*) Then brainstorm major events of personal significance and write them on the board. (Example: *the birth of a child, a surprise party/gift/phone call, a competition, a graduation*)

• Have students choose an event from the board and think of when they learned about it. Encourage them to recall exactly where they were and what they were doing at that time. Have them write notes about it.

• Students report to the class on the event they remember and what they were doing.

Reading and Speaking

• Bring in photocopies of the beginning of a story and have students study how the past progressive and the simple past are used to set the scene. *(The past progressive describes the actions in progress at the moment when the story starts, and the simple past describes the sequence of events that take place.)*

• Then have students discuss why setting the scene for a story is important and what effect it has on the reader.

Go to **www.myfocusongrammarlab.com** for additional listening, pronunciation, speaking, and writing practice.

Note:

• See the *Focus on Grammar Workbook* for additional in-class or homework grammar practice.

Unit 3 Review (page 44)

Have students complete the Review and check their answers on Student Book page UR-1. Review or assign material as needed.

Go to **www.myfocusongrammarlab.com** for the Unit Achievement Test.

UNIT 4 OVERVIEW

Grammar: *Used to* AND *Would*

Unit 4 focuses on the meanings and uses of *used to* and *would*.

• *Used to* describes repeated past activities or situations that no longer exist in the present.

• It is often used in sentences that contrast the past and the present. Time expressions such as *now, no longer,* and *anymore* are often used to emphasize the contrast.

• *Would* describes repeated past activities that no longer exist in the present.

• It is often used to tell past stories.

Theme: MEMORIES

Unit 4 focuses on language that describes life in the past and contrasts it with life in the present. It focuses on memories from the 1980s, such as computer games, vinyl records, early computers, and class reunions.

   He-Man and the Masters of the Universe was a TV cartoon in which He-Man, the most powerful man in the universe, fought the evil forces of Skeletor and other villains. *She-Ra Princess of Power* was created after He-Man for a new target audience—girls. She-Ra was He-Man's twin sister. As the cartoons became popular, action figures of the main characters from both series were manufactured and sold for children to play with.

Step 1: Grammar in Context (pages 45–46)

See the general suggestions for Grammar in Context on page 1.

Before You Read

- Ask: "What is a blog?" Write students' ideas on the board. (Example: *a personal website, a website that is changed regularly, a journal on the Internet, a website where you can post personal comments*)
- Have students look at the reading and say what they think Sandra's blog is about.
- To get students to share their own experience, ask them to say what toys, TV shows, clothes, and hairstyles they remember from childhood. Students can also share other memories from their childhood. (Example: *a band, a type of music, a book, a comic*)

Read

- To encourage students to read with a purpose, write these questions on the board:
  1. What time of her life does Sandra write about? *(her childhood/the time when she was a kid)*
  2. What does she remember doing in her childhood? *(watching cartoons, collecting the toys, and acting out the stories)*
  3. What did her sister use to do? *(play with a puzzle/a cube/a Rubik's Cube)*
  4. What did her mother use to wear? *(suits with big shoulders)*
  5. What did her brother use to do? *(practice with his rock band/play in a rock band)*
- Have students read the text. (OR: Play the audio and have students follow along in their books.) Then call on students to share their answers to the questions on the board.
- To get students to share their ideas on the reading, have them discuss the following topics in pairs or small groups. Write them on the board if necessary.
  1. Compare what kids play with today with what kids used to play with in the past. Which toys require more imagination and creativity? Why?
  2. Compare your grandparents' lifestyles with your own. Is life better now, or was it better then?
- Encourage students to support their views.

After You Read

A. Vocabulary

- Have students complete the exercise individually. Encourage them to use context clues to help.

- Have students compare answers in pairs. Then call on students to read their answers aloud.
- ⏱ Books closed. Play a memory game as a class by using the vocabulary words in questions about the reading. Ask: "What does Sandra say is awesome?" *(the eighties)* "What did she use to collect?" *(She-Ra toys)* "What does Sandra say is weird?" *(her brother's haircuts)* "Which puzzle was very popular in the 1980s?" *(the Rubik's Cube)* "Does Sandra have good or bad memories of her childhood?" *(good memories)* "Why did Sandra's mother call one of her suits her 'power suit'?" *(because it made her feel strong)*

B. Comprehension

- Have students complete the exercise individually.
- Have students compare answers in pairs. Then call on students to correct the false statements. (Example: *Sandra watched TV on Saturdays. She always watched* She-Ra, Princess of Power.)

Go to **www.myfocusongrammarlab.com** for an additional reading, and for reading and vocabulary practice.

Step 2: Grammar Presentation (pages 47–48)

See the general suggestions for Grammar Presentation on page 2.

Grammar Charts

- To explain affirmative and negative statements with *used to*, write on the board:
  When I was a kid, I used to watch *She-Ra*.
  My brother used to watch *He-Man*.
  My sister didn't use to watch cartoons.
  — Ask: "How do you form affirmative statements with *used to*?" (used to + *base form of verb*) "Does *used to* change when the pronoun changes?" (*No. Used to is the same for all pronouns.*) "How do you form negative statements?" (didn't + use to + *base form of verb*)
- To explain *yes/no* and *wh-* questions with *used to* and *use to*, write on the board:
  Did you use to watch cartoons when you were a kid?
  What did you use to watch?
  — Ask: "How do you form *yes/no* questions?" (did + *subject* + use to + *base form of verb*)
  — Call on a student to come to the front and write the two possible answers to the question on the board:
  Yes, I did. / No, I didn't.

— Then ask: "How do you form *wh*-questions?" (wh- *word* + did + *subject* + use to + *base form of verb*)

- To explain statements with *would*, write on the board:
  I would visit my grandmother every Sunday.
  She would prepare a special dinner for us.
  — Ask: "How do you form statements with *would*?" (would + *base form of verb*) "Does *would* change when the pronoun changes?" (*No. Would is the same for all pronouns.*)
  — Go over the Contractions chart with students.

Grammar Notes

Note 1

- To explain the use of *used to*, draw two timelines on the board:

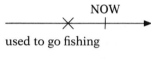

used to go fishing

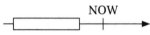

used to live near the sea

- To explain the first timeline, point to the cross. Explain that *used to* can indicate that an action happened several times in the past. Write to the right of the timeline on the board:
  I used to go fishing. = I went fishing several times in the past.

- Point out that there are no crosses on *NOW* or after *NOW*. This is because *used to* indicates that the action is no longer true in the present. Add a new sentence to the explanation on the board:
  I used to go fishing. = I went fishing several times in the past. = I no longer go fishing.

- To explain the second timeline, point to the bar. Explain that *used to* can indicate that a situation existed for some time in the past and no longer exists. Write below the timeline on the board:
  I used to live near the sea. = I lived near the sea for some time in the past. = I no longer live near the sea.

Note 2

- To explain that *used to* can be used only for the past, write on the board:
  Past: She used to ride her bike.
  Present: She (always) rides her bike. ~~She use to ride her bike.~~

- Point to the first example and ask: "What do we use for past habits?" (*used to*) Point to the second example and ask: "What do we use for present habits?" (*the simple present, with or without an adverb of frequency*)

- To explain negative statements, write on the board:
  We didn't use(d) to play video games.
  We never used to play video games.

- Point to *use(d) to* in the first example. Explain that a *-d* on *use* is not necessary because *did* in *didn't* expresses the past, but many people use it.

- Point to *never used to* in the second example. Explain that *never used to* is more common than *didn't use(d) to*.

- To explain questions, write on the board:
  <u>Did you use</u> to watch cartoons?
  What <u>did</u> you <u>use to play</u>?

- Point to *use* in the first question and ask: "Why isn't there a *-d* on *use*?" (*because* did *expresses the past*)

Note 3

- To explain the use of *would*, draw a new timeline on the board:

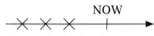

play with my brother

- Point to the three crosses. Explain that *would* is used for repeated past activities (habits) that no longer happen in the present. Write below the timeline on the board:
  I used to play with my brother. = I would play with my brother.

- Write on the board:
  We used to have a great time. ~~We would have a great time~~.

- Draw attention to the *Be Careful!* note. Explain that *would* cannot be used for past situations. *Used to* is used instead.

- Explain that we often use *would* to describe past memories. We start with *used to* and then continue with *would*. (Example: *When I was a kid, I used to collect cans, screws, and bolts. Then I would give them to my brother to make robots.*)

🕐 **Identify the Grammar:** Have students identify the grammar in the opening reading on page 45. For example:
  What toys **did** you **use to play** with?
  I **used to love** She-Ra . . .
  I **would collect** all the toys . . .

Go to **www.myfocusongrammarlab.com** for grammar charts and notes.

Step 3: Focused Practice (pages 49–52)

See the general suggestions for Focused Practice on page 4.

Exercise 1: Discover the Grammar

- Go over the example with the class. Remind students to underline the complete expressions: *used to* plus a base form or *would* plus a base form. Point out that the expressions can be affirmative, negative, or questions.
- If needed, explain the meaning of *vinyl* (a type of strong plastic) and *record* (a round, flat piece of vinyl on which music is stored).
- Have students complete the exercise individually and then discuss their answers with a partner.

Exercise 2: Forms of *Used to*

- Have students complete the conversations that take place at a class reunion, which is a meeting of people who used to be in the same class and have not met for a long time.
- Go over the example with the class.
- Have students complete the conversations in pairs. Then call on pairs to read the conversations aloud.

Exercise 3: *Used to* or *Would*

- Go over the example with the class. Ask: "Is *would* also possible in item 1?" *(no)* "Why not?" *(because* would *cannot be used for past situations)*
- Have students complete the exercise individually. Then have students compare answers in pairs.
- Ⓘ Say statements describing CityGal's life today and have the class contribute related sentences describing her life in the past. Say: "She lives in the city." *(In the past, she used to live on a farm.)* "She gets up at 8:00." "She sits at her desk all day and does very little exercise." "She has long, dark hair." "She wears contact lenses."

Exercise 4: Contrast: *Used to* or *Would*

- Go over the example with the class.
- Have students complete the exercise individually.
- Have students role-play the conversation in pairs. Then call on a pair to read the conversation aloud.

Exercise 5: Editing

- Have students read the journal entry quickly to find out what it is about. Then ask: "Who is Shania Twain?" *(a country pop singer)* "Where does she live now?" *(in a chateau/large house in Switzerland)* "Why did her grandmother use to make her clothes?" *(because she used to be poor and her family could not afford to buy them)* "How did she use to earn money for her family?" *(She performed with a local rock band.)* "Does she care for her hometown?" *(Yes, she uses her power to do good things for her community.)*
- Go over the example with the class.
- Have students find and correct the mistakes individually. Then call on students to explain why the mistakes are wrong.
- Ⓘ Have students point out examples of correct usages of *used to* and *would*.

Go to **www.myfocusongrammarlab.com** for additional grammar practice.

Step 4: Communication Practice (pages 53–56)

See the general suggestions for Communication Practice on page 5.

Exercise 6: Listening

A

- Write these topics on the board:
  1. getting up
  2. having breakfast
  3. going out
  4. shopping
  5. having energy
  6. going to bed
- Play the audio. Have students listen for which topics from the board the women talk about. Review as a class. *(1, 2, 3, 5)*

B

- Have students read the statements and then listen for specific information. Have students compare answers in pairs.

C

- Have students read the activities and then listen again to check the correct column. Then call on students to say full sentences and use *used to* where appropriate. *(They used to get up early without an alarm clock. Now they use an alarm clock.)*
- Ⓘ Small groups. For further practice, have students share their own past and present habits in connection with getting up, having breakfast, and having energy.

Exercise 7: Pronunciation

A

- Play the audio. Have students read along as they listen to the Pronunciation Note.

B

- Play the audio. Have students listen, noting the pronunciation of *used to* and the contraction of *would*.

C

- Play the audio. Have students listen and repeat the sentences. Be sure they pronounce *used to* and contract *would* correctly.

Exercise 8: Picture Discussion

- Go over the example with the class. Have students say more things about Sharifa. Encourage them to use their imagination. (Example: *She used to wear business clothes, but now she wears casual, comfortable clothes. She used to work every day. Now she works three times a week.*)
- ⏱ Small groups. For further practice, write on the board:
  She/He used to _____, but now _____.
- Form small groups. Have each student complete the statement on the board to describe a famous person (they should not say the person's name). Point out that students can give more than one clue by saying more than one sentence, for example, one about the person's appearance and one about his/her habits. (Example: *She used to have dark hair, but now she is blonde. She used to be a model, but now she is an actress.*) The other students in the group guess who the person is.

Exercise 9: Compare and Contrast

- To set up the activity, brainstorm topics students can talk about. Write them on the board; for example:
hairstyle	tastes in music
clothes	hobbies
eating habits	free time activities
- Go over the example with the class. Form small groups. Encourage students to keep the conversation going by asking follow-up questions.
- Have students share with the class what their classmates used to do or what they used to be like.

Exercise 10: Writing

A

- Write these questions on the board to elicit vocabulary and help students generate ideas:
  Where did you use to live?

Who did you use to live with?
What did you use to like/hate?
How did you use to spend your time?

- Have students make notes for each question and then use them as a guide as they write. Remind students that they will often want to begin with *used to* and then change to *would*.

B

- Have students correct their work using the Editing Checklist.

OUT OF THE BOX ACTIVITIES

Speaking and Listening

- If your students are in the work force, have them talk in small groups about a past work experience they had. Encourage them to be specific and say the tasks they used to do at work. (*I used to answer the phone. I also used to address envelopes and mail out letters and notices.*)
- If your students are still in school and have not yet begun working, have them talk about elementary school. Encourage them to be specific and talk about the things they used to do in elementary school. (*On rainy days I used to play cards at recess. On sunny days I used to play baseball with my friends.*)

Reading and Speaking

- Bring in printouts of magazines from the 1950s or 1960s.
- Form small groups and give each group at least one magazine.
- Have students flip through the magazine(s). Have students talk about what magazines used to be like and compare them with magazines today. (Some of the aspects students can compare are colors, illustrations, photographs, and advertisements.)

Go to **www.myfocusongrammarlab.com** for additional listening, pronunciation, speaking, and writing practice.

Note:
- See the *Focus on Grammar Workbook* for additional in-class or homework grammar practice.

Unit 4 Review (page 57)

Have students complete the Review and check their answers on Student Book page UR-1. Review or assign material as needed.

Go to **www.myfocusongrammarlab.com** for the Unit Achievement Test.

UNIT 5 OVERVIEW

Grammar: *Wh-* Questions

Unit 5 focuses on the meanings and uses of *wh-* questions—specifically the comparison between questions about the subject and questions about the object.

- *Wh-* questions begin with *wh-* words—*who, what, where, when, why, which, whose, how, how many, how much,* and *how long.*
- They are used to ask specific information.
- *Wh-* questions that ask about the subject need statement word order.
- *Wh-* questions that ask about the object need *yes/no* question word order.

Theme: In Court

Unit 5 focuses on the language that is used to ask questions to get information—specifically, about criminal cases and traffic accidents.

In a criminal trial, the government makes an accusation of guilt and the accused (the defendant) defends himself/herself (usually with the help of a lawyer) against the accusation. Both sides present arguments, witnesses, and evidence. During the trial, a court reporter sits near the judge and records everything that is said and done during the trial. The record is called a transcript. After both sides have presented their case, a jury decides if the defendant is guilty or not guilty of the crime.

Step 1: Grammar in Context (pages 58–59)

See the general suggestions for Grammar in Context on page 1.

Before You Read

- As a class discuss what a *lawyer* (someone whose job is to advise people about laws, write formal agreements, or represent people in court), a *judge* (the official in control of a court who decides how criminals should be punished), and a *witness* (someone who describes in a court of law what she/he has seen or knows about a crime) are.
- Have students discuss the questions in pairs. Encourage them to make notes of some possible answers.

- Call on pairs to share their answers with the class.

Read

- To encourage students to read with a purpose, write these questions on the board:
  1. Where was the witness? *(in a restaurant/at Al's Grill)*
  2. Who did he see there? *(a man/Mr. Adams/Harry Adams and a woman)*
  3. What did he see the people do? *(The man received a box from the woman, went to the parking lot, and drove away.)*
- Have students read the text. (OR: Play the audio and have students follow along in their books.) Then call on students to share their answers to the questions on the board.
- To get students to share their ideas on the reading, have them discuss the following questions in pairs or small groups. Write them on the board if necessary.
  1. What do you think was in the box?
  2. What crime do you think Harry Adams was accused of?
- ⏱ Tell students that in the United States, the jury (the people who listen to details of a case in court and decide whether someone is guilty) is usually a group of 12 people. These people are ordinary citizens who are selected from tax rolls or voting registers. Have students discuss whether they would like to be a member of the jury in a criminal case such as Harry M. Adams's. Encourage them to support their view.

After You Read

A. Vocabulary

- Have students complete the exercise individually. Encourage them to use context clues to help.
- Have students compare answers in pairs. Then call on pairs to give answers.
- ⏱ For further practice, use the vocabulary words in false sentences about the court transcript and have students correct them. Say: "The defendant is a woman." *(No, the defendant is a man.)* "What the witness said was recorded on a video." *(No, what he said was written on the record.)* "The witness said the woman looked frightened when she handed him the box." *(No, he said the man/Adams/the defendant looked frightened when he received the box.)* "The witness said the woman left in a hurry." *(No, he said Adams left in a hurry.)* "When the witness was testifying, he indicated the box that was on the table." *(No, he indicated the defendant who was sitting in the courtroom.)*

B. Comprehension
- Have students complete the exercise individually.
- Have students compare answers in pairs. Then call on pairs to give answers and correct the false statements.

Go to **www.myfocusongrammarlab.com** for an additional reading, and for reading and vocabulary practice.

Step 2: Grammar Presentation (pages 60–62)

See the general suggestions for Grammar Presentation on page 2.

Grammar Charts
- To explain questions about the subject, on the left of the board write:
  Who saw you?   A woman saw me.
  — Direct attention to the answer. Ask: "Is *a woman* the subject or the object of the sentence?" *(the subject)* "Which is the object of the sentence?" *(me)*
  — Underline the subject and the object, and write *subject* below *A woman* and *object* below *me*, as shown:
  Who saw you?   A woman saw me.
                     subject   object
  — Point to the question *(Who saw you?)* and ask: "Does this question ask about the subject or about the object?" *(the subject)*
  — Draw an arrow from *Who* in the question to *A woman* in the answer, as shown:

  Who saw you?   A woman saw me.
                     subject   object
  — Then ask: "What is the word order of this type of question?" (wh- *word + verb + subject*)
- Do not erase the board. To explain questions about the object, to the right of the board write:
  Who did you see?   I saw a woman.
  — Direct attention to the answer. Ask: "Is *a woman* the subject or the object of the sentence?" *(the object)* "Which is the subject of the sentence?" *(I)*
  — Underline the subject and the object, and write *subject* below *I* and *object* below *a woman*, as shown:
  Who did you see?   I saw a woman.
                     subject   object
  — Point to the question *(Who did you see?)* and ask: "Does this question ask about the subject or about the object?" *(the object)*
  — Draw an arrow from *Who* in the question to *a woman* in the answer, as shown:

  Who did you see?   I saw a woman.
                     subject   object
  — Then ask: "What is the word order of this type of question?" (wh- *word + auxiliary verb + subject + main verb*)
- To explain *wh-* questions with *which, whose,* and *how many* plus nouns, write below the question and answer on the left:
  Which woman saw you? Mrs. Kent saw me.
  — Then write below the question and answer on the right:
  Which woman   I saw
    did you see?   Mrs. Wayne.
  — Point to *woman* after *which* in both questions. Tell students that *which, whose,* and *how many* can be followed by nouns. Give more examples: *Whose boss did you see? Whose boss saw you? How many people did you see? How many people saw you?*
  — Ask: "What is the word order of these questions?" (wh- *word + noun + subject + main verb if they ask about the subject* OR wh- *word + noun + auxiliary verb + subject + main verb if they ask about the object*)
- To explain *wh-* questions with *when, where,* or *why,* write on the board:

When		I spoke to her on Sunday.
Where	did you speak to her?	I spoke to her at the bar.
Why		I spoke to her because she looked familiar.

  — Ask: "What is the word order of these questions?" (wh- *word + auxiliary verb + subject + main verb*)
  — Point out that questions with *when, where,* and *why* ask about times, places, and reasons. They always need an auxiliary.

Grammar Notes

Note 1
- To compare *yes/no* questions and *wh-* questions, write on the board:
  Did he go to the   Yes, he did.
    parking lot?
  Where did he go?   To the parking lot.
- Point out how *yes/no* questions seek to confirm information *(yes or no)* and *wh-* questions ask for specific information *(the parking lot)*.

Note 2
- To review questions about the subject, write on the board:
  Who gave him the box?
  What happened?

- Have students say the pattern of the question on the board. Write the pattern to the right of the question:

subject

wh- word + verb (+ rest of the sentence)
- Remind students that there is no change in word order when the question word refers to the subject of the sentence.
- To review questions about the object, write on the board:
  Who did the man meet?
  What does the witness know?
- Have students say the pattern of the question on the board. Write the pattern to the left of the question:

object

wh- word + auxiliary verb + subject + main verb (+ rest of the sentence)
- To review auxiliaries, have students name the auxiliaries in the questions. *(did, does)* Name other auxiliaries. *(has, had, can, will, am, is, are)* Give examples with other auxiliaries. *(Where do you work? Where have you been? What had she done? What can he do? Where is she going?)*
- To explain the use of *whom*, write on the board.
  a. Whom did you meet?
  b. Whom is at the door?
  c. Whom gave it to you?
  d. Whom did you interview?
- Tell students that *whom* can be used instead of *who* in questions about the object that do not use *be*. Then have students decide in pairs which questions are correct. (a *and* d)
  To review as a class, have students explain why b and c are incorrect. (b *is incorrect because you cannot use* whom *if the main verb is a form of* be; c *is incorrect because you cannot use* whom *when asking about someone as subject*)

Note 3
- To review questions with *which, whose,* and *how many,* write on the board:
  Which witness
  Whose witness   told lies?
  How many witnesses
- Ask: "Do these questions ask about the subject or the object?" *(the subject)*
  Have students say the pattern of the questions on the board. Write the pattern to the right of the questions:

subject

wh- word + noun + verb (+ rest of the sentence)
- Then write on the board:
  Which witness
  Whose witness   did you question?
  How many witnesses
- Ask: "Do these questions ask about the subject or the object?" *(the object)*
  Have students say the pattern of the questions on the board. Write the pattern to the right of the questions:

object

wh- word + noun + auxiliary verb + subject + main verb (+ rest of the sentence)

Note 4
- To review questions with *when, where,* and *why,* give more examples. Ask: "When did he call you? Where did he go? Why did he call?"

Note 5
- To explain *wh-* questions with a form of *be,* write on the board:
  Jay Bell is the witness.
   subject   object
  Who is Jay Bell?
  Who is the witness?
- Ask: "Do both questions have the same word order?" *(yes)*
  Point out that the word order never changes with a form of the verb *be.*

🕐 **Identify the Grammar:** Have students identify the grammar in the opening reading on page 58. For example:
  What happened on the night of May 12?
  Who did you see there?
  Which one did you see?
  Who saw you?

Go to **www.myfocusongrammarlab.com** for grammar charts and notes.

Step 3: Focused Practice (pages 62–64)

See the general suggestions for Focused Practice on page 4.

Exercise 1: Discover the Grammar
- Go over the example with the class. Ask: "Is this a question about the subject or the object?" *(the object)*
- Have students complete the exercise individually.
- Have students compare answers in pairs. Then call on pairs to give answers.

Exercise 2: Questions

- Have students complete the cross-examination questions. Explain that a cross-examination is when a lawyer asks a person questions in a court of law to see if he/she is telling the truth.
- Have students complete the exercise individually and then compare answers in pairs. Have students check that they have used the correct word order. Then call on a pair to role-play the cross-examination for the class.
- ⏱ Have pairs write three more questions to ask the witness and make up the answers. Call on pairs to share their questions with the class.

Exercise 3: Questions

- Go over the example with the class.
- Encourage students to follow these steps to write the questions: (1) Choose the correct *wh-* word for the underlined words (2) Decide on the correct word order for the question and (3) Write the question.
- If necessary, explain the meaning of *district attorney* (a lawyer who works for the government in a particular district and brings criminals to court), *verdict* (an official decision that is made by a jury in a court of law about whether someone is guilty of a crime), and *trial* (a legal process in which a court of law examines a case to decide whether someone is guilty of a crime).

Exercise 4: Editing

- Have students read the questions quickly to find out what they are about.
- Go over the example with the class.
- Have students find and correct the mistakes individually. Then have students compare answers in pairs.

Go to **www.myfocusongrammarlab.com** for additional grammar practice.

Step 4: Communication Practice (pages 65–67)

See the general suggestions for Communication Practice on page 5.

Exercise 5: Listening

A

- Go over the example with the class. Then play the audio and have students complete the exercise individually.

- Call on students to give answers. If students disagree on the answers, play the segment in question again and have them write what they hear. Have students use what they wrote to support their answers. (Example: *1. The correct question is "Who did you see at the restaurant?" The listener heard "I saw . . . at the restaurant." Nobody saw the speaker. The speaker saw someone.*)

B

- Play the audio and have students write the correct answers. If necessary, stop after each conversation to allow students time to write.

Exercise 6: Pronunciation

A

- Play the audio. Have students read along as they listen to the Pronunciation Note.
- To check comprehension, ask: "When does intonation fall in *wh-* questions?" *(when we ask for information)* "When does intonation rise in *wh-* questions?" *(when we ask someone to repeat information)*

B

- Play the audio. Have students check the correct box. If necessary, play the audio again so that students can confirm their answers.

C

- Play the audio. Have students listen and repeat the questions. Be sure they use the correct intonation.

Exercise 7: Role Play: On the Witness Stand

- Have students work in pairs to continue the questions. Encourage students to use different *wh-* words and to use both subject and object questions.
- Have pairs practice the conversation they created. Then call on pairs to perform their conversation for the class.

Exercise 8: Game: To Tell the Truth

A

- Form groups of three and have each student share an interesting fact about himself/herself. Encourage students to show interest and ask one another questions to find out more about the interesting facts their classmates have shared.

B

- Have groups choose the interesting fact they will state in front of the class. Encourage students to think of possible questions the class will ask them and then make up answers for those questions.

C

- Have the class ask as many questions as necessary to find out who is telling the truth.

Exercise 9: Writing

A

- Have pairs take turns telling each other about something interesting or exciting they saw. Have students be brief at this stage and not give too many details.
- Have students work individually to write the questions they would like to ask their partner.
- Have pairs take turns interviewing each other. Remind students to take notes of their partners' answers. Have students use their notes as a guide to write their interview.

B

- Have students correct their work using the Editing Checklist.

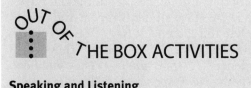

OUT OF THE BOX ACTIVITIES

Speaking and Listening

- Have students imagine they could interview a person in history. Brainstorm people in history and list them on the board. (Examples: *Leonardo da Vinci, Moses, Joan of Arc, Lao Tzu*)
- Have students choose a person from the board and write down ten questions they would like to ask this person.
- Have students share their questions in groups.

Reading and Speaking

- Bring in newspaper articles about criminal cases. Then form small groups and give each group one article.
- Have students imagine they will interview a witness of the crime in their article and have them write down the questions they would ask the witness.
- Have students report to the class on the crime they read about and share the questions they prepared for the witness. **Note:** You can also bring in just one criminal case and give each group a photocopy of the case. After writing the questions, students join another group and compare the questions they wrote.

Go to **www.myfocusongrammarlab.com** for additional listening, pronunciation, speaking, and writing practice.

Note:

- See the *Focus on Grammar Workbook* for additional in-class or homework grammar practice.

Unit 5 Review (page 68)

Have students complete the Review and check their answers on Student Book page UR-2. Review or assign material as needed.

Go to **www.myfocusongrammarlab.com** for the Unit Achievement Test.

From Grammar to Writing (pages 69–71)

See the general suggestions for From Grammar to Writing on page 9.

Go to **www.myfocusongrammarlab.com** for an additional From Grammar to Writing Assignment, Part Review, and Part Post-Test.

PART II OVERVIEW

THE FUTURE

UNIT	GRAMMAR FOCUS	THEME
6	Future	Space Travel
7	Future Time Clauses	Setting Goals

Go to **www.myfocusongrammarlab.com** for the Part and Unit Tests.

Note: PowerPoint® grammar presentations, test-generating software, and reproducible Part and Unit Tests are on the *Teacher's Resource Disc*.

Grammar: FUTURE

Unit 6 focuses on different ways to talk about
the future.

- *Be going to* and *will* express predictions
  about the future.
- *Be going to* and the present progressive
  express plans or things that have already
  been decided.
- *Will* expresses quick decisions and offers or
  promises.
- The simple present expresses scheduled
  future events.

Theme: SPACE TRAVEL

Unit 6 focuses on language used to describe
the future of space travel as well as future
activities in everyday life. It covers the use of
future forms to talk about facts, predictions,
plans, quick decisions, and scheduled events.

Step 1: Grammar in Context (pages 74–75)

See the general suggestions for Grammar in
Context on page 1.

Before You Read

- Have students look at the photo and discuss
  the questions in pairs. Encourage students to
  write notes of reasons people want to travel
  into space and reasons they would/wouldn't
  like to do so.
- Call on pairs to share their answers with the
  class.
- ⏱ Take a poll of the class to find out if most
  students are/aren't interested in traveling into
  space.

Read

- To encourage students to read with a purpose,
  write these questions on the board:
  1. Where will space tourists travel? *(100 km/
     70 miles above the Earth/to the edge of
     space)*
  2. How long will trips last? *(about three
     hours)*
  3. How much will it cost? *($200,000, but
     costs will fall in time)*
  4. What will people do during the trip?
     *(experience zero gravity and view the Earth
     from space)*
- Have students read the text. (OR: Play the
  audio and have students follow along in their
  books.) Then call on students to share their
  answers to the questions on the board.

- To get students to share their ideas on the
  reading, form pairs or small groups. Write
  the following facts on the board and have
  students discuss how much they would be
  prepared to pay for a trip in space. Encourage
  them to support their views.

  In 2001, U.S. businessman Dennis Tito paid
  $20 million for a trip into space.
  Some scientists predict that a trip into space
  will cost about $50,000 in the near future.

After You Read

A. Vocabulary

- Have students complete the exercise
  individually. Encourage them to use context
  clues to help.
- Have students compare answers in pairs.
  Then call on pairs to give answers.
- ⏱ For further practice, use the vocabulary
  in incomplete sentences about the interview
  on page 74. Have students repeat and
  complete the sentences. Say: "Tourists will
  travel to the edge . . ." *(of space)* "They will
  experience . . ." *(zero gravity)* "They will float
  . . ." *(in the cabin/spaceplane)* "It will be an
  incredible . . ." *(trip/experience)* "The first ten
  flights are sold out, so tourists can . . ." *(get
  tickets for the eleventh flight)* "During takeoff
  tourists have to . . ." *(wear a seatbelt)*

B. Comprehension

- Have students complete the exercise
  individually.
- Have students compare answers in pairs.
  Then call on pairs to give answers. Encourage
  students to support their answers. (Example:
  *The correct answer is "Now" because Dr. Starr
  says they are already building the space planes.*)

Go to **www.myfocusongrammarlab.com** for an
additional reading, and for reading and vocabulary
practice.

Step 2: Grammar Presentation (pages 76–79)

See the general suggestions for Grammar
Presentation on page 2.

Grammar Charts

- To explain *be going to* for the future, write on
  the board:
  I am going to take the next flight.
  We are going to leave from Terminal B.
  — Ask: "How do you form future statements
    with *going to*?" *(form of* be + going to +
    base form of verb) "Is the future with *going
    to* the same for all pronouns?" *(no)*

— Erase "I am." Elicit the full conjugation of *be going to*. Have students say full sentences. *(You are going to take the next flight, he is going to take the next flight,* and so on.)

- To explain *will* for the future, write on the board:
  I will take the next flight.
  We will leave from Terminal B.
  — Ask: "How do you form future statements with *will*?" (will + *base form of verb*) "Does *will* change when the pronoun changes?" *(no)*

- To explain the present progressive for the future, write on the board:
  I'm taking the next flight.
  We're leaving from Terminal B.
  — Ask: "Does the present progressive have present or future meaning in the first sentence?" *(future)* "How do you know?" *(because it says* next flight) "Does the present progressive have present or future meaning in the second sentence?" *(future)* "How do you know?" *(because of the context/situation)*

- To explain the simple present for the future, write on the board:
  The next flight leaves at 9:00.
  — Ask: "Does the simple present have present or future meaning in this sentence?" *(future)* "What future time expression is there in the sentence?" *(at 9:00)*

- To review negative forms, call on students to turn each of the examples on the board into negative sentences. (Example: *I am not going to take the next flight. I will not take the next flight.)*

- To review *yes/no* questions, call on students to turn each of the examples on the board into *yes/no* questions and provide possible answers. (Example: *Are you going to take the next flight? Yes, I am. / No, I'm not. Will you take the next flight? Yes, I will. / No, I won't.)*

- To review *wh-* questions, call on students to turn each of the examples on the board into *wh-* questions and provide possible answers. (Example: *Why are you going to take the flight? Why will you take the next flight?)*

Grammar Notes

Note 1
- Draw a new timeline on the board:

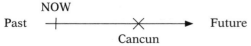

- To review the ways to talk about the future, give examples related to the timeline on the board. Say: "I'm going to go to Cancun next week. I think I'll have fun. I'm catching a 5:00 flight. I come back at 8:00 on Sunday." If necessary, write the examples on the board and have students identify the future forms.

Note 2
- To explain the use of *be going to* and *will* for future facts or things that one is certain will happen in the future, write on the board:
  Lin is going to turn 20 next week.
  Alan will turn 30 in April.
- Point out that the facts in the example will happen for sure. Ask: "What future forms are used in the example?" (be going to *and* will)

Note 3
- To explain the use of *be going to* and *will* for predictions or things one is quite sure will happen in the future, write on the board:
  I think the number of space tourists is going to increase.
  I think the number of space tourists will increase.
- Point out that both sentences have the same meaning—they express predictions. Ask: "What future forms are used for predictions?" (be going to *and* will)
- Draw attention to the *Be Careful!* note. Give more examples. Say: "I'm not feeling well. I think I'm going to be sick." "It's 5:55! We're going to miss the 6:00 train!"

Note 4
- To explain the use of *be going to* and the present progressive for future plans or things one has already decided, write on the board:
  I'm going to give a party in May.
  I'm giving a party in May.
- Point out that both sentences have the same meaning—they express plans. Ask: "What future forms are used in the examples?" (be going to *and the present progressive)*

Note 5
- To explain the use of *will* for quick decisions, write on the board:
  A: That looks like a good movie.
  B: It does. I think I'll go.
- Point out that we use *will* when we make a decision at the moment of speaking.
- To explain the use of *will* for offers or promises, write on the board:
  A: I don't understand this exercise.
  B: Don't worry. I'll help you.

Note 6

- To explain the use of the simple present for scheduled future events, write on the board:
The plane leaves at 4:00.
The zoo closes at 5:00.
- Point out that we use the simple present for timetables, programs, and schedules. Point out that we often use verbs such as *start, leave, end,* and *begin* this way.
- 🕐 Summarize the ways to express the future on the board.

Future facts	→	*Be going to/will*
Predictions	→	*Be going to/will*
Future plans	→	*Be going to*/present progressive
Quick decisions	→	*Will*
Offers or promises	→	*Will*
Scheduled events	→	Simple present

🕐 **Identify the Grammar:** Have students identify the grammar in the opening reading on page 74. For example:

... **is going to talk** to us about space tourism.
... **is** this really **going to happen**?
... our training program for passengers **is starting** next January.
Where **will** these tours **go**?

Go to **www.myfocusongrammarlab.com** for grammar charts and notes.

Step 3: Focused Practice (pages 79–85)

See the general suggestions for Focused Practice on page 4.

Exercise 1: Discover the Grammar

A

- Go over the example with the class. Point out that this is an example of *be going to*. Ask: "What other future forms will you probably find in the transcript?" *(the present progressive for the future, the simple present for the future, and* will + *base form)*
- Have students complete the exercise individually. Then call on students to give answers.

B

- Have students complete the chart in pairs. Have students refer to Grammar Notes 2 through 6 on pages 78–79 if necessary.

Exercise 2: *Will* for Facts and Predictions

- Go over the example with the class. Point out that students have to use affirmative, negative, and interrogative forms of *will*, as needed. Point out that a *Q & A session* is a period of time a group of people can ask an expert questions.
- Have students complete the exercise individually.
- Have students compare answers in pairs. Then have pairs role-play the conversations.

Exercise 3: *Be going to* for Prediction

- Go over the example with the class. Point out that some statements are negative.
- Have students complete the exercise individually.
- Have students compare answers in pairs. Then go over the answers as a class.

Exercise 4: Present Progressive for Plans

- Go over the example with the class.
- Have students complete the exercise in pairs. Then call on pairs to give answers.
- 🕐 Have pairs talk about their plans for today, after their English lesson. Have them use the present progressive.

Exercise 5: Simple Present for Schedules

- Have students study the schedule. To check comprehension, ask: "Which season is this schedule for?" *(fall)* "Where does the shuttle go?" *(to the moon)* "How long does it take to get to the moon?" *(more than three days)* "How often does it travel to the moon?" *(twice a month)*
- Go over the example with the class.
- Have students complete the activity in pairs. Then go over the answers as a class.

Exercise 6: Forms of the Future

- Go over the example with the class. Ask: "Why is *It's going to rain* the correct answer?" *(because Jason is almost certain that it's going to happen—he has heard the weather report)*
- Have students complete the exercise individually.
- Go over the answers as a class. Then have pairs role-play the conversations.

Exercise 7: Editing

- Have students read the report quickly for meaning. Then ask: "What will the differences between space tourists and astronauts be?" *(Space tourists won't work, worry about technical problems, or go outside the spacecraft to make repairs.)* And the similarities? *(They will both do the same regular activities and exercises to stay fit. They will both have new adventures.)*
- Go over the example with the class.
- Have students find and correct the mistakes individually. Then go over the answers as a class, having students explain why the incorrect structures are wrong.
- ⏱ Have students point out examples of correct usages of the future forms.

Go to **www.myfocusongrammarlab.com** for additional grammar practice.

Step 4: Communication Practice (pages 86–89)

See the general suggestions for Communication Practice on page 5.

Exercise 8: Listening

A

- Play the audio. Have students listen to the conversations. Then have them listen again to complete the exercise individually.
- Have students listen a third time and write brief notes about what the people are talking about in each conversation.
- Go over the answers as a class, having students use their notes to support their answers. (Example: *1. They are talking about the future—what one woman is doing tonight. 2. They are talking about what is happening now—what Pete is watching on TV.*)

B

- Have students read the statements quickly for meaning. Play the audio. Have students listen and complete the exercise individually.
- Call on students to correct the false statements.

Exercise 9: Pronunciation

A

- Play the audio. Have students read along as they listen to the Pronunciation Note. Be sure students identify the contractions.

B

- Play the audio. Have students listen.

C

- Play the audio. Have students listen and repeat.
- Have students practice the conversations with a partner. Be sure students play both roles.

Exercise 10: Making Plans

A

- Have students work individually to complete their weekend schedules. Point out that they should write in note form. Write a few examples on the board:
  Buy gift for mom
  Lunch with Jean at Rock Café
  Meeting with Joe Pegs

B

- Brainstorm with the class ways to invite someone and ways to accept an invitation. Write students' ideas on the board, for example:
  Do you want to _____ ? I'd love to.
  Would you like to _____ ? That would be nice.
  Why don't we _____ ? Sounds great.
- Go over the example with the class.
- Have students complete the exercise in pairs. Then have pairs role-play their conversations.

Exercise 11: Reaching Agreement

- Have pairs look at their own weekend schedule on page 87 and the schedule of events on page 88 and decide which events they will attend together this weekend.
- Go over the example with the class. Have students decide which two or three events from the schedule to attend.
- Follow up by asking each pair which events they will attend. Have students explain why they chose a particular event.

Exercise 12: Writing

A

- Write questions on the board to help elicit vocabulary and generate ideas:
  Who will you live with?
  What will you do in your free time?
  What will you spend your money on?
  Where will you go on vacation?
- Have students make notes to answer questions of their choice from the book or the board. Then have students use their notes as a guide when they write.

B

- Have students correct their work using the Editing Checklist.

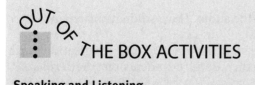

OUT OF THE BOX ACTIVITIES

Speaking and Listening

- Have students who have brought a personal organizer or a datebook to class raise their hands. Have them form small groups with students who don't have one. (If half the class has a personal organizer or datebook, students should work in pairs.)
- Have students open their datebooks or turn on their organizers and talk about their plans for the coming weeks. Encourage students to ask follow-up questions. (Example: Student A: *I'm going out for dinner on Friday.* Student B: *Who are you going with?* Student A: *My mom.* Student B: *I'm going to the movies on Saturday.* Student A: *What time does the movie start?*)

Reading and Speaking

- Bring in today's or yesterday's newspapers.
- Explain the game: Each group will get a newspaper and will have 15 minutes to circle in their newspaper three scheduled events, three plans or arrangements, and three predictions about the future. Have them write a sentence about each on a separate sheet of paper. Have students use the ways to express the future they learned in this unit. If necessary, give an example of each category: *The conference on globalization starts at 8:00 A.M.* (scheduled event); *The president is traveling to Spain next week.* (arrangement); *Scientists say they will soon find a cure for cancer.* (prediction)
- When time is up, collect the sentences. The group with the most correct sentences wins.

Go to **www.myfocusongrammarlab.com** for additional listening, pronunciation, speaking, and writing practice.

Note:
- See the *Focus on Grammar Workbook* for additional in-class or homework grammar practice.

Unit 6 Review (page 90)

Have students complete the Review and check their answers on Student Book page UR-2. Review or assign additional material as needed.

Go to **www.myfocusongrammarlab.com** for the Unit Achievement Test.

UNIT 7 OVERVIEW

Grammar: FUTURE TIME CLAUSES

Unit 7 focuses on the meanings and uses of future time clauses.

- Future time clauses begin with time expressions such as *when, after, as soon as, before, until,* and *while.*
- The verb in future time clauses is normally in the simple present tense.
- Future time clauses can come at the beginning or end of sentences.

Theme: SETTING GOALS

Unit 7 focuses on language used to describe future goals, such as starting a job, getting married, and buying a house.

Step 1: Grammar in Context (pages 91–92)

See the general suggestions for Grammar in Context on page 1.

Before You Read

- Write the word *goal* on the board. Elicit or explain its meaning. (*something that you hope to succeed in doing in the future*)
- Have students look at the picture in the reading and discuss the questions in pairs. As students discuss, have them take notes about typical goals and steps to reach them.
- Call on pairs to give answers. Write the goals students mention on the board. (Example: *graduating, getting a degree, getting married, having a family, buying a car/house/apartment, going on a trip, getting a job, getting a promotion*)

Read

- To encourage students to read with a purpose, write these questions on the board:
  1. According to the article, what four steps should you take to change your dream into a goal? *(write down your dream, list your reasons, write down an action plan, and take your first steps today)*
  2. What is Latoya's dream/goal? *(becoming a successful businessperson)*

3. What are some of the things she plans to do to reach it? *(save money, go to business school, get her degree, get a job with a big company)*
- Have students read the text. (OR: Play the audio and have students follow along in their books.) Then call on students to share their answers to the questions on the board.
- To get students to share their ideas on the reading, form pairs or small groups. Have students discuss which two steps from the article they consider most important. Encourage them to support their views. Have them also think about other steps that could have been included in the article.
- ⏱ Have students discuss the following questions in small groups:
  What does achieving a goal depend on? Does it only depend on yourself? Does it also depend on luck? Can a goal be achieved in spite of the obstacles?
- Call on students from various groups to share their conclusions with the class.

After You Read

A. Vocabulary
- Have students complete the exercise individually. Encourage them to use context clues to help.
- Have students compare answers in pairs. Then call on pairs to give answers.

B. Comprehension
- Have students complete the exercise individually.
- Have students compare answers in pairs. Then call on pairs to read the action plan in the correct order.

Go to **www.myfocusongrammarlab.com** for an additional reading, and for reading and vocabulary practice.

Step 2: Grammar Presentation (pages 93–94)

See the general suggestions for Grammar Presentation on page 2.

Grammar Charts
- To explain future time clauses, write on the board:
  1. <u>When I have my degree</u>, I'll get a job with a big company.
  2. She's going to go on a trip <u>as soon as she graduates</u>.

— Ask: "How many clauses does each sentence have?" *(two)* "Which part of each sentence is the time clause?" *(the part that is underlined)* "How do time clauses start?" *(with a time expression)* "What time expressions are used in the examples?" *(when and as soon as)*
— Point to the verb in the first time clause *(have)* and ask: "What verb form is this?" *(simple present)* "Does the other time clause also have a present verb form?" *(yes)* "What's the verb in the present in the other time clause?" *(graduates)* "Do main clauses also have present verb forms?" *(no)* "What verb forms do they have?" *(future forms: will or be going to)*
— Do not erase the board.
- To explain *yes/no* and *wh-* questions with future time clauses, write on the board:
  3. Will you start your own business before you turn 40?
  4. What are you going to do when you finish high school?
— Ask: "What are the time clauses in the examples?" *(before you turn 40, when you finish high school)* "Which part of the sentence needs inversion when you make a question—the main clause or the future time clause?" *(the main clause)*
— Call on a student to come to the front and turn the affirmative sentences on the board (1 and 2) into questions. *(Will you get a job with a big company when you have your degree? Is she going to go on a trip as soon as she graduates?)*
— Call on another student to write the possible short answers. *(Yes, I will. / No, I won't. Yes, she is. / No, she isn't.)*
— Have another student turn the *yes/no* questions on the board (3 and 4) into *wh-* questions. *(Where will you get a job when you have your degree? What is she going to do as soon as she graduates?)*

Grammar Notes

Note 1
- To explain the use of future time clauses, write on the board:
  She will buy a car as soon as she saves enough money.
- Ask: "What two future events does the sentence express?" *(buying a car and saving enough money)* "Which event will happen first?" *(saving enough money)*
- Point out that future time clauses show the time relationship between two future events.

- To review the verb form in future time clauses, write on the board:
  She will reserve the hotel after she buys the plane ticket.
- Ask: "Is the verb in the time clause in the present or in the future?" *(the present)*
- Remind students that *be going to* and *will* are never used in future time clauses. (They are used in main clauses.)
- To explain the order of the clauses, write the following example on the board:
  After she buys the plane ticket, she will reserve the hotel.
- Point out that the time clause can come at the beginning or at the end of a sentence. If it comes at the beginning, a comma is needed following the time clause.

Note 2
- To explain future time clauses with *when*, *after*, *as soon as*, and *before*, write the following sentences on the board, leaving space above them:
  When/As soon as/After Tom finishes his French course, he'll travel to Paris.
  Before Tom travels to Paris, he will finish his French course.
- Have students study the first example. Ask: "What will happen first?" *(Tom will finish his French course.)* Write *1* above the time clause as shown below. Then ask: "What will happen next?" *(Tom will travel to Paris.)* Write *2* above the main clause as shown.

1
[When/As soon as/After Tom finishes his French course,]
2
[he'll travel to Paris.]

- Have students study the second example. Ask: "What will happen first?" *(Tom will finish his French course.)* Write *1* above the main clause. Then ask: "What will happen next?" *(Tom will travel to Paris.)* Write *2* above the time clause.

2
[Before Tom travels to Paris,]
1
[he will finish his French course.]

- Then ask: "Do *when*, *as soon as*, and *after* introduce the first event or the second event?" *(the first event)* "Does *before* introduce the first event or the second event?" *(the second event)*

- To explain time clauses with *until*, write on the board:
  Tom will keep taking his driving test until he passes it.
- To help clarify, say: "A time clause with *until* indicates that something will continue to happen until something else happens: Tom will stop taking his driving test only when he passes it."
- To explain time clauses with *while*, point out that *while* in a time clause indicates that something will happen at the same time as the event in the main clause. Give an example. Say: "While Tom is in Paris, he will keep on learning French."

🕐 **Identify the Grammar:** Have students identify the grammar in the opening reading on page 91. For example:
  . . . **when you're 22?**
  . . . **before you turn 40?**
  . . . **until we change them to goals.**

Go to **www.myfocusongrammarlab.com** for grammar charts and notes.

Step 3: Focused Practice (pages 95–97)
See the general suggestions for Focused Practice on page 4.

Exercise 1: Discover the Grammar
- Go over the example with the class.
- Have students complete the exercise individually.
- Call on students to give answers.

Exercise 2: Simple Present or Future
- Have students read the worksheet for meaning.
- Go over the example with the class. Ask: "What is the future time clause?" *(after I graduate)* "What time expression introduces the clause?" *(after)* "What verb form does it need?" *(simple present)*
- Have students do the exercise individually. Encourage them to find and circle the time expressions that introduce future time clauses. Then go over the answers as a class.

Exercise 3: Order of Events
- Go over the example with the class. Point out that students may need to change the order of clauses.
- Have students do the exercise individually.
- Have students compare answers in pairs. Then go over the answers as a class.

Exercise 4: Editing

- Have students read the journal entry quickly for meaning. Then ask: "What is the journal entry about?" *(what the student will do when he/she finishes high school)* "Has the student made plans already, or is he/she still making decisions?" *(He/she is still making decisions.)*
- Go over the example with the class.
- Have students find and correct the mistakes individually. Then call on students to explain why the incorrect structures are wrong.
- ⏱ Have students point out examples of correct usages of the future time clauses.

Go to **www.myfocusongrammarlab.com** for additional grammar practice.

Step 4: Communication Practice

(pages 98–101)

See the general suggestions for Communication Practice on page 5.

Exercise 5: Listening

A

- Ask: "What services do employment agencies provide?" *(Example: They find jobs for people; they suggest additional training; they give people advice on the most suitable kind of work.)*
- If (some of) your students are in the work force, you can draw on their previous experience by asking them if they ever got a job through an employment agency. Have them briefly describe their experience.
- Play the audio. Have students listen and put the events in order. Then go over the answers as a class.

B

- Have students read the sentences so that they can listen for specific information.
- Play the audio. Have students listen and complete the exercise individually.
- Have students compare answers in pairs. Then call on pairs to give answers.

Exercise 6: Pronunciation

A

- Play the audio. Have students read along as they listen to the Pronunciation Note. Be sure students understand that intonation drops at the end of both clauses, but it drops more at the end of the last clause to mark the end of the statement.

B

- Play the audio. Have students listen and notice the intonation in the answers.

C

- Play the audio. Have students listen and repeat.
- Have students practice the conversations with a partner. Be sure students play both roles.

Exercise 7: What About You?

A

- Have students read the incomplete sentences and decide if they need a future time clause or a main clause. Then have them complete the sentences. Remind students that future forms are not used in future time clauses.
- Have students complete the sentences individually.

B

- Go over the example as a class.
- Form small groups and have students share their sentences. Encourage them to keep the conversation going by making relevant comments and asking follow-up questions.

Exercise 8: Game: What's Next?

- Go over the example with the class. Be sure students understand they have to start their sentence with a future time clause that uses information from the main clause of the previous student's sentence.
- Encourage students to be creative and to continue playing until they run out of ideas.

Exercise 9: Writing

A

- Have students complete the worksheet individually. Remind students to use future time clauses. Refer students to the reading on page 91 and to Exercise 2 on page 96, which illustrate how future time clauses can be used in this context.

B

- Have students correct their work using the Editing Checklist.
- ⏱ Form small groups and have students share their plans. Encourage students to give their classmates any advice or information that can help them reach their goals.

OUT OF THE BOX ACTIVITIES

Speaking and Writing

- Explain what a time capsule is *(a container that is filled with objects from a particular time so that people in the future will know what life was like then).*
- Have students predict the sequence of life events that they expect to experience in the next ten years. (Example: *marriage, homes, jobs, children*) Have students write their predictions.
- Form small groups and have students discuss their predictions. Then have students seal their predictions in an envelope and write on the front "Time Capsule: Open Ten Years From [today's date]." Suggest that they put it in a place where they will remember to look at it in ten years.

Reading and Speaking

- Bring in travel magazines or brochures of places to go on vacation. (Example: *hotels, resorts, theme parks*) Hand out the magazines and/or brochures.
- Form pairs or small groups and have students imagine they will go on vacation to the place in their brochure or a place of their choice from the travel magazine. Have students plan their vacation by writing down notes of the things they will do in the order in which they will do them, for example:
  1. Arrive at Heathrow airport
  2. Buy a camera at duty-free shop
  3. Get to hotel
  4. Take a nap!
  5. Go sightseeing: Visit the Tower of London
- Have students join another pair or group and share their vacation plans, using their notes as a guide. Encourage students to use future time clauses. (Example: *When we arrive at the airport, we'll buy a camera at the duty-free shop. As soon as we get to the hotel, we'll take a nap.*)

Go to **www.myfocusongrammarlab.com** for additional listening, pronunciation, speaking, and writing practice.

Note:
- See the *Focus on Grammar Workbook* for additional in-class or homework grammar practice.

Unit 7 Review (page 102)

Have students complete the Review and check their answers on Student Book page UR-2. Review or assign additional material as needed.

Go to **www.myfocusongrammarlab.com** for the Unit Achievement Test.

From Grammar to Writing (pages 103–105)

See the general suggestions for From Grammar to Writing on page 9.

Go to **www.myfocusongrammarlab.com** for an additional From Grammar to Writing Assignment, Part Review, and Part Post-Test.

PART III OVERVIEW

PRESENT PERFECT

UNIT	GRAMMAR FOCUS	THEME
8	Present Perfect: *Since* and *For*	Careers
9	Present Perfect: *Already, Yet,* and *Still*	Party Planning
10	Present Perfect: Indefinite Past	Adventure Travel
11	Present Perfect and Simple Past	Long-Distance Relationships
12	Present Perfect Progressive and Present Perfect	Climate Change

Go to **www.myfocusongrammarlab.com** for the Part and Unit Tests.

Note: PowerPoint® grammar presentations, test-generating software, and reproducible Part and Unit Tests are on the *Teacher's Resource Disc.*

Grammar: PRESENT PERFECT: *Since* AND *For*

Unit 8 focuses on the uses of the present perfect with *since* and *for*.

- The present perfect describes an action that began in the past and continues into the present (and may continue into the future).
- It is used with *since* to show when something started and with *for* to show how long a present condition has lasted.

Theme: CAREERS

Unit 8 focuses on language used to talk about people's lives, careers, and accomplishments.

Step 1: Grammar in Context (pages 108–109)

See the general suggestions for Grammar in Context on page 1.

Before You Read

- Have students look at the photo and the text on the sports card and discuss the questions in pairs.
- Call on pairs to give answers. Make a list of students' interests on the board.

Read

- To encourage students to read with a purpose, write these questions on the board:
  1. Why did Bob Burnquist's life change when he was 11 years old? *(because he started skating and he has never stopped since then)*
  2. How does he support himself? *(doing his favorite sport—skateboarding)*
- Have students read the text. (OR: Play the audio and have students follow along in their books.) Then call on students to share their answers to the questions on the board.
- To get students to share their ideas on the reading, form pairs or small groups. Have them discuss one or both of the following topics:
  1. Bob Burnquist supports himself doing what he loves the most. What do you love the most? Would you like to support yourself doing that? Explain why or why not.
  2. What are the advantages and disadvantages of being a professional sportsperson? Consider such aspects as fame, ups and downs, and so on. Give examples to support your view.

After You Read

A. Vocabulary

- Have students complete the exercise individually. Encourage them to use context clues to help.
- Have students compare answers in pairs. Then call on pairs to give answers.
- ⏱ Books closed. For further practice, say sentences using the definitions in Part A and have students restate them using the vocabulary words. Say: "Bob's life changed a lot when he was a kid." *(Bob's life changed dramatically when he was a kid.)* "He pays for his food, clothing, and home." *(He supports himself.)* "He thinks he is a citizen of the world." *(He considers himself a citizen of the world.)* "International contests provide good chances for gaining fame." *(International contests provide the opportunity to gain fame.)* "His home is in the United States." *(His residence is in the United States.)* "He always believes good things will happen." *(He's always positive.)*

B. Comprehension

- Have students complete the exercise individually.
- Have students compare answers in pairs. Then call on pairs to correct the false statements.

Go to **www.myfocusongrammarlab.com** for an additional reading, and for reading and vocabulary practice.

Step 2: Grammar Presentation

(pages 110–111)

See the general suggestions for Grammar Presentation on page 2.

Grammar Charts

- To explain the present perfect affirmative with *for* and *since*, write on the board:
  Bob has lived in California since 1995.
  His friends have lived in Brazil for about 30 years.
  — Have students study the examples. Then ask: "How many words are needed for the present perfect?" *(two)* "How do you form the present perfect?" *(form of* have + *past participle)*

— Underline *since 1995* and *for about 30 years* in the examples and ask: "What does *since 1995* express?" *(the moment when Bob started living in California)* "Does Bob still live in California?" *(yes)* "What does *for about 30 years* express?" *(how long Bob's friends have lived in Brazil)* "Do Bob's friends still live in Brazil?" *(yes)*

— Emphasize that the present perfect with *for* and *since* expresses things that began in the past and *continue into the present*.

— Erase *Bob has* and *His friends have* and replace them with *He's* and *They've*. Point out that *have* and *has* are contracted in everyday speech—especially after pronouns.

— Point out that the contraction for *has* is the same as for *be*: *he's, she's, it's*. Use of the past participle marks the present perfect.

• To explain the present perfect negative, write on the board:

Bob and Jen <u>have</u>   Bob <u>has not stopped</u>
<u>not married</u>.   since then.
They <u>haven't</u>   He <u>hasn't stopped</u>
<u>married</u>.   since then.

— Ask: "How do you form the negative present perfect?" (*form of* have + not + *past participle*) "What are the contractions?" (haven't *or* hasn't + *past participle*)

• To explain *yes/no* and *wh-* questions with present perfect, write on the board:
Has he won any prizes?
How long have they been in California?

— Ask: "How do you form *yes/no* questions?" (*form of* have + *subject* + *past participle*) "How do you form *wh-* questions?" (wh- *word* + *form of* have + *subject* + *past participle*)

— Call on a student to write on the board the two possible answers to the *yes/no* question. (*Yes, he has. / No, he hasn't.*)

— Call on another student to provide the two possible short answers for the *wh-* question. (Example: *since 1991; for 16 years.*)

Grammar Notes

Note 1

• Remind students that the present perfect with *since* and *for* expresses something that started in the past and continues into the present. It may also continue into the future. To illustrate your point, draw a timeline on the board with information about yourself:

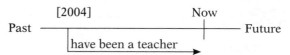

```
        [2004]                 Now
Past ─────────────────────────────┬──── Future
     │ have been a teacher         │
     └────────────────────────►
```

• Say: "I have been a teacher since [2004]. I started being a teacher in [2004], and I'm still a teacher."

Note 2

• Point out that *since* + a point in time is used to show *when* something started. Write examples on the board:
since July
since spring
since I graduated
since last week
since they were born
since my parents moved here

• Explain that the point in time can be expressed with a time clause. Have students say which examples from the board contain time clauses. (*since I graduated, since they were born, since my parents moved here*)

• Point out that *for* + a length of time is used to show *how long* something has lasted. Write examples on the board:
for three hours
for several weeks
for two months
for a year

• Point out that *for* + a length of time can express the same idea as *since* + a point in time. Write two contrasting examples on the board:
I have lived here since 2008. = I have lived here for [insert correct number of years].

Note 3

• To review how the present perfect is formed, write on the board:
They <u>have worked</u> for a big company for several years.
He <u>has won</u> a lot of competitions.

• Ask: "How do you form the present perfect?" (*form of* have + *past participle*)

• Remind students that verbs can be regular or irregular. Ask: "What is *worked* the past participle of?" (work) "Is it regular or irregular?" *(regular)* "What is *won* the past participle of?" (win) "Is it regular or irregular?" *(irregular)*

• To explain how to form the past participle of regular verbs, write on the board:

Base Form	Simple Past	Past Participle
work	worked	worked
live	lived	lived
decide	decided	decided

- Point out that the past participle of regular verbs is formed by adding *-ed* or *-d*. It is the same as the past form.
- Draw a horizontal line below the *decide* row and add more verbs in each column:

spend	spent	spent
meet	met	met
go	went	gone
give	gave	given

- Point out that the past participle of irregular verbs is not formed by adding *-ed* or *-d*. The past participle of *some* irregular verbs is the same as the past form.
- If needed, refer students to Appendix 1 on page A-1 for a list of irregular past participles.

(!) **Identify the Grammar:** Have students identify the grammar in the opening reading on page 108. For example:

He's **been** a skater **since then**.
Bob **has lived** in California **since 1995** . . .
He's **had** dual citizenship (Brazil and the United States) **for many years**.

Go to **www.myfocusongrammarlab.com** for grammar charts and notes.

Step 3: Focused Practice (pages 112–116)

See the general suggestions for Focused Practice on page 4.

Exercise 1: Discover the Grammar
- Go over the example with the class. Ask: "Why is *She is still a skater* the correct answer?" *(because the present perfect expresses actions or situations that continue into the present)*
- Have students complete the exercise individually.
- Have students compare in pairs. Then go over the answers as a class.

Exercise 2: *Since or For*
- Go over the example with the class. Remind students that correct sentence structures use *since* + a point in time or *for* + a length of time.
- Have students complete the exercise individually. Then go over the answers as a class.
- (!) For further practice, have pairs restate the sentences using *since* or *for*, as appropriate. (Example: *Mariana Andrade has lived in São Paulo for [number of years up to now]*.)

Exercise 3: Forms of the Present Perfect
- Go over the example with the class. Have students read the article for general meaning.

- Have students complete the exercise individually. Then go over the answers as a class.
- (!) For further practice, personalize the information in the article by asking questions. Address different students and say: "Roque Guterres has loved skating since he was a boy. And you? What have you loved doing since you were a child?" "He's had the same apartment for five years. And you? How long have you lived in the same place?" "He hasn't taken a vacation for many years. And you? How long has it been since you last took a vacation?" Have various students answer the same questions.

Exercise 4: Forms of the Present Perfect with *Since* or *For*
- Go over the example with the class.
- Have students complete the exercise in pairs. Then call on pairs to give answers.
- (!) Books closed. Have students say interesting facts about skateboarding that they remember from the exercise. Encourage them to use the present perfect with *since* or *for*.

Exercise 5: Questions, Statements, and Short Answers

A
- Elicit from the class what a résumé is *(a written list and description of a person's education and previous jobs, usually in chronological order with the most recent experience in each category first)*
- If necessary, explain that M.A. means master of arts, a university degree in a subject such as literature or history that you can get after you have your first degree.
- Have students look at the résumé and the interviewer's notes. Ask: "Where does Amy Lu live?" *(in Honolulu)* "What job is she applying for?" *(college sports instructor)* "Does she have any previous experience?" *(Yes, she's been a teacher and a sports trainer.)* "What other important qualifications does she have?" *(She has a certificate. She has an M.A. in physical education. She's won two awards.)*

B
- Go over the example with the class. If necessary, point out the word order for questions.
- Have students do the exercise individually. Then have them compare answers in pairs.

C

- Go over the example with the class. Remind students to use contractions when possible.
- Have students do the exercise in pairs. Then call on pairs to give answers.
- ⏱ Have pairs role-play the interview.

Exercise 6: Editing

- Have students read the posts to the online message board quickly to find out what they are about.
- Ask the following questions and have the class scan the text for the answers: "Who has broken three boards so far?" *(Sang-Ook)* "Who has gone to a skate park every day since it opened?" *(Sylvie)* "Who has won two contests?" *(Paulo)* "Who was a surfer before becoming a skater?" *(Ming)* "Who has broken a part of their body twice?" *(Marta)*
- Have students do the exercise individually. Then go over the answers as a class, having students explain why the incorrect structures are wrong.
- ⏱ Have students point out examples of correct usages of the present perfect with *since* or *for*.

Go to **www.myfocusongrammarlab.com** for additional grammar practice.

Step 4: Communication Practice

(pages 117–119)

See the general suggestions for Communication Practice on page 5.

Exercise 7: Listening

A

- Have students read the sentences. Then play the audio. Have students listen.
- Have students listen again and complete the exercise individually.
- Have students compare answers in pairs. Then go over the answers as a class.

B

- Play the audio. Have students listen and complete the exercise individually. Point out that there may be more than one way to complete each sentence. (Example: *since Monday* is the same as *for [number] days*.)
- Go over the answers as a class.
- ⏱ Follow up with a brief discussion. Ask: "Is Eliana Serrano a good candidate for the job?" Encourage students to support their answers.

Exercise 8: Pronunciation

A

- Play the audio. Have students read along as they listen to the Pronunciation Note. Check comprehension by asking: "Does the voice go up or down at the end of a *yes/no* question?" *(up)* "And at the end of a *wh-* question?" *(down)*

B

- Play the audio. Have students listen, notice the intonation, and draw the arrows going up or down.

C

- Play the audio. Have students listen and repeat the questions.
- Have students practice the conversations with a partner. Be sure students play both roles.

Exercise 9: Role Play: A Job Interview

A

- Go over the résumés with the class and answer any questions. Point out that a publication is something that the person has written and has appeared in a magazine, journal, or other media.
- Go over the example with the class. Point out the *wh-* word *how long* and the present perfect verb form.
- Have pairs write the questions to ask the candidates. Remind them to ask questions starting with *How long, How many,* and *Have you . . . since?* Then call on pairs to give answers. (Example: *How many courses have you taught? How long have you worked since you graduated?*)

B

- Have pairs role-play the interviews using the questions they wrote as a guide.

C

- Form small groups. Have groups complete the exercise. Then have them present their decision and explain their choice to the class.

Exercise 10: Writing

A

- Before students write their paragraph, write the following questions on the board to help elicit vocabulary and generate ideas:
  How long has the person been a/an [job or profession]?
  How long has the person worked in/for [company or person]?
  How many prizes/awards has the person received since _____ ?

How many books has the person written since
_____ ?

How many times has the person appeared on
TV since _____ ?

What important things has the person
achieved since _____ ?

How long has the person been a member of
[institution]?

• Have students make notes for each question
  and then use them as a guide as they write.

B
• Have students use the Editing Checklist to
  correct their work.

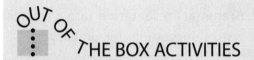

OUT OF THE BOX ACTIVITIES

Writing and Speaking
• Have students write three statements about
  themselves with *since* or *for*. (Example:
  *I've lived in this city since 2008. I've been a
  teacher since 2004. I've been married since
  I graduated from college.*) Have them write
  each sentence on a separate slip of paper.
• Collect the slips, shuffle, and redistribute
  them.
• Have students read the statements and
  identify the person.

Reading and Speaking
• Bring in biographies of contemporary
  people from magazines or websites.
  Form small groups and give each group a
  biography.
• Have students find in the biography things
  about the person's life that started in the
  past and continue into the present. Write
  the following on the board for students to
  use as a guide:

	been a		
	lived in		
	had		
	studied		
	won	____ since ____.	
He/She has	been married	____ for ____.	
	to		
	worked		
	in/for/as		
	liked		

• Have students use the information they
  found and write at least four sentences with
  since and *for*.

• Have students from each group report to
  the class on the biography they read. Point
  out that students should say only sentences
  that use the present perfect with either
  since or *for*.

Go to **www.myfocusongrammarlab.com** for
additional listening, pronunciation, speaking, and
writing practice.

Note:
• See the *Focus on Grammar Workbook* for
  additional in-class or homework grammar
  practice.

Unit 8 Review (page 120)
Have students complete the Review and check
their answers on Student Book page UR-2.
Review or assign additional material as needed.

Go to **www.myfocusongrammarlab.com** for the
Unit Achievement Test.

UNIT 9 OVERVIEW

Grammar: PRESENT PERFECT: *Already, Yet,*
AND *Still*

Unit 9 focuses on the uses of the present
perfect with *already, yet,* and *still.*

• Affirmative and present perfect statements
  with *already* express something that has
  happened before now.

• Negative present perfect statements with *yet*
  express something that has not happened
  before now.

• Negative present perfect statements with *still*
  have a similar meaning to *not yet* but express
  that the speaker is surprised or unhappy.

• Present perfect questions with *yet* ask
  whether something has happened before
  now.

Theme: PARTY PLANNING

Unit 9 focuses on language used to talk about
people's goals and what they have done to
reach them, especially as related to planning a
party.

Step 1: Grammar in Context (pages 121–122)

See the general suggestions for Grammar in Context on page 1.

Before You Read

- Give students a few minutes of silent time to think of their answers to the questions. Encourage them to make notes of reasons why they like/don't like parties and why they prefer to give/go to parties.
- Have students discuss the questions in pairs or small groups.
- Call on students to share their answers. As you get feedback from students, on the board make two lists of reasons why students prefer giving or going to parties.

Read

- To encourage students to read with a purpose, write these questions on the board:
  1. According to the article, is giving a party a very difficult task? *(no)*
  2. Who is Patty Cake? *(a professional party planner)*
  3. Does she think giving a party requires a lot of new skills? *(no)*
  4. What skills do we already have? *(shopping for food, putting food on plates, introducing friends to one another)*
  5. What kind of help can you find on Patty Cake's website? *(free advice, handy lists to check out what you have done/haven't done)*
- Have students read the text. (OR: Play the audio and have students follow along in their books.) Then call on students to share their answers to the questions on the board.
- To get students to share their ideas on the reading, have them imagine that they will give a party for their next birthday. Form small groups and have students tell their classmates what kind of party they would give and if they would hire a party planner. Encourage students to support their views.

After You Read

A. Vocabulary

- Have students complete the exercise individually. Encourage them to use context clues to help.
- Have students compare answers in pairs. Then call on pairs to give answers.
- ⏱ For further practice, write on the board: Think of someone you know who:
  is always available when you need him/her.
  is very organized.
  is successful in his/her career.
  is really professional.

- Have students form small groups and discuss people they know. Have them give examples to explain why they consider these people available, organized, successful, and/or professional.

B. Comprehension

- Have students complete the exercise individually.
- Have students compare answers in pairs. Then call on pairs to give answers.

Go to **www.myfocusongrammarlab.com** for an additional reading, and for reading and vocabulary practice.

Step 2: Grammar Presentation (pages 123–124)

See the general suggestions for Grammar Presentation on page 2.

Grammar Charts

- To explain present perfect statements with *already*, *yet*, and *still*, write on the board:

Present Perfect: Already	Present Perfect: Yet	Present Perfect: Still
I've already sent the invitations. I've sent the invitations already.	I haven't decided on the menu yet.	I still haven't hired a DJ.

  — Point to the first example and ask: "How do you form present perfect statements with *already*?" (*form of* have + already + *past participle*) "Is *already* used in affirmative or in negative statements?" (*affirmative statements*) "In what two positions can *already* go?" (*between a form of* have *and the past participle* OR *at the end of a clause*)
  — Point to the second example and ask: "How do you form present perfect statements with *yet*?" (*form of* have + not + *past participle* + yet) "Is *yet* used in affirmative or in negative statements?" (*negative statements*) "In what position does *yet* normally go?" (*at the end of a clause*)
  — Point to the third example and ask: "How do you form present perfect statements with *still*?" (still + *form of* have + not + *past participle*) "Is *still* used in affirmative or negative statements?" (*negative statements*) "In what position does *still* normally go?" (*before a form of* have)

- To explain present perfect *yes/no* questions with *yet*, write on the board:
  Have you chosen the date yet?
  Has Patty Cake replied to your email yet?
  — Have students study the examples. Then ask: "How do you form present perfect questions with *yet*?" (*form of* have + *subject* + *past participle* + yet)
  — Call on a student to come to the front and write the two possible short answers to the first question on the board. *(Yes, I have. / No, I haven't.)* Do the same for the second question. *(Yes, she has. / No, she hasn't.)*
  — Point out that *yet* can also be used in negative short answers. Write on the board:
    No, I haven't. = No, not yet.
    No, she hasn't. = No, not yet.

Grammar Notes

Note 1
- To help clarify the meaning of present perfect statements with *already*, write an example on the board and draw a timeline:
  1. I've already hired a party planner.

  Past ———————X———————|———— Future
  　　　　hire a party
  　　　　planner

- Point out that the present perfect with *already* expresses that something has happened *some time before now*. (Some time before now, the person hired a party planner.)
- To help clarify the meaning of present perfect statements with *yet* and *still*, write two new examples and draw a new timeline:
  2. I haven't mailed the invitations yet. / I still haven't mailed the invitations.

  　　　　　　　　Now
  Past ———————————|———— Future
  　　~~mail the invitations~~

- Point out that the present perfect with *yet* or *still* expresses that something has *not* happened *some time before now*. (Some time before now, the person did not mail the invitations.)
- Point out that negative statements with *still* express that the speaker is surprised or unhappy.
- Point out that present perfect questions with *yet* are used to ask if something has happened *some time before now*.
- Point out that "Not yet" by itself is commonly used.

Note 2
- To compare questions with *already* and *yet*, write two contrasting conversations on the board:
  1. LYNN: I'm giving a party next month.
     MAX: <u>Have you mailed the invitations yet</u>?
     LYNN: Yes, I have.
  2. LYNN: I'm giving a party for my birthday. I mailed the invitations this morning.
     MAX: You<u>'ve mailed them already</u>? Your birthday is three months away!
- Have students compare the conversations. Then ask: "In which of the two conversations is Max surprised?" *(in the second)* "Why?" *(because Lynn's birthday is three months away and she has already sent the invitations)*
- To explain the use of *already* in American English, write two contrasting examples on the board:
  He has already chosen the music.
  He already chose the music.
- Ask: "Which example uses the present perfect?" *(the first)* "Which example uses the simple past?" *(the second)* "Do both examples use *already*?" *(yes)* "Do they have the same meaning?" *(yes)*
- Point out that the use of *already* with the simple past is possible in American English.
- Point out that the simple past—not the present perfect—is used with past time expressions. To clarify, write on the board:
  Unspecified time in the past: present perfect + already
  Specific time in the past: simple past + time expression

Note 3
- To review the placement of *already*, write on the board:
  have/has + already + past participle + (. . .)
  have/has + past participle + (. . .) + already
- Point out that the usual placement of *already* is between a form of *have* and the past participle. The end position is usually emphatic.
- To review the placement of *yet* and *still*, write on the board:
  haven't/hasn't + past participle + (. . .) + yet
  still + haven't/hasn't + past participle + (. . .)
- Point out that the usual placement of *yet* is at the end of a clause and that the placement of *still* is before the present perfect form of a verb.
- If needed, refer students to Appendix 1 on page A-1 for a list of irregular past participles.

⏱ **Identify the Grammar:** Have students identify the grammar in the opening reading on page 121. For example:

. . . you**'ve already been** to several parties . . .

. . . you **haven't given** one **yet**.

Have you **chosen** the day **yet**?

You**'ve already chosen** the date and the time . . .

Go to **www.myfocusongrammarlab.com** for grammar charts and notes.

Step 3: Focused Practice (pages 124–127)

See the general suggestions for Focused Practice on page 4.

Exercise 1: Discover the Grammar

- Go over the example with the class. Ask: "Why is the second statement false?" *(because the first statement says the person has already given parties)*
- Have students complete the exercise individually.
- Have students compare answers in pairs. Then call on pairs to give answers.

Exercise 2: Questions, Statements, and Short Answers

- Go over the example with the class. Then have students read the conversations quickly for meaning.
- Have students complete the exercise individually. Remind students to use contractions and, if needed, refer students to Appendix 1 on page A-1. Point out that if a verb is not in the appendix, it is regular.
- ⏱ For further practice, have pairs role-play the conversations.

Exercise 3: Affirmative and Negative Statements

- Go over the list and the examples with the class.
- Have students complete the exercise individually. Remind students to use contractions and to refer to Appendix 1 on page A-1 if necessary. Remind students that if a verb is not in the appendix, it is regular.
- ⏱ For further practice, have students think of a task they have to do for school or work. Have them write a checklist of four to five things they need to do to complete the task. Have pairs use their checklist as a guide to tell their partners what they have already done and what they haven't done yet/still haven't done.

Exercise 4: Editing

- Have students read the online bulletin board quickly for meaning.
- Ask the following questions and have the class scan the text for the answers: "Who hasn't decided on a theme for their party yet?" *(Rosa)* "Who hasn't figured out the food yet?" *(Doug)* "Who has already had a pasta party?" *(Rosa)* "Who hasn't met anyone who doesn't like pizza?" *(the party planner)*
- Have students find and correct the mistakes individually. Then go over the answers as a class, having students explain why the incorrect structures are wrong.
- ⏱ Have students point out examples of correct usages of the present perfect with *already, yet,* or *still.*

Go to **www.myfocusongrammarlab.com** for additional grammar practice.

Step 4: Communication Practice

(pages 127–131)

See the general suggestions for Communication Practice on page 5.

Exercise 5: Listening

A
- Have students read the To Do list quickly for meaning.
- Play the audio. Have students listen and complete the exercise individually.
- Go over the answers as a class.

B
- Have students read the questions before listening again. Then play the audio. Have students listen and complete the exercise individually.
- To go over the answers, have students say complete sentences and use *already* or *yet* (or *still*) when appropriate. *(Example: Jason has already borrowed extra chairs.)*

Exercise 6: Pronunciation

A
- Play the audio. Have students read along as they listen to the Pronunciation Note.

B
- Play the audio. Have students listen. Be sure they notice the contractions of *have.*

C
- Play the audio. Have students listen and repeat.
- Have students practice the conversations with a partner. Be sure students play both roles.

Exercise 7: Information Gap: Chores

Step 1

- Divide the class into two groups—Students A and Students B—and then form pairs.
- Ask Students A to stay on the page and Students B to go to page 131.
- Have Students A look at the picture and cross out the things Gisela has already done. Have Students B look at the picture and cross out the things Helmut has already done.
- Go over Helmut and Gisela's To Do lists and elicit from students the past participles of the verbs on the lists. Write them on the board as students say them. For example:

Base Form	Past Participle
bake	baked
put	put
mop	mopped

- To provide practice pronouncing the past participles, read them aloud and have students repeat. You may want to leave the lists on the board for students to refer to as they interact.

Step 2

- Go over the example with the class. Have Students B ask questions. Have Students A answer them and cross out the chores that have already been done.

Step 3

- Go over the example with the class. Have Students A ask questions. Have Students B answer them and cross out the chores that have already been done.
- To finish, have students compare their lists.
- 🕐 Have students close their books and play a memory game. Call on students to say a sentence each about the things Helmut and Gisela have already done and haven't done yet / still haven't done.

Exercise 8: What About You?

- Brainstorm with the class possible items for students to put on their lists. Write a list on the board, for example:
  buy a new computer
  plan my birthday party
  get a gift for Mom
  take driving lessons
  choose a college
  plan my vacations
  save money for a car

- Have students write their own lists individually. Point out they can use some of the ideas on the board. Have them include six to eight items on their lists.
- Have students exchange lists with a classmate and ask and answer questions. Encourage them to keep their conversation going by asking follow-up questions.

Exercise 9: Writing

A

- Go over the example with the class.
- Have students choose a goal from the list or write their own goal. (Example: *planning a vacation*)

B

- Have students who have chosen the same goal work in groups to write their lists of things to do. Students can also complete the exercise individually.

C

- Go over the example with the class.
- Have students write their paragraphs individually.

D

- Have students use the Editing Checklist to correct their work.

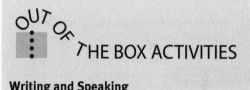

OUT OF THE BOX ACTIVITIES

Writing and Speaking

- Have students think of a homework assignment or task at work. Then have them write down the things they have already done and the things they haven't done yet, for example:
  For geography, I must write a paragraph about a big city and include a picture.
  I've already chosen the city.
  I've already done a search on the Internet.
  I've already selected the picture.
  I haven't written the paragraph yet.
  I haven't chosen a title for my paragraph yet.
- Have pairs take turns talking about the things they have to do and what they have already done and haven't done yet.

Reading and Speaking

- Bring in newspapers. Form small groups and give each group a newspaper.

(continued)

- Have students browse the newspaper in search of a project. Have them use *already, yet,* and *still* to write four to six statements to describe the development of the project, for example:

  They are going to build a dam in India.
  They have already chosen the place.
  They have already told the villagers about the project.
  They haven't started building the dam yet.
  The villagers still haven't moved somewhere else.
- Have students tell the class about the project they read about using sentences with *already, yet,* and *still,* as appropriate.

Go to **www.myfocusongrammarlab.com** for additional listening, pronunciation, speaking, and writing practice.

Note:
- See the *Focus on Grammar Workbook* for additional in-class or homework grammar practice.

Unit 9 Review (page 132)

Have students complete the Review and check their answers on Student Book page UR-3. Review or assign additional material as needed.

Go to **www.myfocusongrammarlab.com** for the Unit Achievement Test.

UNIT 10 OVERVIEW

Grammar: PRESENT PERFECT: INDEFINITE PAST

Unit 10 focuses on the use of the present perfect to express what happened at an indefinite time in the past.

- The present perfect is used for repeated actions at some indefinite time in the past with adverbs such as *twice, always, often,* and *many times.*
- It is used for actions in the very recent but still indefinite past with *just, recently,* and *lately.*

Theme: ADVENTURE TRAVEL

Unit 10 focuses on language used to talk about exciting or unusual experiences people have had, for example, global travel and hot-air ballooning.

Step 1: Grammar in Context (pages 133–134)

See the general suggestions for Grammar in Context on page 1.

Before You Read
- Draw attention to the photos and have students name the activities. *(riding a camel, hot-air ballooning, ice climbing)* To help students with the language they will need for the discussion, write on the board:

  I would/wouldn't like to:
  ride a camel
  go up in a hot-air balloon
  go ice climbing
- Have students discuss the questions in pairs or small groups. Encourage them to give reasons they would like/wouldn't like to do the things in the photos.

Read
- To encourage students to read with a purpose, write these questions on the board:
  1. Why are people looking for new places to see and new things to do? *(because they've already traveled the globe/been to typical vacation places)*
  2. What is the *Travel Today* survey about? *(what people would like to do that they've never done before)*
  3. What did some of the people who took the survey answer? *(that they'd like to ride a camel, go hot-air ballooning, and go ice-climbing)*
  4. Are those activities expensive? *(yes)*
  5. What other less expensive activities are suggested in the article? *(walking in the woods, listening to the wind, watching the sun set over the ocean)*
- Have students read the text. (OR: Play the audio and have students follow along in their books.) Then call on students to share their answers to the questions on the board.
- To get students to share their ideas on the reading, have them discuss the following questions in pairs or small groups. Write the questions on the board if necessary.
  1. What is your ideal vacation? Would you rather go sightseeing in traditional places or try new experiences?
  2. What are some ways to have a great vacation without spending much money? Make a list of ideas.

After You Read

A. Vocabulary
- Have students complete the exercise individually. Encourage them to use context clues to help.
- Have students compare answers in pairs. Then call on pairs to give answers.
- ⏱ To reinforce the vocabulary, as a class, have students name:
  1. four forms of transportation
  2. three ancient places located in different countries
  3. two affordable restaurants in the area where they live
  4. two annual events in their country
  5. three vacation destinations where tourists can have great adventures

B. Comprehension
- Have students complete the exercise individually.
- Have students compare answers in pairs. Then call on pairs to give answers.

Go to **www.myfocusongrammarlab.com** for an additional reading, and for reading and vocabulary practice.

Step 2: Grammar Presentation (pages 134–136)

See the general suggestions for Grammar Presentation on page 2.

Grammar Charts
- To explain the use of the present perfect for the indefinite past, write on the board:
  They've been to Rome.
  - Point to 've been in the example and ask: "What tense is this?" (present perfect) "Is the action past, present, or future?" (past) "Do we know exactly when the action happened?" (no)
  - Emphasize that the present perfect describes things that happened at an indefinite past time.
- To explain negative present perfect statements, write on the board:
  He hasn't been to Egypt.
  He's never ridden a camel.
  - Have students study the examples. Then ask: "What tense do we use for something that *did not happen* at an indefinite time in the past?" (present perfect) "What two ways are there to express this?" (form of have + not + present perfect OR form of have + never + present perfect)

- To teach adverbs that are normally used with the present perfect, write on the board:
  She has just gotten back from a trip.
  She has recently made a trip.
  She has made a trip recently.
  She has made several trips lately.
  She has been abroad twice.
  - Have students study the examples. Then ask: "What adverbs can be used with the present perfect?" (just, recently, lately, twice) "What do the adverbs *just, recently,* and *lately* express?" (that the action happened in the recent past) "Do we know exactly when the action happened?" (no) "What does the adverb *twice* express?" (that the action happened twice sometime in the past)
  - Have students look at the examples again and have them find:
    a. an adverb that goes between a form of *have* and the past participle or at the end of the sentence (for example, *recently*).
    b. an adverb that goes between a form of *have* and the past participle (for example, *just*).
    c. two adverbs that go at the end of the sentence (for example, *lately, twice*).
- To explain present perfect *yes/no* and *wh-* questions, write on the board:
  Have you ever climbed a mountain?
  How often have you been on safari?
  - Have students study the questions and ask: "Which question seeks to find out if something happened?" (the first) "Which question seeks to find out if something happened several times?" (the second)
  - Call on a student to provide the two possible short answers to the first question. (Yes, I have. / No, I haven't.)
  - Point out that *never* can also be used in short answers. Write on the board:
    No, I haven't. = No, never.
  - Call on another student to provide an answer to the second question. (Example: *Twice.*)

Grammar Notes

Note 1
- To explain the present perfect for the indefinite past, write on the board:
  I've visited the Metropolitan Museum in New York.
  Bruce has been to the Tate Museum in London.

- Point out that the present perfect expresses that something happened at an indefinite time in the past. The time is not important. What matters is the action. (**Note:** If necessary, point out that when the time is important, the simple past should be used.)
- Point out that the speaker may or may not know when the action happened. Ask: "In the first example, do you think the speaker knows when the action happened?" *(yes)* "Why doesn't he/she say it then?" *(because it is not important)* Point out that in the second example the speaker may or may not know when Bruce visited the museum. Anyway, it is not important.
- To explain the present perfect for actions that have a result in the present, write on the board:
  The flight has been canceled.
- Point out that the present perfect is used when the result of the action is important in the present. Add to the example on the board:
  The flight has been   Present result: We
    canceled.   won't be able to fly.
- To explain the difference between *been to* and *gone to*, write on the board:
  She's been to the supermarket.
  She's gone to the supermarket.
- Point out that for some speakers, *been to* means that the person is back and *gone to* means that the person is still there.
- Add to the examples on the board:
  She's been to the supermarket. (She's back.)
  She's gone to the supermarket. (She's still there.)
- Have students use *been + to +* a place. Write on the board:
  I've been ~~in~~ Australia.
  I've been <u>to</u> Australia.

Note 2
- To explain the use of the present perfect with adverbs, write these contrasting examples on the board.

1. I've | often
always
never | traveled by plane.

2. I've traveled by plane | twice.
many times.

- Point out that we use the present perfect with *often*, *twice*, or *many times* for something that happened several times at an indefinite past time. Draw attention to the *Be Careful!* note.
- We also use it with *always* for something that continues up to the present and with *never* for something that did not happen before now.

- Do not erase the first two examples.
- To explain questions with *ever*, write on the board:

Have you ever ridden an elephant? | Yes, once.
Yes, I once rode an elephant in India.
No, never.
No, I've never ridden an elephant.

- Point out that when we answer positively, we normally add more information. To answer negatively, we normally use *never*.
- Write these examples on the board:
  3. I haven't been to the beach lately.
  4. I've been to the beach recently. / I've recently been to the beach.
  5. I've just been to the beach.
- Ask: "Which sentence means I've been to the beach a very short time ago?" *(5)* "Which sentence means I've been to the beach in the near past?" *(4)* "Which sentence means I've not been to the beach in the near past?" *(3)*
- Point out that *just* and *recently* are sometimes used in the simple past in American English.
- Do not erase examples 3 through 5.

Note 3
- Have students study the examples 1 through 5 on the board. Then ask:
  1. Where do frequency adverbs go? *(between a form of* have *and the past participle)*
  2. Where do adverbs such as *once*, *twice*, or *many times* go? *(at the end of the sentence)*
  3. Where does *just* go? *(between a form of* have *and the past participle)*
  4. Where does *recently* go? *(between a form of* have *and the past participle or at the end of the sentence)*
  5. Where does *lately* go? *(at the end of the sentence)*
- If needed, refer students to Appendix 1 on page A-1 for a list of irregular past participles.

⏱ **Identify the Grammar:** Have students identify the grammar in the opening reading on page 133. For example:
  They**'ve been** to Rome.
  They**'ve visited** Greece.
  Travel Today **has just come out** . . .
  Have you **ever spent** the day walking in the woods . . . ?

Go to **www.myfocusongrammarlab.com** for grammar charts and notes.

Step 3: Focused Practice (pages 137–141)

See the general suggestions for Focused Practice on page 4.

Exercise 1: Discover the Grammar
- Go over the example with the class. Ask: "Why is the statement true?" *(because the present perfect has some connection to the present)*
- Have students complete the exercise individually.
- Have students compare answers in pairs. Then call on pairs to give answers.

Exercise 2: Statements and Questions
- Go over the example with the class. Then have students read the interview quickly for meaning.
- Have students complete the exercise individually. Remind students to use contractions and, if needed, refer students to Appendix 1 on page A-1. Point out that if a verb is not in the appendix, it is regular.
- ⏱ Books closed. Call on students to say what they remember about Rosa García's travel experiences. Point out that they should use the present perfect. (Example: *She has swum near sharks*.)

Exercise 3: Affirmative and Negative Statements
- Go over the survey and the examples with the class.
- Go over the past participles of the verbs on the list. Write them on the board: *rent, rented,* and so on.
- Have students complete the exercise individually.
- ⏱ For further practice, have students choose *one* item from the survey that they have never done and would like to do. Write on the board:
  I have never [activity]. I would like to do it / try it because [reason].
- In pairs, have students tell each other what they have never done and would like to do and why.

Exercise 4: Word Order
- Go over the example with the class. Then have students read the conversation quickly for meaning.
- Have students complete the exercise individually.
- Have students compare answers in pairs. Encourage students to refer to Grammar Note 3 to clarify doubts. Then go over the answers as a class.

Exercise 5: Statements
- Go over the example with the class.
- Have students complete the exercise individually.
- Have students compare answers in pairs. Then go over the answers as a class.

Exercise 6: Editing
- Have students read the comments on the website quickly for meaning. Then ask the following questions and have students scan the text for the answers: "Who has just returned from a fantastic vacation?" *(James)* "Who has given a balloon trip as a gift?" *(Pat)* "Who has always wanted to go up in a balloon?" *(Antonio)* "Who hasn't been able to do sports lately?" *(May)*
- Have students find and correct the mistakes individually. Then go over the answers as a class, having students explain why the incorrect structures are wrong.
- ⏱ Have students point out examples of correct usages of the present perfect and adverbs.

Go to **www.myfocusongrammarlab.com** for additional grammar practice.

Step 4: Communication Practice
(pages 142–144)

See the general suggestions for Communication Practice on page 5.

Exercise 7: Listening

A
- Have students read the statements. Then play the audio. Have students listen and complete the exercise individually.
- Have students compare answers in pairs. Then go over the answers as a class.

B
- Have students look at the pictures. Then play the audio. Have students listen and complete the exercise individually.
- Call on students to give answers, saying full sentences. *(She's tried white water rafting. She has never tried sky diving.)* Have students support their choice of the best vacation for Olivia.
- ⏱ Working in pairs, have students take turns saying which activities in the pictures they have done / have never done.

Exercise 8: Pronunciation

A
- Play the audio. Have students read along as they listen to the Pronunciation Note.

- Write "v", "s", "z", and "iz" on the board. Have pairs choose the correct contraction for each boldfaced item and make notes above each statement. Write an example on the board:

"v"

My <u>friends have</u> just returned from their trip.

B

- Play the audio. Have students listen. Be sure they notice the pronunciation of the *have* contractions.

C

- Play the audio. Have students listen and repeat.
- Have students practice the conversations with a partner. Be sure students play both roles.

Exercise 9: Find Someone Who . . .

A

- Go over the example with the class. Point out that they should use the simple past to find out more. Write a new example on the board for reference as students interview their classmates:
  A: <u>Have</u> you ever <u>climbed</u> a mountain?
  B: Yes, I have.
  A: Where <u>was</u> that?
  B: In the Andes.
  A: <u>Did</u> you <u>reach</u> the top?
- Have students complete the exercise. Encourage them to ask follow-up questions.

B

- Have students choose an interesting activity a classmate has done and share the story with the class.

Exercise 10: Writing

A

- Write the following questions on the board to help elicit vocabulary and generate ideas:
  What did you like about the place(s) you have been?
  Why would you like to go to [the place you chose that you have never been to]?
  What have you heard/read about it?
  Do you think you will ever be able to go? If so, when?
  Who would you like to go with?
- Have students make notes for each question and then use them as a guide as they write.

B

- Have students use the Editing Checklist to correct their work.
- Call on students to share with the class the places they have never been that they would like to go to. Write a list of places on the board. Is there a place that several students would like to visit?

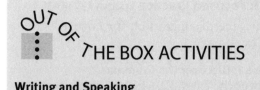

OUT OF THE BOX ACTIVITIES

Writing and Speaking

- Write the following chart on the board:

| Something I've never done that I hope to be able to do: _____ |
| Something I've never done that I don't think I'll ever do: _____ |
| Something I've done that I don't want to try again: _____ |
| Something I've done that I hope to be able to do again: _____ |

- Have students complete the chart with information about themselves.
- Form small groups. Have students use the present perfect to talk about the information in their chart. Encourage students to explain why they would like/wouldn't like to do the activities.

Reading and Speaking

- Bring in science and technology magazines. Form small groups and give each group a different magazine.
- Have students browse the magazine, choose two recent developments in different fields, and read about them. (Example: *cars, aviation, electronics, space exploration, communications*) Have students write a few notes about the developments.
- Have each group join another group. Students from Groups A and B take turns asking each other if they have ever heard about the developments they read about. (Example: Student A: *Have you ever heard about the Five-Billion-Star Hotel?* Student B: *No. What's that?* Student A: *A prototype space hotel. It was designed by a former NASA engineer.*)

Go to **www.myfocusongrammarlab.com** for additional listening, pronunciation, speaking, and writing practice.

Note:

- See the *Focus on Grammar Workbook* for additional in-class or homework grammar practice.

Unit 10 Review (page 145)

Have students complete the Review and check their answers on Student Book page UR-3. Review or assign additional material as needed.

Go to **www.myfocusongrammarlab.com** for the Unit Achievement Test.

UNIT 11 OVERVIEW

Grammar: PRESENT PERFECT AND SIMPLE PAST

Unit 11 focuses on the comparison between the present perfect and the simple past.

- Present perfect statements with *for* express things that started in the past and continue into the present. Simple past statements with *for* express things that started and finished in the past.

- Present perfect statements express things that happened at an unspecified time in the past. Simple past statements express things that happened at a specific time in the past.

- Present perfect statements express things that happened in a period of time that is not finished. Simple past statements express things that happened in a period of time that is finished.

Theme: LONG-DISTANCE RELATIONSHIPS

Unit 11 focuses on language used to talk about long-distance relationships and modern lifestyles.

Long-distance relationships have become more common as women have entered professional careers. Advances in technology—specifically in the fields of transportation and communications—have made these kinds of relationships possible.

Step 1: Grammar in Context (pages 146–147)

See the general suggestions for Grammar in Context on page 1.

Before You Read

- Have students look at the picture and read the title of the article. Then have them discuss the questions in pairs and make notes of the answers.
- Call on pairs to give answers. Make a list on the board of reasons married people might live apart.

Read

- To encourage students to read with a purpose, write these questions on the board:
  1. Where does he live? Where does she live? *(He lives in South Korea. She lives in Canada.)*

  2. Why are they living apart? *(because she lost her job in South Korea and got a new job in Canada)*
  3. Do they see each other often? Why or why not? *(no, because airfares are very high)*
  4. What do they do to keep in touch? *(They send each other emails, instant messages, and text messages. They talk on the phone.)*
  5. Is there any advantage to this kind of arrangement? *(Yes, they both have jobs they really like.)*

- Have students read the text. (OR: Play the audio and have students follow along in their books.) Then call on students to share their answers to the questions on the board.

- To get students to share their ideas on the reading, form pairs or small groups. Have them discuss one or both of the following topics:
  1. In the past, long-distance relationships were not common. Why have they become more common? What causes them? What makes them possible?
  2. What are the advantages and disadvantages of long-distance relationships? What would you have done if you had been in Shinjeng and Sunmi's shoes?

After You Read

A. Vocabulary

- Have students complete the exercise individually. Encourage them to use context clues to help.
- Have students compare answers in pairs. Then call on pairs to give answers.
- ⏱ To reinforce the vocabulary, use the words and phrases in questions about the reading. Ask: "What arrangement have Shinjeng and Sunmi made?" *(to have a long-distance marriage)* "Is this a temporary or a permanent solution?" *(a temporary solution)* "How long have they been living apart?" *(for about three years)* "Where did Sunmi manage to get a job?" *(in Canada)* "Why couldn't she turn down the offer?" *(because she needed a job and she was not able to find a job in her own country)*

B. Comprehension

- Have students complete the exercise individually.
- Have students compare answers in pairs. Then call on pairs to give answers.

Go to **www.myfocusongrammarlab.com** for an additional reading, and for reading and vocabulary practice.

Step 2: Grammar Presentation (pages 148–149)

See the general suggestions for Grammar Presentation on page 2.

Grammar Charts

- To compare the present perfect and the simple past, write on the board:

Present Perfect	Simple Past
1. Maria has lived in Boston for three years.	Maria lived in Detroit for three years.

- Have students study the examples. Then ask: "Which example describes something that has no connection with the present?" *(Maria lived in Detroit for three years.)* "What tense does it use?" *(simple past)* "Which example describes something that continues up to the present?" *(Maria has lived in Boston for three years.)* "What tense does it use?" *(present perfect)* "From which example do we learn where Maria lives now?" *(the one that uses the present perfect)*

- Write two new examples below the ones already on the board:

2. They've found new jobs.	They changed jobs in 2009.

- Have students study the examples. Then ask: "Which example describes something that happened at a specific time in the past?" *(They changed jobs in 2009.)* "What tense does it use?" *(simple past)* "Which example describes something that happened at an unspecified time in the past?" *(They've found new jobs.)* "What tense does it use?" *(present perfect)* "Which example focuses on *what* happened and *when* it happened?" *(the one that uses the simple past)* "Which example focuses on *what* happened only?" *(the one that uses the present perfect)*

- Write two new examples below the ones on the board:

3. This month they've seen each other twice.	Last month they saw each other once.

- Have students study the examples. Then ask: "Which example expresses what happened in a time period that is finished?" *(Last month they saw each other once.)* "What tense does it use?" *(simple past)* "Which example expresses what happened in a time period that is not finished?" *(This month they've seen each other twice.)* "What tense does it use?" *(present perfect)*

Grammar Notes

Note 1

- To explain use of the present perfect, write the following sentences on the board. You may want to use true information about yourself.
  I <u>lived</u> in Brasilia for ten years. Then I moved to São Paulo. I've <u>lived</u> here for six years.
- Draw a timeline to clarify the information on the board.

Note 2

- To explain the use of the present perfect to talk about things that happened at an indefinite time in the past, write two contrasting examples on the board:
  She <u>has found</u> a job in Mexico.
  He <u>lost</u> his job in 2008.
- To help clarify, say: "Use the present perfect to say *what* happened. Use the simple past to say *what* happened and *when* it happened." Point out that the present perfect is used when the specific time in the past is either not known or not important.
- Write next to each example on the board:
  present perfect = what happened
  simple past = what happened + when it happened
- Write two contrasting examples on the board:
  1. They <u>have lived</u> apart <u>since 2008</u>.
  2. They <u>lived</u> apart in 2008.
- Point out that the present perfect can be used with *since* with a specific point in time. This is because the present perfect with *since* describes an action that started in the past and continues into the present.

Note 3

- To explain the use of the present perfect to talk about things that have happened in a time period that is not finished, write two contrasting examples on the board:
  Today I've received 20 emails.
  Yesterday I received 10 emails.
- To help clarify, say: "Use the present perfect for periods of time that are *not* finished, for example, *today*. Use the simple past for periods of time that are finished, for example, *yesterday*."
- Write next to each example on the board:
  present perfect + unfinished time period
  simple past + finished time period

🕐 **Identify the Grammar:** Have students identify the grammar in the opening text on page 146. For example:

> . . . Lee Shinjeng and Park Sunmi **have been** married for four years.

> Many couples around the world **have found** this arrangement to be a temporary solution . . .

> When they **got** married, both Shinjeng and Sunmi **had** very good jobs.

Go to **www.myfocusongrammarlab.com** for grammar charts and notes.

Step 3: Focused Practice (pages 149–154)

See the general suggestions for Focused Practice on page 4.

Exercise 1: Discover the Grammar
- Go over the example with the class. Ask: "Why is *b* the correct answer?" *(because the present perfect indicates that the action continues up to the present, and we know that Sunmi still lives there)*
- Have students complete the exercise individually.
- Have students compare answers in pairs. Then go over the answers as a class.

Exercise 2: Present Perfect or Simple Past
- Go over the example with the class. Ask: "Why is the present perfect—*have been*—the correct verb form?" *(because the posting says* for just two months, *and the person is finding it hard now)* Then have students read each posting quickly for meaning.
- Have students do the exercise individually. Have them find and circle key words that help them choose the correct verb forms. (Example: *for two months, last week, yesterday, so far*)
- Call on students to read the postings.

Exercise 3: Present Perfect or Simple Past Statements
- Go over the example with the class. Ask: "Why is the simple past—*found*—the correct verb form?" *(because the entry says* yesterday*)* Have students read the journal entry quickly for meaning and complete the exercise individually. Have them find and circle key words that help them choose the correct verb forms.
- Have students compare answers in pairs. Then go over the answers as a class.

- 🕐 For further practice, write the following on the board to personalize the information in the journal entry:
Think about this week.
Has it been a difficult week?
Have you gotten up early?
Have you worked/studied late?
Have you had a lot of meetings/exams/ homework?
What other things have you done?
- Have students write a few sentences describing their week and then tell their partner about it.

Exercise 4: Present Perfect or Simple Past Contrast
- Have students look at the pictures and describe Shinjeng now and in the past.
- Go over the example with the class.
- Have students write the sentences individually. Then call on students to give answers.

Exercise 5: *Wh-* Questions
- Go over the example with the class. Ask: "Why is the present perfect the correct verb form?" *(because they are still married)*
- Have students write the sentences individually. If necessary, remind students to use the simple past (did + *subject* + *base form*) for finished actions and the present perfect for unfinished actions or unfinished periods of time.
- Have students compare answers in pairs. Then call on pairs to give answers.

Exercise 6: Editing
- Have students read the blog post quickly for meaning. Ask: "What do Park Sunmi and Felicia Mabuza-Suttle have in common?" *(Felicia has also had a long-distance marriage.)* "Is Felicia a talk-show host now?" *(no)* "Does she still have a long-distance marriage?" *(no)* "How long did she and her husband live apart?" *(about ten years)* "How long have they lived together in the States?" *(since 2003/for [number of years])* Then go over the example with the class.
- Have students find and correct the mistakes individually. Then go over the answers as a class, having students explain why the incorrect structures are wrong.
- 🕐 Have students point out examples of correct usages of the present perfect and the simple past.

Go to **www.myfocusongrammarlab.com** for additional grammar practice.

Step 4: Communication Practice

(pages 154–157)

See the general suggestions for Communication Practice on page 5.

Exercise 7: Listening

A
- Have students read the list. Then play the audio. Have students first listen for meaning and then listen again after reading the items to complete the exercise individually.
- Go over the answers as a class.

B
- Have students read the statements before listening. Then play the audio. Have students listen and complete the exercise individually.
- Go over the answers as a class.
- ⏱ Books closed. Have pairs write sentences using the information they remember about the professors. Have students write only sentences that use the present perfect or the simple past. Call on students to give answers. Write them on the board, making any necessary corrections.

Exercise 8: Pronunciation

A
- Play the audio. Have students read along as they listen to the Pronunciation Note.
- Point out that students should use /t/ after a voiceless sound (sound that does not vibrate), /d/ after a voiced sound (sound that vibrates), and /ɪd/ after /t/ or /d/. Write examples on the board:
  1. reach (no vibration)   reached /t/
  2. learn (vibration)   learned /d/
  3. want (final /t/)   wanted /ɪd/
  4. end (final /d/)   ended /ɪd/

B
- Play the audio. Have students listen and choose the correct pronunciation.

C
- Play the audio. Have students listen and repeat.
- Have students practice the conversations with a partner. Be sure students play both roles.

Exercise 9: Compare and Contrast
- Briefly go over the chart with the class. Then go over the example with the class.
- Have students complete the exercise in pairs. Remind students that they should use the simple past to talk about last year and the present perfect for this year so far.
- ⏱ Have students write similar records about themselves and discuss them in small groups.

Exercise 10: Interview

A
- Have students choose a person with whom they have a long-distance relationship.
- Have students answer the questions in note form to get ready for the interview. Then have students complete the exercise in pairs.

B
- Have students continue the conversation with more questions based on the information they have found.
- Have students change roles.
- Call on students to share with the class what they have found out about their partner's long-distance relationship.

Exercise 11: Writing

A
- Write the following questions on the board to help elicit vocabulary and generate ideas:
  Who has moved away?
  Why has he/she moved away?
  How long has he/she been away? OR When did he/she move away?
  How often have they seen each other?
  When did they last see each other?
  How have they managed to stay close?
  Has it been easy/difficult?
- Have students make notes for each question and then use them as a guide as they write. Then have students complete the exercise individually.

B
- Have students use the Editing Checklist to correct their work.

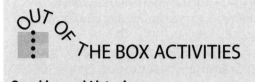

OUT OF THE BOX ACTIVITIES

Speaking and Listening

- If possible, have students bring to class photographs of themselves when they were young. Mix the photographs up and put them on display for a few minutes.
- Have students look at the display and try to identify their classmates.
- Then select a picture and ask: "Who is this?" Once the person has been identified, have that student describe himself/herself as a child and then describe how he/she has changed. (**Note:** If necessary, refer students to Exercise 4 on page 152 to see how descriptions are given using the simple past and the present perfect.) Encourage the class to ask questions about the student's childhood.

Reading and Speaking

- Bring in magazines that have a section about lifestyles. Form small groups and give each group a magazine.
- Summarize on the board the uses of the present perfect and the simple past that students learned in this unit.
  1. a. Present perfect + *for*: action that continues into the present
     b. Simple past + *for*: action that started and finished in the past
  2. a. Present perfect + past action at an indefinite past time
     b. Simple past + past action at a specific past time
  3. a. Present perfect + time period that is not finished
     b. Simple past + time period that is finished
- Have students find in the article examples that match (some of) the uses in the list.

Go to **www.myfocusongrammarlab.com** for additional listening, pronunciation, speaking, and writing practice.

Note:
- See the *Focus on Grammar Workbook* for additional in-class or homework grammar practice.

Unit 11 Review (page 158)

Have students complete the Review and check their answers on Student Book page UR-3. Review or assign additional material as needed.

Go to **www.myfocusongrammarlab.com** for the Unit Achievement Test.

UNIT 12 OVERVIEW

Grammar: PRESENT PERFECT PROGRESSIVE AND PRESENT PERFECT

Unit 12 focuses on the comparison between the present perfect progressive and the present perfect.

- The present perfect progressive often shows that an action is unfinished. The present perfect often shows that an action is finished.
- The present perfect progressive is often used to talk about how long something has been happening. The present perfect is often used to talk about how much someone has done, how many things someone has done, or how many times someone has done something.
- Both the present perfect progressive and the present perfect are used with *for* or *since* for an action that started in the past and continues into the present.

Theme: CLIMATE CHANGE

Unit 12 focuses on language used to talk about changes, especially changes that people or the environment have made or experienced lately; for example, global warming and solar houses.

Step 1: Grammar in Context (pages 159–160)

See the general suggestions for Grammar in Context on page 1.

Before You Read
- Have students look at the picture and discuss the questions in pairs. Have them share what they already know about global warming.
- Call on pairs to give answers. Elicit from students that a hot topic is an important topic that causes arguments because people have different opinions.

Read

- To encourage students to read with a purpose, write these questions on the board:
  1. What are some possible causes of global warming? *(There are natural causes, such as changes in the sun, and human causes, such as burning oil and coal for energy, which sends gases into the atmosphere.)*
  2. What are some effects of global warming? *(Ice has been melting in the Arctic and rainfall has decreased in Africa.)*
  3. What can people do to reduce global warming? *(Use clean solar energy and design homes and cars that use less energy.)*
- Have students read the text. (OR: Play the audio and have students follow along in their books.) Then call on students to share their answers to the questions on the board.
- To get students to share their ideas on the reading, form pairs or small groups. Have them discuss the following topics. Have them write their ideas in note form.
  1. The article mentions some effects of global warming. Do you know any others? Do you think it is important to stop global warming? Why or why not?
  2. The article also mentions some solutions to the problem. What else can people do to help reduce global warming?

After You Read

A. Vocabulary

- Have students complete the exercise individually. Encourage them to use context clues to help.
- Have students compare answers in pairs. Then go over the answers as a class.
- (!) To reinforce the vocabulary, use it in questions about the reading. Have students give full answers. Ask: "How long has the climate been changing?" *(The climate has been changing for billions of years.)* "What causes air pollution?" *(Burning coal and oil causes air pollution.)* "Have people developed ways to use solar energy yet?" *(Yes, people have developed ways to use solar energy.)* "What kind of homes have people designed?" *(People have designed homes that use less energy.)*

B. Comprehension

- Have students complete the exercise individually. Have them underline the information in the text that supports their answers.
- Have students compare answers in pairs. Then call on students to give answers.

Go to **www.myfocusongrammarlab.com** for an additional reading, and for reading and vocabulary practice.

Step 2: Grammar Presentation (pages 161–163)

See the general suggestions for Grammar Presentation on page 2.

Grammar Charts

- To compare the present perfect progressive and the present perfect, write two contrasting sentences on the board:

Present Perfect Progressive	Present Perfect
The climate has been changing for many years.	The climate has changed many times.

  — Have students study the examples. Then ask: "How many words are needed for the present perfect?" *(two)* "How do you form the present perfect?" *(form of* have *+ past participle)* "How many words are needed for the present perfect progressive?" *(three)* "How do you form the present perfect progressive?" *(form of* have *+ been + present participle)*
- To explain negative present progressive statements, write on the board:
  The climate has not been getting cooler.
- Have students study the example. Then ask: "How do you form the negative present perfect progressive?" *(form of* have *+ not + been + present participle)*
- To explain *yes/no* and *wh-* questions, point to the first example under Present Perfect Progressive *(The climate has been changing for many years.)* and turn it into a *yes/no* question. *(Has the climate been changing for many years?)*
- Write on the board:
  It has been raining for over a week.
- Have students turn the example on the board into a *yes/no* question. Have a student write the question on the board. *(Has it been raining for over a week?)*
  —Ask: "How do you form *yes/no* questions?" *(form of* have *+ subject + been + present participle)*
  — Elicit from the class the two possible short answers to the question on the board. *(Yes, it has. / No, it hasn't.)* Have a student write them on the board.
  — Have students turn the same example into a question starting with *How long.* Have a student write the question on the board. *(How long has it been raining?)*

— Ask: "How do you form *wh-* questions?" (wh- *word + form of* have + *subject* + been + *present participle*)

Grammar Notes

Note 1

- To compare the use of the present perfect progressive for unfinished actions and the present perfect for finished actions, write on the board:

  People <u>have been designing</u> homes that use less energy.

  An engineer <u>has designed</u> a new solar car.

- Point to *have been designing* in the first example. Ask: "What tense is this?" *(present perfect progressive)* "Are people still designing homes that use less energy?" *(yes)* Write at the end of the first example:

  = unfinished action

- Point to *has designed* in the first example. Ask: "What tense is this?" *(present perfect)* "Is the engineer still designing the car?" *(No. He/She has already designed it.)* Write at the end of the second example:

  = finished action

- **Note:** Students learned in previous units that the present perfect is used for actions that are not finished, that is, actions that started in the past and continue into the present. If necessary, clarify that for the present perfect to describe an unfinished action it must be used with *for* or *since*.

- To explain the use of the present progressive for finished actions that ended in the recent past, write on the board:

  A: You look tired.

  B: I am! I<u>'ve been exercising</u>.

- Ask: "When do you think B finished exercising—an hour ago or just a few minutes ago?" *(just a few minutes ago)* Point out that we use the present perfect progressive for actions that ended in the very recent past. We can often see their result in the present: the person looks tired now. Write at the end of the third example:

  = action that ended in the very recent past

- Draw attention to the *Be Careful!* note. Elicit non-action verbs from the students. If needed, refer students to Appendix 2 on page A-2. Write some verbs on the board as students say them. Have students use some of the verbs in present perfect statements.

Note 2

- To summarize the uses of the present perfect progressive and the present perfect, write on the board:

  Present perfect progressive: how long + unfinished action

  Present perfect: how much, how many things, or how many times + finished action

- Point to the first summary and give examples: "I've been studying for three hours." "He's been cooking for an hour." "They've been working all day." Write one example on the board.

- Point to the second summary and give more examples: "I've talked to a lot of people." "I've mailed three packages." "He's called me twice." If necessary, write the examples on the board.

Note 3

- Write on the board:

  She <u>has been working</u> in Africa for a year. = She <u>has worked</u> in Africa for a year.

- Explain that the present perfect progressive and the present perfect can sometimes have the same meaning.

- Point out that with verbs such as *live, study, teach,* and *work* plus *since* or *for*, the present perfect progressive and the present perfect have the same meaning.

- Write on the board:

  She<u>'s been teaching</u> French since she got her degree.

  She<u>'s</u> always <u>taught</u> Spanish.

- Write at the end of the first example:

  (She hasn't always taught French. = temporary)

- Write at the end of the second example:

  (She has taught Spanish since she started teaching. = permanent)

- Explain that the present perfect progressive can express that the action is temporary and the present perfect can express that the action is permanent.

🕐 **Identify the Grammar:** Have students identify the grammar in the opening reading on page 159. For example:

  The Earth's climate **has changed** many times.

  . . . the climate **has been changing** for five billion years . . .

  . . . the Earth **has been getting** hotter.

  . . . human activities **have added** to global warming.

Go to **www.myfocusongrammarlab.com** for grammar charts and notes.

Step 3: Focused Practice (pages 163–167)

See the general suggestions for Focused Practice on page 4.

Exercise 1: Discover the Grammar

- Go over the example with the class. Ask: "Why is the action unfinished?" (because the present perfect progressive expresses that the action is unfinished)
- Have students complete the exercise individually.
- Have students compare answers in pairs. Then call on pairs to give answers.

Exercise 2: Present Perfect Progressive or Present Perfect

- Go over the example with the class. Ask: "Is Professor Owen still working on the articles?" (yes) "Which tense do we use for unfinished actions?" (the present perfect progressive)
- Have students read each item quickly for meaning and then choose their answers.
- Go over the answers as a class

Exercise 3: Present Perfect Progressive

A

- If necessary, review how to form the present perfect progressive affirmative and negative. (form of have + [not] + been + present participle)
- Have students look at the pictures.

B

- Go over the example with the class.
- Have students complete the exercise individually, choosing between affirmative and negative forms. Then go over the answers as a class.
- ⏱ For further practice, have students cover the sentences. In pairs, have students take turns describing the pictures using present perfect progressive statements.

Exercise 4: Statements

- Have students read the blog quickly for meaning. Then have students complete the exercise individually.
- Have students compare answers in pairs. Then call on a student to read the text.

Exercise 5: Questions and Answers

- Go over the example with the class.
- Have students complete the exercise in pairs. Then call on pairs to read the questions and answers.
- ⏱ For further practice, have students role-play the interview.

Exercise 6: Editing

- Have students read the email quickly for meaning. Then ask: "Where is the person who writes the email?" (in Madrid) "Why is she there?" (to participate in the solar house competition) "What kind of house has her team designed?" (a house that is beautiful and reduces pollution)
- Have students find and correct the mistakes individually. Then call on students to explain why the incorrect structures are wrong.
- ⏱ Have students point out examples of correct usages of the present perfect progressive and the present perfect.

Go to **www.myfocusongrammarlab.com** for additional grammar practice.

Step 4: Communication Practice

(pages 168–171)

See the general suggestions for Communication Practice on page 5.

Exercise 7: Listening

A

- Go over the example for picture 1a with the class. Call on a student to describe picture 1b. (Example: In picture 1b, they've planted two trees.)
- Have students work in pairs to describe pictures 2 through 5. Have them write a sentence describing each picture.
- Call on pairs to share their descriptions with the class.

B

- Play the audio. Have students listen and circle the picture the people are talking about. Have students make notes to support their choices.

C

- Have students complete the exercise individually. Then play the audio. Have students listen and check their work.

Exercise 8: Pronunciation

A

- Play the audio. Have students read along as they listen to the Pronunciation Note. If necessary, explain that in present perfect forms the main verb is the past participle and that in present perfect progressive forms the main verb is the present participle.

B

- Play the audio. Have students listen and complete the exercise individually.
- Have students compare answers in pairs. Then call on pairs to give answers.

C

- Have students listen and repeat the answers. Then have pairs role-play the conversations. Circulate as students practice, listening to make sure they stress the correct words or parts of words.

Exercise 9: Find Someone Who . . .

A

- Go over the questions and the example with the class.
- Write *Have you . . . ?* on the board and brainstorm with the class other possible interview questions with the present perfect progressive or present perfect. Write them on the board, for example:

   Have you . . .
   been reading a good book?
   been sleeping late?
   been getting up early?
   been exercising?
   bought something new?
   been to a party?

- Have students use these and other questions to interview their classmates.

B

- Go over the example with the class. As a class, continue the conversation for Student A and B. Write students' ideas on the board, for example:

   B: I usually go to West Park. And you?
   A: I like to go over Point Bridge. Have you ever gone to the other side of the bridge?

- As students interact, encourage them to keep their conversation going by asking follow-up questions.
- Call on students to tell the class what they found out about their partners. Encourage them to say sentences using the present perfect progressive or the present perfect. (Example: *David has been exercising in Green Lake Park.*)

Exercise 10: Picture Discussion

- Have students discuss the questions in pairs. Have them make notes of their answers. Encourage them to use the present perfect continuous to describe what has been happening to the Earth. (Examples: *The Earth's climate has been changing. The Earth's temperature has been rising. Levels of pollution have been increasing. People have been burning coal and oil and sending gases into the atmosphere. Some environmental groups have been taking action. Some people have been expressing their concern.*)

- Have pairs join another pair and discuss the questions. Follow up by having students share their views with the class.
- ⏱ Take a poll of the class to find out if most students agree or disagree with the message of the image.

Exercise 11: Discussion

- Go over the questions and the example with the class.
- Write *Have you changed . . . ?* on the board and brainstorm with the class other possible questions. Write them on the board. For example:

   Have you changed . . .
   the way you go to work?
   your diet?
   your studying/working habits?
   the way you spend your free time?
   the way you spend your money?

- Form small groups. Have students discuss the topic in small groups. Encourage them to keep their conversation going by asking follow-up questions.

Exercise 12: Writing

A

- Have students look at Exercises 9 and 11 and choose the questions they want to write about.
- Have students make notes for each question and then use them as a guide as they write.

B

- Have students correct their work using the Editing Checklist.

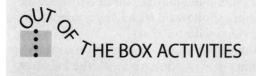

OUT OF THE BOX ACTIVITIES

Speaking and Writing

- Address different students and ask the following questions. You can ask some of the questions to more than one student. Encourage full answers so that students practice the present perfect progressive and the present perfect.
  How long have you been studying English?
  How many English teachers have you had?
  How long have you been reading in English?
  How many books have you read in English?
  How long have you been using *Focus on Grammar*?
  How many units have you done so far?
  How long have you been studying the perfect tenses?
  How much have you learned about the present perfect?
  Have you traveled to any English-speaking countries?
  How many English-speaking countries have you visited?
- Have students use the questions as a guide to write a short paragraph about their English studies.

Reading and Speaking

- Bring in Internet printouts about the work of environmental groups such as Greenpeace. Form small groups and give each group a printout. (You can use the same or different printouts.)
- Have students find in the printout the answers to some of the following questions:
  How long have they been working to protect the environment?
  What action have they taken?
  What are they concerned about?
  Have they published any books or articles?
  Have they taken part in any demonstrations?
  How many different kinds of projects have they been working on?
  What project have they been working on lately?
  How long have they been working on it?
- Follow up by having groups report to the class about their findings.

Go to **www.myfocusongrammarlab.com** for additional listening, pronunciation, speaking, and writing practice.

Note:
- See the *Focus on Grammar Workbook* for additional in-class or homework grammar practice.

Unit 12 Review (page 172)

Have students complete the Review and check their answers on Student Book page UR-3. Review or assign additional material as needed.

Go to **www.myfocusongrammarlab.com** for the Unit Achievement Test.

From Grammar to Writing (pages 173–174)

See the general suggestions for From Grammar to Writing on page 9.

Go to **www.myfocusongrammarlab.com** for an additional From Grammar to Writing Assignment, Part Review, and Part Post-Test.

PART IV OVERVIEW

MODALS AND SIMILAR EXPRESSIONS

UNIT	GRAMMAR FOCUS	THEME
13	Ability: *Can, Could, Be able to*	Dance
14	Permission: *Can, Could, May, Do you mind if*	Roommates
15	Requests: *Can, Could, Will, Would, Would you mind*	Messages
16	Advice: *Should, Ought to, Had better*	Internet Rules

Go to **www.myfocusongrammarlab.com** for the Part and Unit Tests.

Note: PowerPoint® grammar presentations, test-generating software, and reproducible Part and Unit Tests are on the *Teacher's Resource Disc*.

Grammar: ABILITY: *Can, Could, Be able to*

Unit 13 focuses on the uses of *can, could,* and *be able to* to express ability.

• *Can* and *can't* express present ability. They also express future ability when talking about plans or arrangements.

• *Could* and *couldn't* express past ability. *Could* can't be used for single past events— *was/were able to* should be used instead.

• Different forms of *be able to* express present, future, and past ability.

Theme: DANCE

Unit 13 focuses on language used to talk about people's skills and abilities, specifically in this unit, dance—what they can do now, what they could do in the past, and what they will be able to do in the future.

Step 1: Grammar in Context (pages 176–177)

See the general suggestions for Grammar in Context on page 1.

Before You Read

• Have students look at the photo, read the title of the article, and discuss the questions in pairs.

• Have students make notes of what they think the main point is.

• Call on pairs to give answers. Write students' ideas on the board. Accept all possible answers. Example:
The article is about . . .
  a woman who can dance in a wheelchair.
  what a person with a disability can do.
  the life of a woman who can't walk but can dance.
  the achievements of a disabled woman.

Read

• To encourage students to read with a purpose, write these questions on the board:
1. What dream did Verdi-Fletcher achieve? *(to become a dancer)*
2. Why did people think she wouldn't be able to achieve her dream? *(because she couldn't stand or walk)*
3. How did people react when she danced in her first competition? *(They stood and applauded.)*
4. How has Verdi-Fletcher changed the definition of dancing? *(Dancing does not have to be done standing up.)*

5. What does she want to show through her dance? *(that with hard work and dedication dreams can be achieved)*

• Have students read the text. (OR: Play the audio and have students follow along in their books.) Then call on students to share their answers to the questions on the board.

• To get students to share their ideas on the reading, form pairs or small groups. Have them discuss one or all of the following questions:
1. What would you ask Verdi-Fletcher if you had a chance to interview her?
2. Do you know other people with disabilities? If you do, share their achievements—big or small.
3. What kind of example do these people set? What can we all learn from them?

After You Read

A. Vocabulary

• Have students complete the exercise individually. Encourage them to use context clues to help.

• Have students compare answers in pairs. Then call on pairs to give answers.

• ⏱ To reinforce the vocabulary, write the following sentence halves on the board. Have students match them. (Answers: *1. d, 2. e, 3. c, 4. b, 5. a*)

1. Verdi-Fletcher has
2. The audience was confused because
3. Her perception of dance is that
4. Her dance company is integrated because
5. She believes you can achieve your aspirations

a. with dedication.
b. it has two kinds of dancers.
c. it is an emotion.
d. a talent for dancing.
e. they thought she could not dance.

B. Comprehension

• Have students complete the exercise individually.

• Have students compare answers in pairs. Then call on pairs to give answers.

Go to **www.myfocusongrammarlab.com** for an additional reading, and for reading and vocabulary practice.

Step 2: Grammar Presentation (pages 178–180)

See the general suggestions for Grammar Presentation on page 2.

Grammar Charts

- To explain affirmative and negative statements with *can*, write on the board:
  Verdi-Fletcher can't walk, but she can dance.
  You can't take your eyes off her.
  She changed the perception of what we can or cannot do.
  — Have students study the examples. Then ask: "How do you form affirmative statements with *can*?" (can + *base form of verb*) "Does *can* change when the pronoun changes?" (*No. Can is the same for all pronouns.*) "How do you form negative statements?" (can not/cannot + *base form of verb*) "What is the contraction of *can not* and *cannot*?" (can't)
- To explain *yes/no* and *wh-* questions, write on the board:
  Can she dance?
  How well can she dance?
  — Ask: "How do you form *yes/no* questions?" (can + *subject* + *base form of verb*)
  — Call on a student to write the two possible short answers to the question on the board. (*Yes, she can. / No, she can't.*)
  — Ask: "How do you form *wh-* questions?" (wh- *word* + can + *subject* + *base form of verb*)
- To explain statements and questions with *could*, write on the board:
  affirmative statement: Mozart could write music at the age of five.
  negative statement:
  yes/no question:
  wh- question:
  — Call on different students to come to the board and turn the affirmative statement with *could* into a negative statement, a *yes/no* question, and a *wh-* question.
- To explain statements and questions with *be able to*, write on the board:
  affirmative statement: She was able to dance.
  negative statement:
  yes/no question:
  wh- question:
  — Call on different students to come to the board and turn the affirmative statement with *be able to* into a negative statement, a *yes/no* question, and a *wh-* question.

Grammar Notes

Note 1

- Write on the board:
  1. He can speak French.
  2. She could sing really well when she was a child.
  3. After my trip to Italy, I will be able to say a few things in Italian.
- Have students read the sentences. Then point out that *can, could,* and *be able to* all express natural or learned ability.

Note 2

- To explain modals, write on the board:
  She can dance.
  They can sing.
  He can't swim.
  Can they run fast?
  He could play the piano.
  They couldn't swim.
  Could they speak English?
- Have students study the examples. Then ask: "Do modals have the same form for all subjects?" (yes) "How do they form the negative?" (modal + not + base form) "How do we form questions?" (modal + subject + base form)
- To review *be able to*, write on the board:
  She is able to do it.
  They are able to do it.
  She will be able to do it.
  I wasn't able to do it.
  Were they able to do it?
- Point out that although *be able to* is an expression that is similar to a modal, it is not a real modal because it does not have the same form for all subjects.

Note 3

- To explain the use of *can* for present ability, write a list of topics on the board:
  Driving and riding
  Languages
  Sports
  Music and dancing
- Give an example for each topic: *I can ride a motorbike. I can speak two languages. I can ski. I can't play any musical instruments.*
- To explain the use of *am/is/are able to* for present ability, write on the board:
  After two months of physical therapy, he is finally able to walk.
- Point out that in the present, *be able to* implies hard work.

Note 4

- To compare the use of *can* and *will be able to* for future ability, write on the board:
  I <u>can</u> meet him on Friday. (plan or arrangement)
  I <u>will be able to</u> meet him on Friday. (plan or arrangement)
  After taking my driving course, I <u>will be able to</u> drive. (something that you learn)
  Not: After taking my driving course, I ~~can~~ drive. (something that you learn)
- Point out that both *can* and *be able to* can be used to express future ability when talking about plans or arrangements. To talk about things we will learn in the future, we should use *will be able to*.

Note 5

- To explain *could* for past ability, draw a timeline and write information about things you could do at different ages in your childhood, for example:

	4	6	8
I was born.	speak two languages	play the guitar	ski

- Describe the information on the timeline: "When I was four, I could speak two languages. When I was six, I could play the guitar. When I was eight, I could ski really well."
- To compare *could* and *was/were able to* for past ability, write on the board:
  <u>General ability</u>:
  Jessica <u>could run</u> very fast when she was young.
  OR
  Jessica <u>was able to run</u> very fast when she was young.
  <u>Single past event</u>:
  Once she <u>was able to run</u> to the store and back in five minutes.
  ~~Once she could run to the store and back in five minutes.~~
- Draw attention to the *Be Careful!* note. Point out that *could* refers to a general ability but not to a single past event.
- To explain the use of *couldn't* for single events, write on the board:
  I <u>couldn't pass</u> the test.
  I <u>wasn't able to</u> pass the test.
- Make sure students understand that both *couldn't* and *wasn't/weren't able to* can be used for single events in negative statements.
- ⏱ To summarize the Grammar Notes, draw the following chart on the board:

		can	could	be able to
Present ability		can can't	—	am/is/are able to am not/ isn't/ aren't able to (when hard work is implied)
Future ability	(plans or arrangements)	can can't	—	will be able to won't be able to
	(things we learn)	—	—	
Past ability	(general ability)	—	could couldn't	was/were able to wasn't/ weren't able to
	(single event)	—	couldn't	

⏱ **Identify the Grammar:** Have students identify the grammar in the opening reading on page 176. For example:
. . . you **can** only **dance** on your two feet?
. . . she **wasn't able to stand** or **walk**.
You **can't walk** . . .
. . . how **can** you **be** a dancer?

Go to **www.myfocusongrammarlab.com** for grammar charts and notes.

Step 3: Focused Practice (pages 181–184)

See the general suggestions for Focused Practice on page 4.

Exercise 1: Discover the Grammar

- Go over Mary Verdi-Fletcher's biography with the class. Answer any questions. Explain that a keypunch is a machine that puts holes in special cards that are read by computers (no longer in use).
- Go over the example with the class. Ask: "Why is the statement true?" *(because the biography says that she got a job as a keypunch operator after graduating from high school)*
- Have students find and underline phrases with *can, would,* and *be able to*. Then have students complete the exercise individually. As students write their answers, have them underline in the biography the information that supports their choices.

Exercise 2: Statements with *Can* and *Could*

- Go over the example with the class.
- Have students read each item quickly for meaning. Then have them complete the exercise individually.
- Have students compare answers in pairs. Then go over the answers as a class.

Exercise 3: Statements and Questions with *Be able to*

- Go over the example with the class. Have students read the conversations quickly for meaning.
- Have students complete the exercise individually. They will write affirmative, negative, or interrogative forms of *be able to* in the past, present, or future, as appropriate.
- ⏱ Have pairs role-play the conversations.

Exercise 4: *Can, Could,* or *Be able to*

- Go over the example with the class. Point out that when both *can* and *am/is/are able to* are possible, students should use *can*. Similarly, when both *could* and *was/were able to* are possible, students should use *could*.
- Have students complete the conversations in pairs. Then call on pairs to read the conversations aloud.
- ⏱ Have pairs role-play the conversations.

Exercise 5: Editing

- Have students read the review quickly for meaning. Ask: "What did Jennifer Andrews see last night?" *(a performance by the group Pilobolus)* "How many performers are there in the group?" *(six)* "What can they do?" *(dance and make shapes with their bodies)* "Could Jennifer see the entire stage and hear the music from her seat?" *(She was able to see the entire stage but she wasn't able to/couldn't hear the music clearly all the time.)* "Can you get tickets for this week?" *(no)* "And for next week?" *(yes)*
- Have students find and correct the mistakes individually. Then call on students to explain why the incorrect structures are wrong.
- ⏱ Have students point out examples of correct usages of *can, could,* and *be able to.*

Go to **www.myfocusongrammarlab.com** for additional grammar practice.

Step 4: Communication Practice

(pages 185–188)

See the general suggestions for Communication Practice on page 5.

Exercise 6: Listening

- **Note:** Students might not know some of the vocabulary in the conversation, but they should still be able to do the task successfully. After listening and reviewing answers, you can clarify the meaning of the following words: *word processing:* using computer software for writing; *spreadsheet:* a document that contains rows and columns of numbers that can be used to calculate something; *desktop publishing:* the work of producing magazines, books, and so on, with a computer that is designed to be used on a desk.

A

- Have students read the statements. Then play the audio. Have students listen.
- Play the audio again. Have students listen and complete the exercise individually.
- Go over the answers as a class, having students support their choices with information from the audio.

B

- Have students read the list of skills and abilities. If necessary, explain that a *newsletter* is a short written report of news about a club, organization, or particular subject that is sent regularly to people. Point out that Karl talks about things he can do now and things he will be able to do soon. Have students check only the things he can do *now.*
- Play the audio. Have students listen and complete the exercise individually. Then call on students to say full sentences about what Karl can and cannot do. (Example: *Karl can answer the phone.*)
- ⏱ Ask: "Why does Karl think he will soon be able to design a newsletter and dance?" *(because he's taking a course in desktop publishing and he's applying for a job in a dance studio)*

Exercise 7: Pronunciation

A

- Play the audio. Have students read along as they listen to the Pronunciation Note.
- Be sure students understand that:
  1. In affirmative sentences, the pronunciation of *can* is with a relaxed vowel /kən/ and is brief. The main stress is in the base form (not in *can*).
  2. In negative sentences, the pronunciation of *can't* is with an open vowel /kænt/ and drawn out. The main stress is in *can't* (not the base form).

B

- Play the audio. Have students listen and circle the words they hear.

C

- Play the audio. Have students listen and repeat the statements.
- 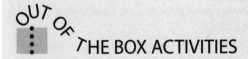 For further practice, write on the board: I can _____ , but I can't _____ .
- Have students complete the gapped sentence on the board twice with true information about themselves. Have students say their sentences to a partner. Circulate, listening to make sure they stress the correct words.

Exercise 8: Information Gap: Can they do the tango?

- Divide the class into Students A and Students B. Have Students A stay on the page and Students B go to page 188.
- Go over the example with the class. Point out the use of present forms *(can)*, future forms *(will be able to)*, and past forms *(could)*.
- Have students complete the exercise in pairs. Encourage them to provide as much information as possible. Point out how in the first example Student A asks about the Argentine tango now and Student B also gives information about the present and the future.

Exercise 9: Ask and Answer

A

- Go over the list of skills and explain any unknown words.
- To help generate ideas, you may want to have students choose an imaginary topic for their presentation.
- Form small groups. Have students complete the exercise as a group.

B

- Have a few students tell the class about their presentations. Encourage the class to ask follow-up questions, for example:
  A: Sonia can type fast, so she's going to type on the computer.
  B: How fast can she type?
  A: Well, she said she can type 70 words per minute.

Exercise 10: Writing

A

- Write the following questions on the board to help elicit vocabulary and generate ideas:
  What did the person want to do or achieve?
  What kind of difficulty or problem did the person have?
  What did the person do to face the problem?

What was this person's key to success?
What can you learn from a story like this?
- Go over the example with the class. Then have students make notes for each question and use them as a guide as they write.

B

- Have students correct their work using the Editing Checklist.

OUT OF THE BOX ACTIVITIES

Speaking and Writing

- Have students choose a topic to survey each other about skills and abilities they developed in their childhood, possess now, or plan for the future. (Example: *music, art, sports, computing, languages*)
- Have them write four questions about the topic they chose. (Example: *When you were a child, were you interested in music? Could you play a musical instrument? Can you play a musical instrument now? What [other] instrument would you like to be able to play?*)
- Have students circulate around the room interviewing their classmates.

Reading and Speaking

- If you have access to a lending library, bring in a copy of the book *Guinness World Records* or do an Internet search on "world records" and bring in printouts (www.guinnessworldrecords.com).
- Form small groups and have students browse the book—or read the printouts—and write notes about an achievement or special feat.
- Have a student from each group report to the class on their findings. (Example: *George Blair can water-ski barefoot. In 2002, he was able to break a record when he successfully skied barefoot on a lake in Florida at the age of 87.*)

Go to **www.myfocusongrammarlab.com** for additional listening, pronunciation, speaking, and writing practice.

Note:

- See the *Focus on Grammar Workbook* for additional in-class or homework grammar practice.

Unit 13 Review (page 189)

Have students complete the Review and check their answers on Student Book page UR-4. Review or assign additional material as needed.

Go to **www.myfocusongrammarlab.com** for the Unit Achievement Test.

UNIT 14 OVERVIEW

Grammar: PERMISSION: *Can, Could, May, Do you mind if*

Unit 14 focuses on ways to ask permission and give and refuse permission.

- The modals *can, could,* and *may* are used in questions to ask permission. *May* is more formal.
- The word *please* makes permission requests more polite.
- Informal expressions such as *sure, certainly,* and *go ahead* are often used to give permission. To refuse permission, we usually apologize and give an explanation.
- The expression *Do you mind if* is also used to ask permission.

Theme: ROOMMATES

Unit 14 focuses on language used to ask permission and give or refuse it politely in different social situations.

People normally know what is considered polite behavior in their own country. They know, for example, what they are expected to ask permission for, or what to say to sound polite. Rules of polite behavior are not the same in every country. Before traveling abroad, it is important to find out about etiquette in other countries. This will help avoid misunderstandings and embarrassing situations.

Step 1: Grammar in Context (pages 190–191)

See the general suggestions for Grammar in Context on page 1.

Before You Read

- Have students look at the cartoons and discuss the questions in pairs. Have students make notes of their answers.
- Call on pairs to give answers.

Read

- To encourage students to read with a purpose, write these questions on the board:
  1. Did Heather and Tara get along at first? *(yes)*
  2. What spoiled their relationship? *(They both did things that annoyed the other.)*
  3. What examples of annoying behavior does the article give? *(Tara ate Heather's cookies, and Heather invited friends without asking.)*
  4. Why is the title of the article "Always Ask First"? *(It's the advice the article gives. Heather and Tara had problems precisely because they didn't ask first.)*
- Have students read the text. (OR: Play the audio and have students follow along in their books.) If necessary, explain that a counselor is someone whose job is to help and support people with problems. Then call on students to share their answers to the questions on the board.
- To get students to share their ideas on the reading, form pairs or small groups. Have them discuss one or both of the following questions:
  1. What would you do if you shared a room and your roommate ate your cookies or invited friends without asking? How would you react? How would you try to resolve the problem?
  2. What other guidelines can a dorm counselor give to help roommates get along with each other? Write a short list of guidelines and rank them in order of importance.

After You Read

A. Vocabulary

- Have students complete the exercise individually. Encourage them to use context clues to help.
- Have students compare answers in pairs. Then call on pairs to give answers.
- (⏱) For further practice, have students match the vocabulary words with the words or phrases that go together. (Answers: *1. f, 2. c, 3. a, 4. b, 5. d, 6. e*)

1. a neat	a. guidelines
2. to look	b. a presentation
3. to follow	c. annoyed
4. to do	d. it's right
5. to assume	e. times
6. to establish	f. person

B. Comprehension

- Have students complete the exercise individually.
- Have students compare answers in pairs. Then call on pairs to give answers.

Go to **www.myfocusongrammarlab.com** for an additional reading, and for reading and vocabulary practice.

Step 2: Grammar Presentation (pages 192–193)

See the general suggestions for Grammar Presentation on page 2.

Grammar Charts

- To explain *yes/no* and *wh-* questions with *can, could,* and *may,* write on the board:
  1. Can I work here tonight?
  2. Could I have a cookie?
  3. May I use your computer?
  4. Where can I sit?
  5. When could I come back?
  — Have students study the examples. Then ask: "How do you ask permission with *can, could,* and *may?*" (can/could/may + subject + base form of verb OR wh- *word* + can/could/may + *subject* + *base form of verb*)
  — Do not erase the questions.
- To explain short answers, write on the board:
  a. Certainly.
  b. Of course.
  c. Sure.
  d. No problem.
  e. Sorry, but . . .
  — Ask: "Which questions go with these answers?" *(1–3)* "Which expressions give permission?" *(a–d)* "Which expression refuses permission?" *(e)*
  — Write below the answers on the board:
  f. At six.
  g. Right here.
  — Ask: "Which question goes with answer *f?*" *(5)* "Which question can be replied with answer *g?*" *(4)*
- To explain statements with *can* and *may,* write on the board:
  1. You can leave a message.
  2. You can not leave earlier.
  3. You may use this phone.
  4. You may not stay in this room.
  5. You can't use that elevator.
  6. You cannot stay here.
  — Ask: "Which sentences give permission?" *(1, 3)* "Which sentences refuse permission?" *(2, 4, 5, 6)* "What are the negative forms of *can?*" (can not, cannot, can't) "What is the negative form of *may?*" (may not) "Can *may not* be contracted?" *(no)*
- To explain questions with *Do you mind if . . .?,* write on the board:

1. Do you mind if I open the window?
2. Do you mind if my friends come over tonight?
— Ask: "How do you ask permission with *do you mind if?*" (do you mind + if + *subject* + *simple present tense*)
— Do not erase the questions.
- To explain short answers, write on the board:
  a. Not at all.
  b. No, I don't.
  c. Go right ahead.
  d. Sorry, but . . .
  — Ask: "Which expressions give permission?" *(a–c)* "Why?" *(because they mean that you don't mind)* "Which expression refuses permission?" *(d)*

Grammar Notes

Note 1

- To review asking permission with the modals *can, could,* and *may,* write on the board:
  Can I . . . ? = Could I . . . ? = May I . . . ?
  less formal ◄─────────────► more formal
- Point out that the three questions have the same meaning—they are all used to ask permission.
- Point out that *can* is less formal than *could,* and *could* is less formal than *may.* Direct students' attention to the arrow on the board.
- Point out that *may* is very formal and is normally used to speak to people in authority.
- Explain that *could* does *not* have a past meaning in questions asking permission.
- To explain the placement of *please,* write on the board:
  Could I <u>please</u> take a photograph?
  Could I take a photograph, <u>please</u>?
- Point out that *please* may be placed just before the main verb or at the end of a question.

Note 2

- To review asking permission with *Do you mind if . . . ?,* write on the board:
  Do you mind if I turn up the TV?
  Do you mind if Lorna stays here?
- To help clarify, say: "If your roommate is studying and you want to turn up the TV, you would say, *Do you mind if I turn up the TV?* because you can anticipate that it will disturb him or her."
- Point out the simple present tense after *if* (*turn up* after *I* and *stays* after *Lorna*).
- Explain that we do not use *please* in questions with *Do you mind if . . . ?*

Note 3

- To review short answers to questions that ask permission with *can, could,* and *may,* write on the board:

Can			Sure.
Could	I close the door?		Of course.
May			Go ahead.
			Certainly.

- Make sure students understand that you can reply to questions with *can, could,* and *may* with any of the four expressions on the board. These expressions are more common than answers with modals.
- Point out that only the modals *can* and *may* can be used in responses. *May* is very rarely used.
- To review short answers to questions with *Do you mind if . . . ?,* write on the board:
  Do you mind if I leave now?
  No, I don't. / Not at all. / Go right ahead.
- Draw attention to the *Be Careful!* note. Ask: "Does *No, I don't* give or refuse permission?" *(It gives permission because you do not mind if the person does what he/she asked permission for.)* "Do *Not at all* and *Go right ahead* give or refuse permission?" *(They give permission.)* "How can you refuse permission?" (I'm sorry, but + *explanation*)
- Point out that when permission is refused, an apology and a brief explanation are expected.

⏱ **Identify the Grammar:** Have students identify the grammar in the opening reading on page 190. For example:
  Could I **have** one?
  . . . **do you mind if** they **hang out** here for a while?
  Could I **use** yours for a few hours?
  Can Luis and Ming-Hwa **work** here tonight?

Go to **www.myfocusongrammarlab.com** for grammar charts and notes.

Step 3: Focused Practice (pages 194–197)

See the general suggestions for Focused Practice on page 4.

Exercise 1: Discover the Grammar

- Go over the example with the class. Point out that some of the modals in the quiz are *not* used for permission. Give an example: In *I may use your computer tonight,* the person is not asking permission, giving permission, or refusing permission, so *may use* should not be underlined.
- Have students complete the exercise individually. Then go over the answers as a class.
- ⏱ Have students take the quiz.

Exercise 2: Questions and Answers

- Have pairs discuss what the signs mean. Have them make notes about the meaning of each sign. Then review the meanings of the signs as a class. *(You cannot eat or drink in the computer lab. You cannot make loud noises between 11:00 P.M. and 7:00 A.M. You can ride your bike. You cannot bring dogs/pets into Kent Hall. You cannot use your cell phone.)*
- Go over the example with the class. Point out that more than one correct short answer may be possible.
- Have students read each conversation. Then have them complete the exercise individually.

Exercise 3: Questions and Answers

- Go over the example with the class. Then have students read the conversations quickly for meaning.
- Have students complete the conversations in pairs.
- ⏱ Have pairs role-play the conversations.

Exercise 4: Editing

- Go over the example with the class. Then have students read Emil's English test quickly for meaning.
- Have students find and correct the mistakes individually. Then go over the answers as a class, having students explain why the incorrect structures are wrong.
- ⏱ Have students point out examples of correct usages of *can, could, may,* and *do you mind if.*

Go to **www.myfocusongrammarlab.com** for additional grammar practice.

Step 4: Communication Practice
(pages 197–200)

See the general suggestions for Communication Practice on page 5.

Exercise 5: Listening

A

- Go over the example with the class. Then play the audio. Stop after each conversation to allow students time to choose their answers.
- For each conversation, ask: "Who was speaking?" If students disagree, play the segment in question again.

B

- Have students listen again and check the correct columns.

- For each conversation, ask: "Was permission given?" If students disagree, have the class recall the conversation. Ask questions, for example: "What request did the person make?" "What did the other person reply?" "Why did he/she refuse permission?"
- (!) Have students listen to the conversations again and write down the permission requests they hear. Have pairs role-play the conversations. Have them take turns asking permission and responding.

Exercise 6: Pronunciation

A
- Play the audio. Have students read along as they listen to the Pronunciation Note.
- Be sure students understand that:
  1. We link *can*, *could*, and *may* with *I* and *he*.
  2. We *don't* link *can*, *could*, and *may* with other pronouns.

B
- Play the audio. Have students listen and circle the words they hear.

C
- Have students identify the requests in which modals are linked.
- Play the audio. Have students listen and repeat the statements.

Exercise 7: Problem Solving
- Review the first situation and the examples. Brainstorm with the class other possible questions for this situation. (Example: *Do you mind if they use the phone? Can Eva use the kitchen to bake a cake for Anton's birthday? Can they put their bags in this closet?*)
- Encourage students to use their imagination and ask as many questions as they can.
- Take notes on the board as groups share their ideas for each situation. For each situation, ask: "What are the possible responses to these requests? How polite is each request? In this situation, which request would you be most comfortable making?"

Exercise 8: Role Play: *Could I . . . ?*
- Review the first situation and the examples. Have students say other possible ways to make the same requests. (Example: *Could I please copy your notes from class yesterday? Can I call you tonight if I have any questions? Do you mind if I call you tonight if I have any questions?*)
- Have students complete the exercise in pairs. Make sure they take turns being Student A and Student B.
- To add a dramatic element to the exercise, you may want to have students read only their own role information, not that of their partner.

Exercise 9: Writing

A
- Brainstorm with the class other situations in which someone might need to write a note asking permission. Write students' ideas on the board, for example:
to borrow a bicycle
to use someone's computer
to borrow money
to invite a friend to stay overnight
to have a party
to borrow clothes
- Have students choose two situations from Exercise 4 or the board to write their notes.

B
- Have students correct their work using the Editing Checklist.
- Have students submit their notes to you. Review them for accuracy.
- Have students trade notes with a classmate. Then have them write responses to their classmates' notes and correct their work using the Editing Checklist.

OUT OF THE BOX ACTIVITIES

Speaking and Writing

- Have groups develop and write out their own situations relating to asking permission to do something (as in Exercise 9 on page 200).
- Then have groups exchange situations and plan how they would respond.

Reading and Speaking

- Bring in enough copies of a museum's FAQs Web page for each group. Many FAQs are framed starting with *Can I . . . ?* (Example: *Can I bring a stroller into the museum?*) Make sure *can* is used for asking permission in some of the questions of the Web page you select. Form small groups and give each group different or the same material.
- Have students read the questions and answers and make up at least four new questions for the Web page starting with *Can I . . . ?*
- Follow up by asking students from each group to read their questions aloud. You may want to write some of the questions on the board.

Go to **www.myfocusongrammarlab.com** for additional listening, pronunciation, speaking, and writing practice.

Note:
- See the *Focus on Grammar Workbook* for additional in-class or homework grammar practice.

Unit 14 Review (page 201)

Have students complete the Review and check their answers on Student Book page UR-4. Review or assign additional material as needed.

Go to **www.myfocusongrammarlab.com** for the Unit Achievement Test.

UNIT 15 OVERVIEW

Grammar: REQUESTS: *Can, Could, Will, Would, Would you mind*

Unit 15 focuses on ways to make requests and respond to them.

- The modals *can, could, will,* and *would* are used in questions to make polite requests.
- The modals *could* and *would* make requests more polite.
- *Sure, certainly, of course, no problem,* and *I'd be glad to* are often used to reply positively to a request. To say *no,* we usually apologize and give an explanation.
- *Would you mind* plus a gerund is also used to make a polite request.

Theme: MESSAGES

Unit 15 focuses on language used to send email and text messages and to ask favors politely in different situations.

Step 1: Grammar in Context (pages 202–204)

See the general suggestions for Grammar in Context on page 1.

Before You Read

- Have students discuss the questions in pairs. For question 4, have students think about when they use text messages and when they use emails. Encourage them to make notes of the different situations.
- Call on pairs to share their answers.

Read

- To encourage students to read with a purpose, write the following names on the board:
  1. Rhea Jones (*Marcia's mother*)
  2. John Sanchez (*Marcia's boss*)
  3. Ann Chen (*Marcia's assistant*)
  4. Ethan Jones (*Marcia's son*)
  5. Jody Jones (*Marcia's daughter*)
- Have students quickly read the messages to find out who these people are.
- Have students read the text. (OR: Play the audio and have students follow along in their books.) Then call on students to share their answers to the questions on the board.
- To get students to share their ideas on the reading, form pairs or small groups. Have them discuss one or both of the following topics:

1. Different methods of communication. (Example: *letters, emails, phones, cell phones, fax machines, pagers*) Have students talk about the different ways they communicate with the different people in their lives. Encourage students to explain why they use different methods for different situations.
2. In some situations it is particularly important to be polite when making requests. Have students also talk about situations in which politeness is not so important. Encourage students to give examples from their everyday life.

After You Read

A. Vocabulary
- Have students complete the exercise individually. Encourage them to use context clues to help.
- Have students compare answers in pairs. Then call on pairs to give answers.
- ⏱ To reinforce the vocabulary, write these questions on the board. Have students scan the text for the answers:
  1. Who texted Marcia to ask a favor? *(her son, Ethan)*
  2. Who did Marcia text to ask a favor? *(her daughter, Jody)*
  3. Who cheers Marcia up? *(her mother, by sending her a cartoon)*
  4. Who appreciates Marcia's help? *(her boss, John)*
  5. Who will deliver a report? *(Ann)*
  6. Who will distribute a report? *(Marcia)*

B. Comprehension
- Have students complete the exercise individually.
- Have students compare answers in pairs. Then call on pairs to give answers.

Go to **www.myfocusongrammarlab.com** for an additional reading, and for reading and vocabulary practice.

Step 2: Grammar Presentation (pages 205–206)

See the general suggestions for Grammar Presentation on page 2.

Grammar Charts
- To explain requests with *can, could, will, would,* and *would you mind,* write on the board:
  Can you drive me to the Burtons?
  Could you make 25 copies?
  Will you pick up dessert?

Would you copy this report?
Would you mind delivering it to me?
- Point to the first four examples and ask: "How do you form requests with *can, could, will,* and *would*?" (can/could/will/would + you + *base form of verb*)
- Point to the last example on the board and ask: "How do you make requests with *would you mind*?" (would you mind + -ing *form of verb*)
- To explain short answers, write below the questions on the board:
  a. Certainly.
  b. No, not at all.
  c. I'm sorry, but I can't.
- Ask:
  "Which questions from the board can be replied with 'Certainly'?" *(the first four)*
  "Does *Certainly* mean you will do what the person asked you to do?" *(yes)*
  "Which question can be replied to with 'No, not at all'?" *(Would you mind delivering it to me?)*
  "Does *No, not at all* mean you will do what the person asked you to do?" *(yes)*
  "Why?" *(because it means that you don't mind doing it)*
  "Which questions can be replied to with 'I'm sorry, but I can't'?" *(all of them)*
  "What does this reply mean?" *(that you can't do what the person asked you to do)*
- Write below the short answers on the board:
  d. I'm afraid I can't.
  e. No problem.
  f. Sure.
- Have students match them to the phrases with similar meaning in *a* through *c*.
  (a–f, b–e, c–d)
- Point out that there are different ways to answer questions expressing requests.

Grammar Notes

Note 1
- To review requests using the modals *can, could, will,* and *would,* write on the board:

Can	you copy this report?
Could	you copy this report, please?
Will	you please copy this report?
Would	

- Point out that requests with *could* and *would* are more formal and polite than requests with *can* and *will*.
- Point out that *please* makes requests more polite. Ask: "Where does *please* normally go?" *(at the end of a question or before the main verb)*

- Call on students to say typical requests they make at home or at work. (Example: *Will you answer the phone? Could you pass the salt, please? Can you pick up something to eat on your way home? Would you give the presentation for me? Could you mail this package, please?*)

Note 2

- To review short answers, write on the board:

Can			Sure.
Could			Certainly.
Will	you open the door?		Of course.
Would			No problem.

- Make sure students understand that requests with *can, will, could,* and *would* can be replied to with any of the four expressions on the board.
- Have students practice responding rapidly to requests. Say: "Could you close the window?" "Can you clean the board?" "Will you lend me your dictionary?" "Would you spell that for me?" "Can you lend me a pen?"
- Point out that in English-speaking cultures, when someone cannot help with a request, an apology and a brief explanation are expected.
- Draw attention to the *Be Careful!* note. Point out that students can answer with the expressions with or without *I* plus *can* or *will* (*Sure* or *Sure I can/will*) but not plus *could* or *would* (*Sure I could/would*).

Note 3

- To review questions with *Would you mind,* write on the board:
  Would you mind calling back later?
- Write the structure of the question on the board and point out the gerund (*verb* + *-ing*) after *mind*:
  Would you mind + gerund . . . ?
- Point out that questions with *would you mind* are even more polite than questions with *could* or *would*.
- Add two replies:
  Not at all.
  Of course not.
- Draw attention to the *Be Careful!* note. Ask: "Do *Not at all* and *Of course not* mean that the person will call back later?" (*yes, because they mean that the person doesn't mind calling back later*) "What should the person say if he/she can't call back later?" (*I'm sorry, I can't.*)

⏱ **Identify the Grammar:** Have students identify the grammar in the opening reading on pages 202–203. For example:
  Can you **drive** me to the Burtons . . . ?
  . . . **will** you **pick up** something special at the bakery . . . ?
  Would you please **copy** and **distribute** the monthly sales report?
  Could you **make** 25 copies?

Go to www.myfocusongrammarlab.com for grammar charts and notes.

Step 3: Focused Practice (pages 206–209)

See the general suggestions for Focused Practice on page 4.

Exercise 1: Discover the Grammar

- Go over the example with the class. Ask: "Why is *I'd be glad to* the correct answer?" (*because we don't reply to a request with* would)
- Have students complete the exercise individually.
- Have students compare answers in pairs. Then call on pairs to give answers.

Exercise 2: Requests

A

- Have students look at the pictures and describe what the people are doing. (Example: *The woman is holding some documents/reports. The man is filing some documents/opening a drawer/looking for something.*)
- Go over the example with the class.
- Have students complete the exercise with a partner.

B

- Go over the example and have students complete the exercise individually.
- Call on students to give answers.
- ⏱ Have pairs use the information in the exercise to create short conversations.

Exercise 3: Requests and Answers

- Go over the example with the class. Have students provide another possible request and short answer. (Example: *Could you please lend me your cell phone? Sure.*) Point out that there is more than one correct answer. Have students choose how to start each request and how to reply to each question.
- Have students read the conversations quickly for meaning. Then have them complete the exercise individually.
- ⏱ Have pairs role-play the conversations.

Exercise 4: Editing

- Have students read the email message quickly for meaning. Then ask: "What does John need to reschedule?" *(the sales meeting)* "What does he need extra copies of?" *(the sales report)* "What message does he have for Emma?" *(that he will call her next week)* "Why does he suggest working on Saturday?" *(because they need extra time to go over new information)* "Why can't he pick up the business cards?" *(because he won't be back in time)*
- Have students find and correct the mistakes individually. Then call on students to explain why the incorrect structures are wrong.
- ⏱ Have students point out examples of correct requests and responses.

Go to **www.myfocusongrammarlab.com** for additional grammar practice.

Step 4: Communication Practice

(pages 210–212)

See the general suggestions for Communication Practice on page 5.

Exercise 5: Listening

A
- Have students read the list. Then play the audio. For reference, have students listen to the four conversations and identify who is speaking with Marcia in each case.
- Play the audio again. Have students listen and complete the exercises individually.
- Call on students to give answers.

B
- Play the audio. Have students listen and complete the exercise individually.
- Have students compare answers in pairs. Call on pairs to give answers.
- ⏱ Divide the class into two groups, A and B. Have students listen to the conversations again. Students in Group A write down the requests they hear. Students in Group B write down the replies to requests that they hear. Have students pair up, A and B, to match the requests they wrote down with possible replies. Then have students role-play similar conversations using their notes as a guide.

Exercise 6: Pronunciation

A
- Play the audio. Have students read along as they listen to the Pronunciation Note. Be sure students notice that the linking sound in *could you* and *would you* is different from the linking sound in *will you* and *can you*.

B
- Play the audio. Have students listen.

C
- Play the audio. Have students listen and repeat.
- Have students practice the conversations with a partner. Be sure students play both roles.

Exercise 7: Making Plans

A
- Ask: "What are you going to do this weekend?" Write some of the plans on the board.
- Have students complete the exercise individually.

B
- Go over the example with the class. Then brainstorm with the class the types of requests students might ask each other. (Example: *give a ride, pick up the kids, return a book to the library, pick up some groceries, stop at the post office, buy a gift, bake a cake, prepare dinner, cancel an appointment*)
- Form small groups and have groups complete the exercise.

Exercise 8: Writing

A
- Go over the first situation and the example. Point out that although the bike is not mentioned in the situation, it appears in the request. Explain that students are expected to use their own ideas when writing the messages.
- Have students complete the exercise individually. Encourage them to use some abbreviations from page 203.

B
- Go over the example response. Point out how Viktor gives an explanation and makes a suggestion. Encourage students to do the same if they give negative answers.
- Have students complete the exercise in pairs.

C
- Have students correct their work using the Editing Checklist.

OUT OF THE BOX ACTIVITIES

Speaking and Writing

- Divide the class into groups of four.
- Have students make polite requests of each other. The student who receives the request must either perform the action or apologize and explain why he/she is refusing, for example:

  A: Kenno, can you open the door?

  B: I'm sorry. I can't get up right now. I have too many papers on my desk.

  A: Andrew, could you please open the door?

  C: No problem!

Reading and Speaking

- Bring in home decorating magazines that include do-it-yourself sections to improve one's home. Hand out the magazines and have each student choose a remodeling or decoration project.
- Point out that students will need help from a classmate to complete the project. Write the following questions on the board:
  1. What are you going to remodel/redecorate?
  2. What do you need to borrow from your friend?
  3. What do you need to buy?
  4. What are you going to ask your friend to get for you?
  5. When are you going to ask your friend to come to your place to help you?
  6. What else are you going to ask your friend to do?
- Have students answer the questions in note form individually and think about the requests they will need to make. Then have students work in pairs to take turns making requests and replying to them. The student who receives the request should either agree to help or apologize and explain why he/she is refusing.

Go to **www.myfocusongrammarlab.com** for additional listening, pronunciation, speaking, and writing practice.

Note:
- See the *Focus on Grammar Workbook* for additional in-class or homework grammar practice.

Unit 15 Review (page 213)

Have students complete the Review and check their answers on Student Book page UR-4. Review or assign additional material as needed.

Go to **www.myfocusongrammarlab.com** for the Unit Achievement Test.

UNIT 16 OVERVIEW

Grammar: ADVICE: *Should, Ought to, Had better*

Unit 16 focuses on ways to give and ask for advice.

- *Should* and *ought to* are used to say something is advisable.
- *Had better* is used to give strong advice. It expresses that something bad will happen if the person does not follow the advice.
- *Should* is used in questions. *Ought to* and *had better* are not normally used in questions.

Theme: INTERNET RULES

Unit 16 focuses on language used to post polite messages on the Internet and give advice in different situations.

Step 1: Grammar in Context (pages 214–216)

See the general suggestions for Grammar in Context on page 1.

Before You Read

- Have students discuss the questions in pairs. Encourage them to make notes about their answers and give examples based on their own experiences.
- Go over the answers as a class and encourage students to give reasons why it is important to be polite on the Internet and some good rules to follow. Write students' ideas in two columns on the board, for example:

  It is important to be polite because . . .
  - you can hurt someone
  - you can get into trouble if you don't
  - you don't know the other person's culture well

  Some rules to follow are . . .
  - respect other people's ideas
  - say "please" and "thank you"
  - don't give personal information

Read
- To encourage students to read with a purpose, write these questions on the board:
  1. What kind of advice does the article give? *(about how to be polite when using the Internet)*
  2. What should you do before posting your own ideas? *(read old messages and/or FAQs)*
  3. Why shouldn't you use capital letters? *(because they seem like shouting)*
  4. Why should you count to 10 before replying to a message that made you angry? *(to avoid sending a reply that can hurt someone)*
  5. What do emoticons show? *(the feelings of the person who is writing a message)*
  6. Why shouldn't you use your real name on the Internet? *(safety/to protect your identity)*
- Have students read the text and the cyber words. (OR: Play the audio and have students follow along in their books.) Then call on students to share their answers to the questions on the board.
- To get students to share their ideas on the reading, form pairs or small groups. Have them discuss one or more of the following questions/topics:
  1. Why is netiquette important? Which rules from the article do you follow? What problems might you have if you don't know or follow the rules of netiquette? If students have had any problems when using the Internet, have them share their experiences.
  2. What other rules of netiquette could have been included in the article? Discuss their importance and rank them in order.

After You Read

A. Vocabulary
- Have students complete the exercise individually. Encourage them to use context clues to help.
- Have students compare answers in pairs. Then call on pairs to give answers.
- (!) To reinforce the vocabulary, write the following sentence halves on the board. Have students match them. (Answers: *1. b, 2. d, 3. e, 4. a, 5. c*)
  1. Don't give   a. a problem.
  2. Protect   b. your real name.
  3. Improve   c. your normal behavior.
  4. Avoid   d. yourself.
  5. Don't change   e. your communication.

B. Comprehension
- Have students complete the exercise individually.

- Have students compare answers in pairs. Then call on pairs to give answers.

Go to **www.myfocusongrammarlab.com** for an additional reading, and for reading and vocabulary practice.

Step 2: Grammar Presentation (pages 216–218)
See the general suggestions for Grammar Presentation on page 2.

Grammar Charts
- To explain *should* for advice, write on the board:
  They should learn the rules of netiquette.
  Should he use capital letters?
  You shouldn't forget that people have feelings.
  When should we post to the bulletin board?
  — Have students study the examples. Then ask: "How do you give advice with *should*?" (should + *base form of verb*) "Does *should* change when the pronoun changes?" (*no—should is the same for all pronouns because it is a modal*) "How do you form the negative of *should*?" (shouldn't *or* should + *not* + *base form of verb*) "How do you form *yes/no* questions?" (should + *subject* + *base form of verb*) "How do you form *wh-* questions?" (wh- *word* + should + *subject* + *base form of verb*)
  — Call on a student to provide the two possible short answers to the *yes/no* questions on the board. (*Yes, they should. / No, they shouldn't.*)
- To explain *ought to* for advice, write on the board:
  You ought to lurk a little first.
  — Ask: "How do you give advice with *ought to*?" (ought to + *base form of verb*) "Does *ought to* change when the pronoun changes?" (*No—ought to is the same for all pronouns because it is a modal.*)
  — Point out that negative statements and questions with *ought to* are not common.
- To explain *had better* for advice, write on the board:
  You had better learn the rules.
  You'd better use a screen name.
  You'd better not reply right away.
  — Have students study the examples. Ask: "What does the *d* in *you'd* stand for?" (had) "How do you give advice with *had better*?" (had better + *base form of verb*) "How do you form the negative of *had better*?" (had better + *not* + *base form of verb*)

— Point out that *had better* does not change when the pronoun changes. *Had better* is not a modal, but it behaves like a modal.

— Point out that *had better* is often contracted in everyday speech and that questions with *had better* are not common.

Grammar Notes

Note 1

• To explain the use of *should* and *ought to* to give advice, write on the board:
  (+) You should remember the rules. = You ought to remember the rules.
  (–) You shouldn't forget the rules.

• Point out that *ought not to* is not common in American English, but it is used in British English.

• Write on the board:

Maybe	you	should	be more polite.
Perhaps		ought to	
I think			

• Point out that when we give advice, we often use *maybe, perhaps,* or *I think* to sound gentler.

Note 2

• To explain the use of *had better* to give advice, write on the board:
  You'd better keep your post short, or no one will read it.
  You'd better write a polite reply, or you might offend him.

• Emphasize that *had better* is used when you believe something bad will happen if the person does not follow the advice. Point out that the undesired consequence is often said, and it is introduced by *or*. Ask: "What are the bad consequences in the examples?" *(that no one will read the post and that someone might feel offended)*

• Point out that the contraction of *had better* (*you'd better, he'd better,* etc.) is normally used in everyday speech.

• Point out that the negative form of *had better* is *had better not* (not ~~had not better~~).

• Draw attention to the *Be Careful!* note. Point out that *had better* always refers to the present or the future, never to the past.

Note 3

• To review questions with *should*, write on the board:

Should I post my opinion?	Yes, you should.
Should I get virus protection?	Why not? Good idea.
Should I tell her my password?	No, you shouldn't.

• Remind students that *ought to* and *had better* are not normally used for questions.

• Point out that *should* can be used in short answers, but we can use other expressions as well. (Example: *Why not? Good idea.*)

Note 4

• To explain informal expressions, write on the board:
  You oughta come.
  You better not go.

• Draw attention to the *Be Careful!* note. Point out that the expressions on the board are informal and should not be used in formal writing.

• Have students say the complete versions of the informal expressions on the board. *(You ought to come. You had better not go.)*

⏱ **Identify the Grammar:** Have students identify the grammar in the opening reading on page 214. For example:
  . . . you **should know** these simple rules of netiquette.
  When **should** you **post** to a bulletin board or chat room?
  . . . they **ought to lurk** a little first.

Go to **www.myfocusongrammarlab.com** for grammar charts and notes.

Step 3: Focused Practice (pages 218–222)

See the general suggestions for Focused Practice on page 4.

Exercise 1: Discover the Grammar

• Go over the example with the class.
• Have students complete the exercise individually.
• Have students compare answers in pairs. Then go over the answers as a class.

Exercise 2: Statements with *Should, Ought to,* and *Had better*

• Go over the example with the class. Then have students read all the posts quickly for meaning. If necessary, clarify the meaning of *Groundhog Day:* February 2, according to American stories, the first day of the year that a groundhog (a small North American animal that has thick brown fur and lives in holes in the ground) comes out of its hole. If it sees its shadow, there will be six more weeks of winter; if it does not, good weather will come early.

- Have students complete the exercise individually, choosing between affirmative and negative forms and using contractions when possible.
- ⏱ Books closed. Have students say pieces of advice they remember from the exercise. Encourage them to use the different ways of giving advice that they learned in this unit.

Exercise 3: Statements with *Should, Ought to,* and *Had better*
- Go over the example with the class. Point out that there can be more than one correct answer.
- Have students complete the exercise individually. Encourage them to use the three ways to give advice they learned in this unit.
- Have students compare answers in pairs. Then go over the answers as a class.

Exercise 4: Questions and Short Answers with *Should*
- Go over the example with the class.
- Have students match the items in the box to the posts. Then have them complete the exercise individually.
- Have students compare answers in pairs. Then call on pairs to read the posts aloud.

Exercise 5: Editing
- Have students read the posts quickly for meaning. Then ask: "What topics do students ask advice about?" *(a dinner party to which the student was asked to bring some food, what to do after losing one's wallet, how to make friends at college, and how to get ready to go to school in Canada)*
- Go over the example with the class. If necessary, explain that *LOL,* a written abbreviation for *laughing out loud,* is used by people communicating in chat rooms on the Internet to say that they are laughing at something that someone else has written.
- Have students find and correct the mistakes individually. Then call on students to explain why the incorrect structures are wrong.
- ⏱ Have students point out examples of correct usages of *should, ought to,* and *had better.*

Go to **www.myfocusongrammarlab.com** for additional grammar practice.

Step 4: Communication Practice
(pages 223–225)

See the general suggestions for Communication Practice on page 5.

Exercise 6: Listening
A
- Go over the questions. Point out that more than one person's name should be checked for some questions.
- Play the audio. Have students listen and complete the exercise individually. If necessary, stop after each call to allow students time to choose their answers.

B
- Play the audio. Have students listen and complete the exercise individually. Then have students give their own opinion about why they agree or disagree with the advice in the list.
- ⏱ Ask: "Do you have any other advice for buying a computer?" Have students brainstorm in small groups and then share their ideas with the class.

Exercise 7: Pronunciation
A
- Play the audio. Have students read along as they listen to the Pronunciation Note. To check comprehension, ask: "How do we often pronounce *ought to?*" *(oughta)* "What are two possible ways to say *had better?*" *(d' better* or just *better)*

B
- Play the audio. Have students listen.

C
- Play the audio. Have students listen and repeat.
- Have students practice the conversations with a partner. Be sure students play both roles.

Exercise 8: Cross-Cultural Comparison
- Go over the list of topics. Brainstorm with the class other topics and write them on the board, for example:
Dressing for work
Punctuality at work
Office schedules
Socializing after work with colleagues
Gift giving
- Go over the examples. Point out the use of *had better* and *should.* Remind students they can also use *ought to.*
- Have students choose two topics from the board and add them to their list. Then have students complete the exercise in pairs.

Exercise 9: Problem Solving

- Go over the example with the class. Brainstorm more advice for the same situation. Write students' ideas on the board. (Example: *Maybe you should buy her a nice gift. You ought to give her a surprise.*)
- Form groups of four and have each group member choose a different problem to ask the group about. Point out that every student should receive advice from his/her group members.
- Have each group present one problem and the corresponding advice to the class. Invite the class to offer additional advice for each problem.

Exercise 10: Picture Discussion

- To help students with unknown vocabulary, have them name the objects that need repairing, cleaning, or arranging. Provide any unknown words. Write a list on the board, for example:

ceiling	notice board
panel	radiator
wallpaper	photocopier
window pane	computer desk
floor	chair
blackboard	wastebasket

- To help students generate ideas, ask what the people in the line could be complaining about. (Example: *The man at the computer is taking too long. He is wasting time as he drinks coffee and eats snacks. The computer desk is messy. There is only one computer in the classroom.*)
- Form small groups and have each group assign a person to write (a scribe). Encourage students to write as many sentences as they can think of.

Exercise 11: Writing

A

- Draw the format of a formal letter on the board:

April 12, 2012
13 Apple Lane
Newtonville, MA 02166

Mr. Edward Thompson
EFL Computer Training Institute
10 Ferry Street
Newbury, MA 01951

Dear Mr. Thompson:
(body of letter)

Sincerely,
(your signature)

- Tell students that Mr. Thompson is the owner of the institute. Point out the date, the address of the person who is writing the letter, the address of the institute, the closing, and the signature.
- Write the following questions on the board to help elicit vocabulary and generate ideas:
  What should they repair?
  What should they clean?
  What should they put in order?
  What new equipment should they buy?
  What rules should there be for computer use?
  What signs should they put up on the walls?
- Have students make notes for each question and then use them as a guide as they write.

B

- Have students correct their work using the Editing Checklist.

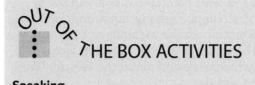

OUT OF THE BOX ACTIVITIES

Speaking

- Have students discuss the following questions in small groups:
  — Have you ever been on a job interview?
  — Was it a good interview? Why or why not?
  — What advice would you give to someone interviewing for the first time?
- Follow up with a class discussion. Encourage students to add other suggestions for job interviews, such as what to wear, how to greet and say goodbye to the interviewer, what to say and not to say, and how to follow up appropriately. Write students' ideas on the board.

Reading and Speaking

- Bring in magazines that have advice columns. (Make sure that the topics covered are appropriate for your group. If necessary, select specific questions and answers and photocopy them for each group.) Form small groups. Have students choose and discuss a problem from the advice column— or the problem in their photocopy—and the advice given by the expert.
- Have students write down a few statements giving their own advice.
- Follow up by asking each group what problem they discussed. Have students give their opinion of the expert's advice and share their own advice.

Go to **www.myfocusongrammarlab.com** for additional listening, pronunciation, speaking, and writing practice.

Note:
- See the *Focus on Grammar Workbook* for additional in-class or homework grammar practice.

Unit 16 Review (page 226)

Have students complete the Review and check their answers on Student Book page UR-4. Review or assign additional material as needed.

Go to **www.myfocusongrammarlab.com** for the Unit Achievement Test.

From Grammar to Writing (pages 227–229)

See the general suggestions for From Grammar to Writing on page 9.

Go to **www.myfocusongrammarlab.com** for an additional From Grammar to Writing Assignment, Part Review, and Part Post-Test.

PART V OVERVIEW

NOUNS, QUANTIFIERS, AND ARTICLES

UNIT	GRAMMAR FOCUS	THEME
17	Nouns and Quantifiers	Time Capsules
18	Articles: Indefinite and Definite	Stories

Go to **www.myfocusongrammarlab.com** for the Part and Unit Tests.

Note: PowerPoint® grammar presentations, test-generating software, and reproducible Part and Unit Tests are on the *Teacher's Resource Disc*.

UNIT 17 OVERVIEW

Grammar: NOUNS AND QUANTIFIERS

Unit 17 focuses on the uses of nouns and quantifiers.

- Proper nouns are names of people, places, or things. Common nouns refer to people, places, and things but are not names.
- Common nouns can be either count or non-count. Count nouns can be singular or plural, and they take singular or plural verbs. Non-count nouns have no plural forms, and they take singular verbs.
- Some quantifiers (e.g., *some, enough, a lot of*) can be used with both count nouns and non-count nouns. Some quantifiers (e.g., *few, several, many*) are used only with plural count nouns, and other quantifiers (e.g., *a little, a great deal of, much*) are used only with non-count nouns.

Theme: TIME CAPSULES

Unit 17 focuses on language used to talk about time capsules and describe things and places, such as Pompeii and a recipe.

Step 1: Grammar in Context (pages 232–233)

See the general suggestions for Grammar in Context on page 1.

Before You Read

- Have students look at the illustration and discuss the questions in pairs.
- To help students with question 2, draw the following diagram on the board and have students complete it with their own ideas:

Time Capsule

    — It is usually filled with _____.
    — It is usually kept _____.
    — Its purpose is to _____.

- Call on pairs to share their answers with the class. As you get feedback from students, complete the diagram on the board. (Example: *It is filled with things from a particular time. It is usually kept underground. Its purpose is to tell the people who will open it in the future what life was like at a particular time.*)

Read

- To encourage students to read with a purpose, write these questions on the board:
  1. Where is the time capsule shown in the picture? *(in Flushing Meadows Park in New York City)*
  2. When was it created? *(in 1939, during the New York's World Fair)*
  3. What and where is Pompeii? *(It is an ancient Roman city in Italy.)*
  4. Why is it a time capsule? *(because it was buried by ash when a volcano erupted in the year 79 and discovered many years later)*
- Have students read the text. (OR: Play the audio and have students follow along in their books.) Then call on students to share their answers to the questions on the board.
- To get students to share their ideas on the reading, form pairs or small groups. Have them discuss one or both of the following questions:
  1. The time capsule in the picture will be opened in 6939. What do you think life will be like then? Will the things in the bottle be useful to tell people about life in 1939? Give your reasons.
  2. Egyptian tombs are time capsules, too. Do you know any other time capsules? Share what you know about them and discuss their importance.

After You Read

A. Vocabulary

- Have students complete the exercise individually. Encourage them to use context clues to help.

- Have students compare answers in pairs. Then call on pairs to give answers.
- ⏱ To reinforce the vocabulary, have students use the words in blue to complete the following paragraph about the Westinghouse Time Capsule:
  The bottle in the picture is an _____ time capsule that was _____ in 1939. The _____ was an international fair. We don't know if the people in 6939 will be able to _____ its English, but we hope they will be _____ by its contents and learn a lot about our _____ !

B. Comprehension

- Have students complete the exercise individually.
- Have students compare answers in pairs. Then call on pairs to give answers.

Go to **www.myfocusongrammarlab.com** for an additional reading, and for reading and vocabulary practice.

Step 2: Grammar Presentation (pages 234–236)

See the general suggestions for Grammar Presentation on page 2.

Grammar Charts

- To explain proper nouns, write on the board:
  The Westinghouse Time Capsule holds a written message from Albert Einstein.
  It is in a park in New York City.
  — Have students find in the example: the name of a person *(Albert Einstein)*, the name of a thing *(Westinghouse Time Capsule)*, and the name of a place *(New York City)*.
  — Point out that the names of people, places, and things are proper nouns.
  — Ask: "Do names of people, things, and places start with a lowercase letter or a capital letter?" *(with a capital letter)*
- To explain common nouns, write on the board:
  Some archeologists are studying an ancient city.
  They found a lot of coins.
  — Have students find in the sentences (a) a noun that refers to people *(archeologists)*, (b) a noun that refers to things *(coins)*, and (c) a noun that refers to a place *(city)*.
  — Point out that nouns that are not names and refer to people, places, and things are common nouns.
  — Ask: "Do common nouns start with a lowercase letter or a capital letter?" *(with a lowercase letter)*

- To explain count and non-count nouns, write on the board:

  They put some books and some money in the capsule.

  They also put in a few magazines and a little rice.

  — Have students study the example. Then ask: "Is it correct to say *a book, two books, three books*?" *(yes)* "Is it correct to say *a money, two moneys, three moneys*?" *(no)*

  — Point out that some common nouns are count nouns; that is, they can be counted and they can be singular or plural. Other common nouns are non-count nouns; that is, they can't be counted and they have no plural forms.

  — Ask: "Is *book* count or non-count?" *(count)* "Does the example on the board use the singular or the plural form of *book*?" *(the plural form)* "Is *money* count or non-count?" *(non-count)* "Does it have a plural form?" *(no)*

  — Ask: "What word comes before *books* and *money* in the example?" *(some)*

  — Point out that *some* is a quantifier and that some quantifiers can be used with both count and non-count nouns.

  — Ask: "Is *magazines* count or non-count?" *(count)* "Is rice count or non-count?" *(non-count)* "What word comes before *magazines* in the example?" *(a few)* "What word comes before *rice*?" *(a little)*

  — Point out that *a few* and *a little* are quantifiers: *a few* is used with count nouns, and *a little* is used with non-count nouns. There are more quantifiers that are used in this way.

- To summarize, draw the following diagram on the board:

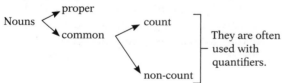

Grammar Notes

Note 1

- To review proper nouns, write on the board the following column heads and one example under each:

People	Places	Things	Months	Nationalities
Sarah	Mexico	Titanic	April	Japanese

- Have students say more nouns for each category. Write the nouns on the board as students say them.

- Point out that the nouns on the board are proper nouns.

- Write on the board:

  Sarah traveled to Mexico in April.

- Have students study the example. Then ask: "Do we usually use articles *(a/an/the)* before proper nouns?" *(no)*

- To review common nouns, write on the board the following column heads and one example under each:

People	Places	Things
student	street	car

- Have students say more nouns for each category. Write the nouns on the board as students say them.

- Point out that the nouns on the board are common nouns.

- Ask: "Are common nouns capitalized?" *(no)*

- If needed, refer students to Appendix 8 on page A-5 for categories of proper nouns.

- If needed, refer students to Appendix 25 on page A-11 for spelling rules for regular plural nouns and to Appendix 6 on page A-4 for a list of irregular plural nouns.

Note 2

- To explain how count nouns are used, write on the board:

  They found a box in the park.

  It has two messages and a coin.

  The notes are not clear.

  The coin is very old.

- Point out that count nouns can be singular or plural. Have students find count nouns in the sentences. *(singular count nouns: box, coin, park; plural count nouns: messages, notes)*

- Point out that count nouns can take singular verbs or plural verbs. Have students find examples in the sentences. *(count noun that takes a singular verb: coin is; count noun that takes a plural verb: notes are)*

- Point out that you can use *a/an* or *the* before count nouns. Have students find examples in the sentences. *(a box, a coin, the notes, the coin, the park)*

- To explain categories of non-count nouns, write on the board the following column headings and one example under each:

Abstract words	Activities	Fields of study	Foods
love	dancing	biology	meat

- Remind students that non-count nouns are things that you cannot count separately.

- Elicit from students more nouns for each category. Write the nouns on the board as students say them.

- To explain how non-count nouns are used, write on the board:

  They don't have plural forms.

  They take singular verbs and pronouns.

  We do not use <u>a/an</u> before them.

- If needed, refer students to Appendix 7 on page A-4 for a list of common non-count nouns.

Note 3
- To explain the use of quantifiers in affirmative sentences, write on the board:

Count nouns

There are	many a lot of a great many some several enough a few	books.

Non-count nouns

There is	a lot of a great deal of some enough a little	time.

- Have students look at the board. Then ask: "Which quantifiers can be used with both count nouns and non-count nouns in affirmative sentences?" (*a lot of, some, enough*) "Which quantifiers are used with count nouns?" (*many, several, a few*) "Which quantifiers are used with non-count nouns?" (*a great deal of, a little*)
- Draw attention to the *Be Careful!* note. To explain the difference between *a few* and *a little*, write on the board:

There are   There is
<u>a few</u> toys.   <u>a little</u> food.
                → some ←

There are   There is
<u>few</u> toys.   <u>little</u> food.
                → not enough ←

- To explain the use of quantifiers in negative statements and questions, write on the board:

Count nouns

There aren't	many a lot of enough any	books.
Are there	any	books?

Non-count nouns

There isn't	much a lot of enough any	time.
Is there	any	time?

- Have students look at the negative sentences. Ask: "Which quantifiers can be used with both count nouns and non-count nouns in negative sentences?" (*a lot of, enough, any*) "Which quantifier is used only with count nouns?" (*many*) "Which quantifier is used only with non-count nouns?" (*much*)
- Have students look at the questions on the board. Ask: "Which quantifier can be used with both count nouns and non-count nouns in questions?" (*any*)
- Point out that in affirmative statements *much* is very formal and not common.

🕐 **Identify the Grammar:** Have students identify the grammar in the opening reading on page 232. For example:
> An **alarm clock, lipstick,** a **toy car,** *some* **fabrics** made out of **cotton** and **wool.**
> A **picture** of a **baseball, money** (a **dollar bill** and **a** *few* **coins**).
> . . . is just one of *many* **capsules** all over the **world.**

Go to **www.myfocusongrammarlab.com** for grammar charts and notes.

Step 3: Focused Practice (pages 237–240)
See the general suggestions for Focused Practice on page 4.

Exercise 1: Discover the Grammar
A
- Go over the examples with the class. Remind students that nouns are words for people, places, and things.
- Have students complete the exercise in pairs. Then call on pairs to give answers.

B
- Go over the examples with the class. Do the first sentence in the article as a class. Ask: "Are *city* and *bay* common nouns or proper nouns?" (*common nouns*) "Are they count or non-count?" (*count*) "Are *Naples* and *Rome* common nouns or proper nouns?" (*proper nouns*)
- Have students complete the exercise in pairs. Then call on pairs to give answers.

Exercise 2: Noun and Verb Agreement
- Go over the example with the class. Then have students read each item quickly for meaning.
- Have students complete the exercise individually. They should decide if they need singular or plural nouns and then choose the correct form of the verb.

- ⏱ Books closed. Write *Shoes, Weather, Picture,* and *Clothes* on the board and have the class say the tips they remember about each topic. Write a few of them on the board.

Exercise 3: Quantifiers

- Go over the example with the class. Ask: "Is *people* a count or non-count noun?" *(count noun)* "Can *much* be used with count nouns?" *(no)*
- Have students read the conversations quickly for meaning. Then have them complete the exercise individually, identifying the nouns and then determining the correct quantifiers.
- ⏱ Have pairs role-play the conversations.

Exercise 4: Editing

- Have students read the email quickly for meaning. Then ask: "Where have Emily and James just gotten back from?" *(Pompeii)* "Did Emily like Pompeii?" *(yes)* "Why?" *(She thinks it's an amazing place. She felt she was communicating with the ancient culture. She was impressed.)* "What is she planning to do with the photos she took?" *(do several blog posts and put them up)* "What did she find in the attic?" *(a trunk)* "What was in the trunk?" *(clothes and letters written by her grandfather)*
- Go over the example with the class. Point out that students can find mistakes in the use of nouns or the quantifiers, verbs, and pronouns that go with them.
- Have students find and correct the mistakes individually. Then call on pairs to explain why the incorrect structures are wrong.
- ⏱ Have students point out examples of correct usages of nouns and the quantifiers, verbs, and pronouns that go with them.

Go to **www.myfocusongrammarlab.com** for additional grammar practice.

Step 4: Communication Practice
(pages 241–244)

See the general suggestions for Communication Practice on page 5.

Exercise 5: Listening

A
- Go over the recipe with the class. Be sure students understand that they are listening for the missing ingredients.
- Play the audio. Have students listen and complete the ingredient list individually.

B
- Play the audio. Have students listen and check the items that Emily and James have enough of. Encourage them to make notes about how many or how much they have of each. Ask: "Do they have a lot?" "Do they have some?" "Do they have a few/a little?" Call on students to say full sentences, using their notes to support their answers.

C
- Play the audio again.
- Have students complete the shopping list. Encourage them to make notes about why Emily and James need to buy each item.
- ⏱ Have students use the list of ingredients to write sentences about what Emily and James are going to buy. They should give reasons Emily and James are/aren't going to buy each ingredient.

Exercise 6: Pronunciation

A
- Play the audio. Have students read along as they listen to the Pronunciation Note.
- Be sure students understand that we sometimes—not always—drop the unstressed vowels in a word.
- To help clarify, write *camera* on the board. Then ask: "Which is the stressed vowel in this word?" (c<u>a</u>mera) "Which are the two unstressed vowels?" (cam<u>e</u>r<u>a</u>) Point out that only the *e* can be dropped.

B
- Have pairs read the sentences and decide which vowel(s) is/are dropped in each sentence.
- Play the audio. Have students listen and check their answers. Pause after each sentence and make sure students made the right choices.

C
- Play the audio. Have students listen and repeat the statements.

Exercise 7: Quotable Quotes

- Elicit or explain that a quote is something that somebody else said and a proverb is a short, well-known statement that contains advice about life in general.
- Go over the example with the class. Brainstorm with the class other ways to explain this proverb. (Example: *You need time and patience to do something well. Important things cannot be done in a rush.*)
- Have pairs write notes about what they think each quote or proverb means. Then call on students to explain each quote or proverb.

Exercise 8: Problem Solving

A

- Go over the categories and questions with the class.
- Draw the following chart on the board for students to use as they discuss the questions. Have them make notes for each item.

a. Ten things—how much or how many of each?	1. 2. 3. 4. 5. 6. 7. 8. 9. 10.
b. Name of time capsule	
c. Date when people will open it	
d. Place where you will put it	

- Form small groups. Have students discuss the items in the chart and encourage them to explain their choice of the things, the name, the place, and the date.

B

- Have each group join another group. Have students use their chart as a guide to share their choices.

Exercise 9: Writing

A

- Have students read the questions and the example. Point out that they can use information from Exercise 8 or their own ideas.
- Have students make notes for each question and then use them as a guide as they write.

B

- Have students correct their work using the Editing Checklist.

OUT OF THE BOX ACTIVITIES

Speaking and Writing

- Brainstorm with the class the major categories of foods. (Example: *appetizers, vegetables, pasta and grains, egg and dairy, poultry and other proteins, desserts*)
- Show several examples of the way recipes are written. Discuss measurements and terms commonly used. (Have students look back at Exercise 5 on page 241.)
- Form small groups. Have students write a recipe, listing the ingredients and quantities first, and then describing the steps in making the recipe.

Reading and Speaking

- Bring in Internet printouts from a website that has information about everyday life in Pompeii. You can print out information about food, work, or the baths. Hand out the material. Form small groups and have students read the material and find proper nouns, count and non-count common nouns, and quantifiers.
- Have students choose two brief pieces of information that contain proper nouns and/or quantifiers plus common nouns to share with the class.
- **Note:** You can go to www.pompeiisites.org and follow this path: Home → archeological sites → Pompeii → visiting the sites → itinerary by topics → everyday life.

Go to **www.myfocusongrammarlab.com** for additional listening, pronunciation, speaking, and writing practice.

Note:
- See the *Focus on Grammar Workbook* for additional in-class or homework grammar practice.

Unit 17 Review (page 245)

Have students complete the Review and check their answers on Student Book page UR-5. Review or assign additional material as needed.

Go to **www.myfocusongrammarlab.com** for the Unit Achievement Test.

Grammar: ARTICLES: INDEFINITE AND DEFINITE

Unit 18 focuses on the uses of indefinite and definite articles.

• Indefinite articles *(a, an)* are used with singular count nouns that are indefinite. (A noun is indefinite if it does not refer to a specific person, place, or thing.)

• The definite article *the* is used with singular and plural count nouns and non-count nouns that are definite. (A noun is definite if it refers to a specific person, place, or thing.)

• Use no article or *some* with plural count nouns and non-count nouns that are indefinite.

Theme: STORIES

Unit 18 focuses on language used to tell stories.
    Aesop was an ancient Greek writer about whom little is known. He is said to have lived from about 620 to 560 B.C.E. and to have been a slave who was then freed. He is credited with the creation of over 600 fables, most of which deal with animals. His fables are often told to children because of the valuable lessons they teach.

Step 1: Grammar in Context (pages 246–248)

See the general suggestions for Grammar in Context on page 1.

Before You Read

• Have students look at the pictures, read the titles of the stories, and discuss the questions in pairs.

• Have students write a sentence explaining what they think a fable is.

• Call on pairs to give answers. Elicit or explain that a fable is a traditional story, often about animals, that teaches a moral lesson.

Read

• To encourage students to read with a purpose, write these questions on the board:
The Ant and the Dove
1. What problem did the ant have? *(He fell into the river when he went to drink water.)*
2. What did the dove do to help him? *(It picked a leaf from the tree and dropped it in the river.)*
3. What problem did the dove have after that? *(A hunter came to catch birds.)*
4. What did the ant do to help the dove? *(He bit the hunter's foot. The hunter shouted in pain, and the noise made the dove fly away.)*

The Town Mouse and the Country Mouse
5. What did the country mouse serve the town mouse? *(the only food he had—some beans and some bread)*
6. Did the town mouse enjoy the meal? *(Yes. He ate and laughed.)*
7. What did the town mouse serve the country mouse? *(the leftovers of a wonderful dinner—jelly, cake, and many nice things)*
8. Did the country mouse enjoy the meal? *(No. A dog ran in and they both had to run away.)*

• Have students read the text. (OR: Play the audio and have students follow along in their books.) Then call on students to share their answers to the questions on the board.

• To get students to share their ideas on the reading, form pairs or small groups. Have them discuss one or both of the following topics:
1. Discuss the moral lesson that each of the fables teaches.
2. Share other fables you know and discuss their moral lessons.

After You Read

A. Vocabulary

• Have students complete the exercise individually. Encourage them to use context clues to help.

• Have students compare answers in pairs. Then call on pairs to give answers.

• 🕐 To reinforce the vocabulary, write the following sentence halves on the board. Have students match them. (Answers: *1. b, 2. a, 3. e, 4. c, 5. d*)

1. Aesop's fables	a. left immediately after dinner.
2. The city mouse	b. are famous all over the world.
3. The ant	c. both mice had a wonderful dinner.
4. At the town mouse's house	d. when an enormous dog came in.
5. Both mice had to run away	e. was struggling in the water.

B. Comprehension

• Have students complete the exercise individually.

• Have students compare answers in pairs. Then call on pairs to give answers.

Go to **www.myfocusongrammarlab.com** for an additional reading, and for reading and vocabulary practice.

Step 2: Grammar Presentation (pages 248–250)

See the general suggestions for Grammar Presentation on page 2.

Grammar Charts

- To explain the indefinite articles *a* and *an*, write on the board:

  a dove   an ant
  a river   an idea

  — Have students study the examples. Then ask: "Do you use *a* before a vowel sound or a consonant sound?" *(before a consonant sound)* "Do you use *an* before a vowel sound or a consonant sound?" *(before a vowel sound)* "What kind of nouns use *a* or *an*—count nouns or non-count nouns, singular nouns or plural nouns?" *(singular count nouns)*

- To explain the definite article, point out that *the* is used with most nouns. To illustrate this point, write on the board:

  the ant   plural count noun
  the food   singular count noun
  the mice   non-count noun

  — Have students match the examples with the nouns. Match the items on the board with arrows as students give their answers.

- To compare indefinite articles with the definite article, write on the board:

  An ant lived next to a river.
  The ant went to the river to drink.

  — Point to the first sentence and ask: "Do we know exactly what ant or river this sentence refers to?" *(no)*
  — Explain that *ant* and *river* are indefinite nouns in this sentence because they do not refer to a specific ant or a specific river. This is why the indefinite articles *an* and *a* are used before them.
  — Point to the second sentence and ask: "Do we know what ant this sentence refers to?" *(yes—the one that lives next to the river)* "Do we know what river this sentence refers to?" *(yes—the one that is near the ant's home)*
  — Explain that *ant* and *river* are definite nouns in this sentence because they refer to a specific ant and a specific river. This is why the definite article *the* is used before them.

- To explain the indefinite article *some*, write on the board:

  The mouse ate beans and bread.
  The mouse ate some beans and some bread.

  — Have students study the examples. Then ask: "Is *bread* a definite or indefinite non-count noun?" *(an indefinite non-count noun)* "Is *beans* a definite or indefinite plural count noun?" *(an indefinite plural count noun)* "Are *beans* and *bread* preceded by any articles in the first example?" *(No. They are used without articles.)* "What comes before *beans* and *bread* in the second example?" *(some)*
  — Explain that indefinite plural count nouns or indefinite non-count nouns can be used with no article or with *some*.

Grammar Notes

Note 1

- To compare definite and indefinite nouns, write on the board:

  "I saw a hunter in the forest," Kim told Joe.

- Ask:

  "Does Kim know the hunter?" *(no)*
  "Is she talking about a specific hunter?" *(no)*
  "Is Kim talking about a specific forest?" *(yes, probably the one in the area)*
  "Does Joe know what forest Kim is talking about?" *(yes)*
  "Is *hunter* a definite or indefinite noun in the sentence on the board?" *(an indefinite noun)*
  "Is *forest* a definite or indefinite noun?" *(a definite noun)*

Note 2

- To compare the use of *a* and *an*, write on the board:

  a horse   an honest man
  a union   an umbrella
  a European writer an excellent book
  a house   an hour

- Draw attention to the *Be Careful!* note. Read the examples so that students can compare and contrast the beginning sound of each word. Then say the words again and have students repeat.

- To explain what article can be used before each type of noun, write on the board:

  a   singular count nouns
  an   plural count nouns
  no article or some non-count nouns

- Have students connect the items, according to what can come before each type of noun. As students give their answers, match the items on the board with arrows. (a: *singular count nouns*; an: *singular count nouns*; some: *plural count nouns and non-count nouns*; no article: *plural count nouns and non-count nouns*)
- If needed, refer students to Appendix 7 on page A-4 for a list of common non-count nouns.

Note 3
- To explain identification, point to a bag and say: "This is a bag."
- To explain generalizations, write on the board:
  I like football.
  I like ~~the~~ football.
  Fruit is good for your health.
  ~~The~~ fruit is good for your health.
- Point out that we don't use articles to make general statements.
- To explain the meaning of *some* in general statements, write on the board:
  I like <u>some</u> impressionist painters. (= not all of them)

Note 4
- Write the following sentences on the board. Have pairs look at Grammar Note 4 and match the uses of *the* to the rules in Note 4. Go over the answers as a class. *(1. b, 2. a, a, 3. b, c, 4. b, 5. d, 6. b, c, c, 7. d, 8. c)*
  1. Can you close <u>the window</u>?
  2. <u>The sun</u> rises in <u>the east</u>.
  3. There are a man and a woman at <u>the door</u>. <u>The man</u> wants to talk to you.
  4. Sam, please clean <u>the board</u>.
  5. I didn't buy <u>the right size</u>.
  6. A cat and a dog were on <u>the doormat</u>. <u>The cat</u> was sleeping, and <u>the dog</u> was eating a bone.
  7. This is <u>the only book</u> I have.
  8. There are many undiscovered places in <u>the world</u>.

Note 5
- To explain the position of adjectives, write on the board:
  <u>a/an</u> + adj. + noun
  <u>the</u> + adj. + noun
  <u>some</u> + adj. + noun
- Point to each pattern and give examples. Say: "a wonderful dinner, the best food, some fresh bread."

🕐 **Identify the Grammar:** Have students identify the grammar in the opening reading on pages 246 and 247. For example:
  An ant lived next to **a river**.
  . . . **the ant** went to **the river** to drink . . .
  . . . **a hunter** came to **the river** to catch **birds**.
  . . . **some beans** and **some bread**.

Go to **www.myfocusongrammarlab.com** for grammar charts and notes.

Step 3: Focused Practice (pages 250–255)
See the general suggestions for Focused Practice on page 4.

Exercise 1: Discover the Grammar
- Go over the example with the class. Ask: "How do we know that Cora isn't talking about a particular story?" *(because she says "could you read me a story")*
- Encourage students to identify the items in the conversations that will help them decide on the correct answers. Then have students complete the exercise individually.
- Have students compare answers in pairs. Then go over the answers as a class.

Exercise 2: Definite Article or No Article
- Review the uses of *the*. Elicit from students the four uses of *the* and summarize them on the board:
  We use <u>the</u> for people or things that are:
    1. unique
    2. defined by the context
    3. mentioned for a second time
    4. defined by a phrase or adjective
- Remind students that we don't use articles in general statements.
- Go over the example with the class. Have students read the conversation quickly for meaning.
- Have students complete the exercise individually. Then call on a pair to read the conversation aloud.

Exercise 3: Indefinite or Definite Article
- Review the uses of the indefinite article. *(when we don't have a specific person, thing, or place in mind; the first time we mention a person, thing, or place)*
- Go over the example with the class. Then have students read the story quickly for meaning.
- Have students complete the exercise individually. Then call on a student to read the story aloud.

Exercise 4: Indefinite, Definite, or No Article

- Go over the example with the class.
- Have students read the article quickly for meaning. Then have them complete the exercise individually.
- Have students compare answers in pairs. Then call on a student to read the article aloud.

Exercise 5: Indefinite, Definite, or No Article

- Go over the example with the class.
- Have students read quickly for meaning. Then have them complete the exercise individually.
- Have students compare answers in pairs.

Exercise 6: Editing

- Have students look at the title of the article. Elicit or explain that a plumber is someone whose job is to repair pipes, sinks, toilets, and so on, and an ape is a large monkey without a tail or with a very short tail, such as a gorilla.
- Go over the example with the class. Then have students read the article quickly for meaning.
- Have students find and correct the mistakes individually. Then call on students to explain why the incorrect structures are wrong.
- ⏱ Have students point out examples of correct usages of *a*, *an*, and *the*.

Go to **www.myfocusongrammarlab.com** for additional grammar practice.

Step 4: Communication Practice
(pages 256–260)

See the general suggestions for Communication Practice on page 5.

Exercise 7: Listening

A
- Go over the example with the class and have students read the sentences.
- Point out that both articles are possible in each context and that students must listen carefully to distinguish the correct article.
- Play the audio. Have students listen and complete the exercise in pairs. If necessary, stop the audio after each conversation and have students discuss the correct answers with their partner.

B
- Go over the example with the class and have students read the statements.
- Play the audio. Have students listen and complete the exercise in pairs. If necessary, stop the audio after each conversation and have students discuss the correct answers with their partner.

- Call on students to give answers, having them support their choices. (Example: *There is more than one princess because the person says she's* the *princess with magic powers. This means that there is at least one more princess who does not have magic powers.*)

Exercise 8: Pronunciation

A
- Play the audio. Have students read along as they listen to the Pronunciation Note.
- To check comprehension, write new examples on the board and have students say the pronunciation of *the* in each case:
the elephant
the story
the apple
the castle

B
- Play the audio. Have students listen and determine the pronunciation of *the* in each case.
- Play the audio again. Have students listen and confirm their choices.

C
- Play the audio. Have students listen and repeat the statements.

Exercise 9: Game: Quiz Show

- Go over the example and have students point out the indefinite and definite articles. As an example, you may want to write three clues on the board for students to guess as a class. (Example: *It's a yellow-white substance. Hunters kill a large animal to get this substance. The animal is now in danger of extinction.* [ivory])
- Circulate as groups write the clues, providing help as needed. Have students pay particular attention to the use of articles in their sentences.
- Have each group share a set of clues with the class. Have students who were not given those clues before guess the thing.

Exercise 10: Information Gap: Story Time

- Explain that the illustrations are the same but each is lacking certain information.
- Go over the examples and point out the definite and indefinite articles.
- Have students complete the exercise in pairs.

Exercise 11: Discussion

A
- Go over the example with the class.
- Form small groups and have them discuss the list of morals. Have them write notes at the end of each moral about what they think it means. Also have them decide which moral from the list could be the moral of "The Ant and the Dove."

B
- Call on students to tell a story that illustrates one of the morals.

Exercise 12: Writing

A
- To help students plan their ideas, draw the following diagram on the board:

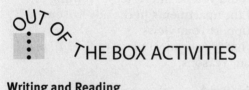

- Have students complete the diagram on the board with notes and use it as a guide as they write their paragraph.

B
- Have students correct their work using the Editing Checklist.
- 🕐 Call on students to share the experience they wrote about.

OUT OF THE BOX ACTIVITIES

Writing and Reading
- Have students work in pairs to write a short fable. Have them either invent a fable or write a version of a fable they know. Point out that students can also write a fable that teaches a moral from the list in Exercise 11.
- Have pairs go over the nouns and articles in their fables to make sure they used *a, an, the, some,* or no article, as appropriate.
- Call on students to read their fables aloud to the class. Then ask: "What moral does the fable teach?"

Reading and Speaking
- Bring in book reviews from newspapers or magazines. (**Note:** If possible, instead of reviews, bring in different kinds of books and have students read the information on the back covers.) Form small groups and give each group member a book review.

- Have students read the review and tell their partners about the book. (Example: *I read a review of a suspense book called* Night Chase. *It is the story of a detective who is chasing a criminal on a dark stormy night. The criminal is very dangerous and . . .*)
- Have students decide which book they would like to read and tell their partners about their choice.

Go to **www.myfocusongrammarlab.com** for additional listening, pronunciation, speaking, and writing practice.

Note:
- See the *Focus on Grammar Workbook* for additional in-class or homework grammar practice.

Unit 18 Review (page 261)

Have students complete the Review and check their answers on Student Book page UR-5. Review or assign additional material as needed.

Go to **www.myfocusongrammarlab.com** for the Unit Achievement Test.

From Grammar to Writing (pages 262–263)

See the general suggestions for From Grammar to Writing on page 9.

Go to **www.myfocusongrammarlab.com** for an additional From Grammar to Writing Assignment, Part Review, and Part Post-Test.

ADJECTIVES AND ADVERBS

UNIT	GRAMMAR FOCUS	THEME
19	Adjectives and Adverbs	Home
20	Adjectives: Comparisons with *As . . . as* and *Than*	Food
21	Adjectives: Superlatives	Cities
22	Adverbs: *As . . . as*, Comparatives, Superlatives	Sports

Go to **www.myfocusongrammarlab.com** for the Part and Unit Tests.

Note: PowerPoint® grammar presentations, test-generating software, and reproducible Part and Unit Tests are on the *Teacher's Resource Disc.*

Grammar: ADJECTIVES AND ADVERBS

Unit 19 focuses on the uses of adjectives and adverbs.

- Adjectives describe or give more information about nouns.
- Adverbs describe or give more information about verbs, adjectives, or other adverbs.
- Adverbs of manner describe or give more information about action verbs.
- Adverbs of degree make adjectives and other adverbs stronger or weaker.
- Participial adjectives (adjectives ending in *-ing* or *-ed*) often describe feelings.

Theme: HOME

Unit 19 focuses on language used to describe apartments, houses, and neighborhoods. Texts used include apartment ads, emails about what one wants in a home, and school dormitory reviews.

Step 1: Grammar in Context (pages 266–267)

See the general suggestions for Grammar in Context on page 1.

Before You Read

- Have students look at the house on page 266 and discuss the questions in pairs.

- Have students make notes of things that are important to them when looking for a home. Call on pairs to share their answers to the questions with the class. Write students' ideas on the board, for example:
a busy/quiet area
nearby shops
comfortable rooms
good value

Read

- To encourage students to read with a purpose, write these questions on the board:
  1. Are the apartments in the advertisement for rent or for sale? *(for rent)*
  2. Where are the apartments located? *(in Wakefield House near Lake Forest Park)*
  3. What is the area like? *(the neighborhood is nice; the streets are safe and quiet; it's a peaceful, residential area)*
  4. What are the apartments like? *(They have big, sunny rooms with high ceilings and modern appliances.)*
  5. Is the rent expensive? *(No. It's affordable.)*
- Have students read the text. (OR: Play the audio and have students follow along in their books.) Then call on students to share their answers to the questions on the board.
- To get students to share their ideas on the reading, form pairs or small groups. Have them discuss one or both of the following questions:
  1. Would you be interested in renting one of the apartments in the advertisement? Support your views.
  2. What is your ideal place to live? Explain your reasons.

After You Read

A. Vocabulary

- Have students complete the exercise individually. Encourage them to use context clues to help.
- Have students compare answers in pairs. Then call on pairs to give answers.
- ⏱ To reinforce the vocabulary, ask different students the following questions. Encourage them to support their answers.
  1. Are you satisfied with your home?
  2. Do you live in a peaceful area?
  3. Where is your ideal home located?
  4. Would you prefer a charming house or a modern apartment building?
  5. Is a convenient transportation system important for you?

B. Comprehension
- Have students complete the exercise individually.
- Have students compare answers in pairs. Then call on pairs to give answers.

Go to **www.myfocusongrammarlab.com** for an additional reading, and for reading and vocabulary practice.

Step 2: Grammar Presentation (pages 268–271)

See the general suggestions for Grammar Presentation on page 2.

Grammar Charts
- To explain adjectives, write on the board:
  Maggie lives in a residential area with safe, quiet streets.
  The house is perfect.
  The people seem friendly.
  — Ask: "What is the area where Maggie lives like?" *(residential)* "What are the streets like?" *(safe and quiet)* "What is the house like?" *(perfect)* "What are the people like?" *(friendly)*
  — Remind students that the words that describe or give information about nouns are called adjectives.
  — Have students name the adjectives in the example. *(residential, safe, quiet, perfect, friendly)*
  — Underline the adjectives as students say them.
- To explain adverbs that describe verbs, write on the board:
  Wakefield House apartments rent quickly.
  — Ask: "How do Wakefield apartments rent?" *(quickly)*
  — Point out that words that give information about a verb are called adverbs.
  — Have students name the adverb in the example. *(quickly)* Underline *quickly*.
- To explain degree adverbs, write on the board:
  Wakefield House apartments rent very quickly.
  — Ask: "How quickly do Wakefield apartments rent?" *(very quickly)*
  — Point out that an adverb can also give more information about another adverb.
  — Have students name the two adverbs in the example. *(very* and *quickly)* Underline both adverbs.
- To explain adverbs that describe adjectives, write on the board:
  The rent is surprisingly affordable.

— Ask: "Is the rent expensive or affordable?" *(affordable)* "How affordable is it?" *(surprisingly affordable)*
  — Point out that an adverb can also give more information about an adjective.
  — Have students name the adjective and the adverb in the example. *(affordable, surprisingly)* Underline both words.
- To explain participial adjectives, write on the board:
  The traffic is annoying.
  The tenant is annoyed by the traffic.
  — Point out that words ending in *-ing* and *-ed* can be adjectives.
  — Have students name the adjectives in the example. *(annoying, annoyed)* Underline both words.
  — Ask: "What does *annoying* describe? *(the traffic)* "What does *annoyed* describe? *(the tenant)*
- To explain word order of adjectives, write on the board:
  She lives in a beautiful residential area.
  She lives in a ~~residential beautiful~~ area.
  — Point out that when more than one adjective describes a noun, we cannot put them in whatever order we would like.
  — Draw attention to the chart on page 268.

Grammar Notes

Note 1
- To review adjectives, write the following examples on the board, leaving space between them:
  It's in a residential area.
  The rooms are sunny.
  The place seems quiet.
- Have students study the examples and name the adjectives. *(residential, sunny, quiet)* Underline the adjectives.
- Ask the following questions and circle the nouns as students say them. Draw arrows from the adjectives to the nouns. "What does *residential* describe?" *(the area)* "What does *sunny* describe?" *(the rooms)* "What does *quiet* describe?" *(the place)*
- To review adverbs, write the following examples on the board, leaving space between them:
  You can walk safely through the park.
  They repaired the building extremely quickly.
  The rooms are really comfortable.
- Have students study the examples and name the adverbs. *(safely, extremely, quickly, really)* Underline the adverbs.

- Ask the following questions and circle the answers as students say them. Draw arrows from the adverbs to the words they describe. Ask: "What does *safely* describe?" *(walk)* "What does *extremely* describe?" *(quickly)* "What does *really* describe?" *(comfortable)*
- Point to the first example and ask: "What kind of word is *walk*?" *(a verb)* Point out that the adverb *safely* describes a verb *(walk)* in this example.
- Point to the second example and ask: "What kind of word is *quickly*?" *(an adverb)* Point out that the adverb *extremely* describes an adverb *(quickly)* in this example.
- Point to the third example and ask: "What kind of word is *comfortable*?" *(an adjective)* Point out that the adverb *really* describes an adjective *(comfortable)* in this example.

Note 2
- To explain the position of adjectives, write the following examples on the board, leaving space between them:
  Maggie lives in a residential area.
  The house is perfect.
  The people seem friendly.
- Direct attention to the first example. Ask: "Does *residential* come before or after the noun it describes?" *(before the noun it describes)*
- Direct attention to the second example. Ask: "Do *perfect* and *friendly* come before nouns in the examples?" *(no)* "Where do they come?" *(after the verbs)*
- Point out that adjectives can also come after *be* or other non-action verbs such as *seem* or *look*.
- To explain the position of adverbs, write the following examples on the board, leaving space between them:
  Wakefield House apartments rent quickly.
  Wakefield House apartments rent very quickly.
  The rent is surprisingly affordable.
- Point to the first example and ask: "Does *quickly* come before or after the verb?" *(after the verb)*
- Point to the second example and ask: "Does *quickly* come before or after the adverb it describes?" *(before the adverb)*
- Point to the third example and ask: "Does *surprisingly* come before or after the adjective it describes?" *(before the adjective)*
- Draw attention to the *Be Careful!* note. Point out that if a verb has no object, the adverb goes right after the verb. If a verb has an object, the adverb goes after the object.

- If needed, refer students to Appendix 2 on page A-2 for a list of non-action verbs.

Note 3
- To explain adverbs of manner ending in *-ly*, write on the board:
  beautiful   nice   absolute
  surprising   complete   quick
- Have students change the adjectives into adverbs by adding *-ly*. *(beautifully, surprisingly, nicely, completely, absolutely, quickly)*
- Point out that there are some adjectives that end in *-ly*. (Example: *friendly*)
- To explain informal forms without *-ly*, write on the board:
  He runs quickly. = He runs quick. (informal)
- To explain irregular adverbs of manner, write on the board:
  He is a <u>good</u> teacher. (adjective). He teaches <u>well</u>. (adverb)
  He has an <u>early</u> breakfast. (adjective) He has breakfast <u>early</u>. (adverb)
- Point out that some adjectives change completely when they are turned into adverbs (Example: *good, well*) and some adjectives have the same form as adverbs (Example: *early, early*)
- Draw attention to the *Be Careful!* note. Point out that not all words that end in *-ly* are adverbs (*hardly, lately*).
- If needed, refer students to Appendix 24 on page A-11 for spelling rules for forming *-ly* adverbs.

Note 4
- To explain adverbs of degree, write on the board:
  It is absolutely perfect.
  It is fairly good.
- Ask: "Does *absolutely* make the adjective *perfect* stronger or weaker?" *(stronger)* "Does *fairly* make the adjective *good* stronger or weaker?" *(weaker)*
- Point out that adverbs that make adjectives stronger or weaker are called adverbs of degree.

Note 5
- To explain participial adjectives, write on the board:
  INTEREST
  The book is _____.
  Sally is _____ in the book.
- As a class, complete the items on the board with adjectives derived from the word *INTEREST*. *(interesting, interested)*

- Point out that the *-ing* adjective describes the person or thing that causes a feeling *(the book)* and the *-ed* adjective describes the person who has the feeling *(Sally)*.
- If needed, refer students to Appendix 11 on page A-6 for a list of participial adjectives.

Note 6
- To explain the order of adjectives, write on the board:
  opinion + size + age + shape + color + origin + material + purpose + noun (used as adjective) + noun
- Brainstorm with the class two adjectives for each category, and write them on the board. (Examples: *nice small old round blue Chinese stone relaxing alarm clock*

  beautiful large new square green ancient metal rocking baby chair)
- Point out that size adjectives can also go first. Write on the board:
  a small nice leather bag = a nice small leather bag
- Point out that we don't use commas between adjectives of different categories but we use them between nouns of the same category. Write two contrasting examples on the board:
  a charming old house (opinion + age)
  a charming, comfortable house (opinion + opinion)
- If needed, refer students to Appendix 12 on page A-6 for the order of adjectives before a noun.

🕐 **Identify the Grammar:** Have students identify the grammar in the opening reading on page 266. For example:
  Are you looking for a **nice** neighborhood with **safe, quiet** streets?
  . . . the **big sunny** rooms . . .
  . . . **high** ceilings in **interesting old** buildings . . .
  Here's your place to relax **completely** . . .

Go to **www.myfocusongrammarlab.com** for grammar charts and notes.

Step 3: Focused Practice (pages 272–275)
See the general suggestions for Focused Practice on page 4.

Exercise 1: Discover the Grammar
- Go over the examples with the class.
- To help students find the words, review what they have learned. Ask: "What do adjectives describe?" *(nouns)* "What can adverbs describe?" *(verbs, adjectives, or other adverbs)*

- Have students complete the exercise individually. Then go over the answers as a class.

Exercise 2: Adjective or Adverb
- Go over the example with the class. Ask: "Why is *large* the correct answer?" *(because it is describing the noun* city; largely *is an adverb, so it cannot describe a noun)* Then have students read the email quickly for meaning.
- Have students complete the exercise individually. Encourage them to find the word that is being described in each case. This will help them choose their answers correctly.
- Have students compare answers in pairs. Then go over the answers as a class.

Exercise 3: Adverbs Before Adjectives and Other Adverbs
- Go over the example with the class. Ask: "What kinds of words are *extremely* and *nice*?" *(adverb, adjective)*
- Have students complete the exercise individually. Have them make any necessary changes to turn adjectives into adverbs. If needed, refer students to Appendix 24 on page A-11.
- 🕐 For further practice, write the following adverb–adjective combinations on the board. Have pairs use them in sentences about their own experiences. (Example: *When I was on vacation in France, I took a train that was incredibly fast.*)
  1. extremely nice
  2. terribly disappointed
  3. surprisingly convenient
  4. incredibly fast
  5. awfully loud
  6. absolutely perfect

Exercise 4: Word Order
- Go over the example with the class. Have students identify the noun *(person)* and the words that describe it *(fairly cheerful)*. Then have students read the journal quickly for meaning.
- Have students complete the exercise individually. Then have students compare answers in pairs.

- ⏱ For further practice, say the following phrases and have students use them in sentences about Sylvie. Say (possible answers are given in parentheses): "fairly cheerful" (*Sylvie is a fairly cheerful person*); "terribly upsetting" (*Some terribly upsetting things happened to her yesterday*); "awfully important" (*She missed an awfully important meeting*); "angry at all" (*Her boss didn't seem angry at all*); "absolutely charming" (*She looked at an absolutely charming apartment*).

Exercise 5: Participial Adjectives
- Go over the example with the class. Remind students that -*ing* adjectives describe the person or thing that causes a feeling and -*ed* adjectives describe the person who has the feeling.
- Have students complete the exercise individually. Then call on a pair to read the conversation.
- ⏱ Have pairs role-play the conversations.

Exercise 6: Word Order: Adjectives + Noun
- Have students complete the exercise individually. Encourage them to use the word order that sounds natural to them.
- Call on students to say the correct order of adjectives. Write it on the board as students say it, making any necessary corrections: opinion + size + age + shape + color + origin + material + purpose + noun (used as adjective) + noun
- Call on a student to read the journal entry aloud.

Exercise 7: Editing
- Have students read the reviews quickly for meaning. To check comprehension, have students say some advantages and disadvantages of the Northwood dorms, Miller and Wyeth Hall. (Example: *The Northwood dorms are clean. At Miller, you can make friends fast. At Wyeth Hall the toilets don't work well.*)
- Go over the example with the class.
- Have students find and correct the mistakes individually. Then call on students to explain why the incorrect structures are wrong.
- ⏱ Have students point out examples of correct usages of adjectives and adverbs.

Go to **www.myfocusongrammarlab.com** for additional grammar practice.

Step 4: Communication Practice
(pages 276–280)
See the general suggestions for Communication Practice on page 5.

Exercise 8: Listening
A
- Have students read the ads quickly for meaning. Ask: "Where do these ads appear?" *(on a website)* "What's its name?" *(Janslist)* "Which section can you find these ads in?" *(apartments/housing to rent)*
- Have students guess the missing adjectives and write them in pencil.

B
- Play the audio. Have students listen and confirm or correct their guesses.

C
- Call on a student to read the opinions in the chart. Clarify meaning as necessary.
- Play the audio. Have students listen and complete the exercise individually.
- ⏱ To personalize, have students tell a partner which of the four apartments they would choose to rent. Have them support their choices.

Exercise 9: Pronunciation
A
- Play the audio. Have students read along as they listen to the Pronunciation Note.
- Be sure students understand that:
  1. Both words—the adjective and the noun—are stressed.
  2. The noun is stressed more strongly.

B
- Play the audio. Have students listen and write small and large dots as indicated.

C
- Play the audio. Have students listen and repeat the statements.
- Have students practice the conversations with a partner. Be sure students play both roles.

Exercise 10: What About You?
- Go over the example with the class. Have students say the adjectives and adverbs that are in the example. *(beautiful, pretty happy, cozy, old)*
- Write the following column heads on the board:

The area | The apartment | Feelings

- Brainstorm with the class adjectives—or phrases—to describe the nouns on the board. If students need ideas, have them look at the ads in Exercise 8 and the readings on pages 266 and 275. Write students' ideas under the corresponding head, for example:

The area
busy
quiet
safe
peaceful
residential
near stores
near schools
near public transportation

The apartment
recently redecorated
beautifully furnished
newly painted
in excellent condition
cute and cozy
sunny and spacious
light and bright
fully equipped

Feelings
(terribly) disappointed
(extremely) confused
(absolutely) fascinated
(very) surprised
(very) pleased
(really) excited
(really) interested
satisfied

- Have students make notes of their answers to questions 1 through 5. Then have them complete the exercise individually.

Exercise 11: Compare and Contrast

- Have students list a few adjectives or adverbs plus adjectives to describe each type of housing. Point out that students can extract these adjectives from dictionary definitions or think them up on their own.
- Go over the example with the class. If necessary, explain the meaning of *nosy* (always trying to find out private information about someone).
- Have students complete the exercise in pairs. Then call on students to share their descriptions of the types of housing with the class. As students speak, they can use their lists as a guide.

Exercise 12: Discussion

- Have students circle in the first chart the adjectives that describe their ideal home. Then have them underline the adjectives that describe their ideal roommates, neighbor, or landlord.
- Form small groups. Have students discuss their ideal homes. As students discuss, encourage them to use words from the charts.
- Write the following questions on the board:
  How similar are your ideal homes?
  Is there one ideal home for everyone?
  How similar are your ideal roommates/ neighbors/landlords?
  Is there an ideal roommate/neighbor/landlord for everyone?
- Have students from different groups use the questions on the board as a guide to report to the class on their discussion.

Exercise 13: Game: A Strange Story

- Form small groups. One member of each group is Student A.
- Have all students except for Students A close their books. Then have Students A ask questions to fill in the blanks and create a story.
- Call on a student from each group to read the story aloud. Vote for the funniest story.

Exercise 14: Writing

A

- Write the following questions on the board to help elicit vocabulary and generate ideas:
  Where is the home located?
  What is the area like?
  What is the apartment/house/room like?
  What are the neighbors like?
- Have students make notes for each question and then use them as a guide as they write.
- Encourage students to use some of the vocabulary from Exercise 12 on page 279 and the ads in Exercise 8 on page 276 as a model.

B

- Have students correct their work using the Editing Checklist.

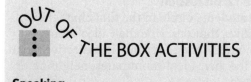

OUT OF THE BOX ACTIVITIES

Speaking

- Divide the class into two teams.
- Call out an adjective or adverb to alternating teams and have the team come up with its opposite within 15 seconds. (Example: *bad, good; easy, hard*) If the team is unable to name an opposite, give the other team a chance to try.
- Each time a team successfully identifies an opposite, it wins 1 point. The team with the most points wins.

Reading and Speaking

- Bring in house and/or apartment ads from the newspaper. Form small groups and give each group a newspaper page or a photocopy containing ads.
- Have students read the ads and figure out the meaning of abbreviations.
- Then have students share with their partners which apartment or house they would be interested in buying or renting. Have students support their views.

Go to **www.myfocusongrammarlab.com** for additional listening, pronunciation, speaking, and writing practice.

Note:
- See the *Focus on Grammar Workbook* for additional in-class or homework grammar practice.

Unit 19 Review (page 281)

Have students complete the Review and check their answers on Student Book page UR-5. Review or assign additional material as needed.

Go to **www.myfocusongrammarlab.com** for the Unit Achievement Test.

UNIT 20 OVERVIEW

Grammar: ADJECTIVES: COMPARISONS WITH *As . . . as* AND *Than*

Unit 20 focuses on the uses of adjectives to make comparisons—specifically comparisons with *as . . . as* and comparative adjectives with *than*.

- *As* + adjective + *as* is used to compare people, places, or things and show how they are the same or equal.
- *Not as* + adjective + *as* is used to compare people, places, or things and show how they are not the same or equal. Similarly, comparative adjectives + *than* show how people, places, or things are different.
- Comparative adjective + *and* + comparative adjective shows how something is increasing or decreasing.
- *The* + comparative adjective + *the* + comparative adjective shows cause and effect.

Theme: FOOD

Unit 20 focuses on language used to describe and compare restaurants and brands of food. Restaurant reviews, consumer magazine product reviews, and menus are presented.

Step 1: Grammar in Context (pages 282–283)

See the general suggestions for Grammar in Context on page 1.

Before You Read

- Have students look at the photo and discuss the questions in pairs.
- Have students make notes for each question. Then have them discuss the questions in pairs.
- Call on pairs to say the types of restaurant food the students enjoy. Then take a poll to find out the most popular restaurant food in the class.

Read

- To encourage students to read with a purpose, write these questions on the board:
  1. What has just opened on Main Street? (*a new Pizza Place restaurant*)
  2. Did Pete Tsa eat there himself? (*yes*)
  3. What does he say about the service? (*It was not as good as at other Pizza Place restaurants. The staff needs to become more professional.*)
  4. What does he say about the food? (*The pizza was incredible. It seemed bigger and better than at other Pizza Place restaurants.*)

5. Is the new restaurant larger or smaller than other Pizza Place restaurants? (*It's larger.*)
6. So why is it more crowded? (*because students love it*)
7. What should you do for a quieter, more relaxed meal? (*go early*)

- Have students read the text. (OR: Play the audio and have students follow along in their books.) Then call on students to share their answers to the questions on the board.
- To get students to share their ideas on the reading, form pairs or small groups. Have them discuss one or both of the following questions:
  1. What is the best restaurant you have ever been to? Briefly describe the place and explain your choice.
  2. Would you like to go to the restaurant in the review? Support your answer.

After You Read

A. Vocabulary

- Have students complete the exercise individually. Encourage them to use context clues to help.
- Have students compare answers in pairs. Then call on pairs to give answers.
- ⏱ To reinforce the vocabulary, have students give specific examples of the following items:
  1. delicious food
  2. fresh food
  3. a place where you can have a relaxed meal
  4. a restaurant where the menu is varied
  5. a restaurant that is usually crowded
  6. a traditional food in their country
- Write students' ideas on the board.

B. Comprehension

- Have students complete the exercise individually.
- Have students compare answers in pairs. Then call on pairs to give answers.

Go to **www.myfocusongrammarlab.com** for an additional reading, and for reading and vocabulary practice.

Step 2: Grammar Presentation (pages 284–286)

See the general suggestions for Grammar Presentation on page 2.

Grammar Charts

- To explain comparisons with *as . . . as*, write on the board:
  The new Pizza Place is as interesting as the other Pizza Place restaurants.

— Have students study the example. Then ask: "How can you make comparisons to show that two things are the same?" (as + *adjective* + as)
- Write a new example on the board:
  The service is not as good as at the other locations.
  — Have students study the example. Then ask: "How can you make comparisons to show that two things are *not* the same?" (not + as + *adjective* + as)
- To explain comparisons with *than* and short adjectives, write on the board:
  The new Pizza Place is bigger and louder than the other Pizza Place restaurants.
  — Have students name the two comparative adjectives in the example (*bigger, louder*). Underline them.
  — Ask: "How do you form the comparative of short adjectives such as *loud*?" (*short adjective* + -er) "What comes after *louder*?" (than + *the other place being compared*) "What spelling change is there in *bigger*?" (*the final g is doubled to form the comparative*)
  — Point out that spelling changes are sometimes necessary to form the comparative of short adjectives.
  — Write additional examples on the board:
  busy—busier
  hot—hotter
- To explain comparisons with *than* and long adjectives, write on the board:
  At the new Pizza Place the choices are more varied than at the other locations.
  The new Pizza Place is less crowded before 1:00 P.M.
  — Have students name the comparative adjectives in the examples (*more varied, less crowded*). Underline them.
  — Ask: "How do you form the comparative of long adjectives such as *varied* or *crowded*?" (more *or* less + *adjective*)
- To explain irregular comparative forms, write on the board:
  At the New Pizza Place the pizza is better than at other locations.
  — Have students name the comparative adjective in the example (*better*). Underline it.
  — Ask: "What is *better* the comparative of?" (*good*)
  — Point out that some adjectives such as *good* have irregular comparative forms.
  — Write a new example on the board:
  bad—worse

Grammar Notes

Note 1

- To review comparisons with *as . . . as*, write on the board:

  The new Pizza Place is as good as the one on Knight Street.

- Have students study the example. Then ask: "Is the restaurant on Knight Street good?" *(yes)* "Is the new Pizza Place equally good?" *(yes)*

- Insert *just* between *is* and *as*. Then ask: "Is the comparison weaker or stronger now?" *(stronger)*

- Write a new example on the board:

  The new Pizza Place is not as quiet as the one on Knight Street.

- Then ask: "Is the Pizza Place on Knight Street quiet?" *(yes)* "Is the new Pizza Place equally quiet?" *(no)*

Note 2

- To review comparisons with *than*, write on the board:

  At the new Pizza Place the choices are more varied than at the other locations.

- Have students study the example. Then ask: "Are the choices varied at the new Pizza Place?" *(yes)* "Are the choices equally varied at the other locations?" *(no)*

- Insert *even* before *more*. Then ask: "Is the comparison weaker or stronger now?" *(stronger)*

- To explain the use of *less . . . than*, write on the board:

  Pizza Place is not as cheap as Crown Pizza.
  Pizza Place is more expensive than Crown Pizza.
  Pizza Place is ~~less cheap than~~ Crown Pizza.

- Point out that we do not use *less . . . than* with one-syllable adjectives such as *cheap*.

- Write on the board:

  Crown Pizza is less expensive than Pizza Place.

- Point out that we do use *less . . . than* with long adjectives such as *expensive*.

- Write on the board:

  BILL: Let's have the one with chicken. It's more interesting than the traditional pizza.

  PAM: But it's also more expensive.

- Ask: "What are Bill and Pam comparing?" *(a pizza with chicken with a traditional pizza)* "Why doesn't Pam mention the traditional pizza?" *(Because it is not necessary. The context makes it clear that she is comparing the pizza with chicken with the traditional pizza.)*

- Underline *it's also more expensive* in the conversation.

- Call on a student to provide the full version of the comparison. *(It's also more expensive than the traditional pizza.)*

Note 3

- To review how to form comparative adjectives, write the following list on the board and explain each category. The adjectives in brackets are additional examples. Don't write them on the board.

  <u>Short adjectives use *-er*</u>:
  one-syllable adjectives: [loud, late, big]
    cheap—cheaper
  two-syllable adjectives   [funny]
    ending in *-y*: easy—easier
  <u>Spelling changes</u>:
  Adjectives ending in *-e*: only
    add *-r*; large—larger
  Adjectives ending in *-y*: change
    y to *i*; pretty—prettier
  Adjectives ending in consonant +
    vowel + consonant: double
    final consonant; thin—
    thinner
  <u>Irregular comparative forms</u>:
  little—less   [good]
  far—farther/further
  <u>Long adjectives use *less/more*</u>:
  crowded—more/less crowded [interesting]
  varied—more/less varied
  <u>Some adjectives can use either *-er* or *more*</u>
  lovely—lovelier, more lovely [quiet]
  cruel—crueler, more cruel

- If needed, refer students to Appendix 23 on page A-11 for spelling rules for the comparative form of adjectives.

- If needed, refer students to Appendix 10 on page A-6 for a list of irregular comparative adjectives.

- If needed, refer students to Appendix 9 on page A-5 for a list of adjectives that use both forms of the comparative.

Note 4

- To explain how comparative adjectives can be repeated to show increase or decrease, write on the board:

  Prices are getting lower and lower.
  At Crown Pizza, the menu is getting more and more varied.
  The staff is becoming less and less professional.

Note 5

- To explain how to use two comparative adjectives to show cause and effect, write on the board:

  The better the pizza, the higher the price.
  The fresher, the better.

- Point out that the nouns are given in the first example because the comparative adjectives *better* and *higher* give information about different things: the pizza and the price.
- Point out that the nouns are left out in the second example because both adjectives give information about the same thing: the ingredients.

🕐 **Identify the Grammar:** Have students identify the grammar in the opening reading on page 282. For example:

> . . . the service was **not as good as** at the other Pizza Place restaurants . . .
>
> . . . needs time to become **more professional**. It seemed **bigger** and **better than** at the other six locations.
>
> . . . **the fresher** the ingredients, **the better** the pizza.

Go to **www.myfocusongrammarlab.com** for grammar charts and notes.

Step 3: Focused Practice (pages 286–290)

See the general suggestions for Focused Practice on page 4.

Exercise 1: Discover the Grammar
- Have students look at the chart. Answer any questions. Then go over the example with the class. Ask: "Why is the statement false?" *(because both pizzas are the same size— 12 inches)*
- Have students complete the exercise individually. Then call on students to give answers.
- 🕐 Ask several students which pizza they would buy and why. (Example: *I'd buy John's pizza because it has fewer calories, and I'm on a diet.*)

Exercise 2: Comparisons with *As . . . as*
- Go over the example with the class.
- Have students complete the exercise individually. Then go over the answers as a class.
- 🕐 Have students compare two brands of cookies, juice, or another type of food using *as . . . as* and *not as . . . as*. Call on students to share some of their sentences with the class. Write some of them on the board.

Exercise 3: Comparisons with *Than*
- Go over the menu with the class. Elicit or explain what a take-out menu is. *(a list of the food that is available for you to buy at a restaurant and eat somewhere else)* To check comprehension of the options on the menu, have students name vegetables *(broccoli, garlic, red pepper, scallions)*; types of meat *(beef, chicken, pork)*; seafood *(shrimp, scallop)*; and words to describe food *(sweet and sour, steamed, hot and spicy)*. Answer any questions about vocabulary.
- Go over the example with the class. Ask: "Why do we use *more* to form the comparative of *expensive*?" *(because expensive is a long adjective)* "How do we form the comparative of one-syllable adjectives and two-syllable adjectives ending in -*y*?" *(adjective + -er or -r)* Warn students about spelling changes.
- Have students complete the exercise individually. Then go over the answers as a class

Exercise 4: Increase or Decrease; Cause and Effect
- Go over the example with the class. Then have students read the conversations quickly for meaning.
- Have students complete the exercise individually. Then have students compare answers in pairs.
- 🕐 Have pairs role-play the conversations.

Exercise 5: Editing
- Have students read the essay quickly for meaning. To check comprehension, ask: "Where did the student grow up?" *(in the Philippines)* "Where is the student now?" *(in the United States)* "What does he think about the snacks he used to eat?" *(that they were very good)* "What does he think about American fast food?" *(He didn't like it a first, but now he does.)*
- Go over the example with the class.
- Have students find and correct the mistakes individually. Then call on students to explain why the incorrect structures are wrong.
- 🕐 Have students point out examples of correct usages of *as . . . as* and comparatives with *than*.

Go to **www.myfocusongrammarlab.com** for additional grammar practice.

Step 4: Communication Practice

(pages 290–294)

See the general suggestions for Communication Practice on page 5.

Exercise 6: Listening

A

- Ask: "Do you comparison-shop for food? What do you compare?" Write students' ideas on the board, for example:

brands	ingredients
prices	number of servings
nutrition information	expiration dates

- Have students read the statements quickly for meaning.
- Play the audio. Have students listen and complete the exercise individually.

B

- Play the audio. Have students listen and complete the exercise individually. Encourage them to take notes to support their answers.
- Go over the answers as a class, having students support their choices with details they remember. (Example: *Di Roma's is cheaper because it costs $4.59 and Angela's costs $5.38.*)
- (🕐) Have students say which brand of fresh or frozen pizza (or another traditional food in their country) they usually buy. Have them explain their choice.

Exercise 7: Pronunciation

A

- Play the audio. Have students read along as they listen to the Pronunciation Note.
- Point out that the schwa sound is used in unstressed syllables. This means that the words *as . . . . as* and *than* are not normally stressed in comparative sentences. The stress is placed on the adjectives.

B

- Play the audio. Have students listen.

C

- Play the audio again.
- Have students practice the conversations with a partner. Be sure students play both roles. Be sure students pronounce the schwa correctly and stress the adjectives.

Exercise 8: Compare and Contrast

- Go over the adjectives in the box. If necessary, clarify the meaning of *filling. (the food that is put inside something such as a pie, cake, etc.)* Have students look at the pizza toppings. Encourage them to use the pictures to figure out the meaning of unknown words. Answer any questions. Students might need help with the following words: *ground beef* (beef that has been cut or ground into very small pieces), *jalapeño pepper* (a small, hot green pepper, used especially in Mexican food), *feta cheese* (a white cheese from Greece made from sheep's milk or goat's milk), *bean curd* (a soft, white food, like cheese, that is made from soy beans).
- Go over the example with the class.
- Have students complete the exercise in pairs. Encourage them to use comparatives as they discuss the pizzas.

Exercise 9: Role Play: Your Restaurant

A

- To make sure students understand the types of food offered on a menu *(Soups and Appetizers/Starters, Entrées, Salads and Side Dishes, Desserts, Beverages)*, elicit from the class an example of each type.
- Brainstorm with the class and write on the board a list of adjectives to discuss food. If necessary, have students look back at the unit and scan it for adjectives of this kind, for example:

interesting	fresh	hot
good	flavorful	sweet
tasty	salty	healthy
spicy	nutritious	expensive
cheap	delicious	traditional
unusual	filling	international

- Form small groups. Have students complete the exercise in groups.

B

- Have servers write down their customers' orders.
- Follow up by having students say which food one of their classmates chose to order. Have them explain their partner's choice using a comparative. Example: *Maria ordered the vegetable soup. She said it was healthier than the beef soup.*
- (🕐) Have students from different groups tell the class the name of their restaurant and what is on the menu. Call on students to say which restaurant they would like to go to and what they would like to eat there.

Exercise 10: Writing

A

- Write these questions on the board to help elicit vocabulary and generate ideas:

  What country would you like to compare your country's food with? What is food like in your country? What is food like in the other country? Which is more varied, spicier, healthier? Which is more flavorful?

  What's the name of a typical dish in your country? What does it consist of?

  What's the name of a typical dish in the other country? What does it consist of?

  Which food do you prefer—the one in your country or the one in the other country? Why?

- Have students make notes for each question and then use them as a guide as they write.

B

- Have students correct their work using the Editing Checklist.

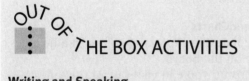

OUT OF THE BOX ACTIVITIES

Writing and Speaking

- Brainstorm with the class different types of restaurants. (Example: *fast food, sandwich or sub shops, fine dining, pizzerias, bars, ethnic restaurants*)
- Have pairs of students choose one type of restaurant to review.
- Have each partner choose a different restaurant within that category and write a review of it according to the following criteria: value, quality of food, service, and location. Then have partners compare their reviews and then report their findings to the class.

Reading and Speaking

- Bring in empty food containers such as boxes or cartons. If you don't have access to containers in English, print out information and/or nutrition facts from websites of companies that produce food. Form small groups and give each group a few containers. If possible, give each group containers of the same food from different brands.
- Have students read the information on the container and compare the food(s) and the information on the container.
- Follow up by having students report to the class on the food(s) they discussed.

Go to **www.myfocusongrammarlab.com** for additional listening, pronunciation, speaking, and writing practice.

Note:

- See the *Focus on Grammar Workbook* for additional in-class or homework grammar practice.

Unit 20 Review (page 295)

Have students complete the Review and check their answers on Student Book page UR-5. Review or assign additional material as needed.

Go to **www.myfocusongrammarlab.com** for the Unit Achievement Test.

UNIT 21 OVERVIEW

Grammar: ADJECTIVES: SUPERLATIVES

Unit 21 focuses on the use of superlative adjectives to make comparisons.

- Superlative adjectives are used to compare one person, place, or thing with other people, places, or things in a group.
- Superlative adjectives are often used with words or expressions such as *in* and *of*; *one of* and *some of*; *second, third,* etc.; and *ever* plus the present perfect. (Example: *the tallest tower in town, one of the tallest towers in the world, the second tallest tower in the world, the tallest tower I have ever visited*)

Theme: CITIES

Unit 21 focuses on language used to describe and compare cities and their features.

The Toronto Transit Commission (TTC) operates the system of subways, buses, and streetcars that constitutes the second largest public transportation system in North America. (The largest is in New York City.) In Toronto there are three subway lines, 161 bus routes, and 11 streetcar routes that operate in the downtown area. Many of the streetcar routes date from World War II.

Step 1: Grammar in Context (pages 296–297)

See the general suggestions for Grammar in Context on page 1.

Before You Read

- Have students look at the photo and discuss the questions in pairs.

- Have students make notes of important features for a city to have.
- Call on pairs to share their answers to the questions with the class. Write students' ideas on the second question on the board, for example:

a convenient transportation system
nice stores
good restaurants
large parks

Read

- To encourage students to read with a purpose, write these questions on the board:
  1. Is Toronto the capital of Canada? (No. It's the capital of the province of Ontario.)
  2. Is Toronto larger than the capital of Canada? (yes)
  3. How do you know? (because the brochure says Toronto is the largest city in Canada)
  4. What proves that Toronto is a multicultural city? (the fact that 100 languages are spoken there)
  5. What makes it easy to get around in Toronto? (its large public transportation system)
  6. Is Toronto the safest city in the world? (No. It's the safest on the continent/in North America.)
  7. What makes Toronto an exciting place to visit? (its many unique features)
- Have students read the text. (OR: Play the audio and have students follow along in their books.) Then call on students to share their answers to the questions on the board.
- To get students to share their ideas on the reading, form pairs or small groups. Have them discuss one or both of the following topics:
  1. Tell your partners about a big city you have been to. Describe the features that make the city an interesting place to visit.
  2. Think about why you would/wouldn't like to visit Toronto. Share with your partners other information you might know about this city.

After You Read

A. Vocabulary

- Have students complete the exercise individually. Encourage them to use context clues to help.
- Have students compare answers in pairs. Then call on pairs to give answers.
- ⏱ To reinforce the vocabulary, have students write down:
  1. An important financial center in their country.

2. A multicultural city in their country or the world.
3. An important feature of the town where they live.
4. A large public building in their town.
5. A reason why they think their town is/is not dynamic.

- Then call on students to share their answers and write some of them on the board.

B. Comprehension

- Have students complete the exercise individually.
- Have students compare answers in pairs. Then call on pairs to give answers.

Go to **www.myfocusongrammarlab.com** for an additional reading, and for reading and vocabulary practice.

Step 2: Grammar Presentation (pages 298–299)

See the general suggestions for Grammar Presentation on page 2.

Grammar Charts

- To explain the superlative of short adjectives, write on the board:

In Toronto you can visit one of the tallest towers in the world.
Toronto is the biggest city in Canada.
Toronto is one of the easiest towns to get around.

  — Have students name the superlative adjectives in the examples. (the tallest, the biggest, the easiest) Underline them as students say them.
  — Then ask: "How do you form the superlative of short adjectives such as tall?" (the + adjective + -est) "What spelling change is there in biggest?" (the final -g is doubled to form the superlative) "What spelling change is there in easiest?" (the -y in easy changes to i)
  — Point out that spelling changes (as with forming the comparative) are sometimes necessary to form the superlative of short adjectives.

- To explain the superlative of long adjectives, write on the board:

Toronto is one of the most exciting cities in the world.
It is the least dangerous city on the continent.

  — Have students name the superlative adjectives in the examples. (the most exciting, the least dangerous) Underline them as students say them.

— Then ask: "How do you form the superlative of long adjectives such as *exciting* or *dangerous*?" (the most *or* the least + *adjective*)
- To explain the superlative of irregular adjectives, write on the board:
Toronto has the second best public transportation system in North America.
  — Have students name the superlative adjective in the example *(best)* and underline it.
  — Then ask: "What is *best* the superlative of?" *(good)*
  — Point out that some adjectives such as *best* have irregular superlative forms. (These adjectives also have irregular comparative forms.)
  — To summarize, write on the board:
Adjective	Comparative	Superlative
good	better	best

Grammar Notes

Note 1
- To review superlative adjectives, write on the board:
Toronto is the largest city in Canada.
- Have students study the example. Then ask: "Is Toronto a large city?" *(yes)* "What is Toronto being compared with in the example?" *(other cities in Canada)* "Are other Canadian cities larger than Toronto?" *(No. Toronto is the largest of all.)*
- Point out that the superlative compares one person, place, or thing with other people, places, or things in a group. In the example, the superlative compares Toronto with other cities in Canada.
- Emphasize that the superlative compares three or more things and that it should not be used to compare only two things. Write two contrasting examples on the board:
Toronto is <u>larger than</u> Montreal. (comparison of two cities)
Toronto is <u>the largest</u> city in Canada. (comparison of more than two cities)

Note 2
- To review how to form superlative adjectives, write the following list on the board. Answer any questions.
<u>Short adjectives that use *-est*</u>:
one-syllable adjectives: cheap—the cheapest
two-syllable adjectives ending in *-y*: easy—the easiest
<u>Spelling changes</u>:
Adjectives ending in *-e*: only add *-est* (large—the largest)

Adjectives ending in *-y*: change *y* to *i* (funny—the funniest)
Adjectives ending in consonant + vowel + consonant: double final consonant (hot—the hottest)
<u>Irregular superlative forms</u>:
little—the least
far—the farthest/furthest
<u>Long adjectives that use *the most/the least*</u>:
peaceful—the most/least peaceful
multicultural—the most/the least multicultural
<u>Adjectives that can use either *-est* or *the most*</u>
lovely—the loveliest, the most lovely
cruel—the cruelest, the most cruel

Note 3
- To explain the words and expressions that are often used with the superlative, write on the board:
It's the safest city <u>in</u> the country.
It's <u>one of</u> the safest cities.
It's the safest city I<u>'ve ever been</u> to.
It's <u>the second</u> safest city.
- Direct attention to the underlined words and expressions in the examples.

🕐 **Identify the Grammar:** Have students identify the grammar in the opening reading on page 296. For example:
  the largest city in Canada
  the most important economic and financial center of the country
  one of **the easiest** places to get around
  the safest city on the continent . . .

Go to **www.myfocusongrammarlab.com** for grammar charts and notes.

Step 3: Focused Practice (pages 299–302)
See the general suggestions for Focused Practice on page 4.

Exercise 1: Discover the Grammar
- Go over the example with the class.
- Have students do the exercise individually. Then go over the answers as a class.

- 🕐 Write the following information on the board. Have pairs match the items in each column and write sentences using the superlative.

CN Tower	historic	buildings/Toronto
Yonge Street	funny	underground shopping complex/world
Path	large	building/Canada
York	tall	bus ride/Toronto
Yuk Yuk Comedy Tour	good	family outing/city
Toronto Zoo	long	street/world

- Go over the answers as a class. *(The CN Tower is the tallest building in Canada. Yonge Street is the longest street in the world. Path is the largest underground shopping complex in the world. York has the most historic buildings in Toronto. The Yuk Yuk Comedy Tour is the funniest ride in the city. The Toronto Zoo is the best family outing in the city.)*

Exercise 2: Superlative Adjectives
- Go over the chart with the class. Answer any questions.
- Go over the example with the class. Ask: "How do we form the superlative of short and long adjectives?" (the + *adjective* + -est; the most + *adjective*) Remind students of spelling changes.
- Have students complete the sentences individually. Then call on students to read the sentences aloud.

Exercise 3: Superlative Adjectives
- Have students read the information quickly for meaning. Then have them complete the exercise individually.
- Call on students to read the sentences aloud.

Exercise 4: *The Most* and *The Least* + *Ever*
- Go over the example with the class. Point out that students should write two sentences for each item—one with *the most* and the other with *the least*.
- Have students complete the exercise individually.
- Call on students to share some of their sentences with the class.

Exercise 5: Editing
- Have students read the postcard quickly for meaning. To check comprehension, ask: "Where is Marissa?" *(in Toronto)* "What did she see from the CN Tower?" *(the neighborhoods, the harbor, the traffic)* "Did she eat at the tower?" *(no)* "Why not?" *(because the restaurant is very expensive)* "Where is she staying?" *(in a bed-and-breakfast in East Toronto)*

- Go over the example with the class.
- Have students find and correct the mistakes individually. Then call on students to explain why the incorrect structures are wrong.
- 🕐 Have students point out examples of correct usages of superlative adjectives.

Go to **www.myfocusongrammarlab.com** for additional grammar practice.

Step 4: Communication Practice
(pages 303–305)

See the general suggestions for Communication Practice on page 5.

Exercise 6: Listening
A
- Have students read the statements quickly for meaning.
- Play the audio. Have students listen.
- Play the audio again. Have students listen and complete the exercise individually.

B
- Play the audio. Have students listen and complete the exercise individually. Point out that the answers are not given in the order in which the items appear in the chart.
- Call on students to give answers (have them say full sentences). (Example: *Westin Harbour Castle has the best view of the three.*)
- 🕐 Ask students which of the three hotels they would like to stay at if they had the chance to visit Toronto. Have students explain their choice.

Exercise 7: Pronunciation
A
- Play the audio. Have students read along as they listen to the Pronunciation Note.
- To check comprehension, ask: "In comparative sentences that use short adjectives, what do we stress?" *(the adjective)* "In comparative sentences that use long adjectives, what do we stress?" (most *or* least)

B
- Have students anticipate which word will receive the main stress in each response.
- Play the audio. Have students listen and put the stress marks.

C
- Play the audio. Have students listen and repeat.
- Have students practice the conversations with a partner. Be sure students play both roles.

Exercise 8: What About You?

- Have pairs take turns asking each other about the information in Exercise 4.
- Encourage them to use the list of questions and their own ideas to keep the conversation going. Remind them to use the superlative.
- Call on students to report to the class on an interesting experience their partner had.

Exercise 9: Discussion

- Brainstorm with the class and write on the board aspects to discuss about a city, for example:

getting around	entertainment
safety	parks and gardens
restaurants	historic buildings
hotels	museums and galleries
shopping	the people
nightlife	zoos

- Go over the example. Point out how reasons are given for each opinion. Ask: "B says Buenos Aires is the most interesting city in Argentina. Why?" *(because there's a lot to do)* "B also says it's the most multicultural city in the country. Why?" *(because people from all over the world live there)*
- Form small groups. Have students do the exercise in groups. Encourage students to give reasons for each opinion and to ask follow-up questions to find out more.

Exercise 10: Writing

A

- Write the following questions on the board to help elicit vocabulary and generate ideas:
  What's the most famous tourist attraction?
  What are the best historic buildings and areas?
  Where can you eat the best food?
  What's the most convenient way to get around?
  Where can you eat the most relaxed meal?
  Where can you find the friendliest atmosphere?
  What's the most interesting tour?
  Where can you get the best views?
  What's the most beautiful park?
  What's the most convenient place to shop?
  Where can you get the best bargains?
- Go over the example with the class. Point out the use of the imperative and the superlative.
- Have students make notes for each question on the board and then use them as a guide as they write.

B

- Have students correct their work using the Editing Checklist.

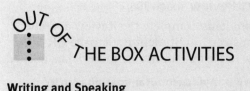

OUT OF THE BOX ACTIVITIES

Writing and Speaking

- Form small groups. Have students create a general-knowledge quiz of six to eight questions using the superlative in all of their questions. Point out that they should know the answers to the questions they write. (Example: *What's the fastest animal in the world? What's the longest river in the world? What's the oldest building in London?*)
- Have groups exchange quizzes and answer the questions.
- Follow up by having students report to the class on some of the questions they answered.

Reading and Speaking

- If you have access to a lending library, bring in a copy of the book *Guinness World Records* or printouts from different sections of its website (www.guinessworldrecords.com).
- Form small groups. Have students browse the book—or read the printouts—and use the superlative to write notes about world records. (If students use the book, have each group choose a different topic to research, for example, sports, travel and transportation, the natural world, or arts and media.)
- Have a student from each group report to the class on their findings. (Example: *At Wimbledon in 2010, American tennis player John Isner defeated Nicolas Mahut from France in the longest professional tennis match ever played. It lasted 11 hours 5 minutes.*)

Go to **www.myfocusongrammarlab.com** for additional listening, pronunciation, speaking, and writing practice.

Note:
- See the *Focus on Grammar Workbook* for additional in-class or homework grammar practice.

Unit 21 Review (page 306)

Have students complete the Review and check their answers on Student Book page UR-5. Review or assign additional material as needed.

Go to **www.myfocusongrammarlab.com** for the Unit Achievement Test.

Go to www.myfocusongrammarlab.com for the Unit Achievement Test.

UNIT 22 OVERVIEW

Grammar: ADVERBS: *As . . . as*, COMPARATIVES, SUPERLATIVES

Unit 22 focuses on the uses of adverbs to make comparisons with *as . . . as*, comparative adverbs with *than*, and superlative adverbs.

- *As* + adverb + *as* is used to compare actions and show how they are similar.

- *Not as* + adverb + *as* is used to compare actions and show how they are not the same or equal. Similarly, comparative adverbs + *than* show how the actions of two people or things are different.

- Superlative adverbs are used to compare one action with the actions of other people or things in a group.

- Comparative adverb + *and* + comparative adverb shows how something is increasing or decreasing.

- *The* + comparative adverb + *the* + comparative adverb shows cause and effect.

Theme: SPORTS

Unit 22 focuses on language used to describe sports games and compare their teams and players. Formats include a transcript of a sports TV program, a story from the sports section of the newspaper, and a questionnaire.

Step 1: Grammar in Context (pages 307–308)

See the general suggestions for Grammar in Context on page 1.

Before You Read

- To prepare students for the discussion, brainstorm with the class names of sports or physical activities. Write a list on the board. (Example: *tennis, soccer, baseball, yoga, basketball, jogging, brisk walking, cycling*)
- Have students look at the photo and discuss the questions in pairs.
- Have students make notes of reasons they play particular sports. Then call on pairs to share their answers to the questions with the class.

Read

- To encourage students to read with a purpose, write these questions on the board:
  1. What two teams are playing? *(the Australian and French teams)*
  2. Who is winning? *(the Australian team)*
  3. Who are the star players? *(Elizabeth Cambage from the Australian team and Maud Medenou from the French team)*
  4. Why can't the sports commentators predict a winner? *(because both teams are playing well)*
- Have students read the text. (OR: Play the audio and have students follow along in their books.) Then call on students to share their answers to the questions on the board.
- To get students to share their ideas on the reading, form pairs or small groups. Have them discuss one or both of the following topics:
  1. Discuss sports programs and sports commentators. Name your favorite sports programs and/or commentators and explain your choices.
  2. Basketball is one of the most popular sports in the United States. What do you know about popular or top sports in other countries? Discuss why each sport is popular.

After You Read

A. Vocabulary

- Have students complete the exercise individually. Encourage them to use context clues to help.
- Have students compare answers in pairs. Then call on pairs to give answers.
- ⏱ To reinforce the vocabulary, write the following sentence halves on the board. Have students match them. (Answers: *1. d, 2. c, 3. e, 4. a, 5. b*)

1. If you play intensely,	a. you do it quite often.
2. If you play aggressively,	b. you achieve the desired results.
3. If you play consistently,	c. you do all you can do to try to win.
4. If you play frequently,	d. you do it with a lot of energy and attention.
5. If you do something effectively,	e. you play the same way throughout the game.

B. Comprehension

- Have students complete the exercise individually.
- Have students compare answers in pairs. Then call on pairs to give answers.

Go to **www.myfocusongrammarlab.com** for an additional reading, and for reading and vocabulary practice.

Step 2: Grammar Presentation (pages 309–311)

See the general suggestions for Grammar Presentation on page 2.

Grammar Charts

- To explain comparisons with *as* + adverb + *as*, write on the board:
  The Australians played as well as the French.
  — Have students study the example. Then ask: "Did the French play well? *(yes)* "Did the Australians play equally well?" *(yes)* "How do you know?" *(because the sentence says that they played as well as the French)* "How can you make comparisons to show that two actions are the same?" (as + *adverb* + as)
  — Underline *as well as* in the example.
- To explain comparisons with *not as* + adverb + *as*, write on the board:
  The French didn't cheer as loud as the Australians.
  — Ask: "Did the Australians cheer loud? *(yes)* "Did the French cheer equally loud?" *(no)* "How do you know?" *(because the sentence says that they didn't cheer as loud as the Australians)* "How can you make comparisons to show that two actions are *not* the same?" (not + as + *adverb* + as)
  — Underline *didn't* and *as loud as* in the example.
  — Be sure students understand that a negative verb is necessary.
  — **Note:** You may want to point out that *loud* is the informal adverb, but in writing and more formal speech *loudly* should be used as the adverb. (See Unit 19, Grammar Note 3, page 270.)
- To explain comparative and superlative forms of short adverbs, write on the board:
  At first, the Australians played harder than the French.
  The Australians cheer the loudest of any fans in the game.
  — Have students name the comparative and superlative adverbs in the examples. *(harder, the loudest)* Underline them as students say them.

- Then ask: "How do you form the comparative of short adverbs such as *hard*?" (*short adverb* + -er) "What comes after *harder*?" (than + *the second part of the comparison*) "How do you form the superlative of short adverbs such as *loud*?" (the + *adverb* + -est)
- To explain the comparative and superlative forms of long adjectives, write on the board:
  The Italians blocked Nixon more effectively than any other team.
  Nixon got the ball less consistently than in other games.
  Trigs scored the most consistently of anyone on the team.
  Nixon played the least intensely of anyone on the team.
  — Have students name the comparative and superlative adverbs in the examples. *(more effectively, less consistently, the most consistently, the least intensely)* Underline them as students say them.
  — Then ask: "How do you form the comparative of long adverbs?" (more or less + *adverb*) "How do you form the superlative of long adverbs?" (the most or the least + *adverb*)
- To explain the comparative and superlative forms of irregular adverbs, write on the board:
  Trigs played better than Nixon.
  Trigs scored the most of her team.
  — Have students name the comparative and superlative adverbs in the examples *(better, the most)*. Underline them.
  — Then ask: "What is *better* the comparative of?" *(well)* "What is *the most* the superlative of?" *(a lot)* Point out that some adverbs have irregular comparative and superlative forms.
  — To summarize, write on the board:

Adverb	Comparative	Superlative
well	better	the best
a lot	more	the most

Grammar Notes

Note 1

- To review comparisons with *as* + adverb + *as*, write on the board:
  Nixon ran as fast as Jones.
- Have students study the example. Then ask: "Did Nixon run fast?" *(yes)* "Did Jones run equally fast?" *(yes)*
- Insert *just* between *ran* and *as*. Ask: "Is the comparison weaker or stronger now?" *(stronger)*

- Write a new example on the board:
  Trigs didn't score as frequently as Jones.
- Ask: "Did Jones score frequently?" *(yes)* "Did Trigs score with the same frequency?" *(no)*

Note 2

- To review comparative adverbs + *than*, write on the board:
  Jones played more intensely than Trigs.
- Have students study the example. Then ask: "Did Jones play intensely?" *(yes)* "Did Trigs play as intensely as Jones?" *(no)*
- Insert *even* between *played* and *more*. Ask: "Is the comparison weaker or stronger now?" *(stronger)*
- To explain the use of *less . . . than*, write on the board:
  The Tigers didn't cheer as loud as the Vikings.
  The Vikings cheered louder than the Tigers.
  The Tigers cheered ~~less loud than~~ the Vikings.
- Point out that we do not use *less . . . than* with short adverbs such as *loud*.
- Write on the board:
  The Tigers played less consistently than the Vikings.
- Point out that we do use *less . . . than* with long adverbs such as *consistently*.
- Write on the board:
  a. Riley played intensely. Nixon played just as intensely.
  b. Trigs played patiently. Jones played less patiently.
- Point out that when the meaning is clear, it is not necessary to mention both parts of the comparison.

Note 3

- Write the following example on the board:
  The whole team played skillfully, but Riley played the most skillfully.
- Have students study the example. Then ask: "Did Riley play skillfully?" *(yes)* "Who is Riley compared with in the example?" *(all the other players on the team)* "Did any of the other players play more skillfully than Riley?" *(no)*
- Point out that the superlative compares one action with the action of other people in a group. In the example, the superlative compares the way Riley played with the way the other players on the team played.
- Emphasize that the superlative compares three or more things. It should not be used to compare only two things. Write two contrasting examples on the board:
  Brad scored <u>more frequently than</u> Rost. (comparison of two people)

Brad scored <u>the most frequently</u> of anyone on the team. (comparison of more than two people)

- To explain the words and expressions that are used with superlative adverbs, write on the board:
  She runs the fastest of all the players.
  She runs the fastest of anyone on the team.
  She runs the fastest of all.
  She runs the fastest of her team.
- Have students study the examples. Then ask: "What preposition is used in expressions that are used with the superlative?" *(of)*

Note 4

- To review how to form comparative and superlative adverbs, draw the following chart on the board. (**Note:** Do not write the comparative and superlative forms. Just fill in text in the first two columns.)

	Adverb	Comparative	Superlative
One-syllable adverbs	soon late loud	sooner later louder	the soonest the latest the loudest
Irregular adverbs	little a lot far	less more farther/ further	the least the most the farthest/ furthest
Long adverbs	cooperatively patiently	more/less cooperatively more/less patiently	the most/least cooperatively the most/least patiently

- Have students say the comparative and superlative forms and fill in the chart.
- To review the word order of adverbs of manner, write on the board:
  a. Jones played more skillfully than Whine.
  b. Jones blocked more skillfully his opponents than Whine.
  c. Jones blocked his opponents more skillfully than Whine.
- Have pairs decide which statements are correct. Go over the answers as a class. *(Correct statements: a and c)*
- If needed, refer students to Appendix 10 on page A-6 for a list of irregular comparative and superlative adverbs.
- Refer students to Unit 19 for more information about adverbs.

Note 5

- To explain how comparative adverbs can be repeated to show increase or decrease, write on the board:
  He is working faster and faster.
  She has been playing more and more intensely.
  They have been playing less and less aggressively.
- Ask: "What word is repeated in the first example?" *(the adverb* faster*)* "What words are repeated in the second and third examples?" (more *and* less)
- Point out that with long adjectives, we repeat *more* or *less*, as appropriate.

Note 6

- To explain how to use two comparative adverbs to show cause and effect, write on the board:
  The <u>better</u> she plays, the <u>more</u> she scores. = comparative adverbs
  The <u>better</u> the pizza, the <u>higher</u> the price. = comparative adjectives
- To clarify the difference between the way comparative adjectives and comparative adverbs are used in this structure, point out that comparative adjectives are followed by nouns *(the pizza* and *the price)*, and comparative adverbs are followed by a subject and a verb *(she plays* and *she scores)*.

⏱ **Identify the Grammar:** Have students identify the grammar in the opening reading on page 307. For example:
  . . . have you ever seen two teams play **more aggressively**?
  . . . the Australians cheer **the loudest** of any fans in the game!
  They've scored almost **as frequently as** the French in the first half.
  . . . she's been playing **more and more intensely** . . .

Go to **www.myfocusongrammarlab.com** for grammar charts and notes.

Step 3: Focused Practice (pages 311–314)

See the general suggestions for Focused Practice on page 4.

Exercise 1: Discover the Grammar
- Go over the example with the class.
- Have students do the exercise individually.
- Have students compare answers in pairs. Then call on students to give answers.

Exercise 2: Comparisons with *As . . . as*
- To help familiarize students with the chart, ask: "Is Z comfortable?" *(no)* "Does X protect your feet?" *(yes)* "Does Z last very long?" *(no)* "Does X support your ankles very well?" *(no)* "And Y?" *(It doesn't support them at all.)*
- Go over the example with the class. Remind students to change the adjectives to adverbs.
- Have students complete the exercise individually. Then go over the answers as a class.

Exercise 3: *As . . . as*, Comparative and Superlative Adverbs
- Go over the example with the class. Then have students read the conversation quickly for meaning.
- Have students complete the exercise in pairs. Then call on a pair to read the conversation aloud.
- ⏱ Have pairs role-play the conversation.

Exercise 4: Comparative and Superlative Adverbs
- Review the sports in the chart with the class. If necessary, explain that broad jump is a sport in which you jump as far as possible and pole vaulting is a sport in which you jump over a high bar using a special long pole (stick).
- Go over the examples with the class. Remind students to use comparative forms to compare two people and superlative forms to compare three or more people.
- Have students do the exercise individually. Then go over the answers as a class.

Exercise 5: Editing
- Have students read the student newspaper article quickly to find out what it is about. To check comprehension, ask: "Which two teams played last night?" *(the Lions and the Cubs)* "Which team won the game?" *(the Lions)* "What might happen if the Lions keep playing so well?" *(They might be this season's new champions.)*
- Go over the example with the class.
- Have students find and correct the mistakes individually. Then call on students to explain why the incorrect structures are wrong.
- ⏱ Have students point out examples of correct usages of adverbs.

Go to **www.myfocusongrammarlab.com** for additional grammar practice.

Step 4: Communication Practice
(pages 314–317)

See the general suggestions for Communication Practice on page 5.

Exercise 6: Listening

A

- Have students practice pronouncing the names of the horses so that they can recognize the names while listening to the audio. Point out that the horses are not mentioned in the order in which they finished the race.
- Play the audio. Have students listen and complete the exercise individually.
- Have students compare answers in pairs. Then call on pairs to give answers.

B

- Have students read the statements.
- Play the audio. Have students listen and complete the exercise individually.
- Have students compare answers in pairs. Go over the answers as a class.

Exercise 7: Pronunciation

A

- Play the audio. Have students read along as they listen to the Pronunciation Note.
- Be sure students understand a final consonant is linked to an initial vowel. The *-ly* ending of adverbs ends in the consonant sound "y".

B

- Have students read the conversations and identify the sounds that are linked.
- Play the audio. Have students listen.

C

- Play the audio again. Have students listen and repeat the responses.
- Have students practice the conversations with a partner. Be sure students play both roles.

Exercise 8: Compare and Contrast

- As a class, have students choose one sport. Write the sport on the board. Then brainstorm with the class names of famous athletes for that sport. Write the names on the board.
- Go over the list of verbs and adverbs. Have students choose verbs that they would like to use to talk about the athletes. Have students match each verb they chose with an adverb from the list or an adverb of their choice. (Example: *kick powerfully*)
- Go over the example with the class. Discuss as a class the athletes you chose. Point out that students should use comparative and superlative adverbs. Then have students write down three statements comparing the athletes.

Exercise 9: Questionnaire: Work and Play

A

- Have students complete the exercise individually.

B

- Have students add three of their own questions to the questionnaire.

C

- Form small groups. Have students discuss their answers to questions 1 through 9.
- Have students ask their classmates the questions they wrote.
- Call on students to report their findings to the class.

Exercise 10: Writing

A

- Write these questions on the board:
  1. Which two sports figures would you like to compare?
  2. What sport do they play?
  3. How well do they play it?
  4. What is one of the players better at?
  5. What is the other player better at?
  6. Who plays more intensely, aggressively, skillfully, or cooperatively?
  7. Who trains more seriously?
  8. Who scores more frequently or more consistently?
- Have students take notes for each question and then use them as a guide as they write.
- Encourage students to use some of the vocabulary from Exercise 8 on page 316.

B

- Have students correct their work using the Editing Checklist.

OUT OF THE BOX ACTIVITIES

Speaking

- Have students form small groups and choose a famous person they like—for example, a sportsperson, movie star, musician, singer, or dancer—and use comparative or superlative adverbs to explain to their classmates why they like this person. (Example: *My favorite ballet dancer is Julio Bocca from Argentina. I think he dances more gracefully than any other dancer I've seen.*)
- Call on students to tell the class about the people they like.

Reading and Speaking

- Bring in the sports section of several newspapers. Form small groups and have students browse the sports section in search of an article that reports on a game.
- Have students find the answers to (some of) the following questions:
  — Who played better?
  — Who began the game more aggressively?
  — Who played more skillfully by the end of the game?
  — Who scored more in the first half/set/ game?
  — Who has been training more seriously?
  — Which player on the team played the hardest?
  — Which player on the team played the least consistently?
- Call on a member from each group to report to the class on the article they read.

Go to **www.myfocusongrammarlab.com** for additional listening, pronunciation, speaking, and writing practice.

Note:
- See the *Focus on Grammar Workbook* for additional in-class or homework grammar practice.

Unit 22 Review (page 318)

Have students complete the Review and check their answers on Student Book page UR-6. Review or assign additional material as needed.

Go to **www.myfocusongrammarlab.com** for the Unit Achievement Test.

From Grammar to Writing (pages 319–320)

See the general suggestions for From Grammar to Writing on page 9.

Go to **www.myfocusongrammarlab.com** for an additional From Grammar to Writing Assignment, Part Review, and Part Post-Test.

PART VII OVERVIEW

GERUNDS AND INFINITIVES

UNIT	GRAMMAR FOCUS	THEME
23	Gerunds: Subject and Object	Health Issues
24	Infinitives after Certain Verbs	Friends and Family
25	More Uses of Infinitives	Smart Phones
26	Gerunds and Infinitives	Procrastination

Go to **www.myfocusongrammarlab.com** for the Part and Unit Tests.

Note: PowerPoint® grammar presentations, test-generating software, and reproducible Part and Unit Tests are on the *Teacher's Resource Disc.*

UNIT 23 OVERVIEW

Grammar: GERUNDS: SUBJECT AND OBJECT

Unit 23 focuses on the use of gerunds as subjects and objects of verbs and prepositions.

- A gerund (base form + -*ing*) can be the subject of a sentence and is always singular.
- A gerund can be the object of certain verbs such as *admit, avoid, consider,* and *deny.*
- *Go* + gerund is often used to describe activities.
- A gerund can be the object of certain prepositions such as *about, before, for,* and *on.*
- A gerund can follow expressions formed by verb + preposition or adjective + preposition such as *advise against* and *afraid of.*

Theme: HEALTH ISSUES

Unit 23 focuses on language used to talk about smoking and staying healthy. Formats include smoking regulations around the world, an online bulletin board about smoking, an ex-smoker's journal entry, and a class survey.

Step 1: Grammar in Context (pages 322–323)

See the general suggestions for Grammar in Context on page 1.

Before You Read

- Have students look at the cartoon and discuss the questions in pairs.
- Have students make notes of how they think smokers and non-smokers feel about laws that limit smoking.
- Call on pairs to share their answers to the questions with the class. Draw the following diagram on the board to organize students' ideas as you get feedback from them.

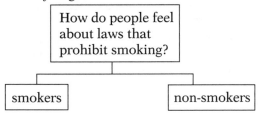

Read

- To encourage students to read with a purpose, write these questions on the board:
  1. Why is the article called "No Smoking—Around the World from A to Z"? *(because more and more countries around the world are introducing laws that limit smoking; the article gives examples of countries from A [Austria] to Z [Zambia])*
  2. What are some examples of public places where people can't smoke? *(trains, train stations, offices, streets, restaurants, malls)*
  3. How do smokers feel about it? *(that some laws go too far and limit personal freedom, and that there are other things that are not healthy—such as eating junk food—that are not regulated by laws)*
- Have students read the text. (OR: Play the audio and have students follow along in their books.) Then call on students to share their answers to the questions on the board.
- To get students to share their ideas on the reading, form pairs or small groups. Have them discuss one or both of the following topics:
  1. Share your thoughts. Are you in favor of or against laws that ban smoking? Explain your view.

2. Share your personal experience. Use these questions as a guide:

Smokers

When did you start smoking? Are you a heavy smoker? Why/When do you smoke? Have you ever tried to stop smoking? Would you like to stop smoking?

Non-smokers

Did you ever try a cigarette? If so, when? Why don't you smoke? If you used to be a smoker, was it easy to quit smoking? What did you do?

After You Read

A. Vocabulary

- Have students complete the exercise individually.
- Have students compare answers in pairs. Then call on pairs to give answers.
- ⏱ To reinforce the vocabulary, write the following sentences on the board. Have students choose answers and complete the sentences with their own ideas, as appropriate. Then call on students to read their sentences aloud.
  1. I approve/don't approve of smoking in public places.
  2. Most of my friends are in favor of/against smoking in public places.
  3. In my town, there are some/no laws that prohibit smoking.
  4. In my town it is/isn't illegal to smoke in _____ .
  5. I think it's OK to ban smoking in _____ .
  6. I think it's OK to permit smoking in _____ .

B. Comprehension

- Have students complete the exercise individually.
- Have students compare answers in pairs. Then call on pairs to give answers.

Go to **www.myfocusongrammarlab.com** for an additional reading, and for reading and vocabulary practice.

Step 2: Grammar Presentation (pages 324–325)

See the general suggestions for Grammar Presentation on page 2.

Grammar Charts

- To explain gerunds as subjects, write on the board:

  Smoking is not permitted in restaurants.

  — Have students study the example. Then ask: "What's the subject of the sentence?" *(smoking)* "What's the verb phrase?" *(is not permitted)*
  — Underline and indicate the subject and the verb phrase in the example:
  <u>Smoking</u> <u>is not permitted</u> in restaurants.
     subject   verb
  — Ask: "Is *smoking* a noun or a gerund?" *(a gerund)* "What's a gerund?" *(a base form of a verb + -ing)*
  — Point out that a gerund is a verb that is used like a *noun*, so it can be a *subject* of a sentence.

- To explain gerunds as objects, write on the board:

  Fumario enjoys smoking.

  — Have students study the example. Then ask: "What's the subject of the sentence?" *(Fumario)* "What's the main verb?" *(enjoys)* "What's the object?" *(smoking)*
  — Underline and indicate the subject, the verb, and the object in the example:
  <u>Fumario</u> <u>enjoys</u> <u>smoking</u>.
    subject   verb   object
  — Point out that a gerund can also be the *object* of a sentence.

- To explain gerunds as objects of a preposition, write on the board:

  I'm in favor of smoking in parks.

  — Have students study the example. Then ask: "What's the gerund in the example?" *(smoking)* "What word comes before the gerund?" *(of)* "What kind of word is *of*?" *(a preposition)*
  — Underline and indicate the preposition and the object of the preposition in the example:
  I'm in favor <u>of</u> <u>smoking</u> in parks.
             prep.   object
                     of the
                     prep.

Grammar Notes

Note 1

- To explain how to form gerunds, write on the board:

  Exercising is healthy.
  I don't like lying.
  He is in favor of banning smoking.

- Have students say the gerunds in the examples. *(exercising, lying, banning, smoking)*
- Draw attention to the *Be Careful!* note. Then write the following base forms and gerunds on the board:

  exercise   exercising
  lie   lying
  ban   banning
  smoke   smoking

- Have pairs study the spelling changes. If needed, refer students to Appendix 21 on page A-10 for spelling rules for verbs + *-ing*. To go over the answers as a class, have students explain the spelling rules.
- To explain how to form negative gerunds, write on the board:

  Not obeying the law can result in fines.

- Ask: "What's the gerund in the example?" *(obeying)* "How do we form the negative of a gerund?" *(not + gerund)*

Note 2

- To review gerunds as subjects, write on the board:

  Reading is fun.
  Smoking is an unhealthy habit.

- Have students study the examples and name the subjects. *(reading, smoking)*
- Point out the singular verb. *(is)*
- Write new examples on the board:

  Reading travel magazines was my favorite pastime.
  Smoking in public places is not allowed.

- Point out that the subject can also be a gerund phrase. Have students name the subjects in the examples. *(reading travel magazines, smoking in public places)*
- Ask students if the verbs are singular or plural. *(singular:* was *and* is*)* Be sure students understand that the verb is always singular, even if the gerund is followed by plural nouns such as *magazines* or *places*.
- Draw attention to the *Be Careful!* note. Point out that gerunds should not be confused with the progressive forms of verbs.
- To review gerunds as objects, write on the board:

  She quit smoking.
  I suggest going to a café.
  He enjoys swimming.

- Have students study the examples and name the gerunds (*smoking, going, swimming*) and the verbs before the gerunds (*quit, suggest, enjoys*).
- Point out that certain verbs such as *quit, suggest,* and *enjoy* are often followed by gerunds.
- Point out that the objects can be either gerunds or gerund phrases. Have students look at the examples on the board again and name the object that is a gerund phrase. (*going to a café*)
- To explain *go* + gerund, write on the board: I like to go fishing.
- Ask: "What kind of word follows *go*?" (*a gerund:* fishing)
- Point out that we use *go* + gerund to describe activities.
- If needed, refer students to Appendix 13 on page A-7 for a more complete list of verbs that can be followed by gerunds.

Note 3

- To explain gerunds as objects to prepositions, write on the board:
  I'm against smoking in parks.
  She complained about having to study.
  She is good at solving problems.
- Have students study the first example. Then ask: "What kind of word is *against*?" (*a preposition*) "What kind of word follows *against*?" (*a gerund*)
- Direct attention to the second example. Ask: What kind of word is *complained*?" (*a verb*) "What preposition is it followed by?" (*about*)
- Point out that certain verbs such as *complain* are followed by a particular preposition. These verb + preposition combinations can be followed by a gerund.
- Write more examples on the board:
  apologize for ⎤
  think about ⎦ + gerund
- Direct attention to last example. Ask: What kind of word is *good*? (*an adjective*) "What preposition is it followed by?" (*at*)
- Point out that certain adjectives such as *good* are followed by a particular preposition. These adjective + preposition combinations can be followed by a gerund.
- Write more examples on the board:
  responsible for ⎤
  interested in ⎦ + gerund

- To explain expressions with the preposition *to*, write on the board:
  I look forward to going on vacation.
  He objects to doing that kind of work.
  I am opposed to working so late.
- Draw attention to the *Be Careful!* note. Make sure students understand that in expressions such as *look forward to, object to,* and so on, *to* is a preposition, not part of the infinitive. Give more examples.

⏱ **Identify the Grammar:** Have students identify the grammar in the opening reading on page 322. For example:
  . . . life has become more and more difficult for people who **enjoy lighting up**.
  . . . for those who want to **quit smoking**, it has become easier . . .
  . . . unless all employees are in favor **of permitting** it.
  . . . smaller ones can choose **between permitting smoking** or **being** smoke-free.

Go to www.myfocusongrammarlab.com for grammar charts and notes.

Step 3: Focused Practice (pages 326–329)

See the general suggestions for Focused Practice on page 4.

Exercise 1: Discover the Grammar

- Go over the example with the class. Ask: "What kind of word comes before *seeing*?" (*a verb*) "Is *seeing those signs* a subject or an object in this sentence?" (*an object*) Remind students that not all words ending in *-ing* are gerunds. If necessary, write two contrasting examples on the board:
  She <u>is eating</u> a hamburger. (present progressive)
  <u>Eating</u> hamburgers is not a healthy habit. (gerund)
- Have students complete the exercise individually.
- Have students compare answers in pairs. Then go over the answers as a class.

Exercise 2: Gerunds: Affirmative and Negative

- Go over the example with the class. Have students read the article quickly for meaning.
- Have students complete the exercise individually. Then go over the answers as a class.

- ⏱ Books closed. For further practice, write the following topics on the board. Have pairs write the tips that they remember for each of the topics. Go over the answers as a class.
  Smoking
  Exercising
  Healthy eating
  Seeing a doctor

Exercise 3: Gerund as Object
- Go over the example with the class.
- Have students complete the exercise individually.
- Have students compare answers in pairs. Then call on pairs to read the conversations and call on a different student to read the summary.

Exercise 4: Gerund as Object of a Preposition
- Go over the example with the class.
- Have students complete the exercise individually. Then have students compare answers in pairs.
- ⏱ For further practice, personalize the ideas in the exercise by having students use the following questions as a guide to talk about their healthy habits:
  What are you most interested in—staying healthy or eating and doing the things you like?
  Do you have any healthy habits? What are you happy about? Are you proud of yourself for something you do to take care of yourself? How can you improve your health? *(I could improve my health by . . .)*

Exercise 5: Editing
- Have students read the journal quickly for meaning. Ask: "What did the person quit?" *(smoking and drinking coffee)* "Has the person gained weight?" *(yes, five pounds)* "What are some advantages of not smoking?" *(he/she doesn't have to stand outside in the cold anymore; he/she doesn't burn holes in his/her clothes anymore)* "Why has he/she decided not to go out to dinner?" *(because he/she doesn't want to risk being around smokers)*
- Go over the example with the class.
- Have students find and correct the mistakes individually. Then call on students to explain why the incorrect structures are wrong.
- ⏱ Have students point out examples of correct usages of gerunds as subject and object.

Go to **www.myfocusongrammarlab.com** for additional grammar practice.

Step 4: Communication Practice
(pages 329–332)

See the general suggestions for Communication Practice on page 5.

Exercise 6: Listening
A
- Have students go over the list and predict what the doctor may say. If necessary, explain the meaning of *complex carbohydrates* (include fiber [found in fruits] and starches [such as rice], vegetables, whole grains, peas, and beans).
- Play the audio. Have students listen and complete the exercise individually. Then ask students whether they were right in their predictions.
- ⏱ Have students listen again and write down at the front of each item the verb the doctor uses before each gerund. Then have students make complete sentences using the verbs they wrote down and the items on the list. (Example: *The doctor said the patient must stop smoking.*)

B
- Have students read the statements quickly for meaning.
- Play the audio. Have students listen and complete the exercise individually.
- Call on students to give answers and encourage students to support their answers with more information from the audio.

Exercise 7: Pronunciation
A
- Play the audio. Have students read along as they listen to the Pronunciation Note. Be sure students notice how the sounds are linked.

B
- Have students read the statements and anticipate which sounds they will hear linked.
- Play the audio. Have students listen and draw the linking lines.

C
- Play the audio. Have students listen and repeat. Be sure they pronounce the words that are linked as one word.

Exercise 8: Survey
A
- Give students a few minutes to look at the survey and think of their answers to the questions. Encourage students to think of reasons to support their views.
- Have students take the class survey.

B

- Have students discuss the survey results as a class. Ask: "Did smokers and non-smokers respond to questions differently? For example, how many smokers agree with opinion 1? How many non-smokers?"
- Have a few students support their answers by saying why they agree or disagree with the statements.

Exercise 9: For or Against

- Form small groups. Have students discuss laws that prohibit smoking. They should take notes on the arguments for and against that are brought up in the discussion. Have students write the arguments in two lists under the headings *For* and *Against*.
- Encourage students to use their lists of arguments for and against to reach a conclusion.
- Call on students from different groups to share their conclusions with the class.

Exercise 10: Writing

A

- Write the following plan on the board to help elicit vocabulary and generate ideas:

```
Topic: _____
1. Are you for or against it? _____ . Some
   reasons:
   _____
   _____
   _____
2. Reasons some people support the
   opposing view:
   _____
   _____
   _____
```

- Have students complete the plan and use it as a guide as they write.

B

- Have students correct their work using the Editing Checklist.

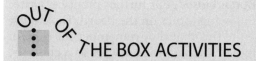

OUT OF THE BOX ACTIVITIES

Speaking and Listening

- Have pairs of students choose a healthy habit to promote to the class.
- Give pairs of students five minutes to explain the habit, its benefits, and any special instructions.
- Possible topics are:
  — Eating five to nine servings of fruit and vegetables a day
  — Not eating snack food while watching TV
  — Exercising most days of the week
  — Drinking eight glasses of water a day

Reading and Speaking

- Bring in self-help articles that deal with a health problem. (Example: *insomnia*, *stress*, or *depression*) Form small groups and hand out the material.
- Have students read the article and write a list of tips for dealing with that problem by completing (some of) the following statements. To help generate ideas, write the following on the board:
  Tips for dealing with _____
      Avoid _____ .
      Consider _____ .
      Enjoy _____ .
      Give up _____ .
      Don't keep _____ .
      Practice _____ .
      When you feel like _____ , you should _____ .
      If you miss _____ , you can _____ .
      Experts recommend _____ .
      They suggest _____ .
      They also advise _____ .
- Have groups report to the class on the problem they read about and the tips for dealing with it.

Go to **www.myfocusongrammarlab.com** for additional listening, pronunciation, speaking, and writing practice.

Note:
- See the *Focus on Grammar Workbook* for additional in-class or homework grammar practice.

Unit 23 Review (page 333)

Have students complete the Review and check their answers on Student Book page UR-6. Review or assign additional material as needed.

Go to **www.myfocusongrammarlab.com** for the Unit Achievement Test.

Grammar: INFINITIVES AFTER CERTAIN VERBS

Unit 24 focuses on the use of infinitives after certain verbs.

- Some verbs can be followed directly by an infinitive.
- Some verbs need an object before the infinitive.
- Some verbs can be followed by either an infinitive or an object + infinitive.

Theme: FRIENDS AND FAMILY

Unit 24 focuses on language used to talk about meeting people and making friends. Formats include an advice column, a diary entry, and an article from an online how-to site.

Step 1: Grammar in Context (pages 334–335)

See the general suggestions for Grammar in Context on page 1.

Before You Read

- Have students look at the advice column and discuss the questions in pairs. Have them make notes of people they ask for advice and places they get advice.
- Call on pairs to share their answers to the questions with the class.
- Write two column headings—*People* and *Places*—on the board. As you get feedback from students, write the people and places students get advice from under each heading. Encourage them to give reasons for their choices.

Read

- To encourage students to read with a purpose, write these questions on the board:
  1. What problem does Lonely in Seattle have? *(she is going to a new school in Seattle and wants to meet new people and make new friends)*
  2. What does Annie advise her to do? *(to relax, do the things she likes to do, and have fun; while doing the things she likes, she will meet people)*

- Have students read the text. (OR: Play the audio and have students follow along in their books.) Then call on students to share their answers to the questions on the board.
- To get students to share their ideas on the reading, form pairs or small groups. Have them discuss one or both of the following topics:
  1. Do you agree with Annie's advice? What is the best way to make friends? Why is it important to make friends when you move to a new place? Is it also important to fall in love? Annie thinks that people shouldn't try to solve the problem of loneliness by falling in love. Do you agree?
  2. Lonely in Seattle chose to write to a newspaper advice column. What would you have done to seek advice if you had been in Lonely's situation?

After You Read

A. Vocabulary

- Have students complete the exercise individually. Encourage them to use context clues to help.
- Have students compare answers in pairs. Then call on pairs to give answers.
- ⏱ To reinforce the vocabulary, write the following words on the board. Have students match the vocabulary words with the words they can go with. Go over the answers as a class. (Answers: *have contact with friends, animals; have similar interests, likes; focus on your problem, your work; solve problems, mysteries*)

a. have contact with	your problem, your work
b. have similar	friends, animals
c. focus on	problems, mysteries
d. solve	interests, likes

B. Comprehension

- Have students complete the exercise individually.
- Have students compare answers in pairs. Then call on pairs to give answers.

Go to **www.myfocusongrammarlab.com** for an additional reading, and for reading and vocabulary practice.

Step 2: Grammar Presentation (page 336)

See the general suggestions for Grammar Presentation on page 2.

Grammar Chart

- To explain infinitives after verbs, write on the board:
  Nothing seems to work.
  I decided not to go.

— Have students study the examples. Then ask: "What's the main verb in each sentence?" *(seems, decided)* "What words follow the main verbs?" *(to work, not to go)* "Are *to work* and *not to go* infinitives or gerunds?" *(infinitives)* Underline the verbs as students say them.

— Point out that some verbs such as *seem* and *decide* are followed by infinitives.

• To explain verbs that need an object before the infinitive, write on the board:
I advise them to make friends first.
I told her to join a club.

— Have students study the examples. Then tell students: "Name the main verb in each sentence." *(advise, told)* "Name the infinitive in each sentence." *(to make, to join)*. Underline the verbs and infinitives as students say them.

— Then ask: "Do the infinitives directly follow the verbs?" *(no)* "What comes before the infinitives?" *(an object: them, her)*

— Point out that some verbs such as *advise* and *tell* need an object before the infinitive.

• To explain verbs that may or may not take an object before the infinitive, write on the board:
I'd just like to make friends.
She would like me to date her friend.

— Have students study the examples. Then ask: "Does the infinitive directly follow the verb in the first example?" *(yes)* "Does it directly follow the verb in the second example?" *(No. There's an object—me—between the verb and the infinitive.)*

— Point out that some verbs such as *would like* can be followed directly by an infinitive or by an object and an infinitive.

Grammar Notes

Note 1

• To review affirmative and negative infinitives after verbs, write on the board:
I decided to stay.
I told her to come.

• Tell students: "Name the main verbs." *(decided, told)* "Name the infinitives that follow them." *(to stay, to come)* "Change *to stay* and *to come* into negative infinitives and say full sentences." *(I decided not to stay. I told her not to come.)*

Note 2

• To review verbs that are followed directly by an infinitive, write on the board:

Lonely in Seattle	has failed	to develop friendships soon.
	refused	not to see that man again.
	decided	to make new friends so far.
	hopes	to lend money to the man she was dating.

• Have students match the second and third columns to make true sentences about Lonely in Seattle. (Answers: *has failed to make new friends so far.; refused to lend money to the man she was dating.; decided not to see that man again.; hopes to develop friendships soon.*)

• Go over the verbs in the list in Note 2 and clarify the meaning of any unknown words. Students might need help with *attempt* (to try to do something) and *refuse* (to say firmly that you will not do or accept something).

• If needed, refer students to Appendix 14 on page A-7 for a list of verbs that are followed by the infinitive.

Note 3

• To review verbs that need an object before the infinitive, write on the board:

I	asked	a few friends	to come with us.
	invited	Alice	
	told	her	

• Point out that the object can be a noun, a noun phrase, or a pronoun.

• Go over the verbs in the list in Note 3 and clarify the meaning of any unknown words. Students might need help with *warn* (to tell someone that something bad or dangerous might happen, so that she/he can avoid it or prevent it) and *urge* (to strongly advise someone to do something).

• If needed, refer students to Appendix 16 on page A-7 for a list of verbs that need an object before the infinitive.

Note 4

• To review verbs that can be followed by an infinitive or an object and an infinitive, write on the board:

| Sarah would like to write a letter to Annie. | = Sarah is interested in writing to Annie. |
| Sarah would like her friend to write a letter to Annie. | = Sarah is not interested in writing a letter herself. She thinks her friend should write to Annie. |

- Point out that a verb followed by an infinitive may have a different meaning from a verb followed by an object and an infinitive.
- If needed, refer students to Appendix 14 on page A-7 for a list of verbs that are followed by infinitives.

🕐 **Identify the Grammar:** Have students identify the grammar in the opening reading on page 334. For example:
I **try to meet** people . . .
. . . nothing **seems to work.**
. . . I **agreed to have** dinner . . .
. . . I **decided not to see** him again.

Go to **www.myfocusongrammarlab.com** for grammar charts and notes.

Step 3: Focused Practice (pages 337–339)

See the general suggestions for Focused Practice on page 4.

Exercise 1: Discover the Grammar
- Go over the example with the class.
- Have students complete the exercise individually. Then call on students to give answers.
- 🕐 For further practice, ask questions about the text. Have students give full answers. Ask: "Which club did Lonely decide to join?" (She decided to join the Outdoor Adventure Club.) "What can't she wait to do?" (She can't wait to go to the hiking trip.) "What did the club decide to do in spring?" (They decided to go rafting.) "What happened after the meeting?" (A group of people asked Lonely to go out with them.) "What didn't Lonely expect?" (She didn't expect everyone to be so friendly.)

Exercise 2: Verb (+ Object) + Infinitive
- Go over the example with the class. Then have students read the article quickly for meaning.
- Have students complete the exercise individually. Then go over the answers as a class.
- 🕐 Follow up with a brief discussion. Ask: "Do you agree with all or some of Dr. Dreyfus's tips? Explain your view."

Exercise 3: Object or No Object
- Go over the example with the class.
- Have students complete the exercise individually.
- Have students compare answers in pairs. Then call on pairs to read the conversations and call on a different student to read the summary.

Exercise 4: Editing
- Have students read the article quickly for meaning. Ask: "What does the article give advice on?" (how to make new friends) Have students mention tips from the article. (Example: *turn off your computer and TV, make real friends, go out with real people, don't refuse invitations, join clubs, volunteer, don't rush to become close friends, listen and encourage people to talk*)
- Go over the example with the class.
- Have students find and correct the mistakes individually. Then call on students to explain why the incorrect structures are wrong.
- 🕐 Have students point out examples of correct usages of infinitives.

Go to **www.myfocusongrammarlab.com** for additional grammar practice.

Step 4: Communication Practice
(pages 340–342)

See the general suggestions for Communication Practice on page 5.

Exercise 5: Listening
A
- Tell students they will listen to a couple talking about their *blended family*. Go over the definition of blended family. Explain that the new child is a stepdaughter or a stepson and the new parent is called a stepmother or stepfather.
- Play the audio. Have students listen and complete the exercise individually.
- Have students go over the answers in pairs. Then call on pairs to give answers.

B
- Play the audio. Have students listen and complete the exercise individually. If necessary, stop after each statement to allow students time to choose their answer.
- Go over the answers as a class.
- 🕐 Follow up with a brief discussion. Ask: "What kind of problem does this family have? What other problems might blended families have? Has this family managed to solve their problem? What would you advise them to do?"

Exercise 6: Pronunciation

A

- Play the audio. Have students read along as they listen to the Pronunciation Note.
- To check comprehension, write the following sentence on the board:
  I wanted them to stay.
- Ask: "Which words are stressed?" *(wanted, stay)* Underline them as students say them. Ask: "Which words are not stressed?" *(them, to)*

B

- Have students read the statements and anticipate which words are stressed. Then play the audio. Have students listen and write the stress marks.

C

- Play the audio. Have students listen and repeat. Be sure they stress the correct words.

Exercise 7: What About You?

- Go over the questions with the class. Then have students add their own questions individually.
- Have them submit the questions to you for correction.
- Have students complete the exercise in pairs. Then call on pairs to report to the class one or two interesting pieces of information about their partners' parents.

Exercise 8: Cross-Cultural Comparison

- Brainstorm with the class useful verbs from this unit that students can use to talk about what parents and young people do. Write the verbs on the board for students to use as reference as they discuss, for example:

Parents		Young people	
allow	warn	want	persuade
forbid	expect	prefer	refuse
force	advise	ask	invite
prefer	encourage	try	choose

- Have students discuss the topic as a class.

Exercise 9: Writing

A

- Write the following questions on the board to help elicit vocabulary and generate ideas:
  What are you planning to do with your classmates?
  What do you want to do after that?
  Why would you like your friend to come?
  Who else did you invite to come with you?
  Where and when did you arrange to meet?
- Have students make notes for each question and then use them as a guide as they write.

B

- Have students correct their work using the Editing Checklist.

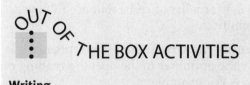

OUT OF THE BOX ACTIVITIES

Writing

- Have students work in pairs to classify some of the verbs in Appendices 14 and 16 on page A-7 into three semantic categories: *Speaking, Making Decisions,* and *Wanting or Expecting.* Tell students that this will help them learn the verbs. (Speaking: *advise, encourage, convince, persuade, promise, remind, tell, urge, warn, ask, refuse, mean, offer, request.* Making decisions: *agree, arrange, decide, plan, prepare.* Wanting or expecting: *want, wish, would like, can't wait, hope, expect*)
- Have students write an example for each category. Each example should be suitable for three verbs from the same category, for example:
  She advised/encouraged/persuaded me to join a club.
  We agreed/decided/are planning to go on vacation.
  I want/would like/can't wait to make new friends.

Reading and Speaking

- Do a search on the Internet on friendship and making friends and bring in several self-help articles about friendship written by psychologists or counselors. The articles should include tips for making new friends. Form small groups and hand out the material.
- Have students read the articles and discuss with their classmates which tips they agree with and which they do not.
- Call on students to report to the class on the tips for making friends suggested by the psychologist/counselor. Challenge students to say only sentences that contain the following verbs, which you should write on the board:

advise	persuade
encourage	teach
expect	tell
help	urge
remind	warn

Go to **www.myfocusongrammarlab.com** for additional listening, pronunciation, speaking, and writing practice.

Note:
• See the *Focus on Grammar Workbook* for additional in-class or homework grammar practice.

Unit 24 Review (page 343)

Have students complete the Review and check their answers on Student Book page UR-6. Review or assign additional material as needed.

Go to **www.myfocusongrammarlab.com** for the Unit Achievement Test.

UNIT 25 OVERVIEW

Grammar: MORE USES OF INFINITIVES

Unit 25 focuses on the uses of the infinitive.

• We use an infinitive (*to* + base form of verb) to explain the purpose of an action.

• In everyday spoken English, we use *because* + a reason to express a negative purpose.

• In formal writing, we often use *in order to* + base form of the verb to express the purpose of an action. A negative purpose is expressed with *in order not to* + base form of verb.

• We use *too* + adjective/adverb + infinitive to show that something is not possible.

• We use adjective/adverb + *enough* + infinitive to show that something is possible.

• *For* + noun/pronoun can be placed before the infinitive to indicate what person, place, or thing the infinitive refers to.

Theme: SMART PHONES

Unit 25 focuses on language used to talk about uses of smart phones and other devices.

Smart phones are computers integrated with a mobile telephone that can run advanced applications based on a specific platform. Advantages are good memory capacity, larger screen size, and open operating systems. "Simon" was the name of the first smart phone, which IBM designed in 1992 and introduced at a trade show in Las Vegas, Nevada.

Step 1: Grammar in Context (pages 344–345)

See the general suggestions for Grammar in Context on page 1.

Before You Read
• Have students look at the photo, read the title of the article, and discuss the questions in pairs.
• Have students write a list of uses of smart phones and cell phones and check the ones they use. Then call on pairs to share their answers to the questions with the class. Write students' ideas on the board.
• Ask: "Which use of the smart/cell phone could you not live without? Why?"

Read
• To encourage students to read with a purpose, write these questions on the board:
  1. What did people use smart phones for when they first came out? (*to make calls, check email, and connect to the Internet*)
  2. What other uses do they have? (*You can also use them to play games, listen to music, watch videos, look up reviews, avoid traffic jams, get directions, and translate words.*)
• Have students read the text. (OR: Play the audio and have students follow along in their books.) Then call on students to share their answers to the questions on the board.
• To get students to share their ideas on the reading, form pairs or small groups. Have them discuss one or both of the following topics:
  1. The article says smart phones have two drawbacks—their cost and the fact that people expect you to be reachable all the time. How important do you think these drawbacks are? Can you think of any others?
  2. The article says phones are getting smarter and smaller all the time. What do you think smart phones will be like in five years' time?

After You Read

A. Vocabulary
• Have students complete the exercise individually. Encourage them to use context clues to help.
• Have students compare answers in pairs. Then call on pairs to give answers.
• To reinforce the vocabulary, write the vocabulary words on the board and have students use four of them to complete the following sentence describing smart phones. (Possible answer: *The smart phone is a multipurpose device that combines many functions.*)
The smart phone is a _____ _____ that _____ many _____ .

B. Comprehension
- Have students complete the exercise individually.
- Have students compare answers in pairs. Then call on pairs to give answers.

Go to **www.myfocusongrammarlab.com** for an additional reading, and for reading and vocabulary practice.

Step 2: Grammar Presentation (pages 346–347)
See the general suggestions for Grammar Presentation on page 2.

Grammar Charts
- To explain the infinitive of purpose, write on the board:
  Anna uses her cell phone to make calls.
  She wants to buy a smart phone to connect to the Internet.
  She asked for advice in order not to buy the wrong phone.
  — Direct attention to the first example. Then ask: "What does Anna use her cell phone for?" *(to make calls)* "Why does Anna want to buy a smart phone?" *(to connect to the Internet)* "Why did Anna ask for advice?" *(in order not to buy the wrong phone / because she doesn't want to buy the wrong phone)*
  — Point out that we use an infinitive to express the purpose of an action.
  — Underline in the examples on the board *to make, to connect,* and *in order not to buy*. Then ask: "How do you form the infinitive of purpose?" *(to + base form of verb)* "How do you express a negative purpose?" *(in order not to + base form of verb)*
- To explain infinitives after adjectives and adverbs, write on the board:
  Some smart phones are easy to use.
  He ran fast to win the race.
  — Have students name the adjective and adverb in each example. *(easy, fast)*
  — Have students name the infinitives that follow them. *(to use, to win)*
  — Point out that infinitives can be used after adjectives and adverbs.
- To explain *too* + adjective + infinitive, write on the board:
  My smart phone is too difficult to use.
  Smart phones are too expensive for many people to afford.
  — Have students name the adjectives in each example. *(difficult, expensive)* Underline them as students say them.

  — Have students name the infinitives. *(to use, to afford)* Underline them as students say them.
  — Direct attention to the first example and ask: "Can the person use the smart phone?" *(no)*
  — Direct attention to the second example and ask: "Can many people afford smart phones?" *(no)*
  — Ask: "How can you show that something is not possible with an infinitive with *too*?" (too + *adjective* + *infinitive* OR too + *adjective* + for + *noun [or pronoun]* + *infinitive*)
- To explain adjective + *enough* + infinitive, write on the board:
  Smart phones are small enough to fit inside your pocket.
  A cell phone is cheap enough for me to buy.
  — Have students name the adjectives in each example. *(small, cheap)* Underline them as students say them.
  — Have students name the infinitives. *(to fit, to buy)* Underline them as students say them.
  — Direct attention to the first example and ask: "Does a smart phone fit inside your pocket?" *(yes)*
  — Direct attention to the second example and ask: "Can the person buy a cell phone?" *(yes)*
  — Ask: "How can you show that something is possible with an infinitive with *enough*?" (*adjective* + enough + *infinitive* OR *adjective* + enough + for + *pronoun [or noun]* + *infinitive*)
  — Be sure students are aware of the different ways in which *too* and *enough* are used: *too* is followed by an adjective or adverb and *enough* is preceded by an adjective or adverb. To summarize, write on the board:
    too + adjective/adverb + (*for* + noun) + infinitive
    adjective/adverb + *enough* + (*for* + noun) + infinitive
- To explain the use of adverbs with *too* or *enough* and infinitives, write on the board:
  1. He worked too slowly to finish on time.
  2. She spoke too quickly for me to understand.
  3. He worked hard enough to finish on time.
  4. She spoke clearly enough for me to understand.
  — Have students name the adverbs in the examples. *(slowly, quickly, hard, clearly)* Underline them as students say them.

— Have students name the infinitives. *(to understand, to finish)* Underline them as students say them.

— Ask: "How can you show that something is not possible with an infinitive with *too?*" (too + *adverb* + *infinitive* OR too + *adjective* + for + *pronoun [or noun]* + *infinitive*)

— Ask: "How can you show that something is possible with an infinitive with *enough*" (adverb + enough + *infinitive* OR adverb + enough + for + *pronoun [or noun]* + infinitive)

Grammar Notes

Note 1

- To review the infinitive of purpose, write on the board:
  Why did Jane go to the mall?
  To buy a gift.
- Point out that the infinitive *(to buy)* expresses the purpose of an action *(why Jane went to the mall).*
- Explain that in conversation we can use an incomplete sentence beginning with *to* to express a purpose.
- Add to the answer on the board:
  Why did Jane go to the mall?
  To buy a gift and book a ticket.
- Point out that we do not repeat *to* to give more than one purpose.

Note 2

- To explain *in order (not) to*, write on the board:
  He asked for advice in order to make the right choice.
  He wrote it down in order not to forget it.
- Emphasize that the longer form *in order (not) to* is formal.
- Point out that in everyday speech we use *because.* You may want to have students restate their answers to the questions in the second step using *because.* (Example: *He got up early because he didn't want to be late.*)

Note 3

- To review the use of *for* + noun/pronoun before the infinitive, write on the board:
  It's late to go out. = General statement = People shouldn't go out.
  It's late <u>for Sarah</u> to go out. = Sarah shouldn't go out.
- Explain that the infinitive can be preceded by a noun to make it clear who (or what) the action expressed by the infinitive refers to.
- Erase *Sarah* in the example and replace it with *her.* Point out that a pronoun is also possible.

- To review *too* + adjective + infinitive, write on the board:
  Micah is too young to own a cell phone.
- Have students name the adjective and the infinitive. *(young, to own)* Underline them.
- Say: "This sentence expresses something that is *not* possible. What is it?" *(Micah can't own a cell phone.)*
- To review *too* + adverb + infinitive, write on the board:
  John drives too slowly to win the race.
- Have students name the adverb and the infinitive. *(slowly, to win)* Underline them.
- Say: "This sentence expresses something that is *not* possible. What is it?" *(John can't win the race.)*
- To review adjective + *enough* + infinitive, write on the board:
  Kyle is old enough to buy a smart phone.
- Have students name the adjective and the infinitive. *(old, to buy)* Underline them.
- Say: "This sentence expresses something that is possible. What is it?" *(Kyle can own a smart phone.)*
- To review adverb + *enough* + infinitive, write on the board:
  Clare trained hard enough to win the competition.
- Have students name the adverb and the infinitive. *(hard, to win)* Underline them.
- Say: "This sentence expresses something that *is* possible. What is it?" *(Clare can win the competition.)*
- To explain that the infinitive is not necessary when the meaning is clear, write on the board:
  Why didn't he catch the bus?
  Because he didn't run fast enough (to catch it).
- Point out that the infinitive *(to catch it)* is not necessary in the answer.

⏱ **Identify the Grammar:** Have students identify the grammar in the opening reading on page 344. For example:
  What's **smart enough to get** all the information you'll ever need . . .
  . . . **small enough to fit** inside your pocket?
  I use my smart phone **to play** games . . .
  It's **easy to see** why these multipurpose devices are so popular.

Go to **www.myfocusongrammarlab.com** for grammar charts and notes.

Step 3: Focused Practice (pages 348–352)

See the general suggestions for Focused Practice on page 4.

Exercise 1: Discover the Grammar
- Go over the example with the class. Remind students that not every *to* introduces an infinitive.
- Have students complete the exercise individually.
- Have students compare answers in pairs. Then go over the answers as a class.

Exercise 2: Affirmative and Negative Purposes

A
- Go over the example with the class.
- Have students complete the exercise individually.
- Have students compare answers in pairs. Then go over the answers as a class.

B
- Go over the example with the class.
- Have students complete the exercise individually. Then go over the answers as a class.
- ⏲ For further practice, personalize the information in the activity. Write the following on the board:
  Think about last week. Write:
  A store you went to: _____
  Purpose: _____
  Something you bought: _____
  Purpose: _____
  A means of transportation you took: _____
  Purpose: _____
  A time of the day you turned on the TV: _____
  Purpose: _____
  A person you called: _____
  Purpose: _____
- Have students write notes about the sentences on the board and then use the information to write sentences with infinitives of purpose.

Exercise 3: Affirmative Statements
- Go over the example with the class.
- Have students decide which words from the box go with each picture. Then have students complete the exercise individually.
- Have students compare answers in pairs. Then call on students to read the sentences.

Exercise 4: Infinitive after Adjectives
- Go over the example with the class. Then have students read all the responses quickly for meaning.

- Have students complete the exercise in pairs. Then call on students to read the sentences.
- ⏲ For further practice, write the following questions on the board and have students use them as a guide to talk about their phones in small groups:
  Is your cell phone or smart phone difficult to use?
  Is it easy to carry around?
  Is the screen big enough to read messages or watch videos?
  Is it necessary for a phone to have a lot of different functions?
  Are you ready to spend money on a new multipurpose phone?

Exercise 5: Infinitive after Adjectives and Adverbs
- Go over the example with the class.
- Have students do the exercise individually. Then have students compare answers in pairs.
- ⏲ Have pairs role-play the conversations.

Exercise 6: Editing
- Have students read the online bulletin board quickly for meaning. Then ask: "What did each person use his/her smart phone for?" *(Jason: to take a picture of a car after a traffic accident and then call police; Emilia: to make a video of a concert and send it to a friend; Andrea: to send photos of houses to her customers; Kim: to search online for a recipe, convert grams to ounces, create a shopping list, remind her when to take the food out of the oven, and listen to songs)*
- Go over the example with the class.
- Have students find and correct the mistakes individually. Then call on students to explain why the incorrect structures are wrong.
- ⏲ Have students point out examples of correct usages of the infinitive of purpose and infinitives after adjectives.

Go to **www.myfocusongrammarlab.com** for additional grammar practice.

Step 4: Communication Practice
(pages 352–355)

See the general suggestions for Communication Practice on page 5.

Exercise 7: Listening

A
- Have students read the statements.
- Play the audio. Have students listen.
- Play the audio again. Have students listen and complete the exercise individually.

B
- Have students read the list of things.
- Play the audio. Have students listen and check the things they remember from the first listening.
- Have students compare answers in pairs. Then go over the answers as a class.

Exercise 8: Pronunciation

A
- Play the audio. Have students read along as they listen to the Pronunciation Note.
- To check comprehension, write the following sentences on the board:
  It's too good to miss.
  She's fast enough to finish.
- Ask: "Which words are stressed in each sentence?" *(good, miss; fast, finish)* Underline them as students say them. Ask: "Are the words *too* and *enough* stressed?" *(no)*

B
- Have students read the statements and anticipate which words they will hear stressed.
- Play the audio. Have students listen and write the stress marks.

C
- Play the audio. Have students listen and repeat. Be sure students stress the correct words.

Exercise 9: Survey
- Go over the example with the class.
- Form small groups and have students share their ideas.
- To go over the answers as a class, ask a question about each sentence:
  1. Are smart phones easy to use?
  2. Is the price low enough for everyone to buy?
  3. What are some important uses of technology?
  4. What do you think about people over age 80?
  5. What are teens responsible enough to do?
  6. What do you think about English—is it easy to learn or understand?
  7. What do you think about the way broadcasters speak?
  8. Does time go by too quickly to do all the things we want to do?

Exercise 10: For or Against

A
- Have students think about their answers to the questions individually.
- Form small groups. Have groups look at the cartoon, consider the questions, and discuss the pros and cons.
- Call on students to share their views with the class.

B
- Have students write a list of the things they will use their new phone for.
- Have students work in pairs to discuss the topic.
- Follow up by having students say the functions they will use and functions they won't use. List the uses on the board and keep a tally of students' answers. As you get feedback, draw checks next to the functions students will use and crosses next to the functions students won't use. Find out what the most popular and least popular functions are.

Exercise 11: Problem Solving

A
- Elicit the names of the objects. Write them on the board.
  1. shell
  2. cork
  3. jar
  4. binder clip
  5. notepad
  6. rubber band
  7. toothbrush
  8. plastic bag
- Go over the example and point out the infinitives of purpose.
- Form small groups. Tell students that they have a time limit of 10 minutes to come up with at least three different purposes for each object. Have students make notes of the purposes, using the infinitive of purpose.

B
- Have groups choose the item they think is the most useful. Have students make notes of the reasons.
- Call on a member from each group to report to the class on their conclusions.

Exercise 12: Discussion

A
- Have students read the ad. Then ask: "What's the ad for?" *(a smart phone)* "What's special about it?" *(It can operate systems in your house.)* "Is it difficult to use?" *(no)*

B

- Have students make notes of smart phone uses they can think of. Encourage them to be creative and write four to five uses.
- Form small groups. Have groups discuss the topic.
- Call on students to share their ideas with the class. Write some of the uses on the board.

Exercise 13: Writing

A

- Write the following questions on the board to help elicit vocabulary and generate ideas:
  Where were you?
  When was that?
  Who were you with?
  What were you doing?
  What did you use your phone (or another device) for?
  Why was your phone (or the other device) helpful?
- Have students make notes for each question and then use them as a guide as they write.

B

- Have students correct their work using the Editing Checklist.

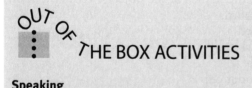
OUT OF THE BOX ACTIVITIES

Speaking

- Write the following pairs of low technology/ high technology items on the board:
  paper dictionary vs. online dictionary
  paper mail vs. email
  bicycle vs. car
  pen and paper vs. calculator
  paper newspaper vs. online news
  personal diary vs. PDA
- Form small groups. Have students in each group discuss what they use each item for.
- Then have students discuss their responses as a class.

Reading and Speaking

- Do a search on antiques and print out pictures of old objects whose uses students can guess at and discuss. They can be objects we no longer use, such as a warming pan (a copper pan that was used in the past to make beds warm), or objects we still use but look different from the ones we use today, for example, a flexible spice container in the shape of a fish. Divide the students into groups, hand out the pictures, and have students discuss what they think the objects were used for in the past. Encourage the use of the infinitive of purpose.
- Have groups exchange pictures to discuss more objects.
- Follow up by having students share with the class what they think each object is and its possible uses. If students didn't guess correctly, provide the correct answer.

Go to **www.myfocusongrammarlab.com** for additional listening, pronunciation, speaking, and writing practice.

Note:
- See the *Focus on Grammar Workbook* for additional in-class or homework grammar practice.

Unit 25 Review (page 356)

Have students complete the Review and check their answers on Student Book page UR-6. Review or assign additional material as needed.

Go to **www.myfocusongrammarlab.com** for the Unit Achievement Test.

Grammar: GERUNDS AND INFINITIVES

Unit 26 focuses on different uses of gerunds and infinitives. Some parts of this unit will be review for your students.

- Some verbs are followed by a gerund.
- Some verbs are followed by an infinitive.
- Some verbs can be followed by either a gerund or an infinitive, and the meaning is the same.
- Some verbs can be followed by either a gerund or an infinitive, but the meanings are different.
- To make general statements, you can use the gerund as subject or *it* + infinitive.

Theme: PROCRASTINATION

Unit 26 focuses on language used to talk about procrastination and ways to prevent it. Formats include a magazine article, a quiz, tips from a website, and a conversation from a procrastinators' support group meeting.

Step 1: Grammar in Context (pages 357–358)

See the general suggestions for Grammar in Context on page 1.

Before You Read

- Have students look at the cartoon, read the title of the article, and discuss the questions in pairs.
- For question 1, write on the board:
  If someone procrastinates, he/she . . .
- Have students complete the sentence with their own ideas. (Example: *doesn't do what he/she has to do; puts off doing what he/she has to do; decides to do things later; does not finish difficult tasks*)
- Call on pairs to share their answers to the questions with the class. As you get feedback from students, write two lists on the board:
  Things people put off   Reasons for putting
                           things off

Read

- To encourage students to read with a purpose, write these questions on the board:
  1. What two examples of procrastination does the article give? (*a woman who puts off studying at the library and a man who puts off making an appointment with the dentist*)
  2. Why do people procrastinate—to have good feelings or to avoid bad feelings? (*to avoid bad feelings*)

3. Does procrastination make people feel better? (*no, they end up feeling even worse*)
- Have students read the text. (OR: Play the audio and have students follow along in their books.) Then call on students to share their answers to the questions on the board.
- To get students to share their ideas on the reading, form pairs or small groups. Have them discuss one or both of the following questions:
  1. The article gives some reasons people procrastinate. Do you agree? Can you think of any others?
  2. Share with your partners methods/ideas you have tried to overcome procrastination. Were they effective? Give concrete examples of your experiences.

After You Read

A. Vocabulary

- Have students complete the exercise individually. Encourage them to use context clues to help.
- Have students compare answers in pairs. Then call on pairs to give answers.
- ⏱ To reinforce the vocabulary, write the following sentence halves on the board. Have students match them. (Answers: *1. f, 2. d, 3. a, 4. e, 5. c, 6. b*)

1. If you are anxious about something,	a. you have to do research and write conclusions.
2. If something is discouraging,	b. a lot of people have it.
3. If you have to work on a project,	c. you will probably procrastinate because you don't like it.
4. If you put things off,	d. you feel that it is useless to try to do it.
5. If you have to do an unpleasant task,	e. you decide to do them later.
6. If a problem is universal,	f. you are worried because you think something bad might happen.

B. Comprehension

- Have students complete the exercise individually.
- Have students compare answers in pairs. Then call on pairs to give answers.

Go to **www.myfocusongrammarlab.com** for an additional reading, and for reading and vocabulary practice.

Step 2: Grammar Presentation (pages 358–360)

See the general suggestions for Grammar Presentation on page 2.

Grammar Charts

- To review verbs followed by gerunds and verbs followed by infinitives, write on the board:

  She put off studying.

  She decided not to study.

  — Have students study the examples. Then ask: "What is *put off* followed by?" (*a gerund*) "What is *decided* followed by?" (*an infinitive*)

  — Point out that some verbs such as *put off* must be followed by gerunds and other verbs such as *decide* must be followed by infinitives.

- To explain verbs followed by gerunds or infinitives, write on the board:

  They prefer going to the park.

  They prefer to go to the park.

  — Ask: "What is *prefer* followed by in the first example?" (*a gerund:* going) "What is *prefer* followed by in the second example?" (*an infinitive:* to go)

  — Point out that a few verbs such as *prefer* can be followed by either a gerund or an infinitive with no change in meaning.

- To explain verbs followed by gerunds or infinitives with a change in meaning, write on the board:

  Brad has stopped studying.

  Tom was watching TV, but he has stopped to study.

  — Ask: "What is *stopped* followed by in the first example?" (*a gerund:* studying) "What is *stopped* followed by in the second example?" (*an infinitive:* to study)

  — Point out that a few verbs such as *stop* can be followed by either a gerund or an infinitive, but the meaning is different.

  — Say: "*Brad stopped studying* means that he is not studying anymore. *Tom stopped to study* means that he is now studying. Tom stopped another activity—watching TV—in order to study."

- To review gerunds as subjects and infinitives after adjectives and prepositions, write on the board:

  Getting started is not easy.

  It's not easy to get started.

  Tom is worried about not passing.

  — Have students name the gerunds (*getting, not passing*) and the infinitive (*to get*) in the examples.

- Remind students that gerunds can be used as subjects, that infinitives can be used after adjectives, and that prepositions such as *about* are followed by gerunds.

Grammar Notes

Notes 1 and 2

(Notes 1 and 2 are review for students.)

- To review verbs followed by a gerund, an infinitive, and an object + an infinitive, write on the board:

  Todd avoided _____ an appointment with the dentist. (make)

  He decided _____ one or two weeks. (wait)

  He promised his wife _____ to the dentist before the end of the month. (go)

  He failed _____ the appointment and _____ his promise. (make, keep)

- Have students complete the sentences with a gerund or infinitive, as appropriate. (*making, to wait, to go, to make, keep*) If necessary, remind students that we do not repeat *to* when there is more than one infinitive.

- If needed, refer students to Appendix 13 on page A-7 for a list of verbs followed by a gerund.

- If needed, refer students to Appendix 14 on page A-7 for a list of verbs followed by an infinitive.

- Refer students to Unit 23 for more information on gerunds as objects.

- Refer students to Unit 24 for more information on infinitives after certain verbs.

Note 3

- To review verbs followed by a gerund or an infinitive with no change in meaning, write on the board:

  Eva hates to go to the library.

  She prefers to go to the park.

  Rod began writing his paper.

  He likes writing papers.

  Sheila loves reading.

  Her teacher encouraged her to continue working hard.

- Have students restate the statements on the board using gerunds or infinitives, as appropriate. Go over the answers as a class. (*Eva hates going to the library. She prefers going to the park. Rod began to write his paper. He likes to write papers. Sheila loves to read. Her teacher encouraged her to continue to work hard.*)

- If needed, refer students to Appendix 15 on page A-7 for a list of verbs followed by a gerund or an infinitive.

Note 4

- Draw attention to the *Be Careful!* note. Then to review verbs followed by a gerund or an infinitive with a change in meaning, write on the board:
  a. Michael <u>stopped talking</u> on the phone.
  b. Michael <u>stopped to talk</u> on the phone.
  1. Michael was studying, but now he's talking on the phone.
  2. Michael was talking on the phone, but now he's studying.
- Have students match the sentences (a, b) with the correct explanation. (a. 2, b. 1)

Note 5

- To review gerunds after prepositions and explain gerunds after phrasal verbs, write on the board:
  He's worried about not passing his exam.
  He put off studying until the last day.
- Direct attention to the first example and ask: "What kind of word follows the preposition *about*?" (*a gerund:* not passing)
- Direct attention to the second example. Underline *put off*. Explain that it is a phrasal verb: a verb + a particle that changes the meaning of the verb.
- Ask: "What kind of word follows the phrasal verb *put off*?" (*a gerund:* studying)
- Refer students to Unit 23 for more information on gerunds after prepositions.

Note 6

- To explain how to make general statements, write on the board:
  Having too little time for a task is discouraging.
  It is discouraging to have too little time for a task.
- Ask: "Which example uses a gerund to make a general statement?" (*the first*) "Which is the gerund?" (*having*) "What does the second example use to make a general statement?" (it + *infinitive*) "Which is the infinitive?" (*to have*)
- Make sure students understand that both sentences have the same meaning.

🕐 **Identify the Grammar:** Have students identify the grammar in the opening reading on page 357. For example:
  Eva doesn't **feel like spending** it at the library.
  . . . he **decided to wait** another week . . .
  Procrastinating . . . is a universal problem.
  Most people **prefer to do** enjoyable things.

Go to **www.myfocusongrammarlab.com** for grammar charts and notes.

Step 3: Focused Practice (pages 360–364)

See the general suggestions for Focused Practice on page 4.

Exercise 1: Discover the Grammar

A
- Go over the example with the class.
- Have students complete the exercise individually.
- Have students compare answers in pairs. Then go over the answers as a class.

B
- Go over the example with the class.
- Have students complete the exercise in pairs. Have them identify information in the text that supports their answers.
- Call on pairs to give answers and explain their choices.

Exercise 2: Gerund or Infinitive

- Go over the example with the class. Explain that in some cases either answer choice can be correct.
- Have students complete the exercise individually. Then go over the answers as a class.
- Have students take the quiz.

Exercise 3: Gerund or Infinitive

- Go over the example with the class. Then have students read the tips quickly for meaning.
- Have students complete the exercise individually. Then go over the answers as a class.
- 🕐 For further practice, have students play a memory game. Have them go over the tips and then close their books and write the ones they remember. Remind them that there are six tips in the exercise. To review, have pairs open their books and check the tips they wrote.

Exercise 4: General Statements: Gerund and Infinitive

- Go over the example with the class.
- Have students complete the exercise in pairs. Then call on pairs to read the conversations.
- 🕐 To extend the activity, have pairs take turns saying their own sentences using a gerund as subject and agreeing by repeating the same idea using *it* + infinitive, as shown in the activity.

Exercise 5: Gerund or Infinitive

- Go over the example with the class.
- Have students complete the exercise individually.
- Have students compare answers in pairs. Then go over the answers as a class.

Exercise 6: Editing

- Have students read the blog entry quickly for meaning. Then ask: "Where did Eva finally decide to go?" (to a support group for procrastinators) "What did she expect people to be like?" (She expected them to be boring.) "What were they actually like?" (They were quite interesting.) "Did she learn anything at the first meeting?" (yes, that she should stop making excuses and start her work)
- Go over the example with the class.
- Have students find and correct the mistakes individually. Then call on students to explain why the incorrect structures are wrong.
- ⏱ Have students point out examples of correct usages of the gerund and infinitive.

Go to **www.myfocusongrammarlab.com** for additional grammar practice.

Step 4: Communication Practice

(pages 365–370)

See the general suggestions for Communication Practice on page 5.

Exercise 7: Listening

A

- Have students read the sentences quickly for meaning.
- Play the audio. Have students listen.
- Play the audio again. Have students listen and complete the exercise individually. If necessary, stop the audio to allow students time to correct the false statements.

B

- Have students read the activities quickly for meaning. Have students check the answers they remember from their first listening.
- Play the audio. Have students listen and complete the exercise individually.
- ⏱ Have students share their study habits with the class. Ask: "Which things from the list don't you do? Why don't you do them? Which things from the list do you do? What else can you do to get better results?"

Exercise 8: Pronunciation

A

- Play the audio. Have students read along as they listen to the Pronunciation Note.
- Point out that the schwa is used in words (or syllables) that are not stressed. In the examples, the stress is placed on the verb that follows the preposition or the *to* in the infinitive.

B

- Play the audio. Have students listen.

C

- Play the audio.
- Have students practice the conversations with a partner. Be sure students play both roles.

Exercise 9: Brainstorming

A

- Go over the examples with the class.
- Have students brainstorm in small groups. Encourage them to use the beginnings from the examples.

B

- Have students share their ideas with the class. Make a list on the board.
- ⏱ Have students write a short paragraph about the kind of breaks they enjoy and the new ideas they would like to try.

Exercise 10: Information Gap: At the Support Group

- Go over the example questions.
- Have students complete the exercise in pairs. Have students decide if each verb is followed by a gerund or an infinitive (or either of them) to frame the questions correctly. Have students choose between: *What did [person] [verb] to do?* and *What did [person] [verb] doing?* as appropriate.
- Follow up with a brief discussion. Have students discuss whether they would like to join a support group. Ask: "Do you like sharing your problems? Do you like sharing ideas about how to solve problems? Do you think that joining a support group can help you solve problems? Why or why not?"

Exercise 11: Quotable Quotes

Note: Students learned to use *advise* followed by an object and an infinitive. In the example, *advise* is followed by a gerund. If necessary, point out that *advise* is followed by an infinitive if it has an object. It is normally followed by a gerund if it has no object.

• Have students complete the exercise in pairs.
• Discuss the meaning of each quote as a class. Encourage students to say why they agree/disagree with them.
• Take a poll to find out which quote is the favorite.

Exercise 12: Problem Solving

A

• Go over the example with the class.
• Form small groups. Have students write a sentence with each of the words in the box.
• Have students use their sentences to guide their group discussion.

B

• Call on students to share their ideas about stopping clutter. Write the ideas on the board.
• ⏱ Follow up by having students say if clutter is a problem for them (or someone they know) and what they try to do (or the person tries to do) about it.

Exercise 13: Writing

A

• Brainstorm with the class some goals to prevent procrastination as a class. Write them on the board.
• Have students complete the exercise individually.

B

• Write the following questions on the board to help elicit vocabulary and generate ideas:
  What will you stop doing to be able to accomplish it?
  What difficult things won't you put off/delay doing?
  What won't you fail to do?
  How long do you promise to spend on the task each day/week?
  What other things do you plan to do in order to achieve your goal?
• Have students make notes for each question and then use them as a guide as they write.

C

• Have students correct their work using the Editing Checklist.

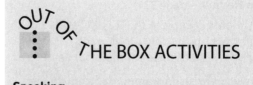

OUT OF THE BOX ACTIVITIES

Speaking

• Form small groups and have students discuss these questions:
  — What do you expect to do this weekend?
  — What do you look forward to doing?
  — What do you need to do?
  — What do you feel like doing?
• Follow up by having students tell the class about their upcoming weekend.

Listening and Speaking

• Bring in a self-help audio recording about how to get organized or stop procrastinating, for example "Getting Organized" by Stephanie Winston; "Doing It Now: How to Cure Procrastination and Achieve Your Goals in 12 Easy Steps" by Edwin Bliss; or "Goals: Setting and Achieving Them on Schedule" by Zig Ziglar. Have students listen to an excerpt and take notes about main ideas.
• To review the tips, read the items below one by one and have different students say ideas about each; for example, *Stephanie Winston said you should remember to set priorities.*
  — What you should remember to do
  — What you should choose to do first
  — What you should stop doing
  — What you should try to do/not to do
  — What you should plan to do
  — What you shouldn't put off doing
  — What you shouldn't forget to do

Note: If you don't have access to self-help CDs in English, conduct an Internet search for tips to stop procrastinating.

Go to **www.myfocusongrammarlab.com** for additional listening, pronunciation, speaking, and writing practice.

Note:
• See the *Focus on Grammar Workbook* for additional in-class or homework grammar practice.

Unit 26 Review (page 371)

Have students complete the Review and check their answers on Student Book page UR-7. Review or assign additional material as needed.

Go to **www.myfocusongrammarlab.com** for the Unit Achievement Test.

From Grammar to Writing (pages 372–373)

See general suggestions for From Grammar to Writing on page 9.

Go to **www.myfocusongrammarlab.com** for an additional From Grammar to Writing Assignment, Part Review, and Part Post-Test.

UNIT 27 OVERVIEW

Grammar: REFLEXIVE AND RECIPROCAL PRONOUNS

Unit 27 focuses on the meanings and uses of reflexive and reciprocal pronouns.

- Reflexive pronouns (*myself, yourself,* etc.) are used when the subject and object of a sentence refer to the same people or things.
- Reciprocal pronouns *(each other, one another)* are used when the subject and the object of a sentence refer to the same people and these have a two-way relationship.
- Reflexive pronouns can also be used to emphasize a person or thing.

Theme: SELF-TALK

Unit 27 focuses on language used to talk about how positive self-talk can help us solve problems.

Psychologists have been studying the effects of hope and optimism on people's lives. Studies indicate that positive attitudes have pervasive (existing or spreading everywhere) effects on many aspects of life, including physical and emotional health and success on the job. Self-talk, one's dialogue with oneself, is an indicator of whether a person is optimistic or pessimistic.

Step 1: Grammar in Context (pages 376–377)

See the general suggestions for Grammar in Context on page 1.

Before You Read
- As a class, discuss the meaning of self-talk. *(to talk to yourself)*
- Write two column heads on the board: Positive Self-Talk   Negative Self-Talk
- Classify the examples of self-talk in the photos.
- Have pairs think of more examples of positive and negative self-talk. Encourage them to write two or three examples of each type on a sheet of paper.

Read
- To encourage students to read with a purpose, write these questions on the board:
  1. What problem did Tom and Sara have? *(They lost their jobs.)*
  2. Who had a positive reaction to the problem? *(Sara)*
  3. What helped Sara have a positive reaction? *(the way she explained the problem to herself)*

- Have students read the text. (OR: Play the audio and have students follow along in their books.) Then call on students to share their answers to the questions on the board.
- To get students to share their ideas on the reading, form pairs or small groups. Have them discuss one or all of the following questions:
  1. Who do you identify with—Tom or Sara? Give reasons for your choice.
  2. Talk about a problem you had and your reaction to the problem. What kind of self-talk did you use? Was it positive or negative?
  3. Explain your views on self-talk. Do you think it is important? Give examples to support your views.

After You Read

A. Vocabulary
- Have students complete the exercise individually. Encourage them to use context clues to help.
- Have students compare answers in pairs. Then call on pairs to give answers.
- (!) To reinforce the vocabulary, write the following paragraph on the board. Have students complete it with the correct form of the vocabulary words. (Answers: *maintained, realized, fault, impact, reaction, finally*)

When Sara lost her job, she _____ her normal life. She _____ it was not her _____ , and she didn't let the problem _____ how she felt. Her _____ was a very positive one. She tried to find a new job, but she _____ got the same job back.

B. Comprehension
- Have students complete the exercise individually.
- Have students compare answers in pairs. Then call on pairs to give answers.

Go to **www.myfocusongrammarlab.com** for an additional reading, and for reading and vocabulary practice.

Step 2: Grammar Presentation (pages 378–379)
See the general suggestions for Grammar Presentation on page 2.

Grammar Charts
- To explain reflexive pronouns, write on the board:
  I talked to myself.
  — Have students study the example and tell them: "Name the subject of the sentence." *(I)* "Name the reflexive pronoun." *(myself)* Draw an arrow from *myself* to *I*.
  — Erase *I* and *myself*. Replace *I* with a blank line and *myself* with *yourself*.
  — Have students say the complete sentence using the correct subject pronoun. *(You talked to yourself.)*
  — Erase *yourself* and replace it with *himself*.
  — Have students say the complete sentence using the correct subject pronoun. *(He talked to himself.)*
  — Follow the same procedure with the reflexive pronouns *herself, itself, ourselves, yourselves,* and *themselves*.
- To explain reciprocal pronouns, write on the board:
  John and Alice met at the party. They talked to each other.
  — Have students study the example and tell them: "Name the subject of the second sentence." *(They)* "Name the reciprocal pronoun." *(each other)*
  — Draw an arrow from *each other* to *They*.
  — Point out that reciprocal pronouns are used with *plural* subject pronouns *(we, you, they)* because they indicate a reciprocal relationship between *two or more people*. (In the example on the board, John talked to Alice, and Alice talked to John.)

Grammar Notes

Note 1
- To help clarify the use of reflexive pronouns, write two contrasting sentences on the board:
  He felt proud of them.   They felt proud of themselves.
- Ask in which sentence the subject and the object refer to the same people. *(They felt proud of themselves.)* Underline the subject *They* and the reflexive pronoun *themselves*.
- Point out that some verbs often take reflexive pronouns. Have students say the verbs that they remember from the previous activity, and write a list on the board. If needed, refer students to Appendix 3 on page A-2 for a list of such verbs.

- Draw attention to the example *My office light turns itself off*. Point out that *itself* can be used with objects to express that objects do something automatically. Tell students that many people will just say "My office light turns off automatically."

Note 2
- To explain reflexive pronouns in imperative sentences, write on the board:
  "Be yourself," Megan   "Be yourselves,"
  said.   Steven said.
- Ask: "How many people did Megan address?" *(one)* "How do you know?" *(because she used a singular reflexive pronoun:* yourself*)* "How many people did Steven address?" *(two or more than two)* "How do you know?" *(because he used a plural reflexive pronoun:* yourselves*)* "Why are *yourself* and *yourselves* the correct reflexive pronouns in imperative sentences?" *(because, although we don't say it, the subject of imperative sentences is always "you")*

Note 3
- To explain how reflexive pronouns can emphasize nouns, write on the board:
  The manager offered   The manager himself
  me a job.   offered me a job.
  I myself made the   I made the cake.
  cake.
- Ask: "In which sentence is the speaker surprised that the manager—and not another person in the company—would have offered him/her a job?" *(in the second)* "How do you know?" *(because he/she used the reflexive pronoun* himself*)* "In which sentence is the speaker particularly proud of having made the cake?" *(in the first)* "How do you know?" *(because he/she used the reflexive pronoun* myself*)*

Note 4
- To explain *by* + reflexive pronoun and *be* + reflexive pronoun, write on the board:
  He's going on vacation <u>by himself</u>
  She decided to <u>be herself</u>.
- Have pairs discuss the meaning of the underlined phrases. Go over the answers as a class. *(He's going on vacation alone. She is going to act in the usual way.)*
- To provide practice of *be* + reflexive pronoun, have students talk about situations in which it is advisable to be yourself. *(Example: It's important to be yourself at a job interview. You should be yourself when you meet someone new.)*

Note 5
- To explain reciprocal pronouns, point to a student and to yourself and say: "We met each other (three months ago)." Write it on the board:
  We met <u>each other</u> three months ago.
- Explain that in this example, *we* refers to (name of the student you pointed to) and you.
- Write next to the example on the board:
  We = (student's name) + I
- Point to the entire class and to yourself and say, "We met one another (three months ago)." Write it on the board:
  We met <u>one another</u> three months ago.
- Explain that in this example, *we* refers to all the students in the class and yourself.
- Write next to the example on the board:
  We = all the students + I
- Point out that some people also use *each other* for more than two people and *one another* for just two people.
- Draw attention to the *Be Careful!* note. To explain the difference between reflexive and reciprocal pronouns, write two contrastive sentences on the board:
  Diana and Ben take   Diana and Ben take
  care of <u>themselves</u>.   care of <u>each other</u>.
- Point out that the second sentence expresses a reciprocal relationship.
- To explain possessive forms of reciprocal pronouns, write on the board:
  Ben and Sue corrected each other's work.
- Say: "Ben corrected Sue's work, and Sue corrected Ben's work."

🕐 **Identify the Grammar:** Have students identify the grammar in the opening reading on page 376. For example:
  . . . we explain a problem to **ourselves**.
  . . . kept **herself** fit.
  Tom . . . spent all of his time at home by **himself** . . .
  Why were their reactions so very different from **one another**?

Go to **www.myfocusongrammarlab.com** for grammar charts and notes.

Step 3: Focused Practice (pages 380–384)
See the general suggestions for Focused Practice on page 4.

Exercise 1: Discover the Grammar
- Go over the example with the class.
- Have students complete the exercise individually.
- Have students compare answers in pairs. Then go over the answers as a class.

Exercise 2: Reflexive or Reciprocal Pronouns

- Have students read the conversations quickly for meaning and decide which person/people the reflexive or reciprocal pronoun refers to.
- Go over the example with the class. Then ask: "Why is *yourselves* the correct answer?" *(because it is part of an imperative sentence)*
- Have students complete the exercise in pairs. Then call on pairs to read the conversations aloud.

Exercise 3: Reflexive or Reciprocal Pronouns

- Go over the example with the class. Then have students read the interview quickly for meaning.
- Have students complete the exercise individually. Then call on two students to read the interview aloud.
- ⏱ For further practice, personalize the information in the exercise. Write the following questions on the board and have students use them as a guide to talk about their experiences at school or at work. Review by having students share their experiences with the class.
  At school/work . . .
  1. Do you keep yourself busy?
  2. Do you and your classmates interfere with one another's work?
  3. Do you learn things by yourself?
  4. What do you pride yourself on?
  5. Is there anything you have to satisfy yourself with because you can't do/have what you want?

Exercise 4: Verbs with Reflexive or Reciprocal Pronouns

- Go over the example with the class.
- Have students decide which verb goes with each picture.
- Have students complete the exercise individually. Then go over the answers as a class.

Exercise 5: Editing

- Have students read the diary quickly for meaning. Then ask: "What problem did the woman have?" *(She forgot to call a friend on his birthday.)* "How did she feel at first?" *(terrible, she was very hard on herself)* "What did her friend forget two weeks before?" *(a dinner date)* "What happened in the end?" *(They forgave each other for their mistakes.)*
- Go over the example with the class.
- Have students find and correct the mistakes individually. Then go over the answers as a class, having students explain why the incorrect structures are wrong.

- ⏱ Have students point out examples of correct usages of reflexive and reciprocal pronouns.

Go to **www.myfocusongrammarlab.com** for additional grammar practice.

Step 4: Communication Practice

(pages 384–389)

See the general suggestions for Communication Practice on page 5.

Exercise 6: Listening

A
- Go over the example with the class. Point out that both pronouns are possible in each context and that students must listen carefully to distinguish the correct pronoun.
- Have students read the sentences.
- Play the audio. Have students listen and complete the exercise individually.

B
- Play the audio. Have students listen and complete the exercise individually. If necessary, stop after each conversation to allow students time to choose their answers.
- Have students compare answers in pairs. Then call on pairs to give answers.

Exercise 7: Pronunciation

A
- Play the audio. Have students read along as they listen to the Pronunciation Note.
- Point out the pronunciation of *-self* and *-selves*. Write the following pronouns on the board, read them aloud, and have students repeat after you:
  my<u>self</u> /self/
  our<u>selves</u> /selvz/

B
- Have students read the statements and anticipate the parts of the pronouns that they will hear stressed.
- Play the audio. Have students listen and write dots where indicated.

C
- Play the audio. Have students listen and repeat. Be sure students stress the correct parts of words.

Exercise 8: Questionnaire

A
- Have students complete the questionnaire, work out their score, and write notes about why they agree/don't agree with their result.

B

- Have students complete the exercise with a partner. Have them say why they would/ wouldn't like to change the way they see some bad situations. As students interview their partners, have them write notes about their partners' answers.

C

- Have students reread the test and underline the verbs or expressions that are used reflexively. Encourage students to use these verbs and expressions as they report to the class.
- Have students interview five classmates and then report the results to another group.

Exercise 9: Game: Who Remembers More?

A

- Have students look at the picture. Encourage them to use the verbs in the labels to help describe the picture silently to themselves. This will help them to remember what the people are doing.
- Have students shut their books and complete the exercise in pairs.

B

- Have students open their books and check their answers in pairs.
- Call on students to read a sentence aloud. As students read the sentences, write them on the board, making any necessary corrections.

Exercise 10: Picture Discussion

- Have students write some self-talk for most of the people at the party. Point out that even if a person is talking to another person, he/she can still be saying something to himself/herself.
- Have students complete the exercise in pairs.
- Go over the answers as a class by calling out each person—for example, "the man at the mirror"— and having various students say what he could be saying to himself. Write students' ideas on the board.

Exercise 11: Problem Solving

A

- Have students read over the situations individually and think about what they would tell themselves in each of the situations. Have them write a few notes for each.

- Point out the reflexive pronouns in the example and encourage students to use as many reflexive pronouns as they can in their conversations. Elicit verbs that can be used with reflexive pronouns and will be useful for students while doing this activity. Write the following list on the board. If necessary, explain the meaning of *push yourself* (work hard).
  tell yourself
  talk to yourself
  prepare yourself well
  believe in yourself
  (don't) blame yourself
  imagine yourself
  push yourself
  remind yourself
  see yourself
- Have students complete the exercise in small groups.

B

- Call on students to report on what their classmates said about the different situations. As students speak, check the use of reflexive pronouns and make a class list on the board of the best self-talk for each situation.

Exercise 12: Writing

A

- Write the following questions on the board to help elicit vocabulary and generate ideas:
  What do you tell yourself when you have problems at school/work?
  How does it help?
  What do you tell yourself when you have problems with a boyfriend or girlfriend?
  How does it help?
- Have students make notes for each question and then use them as a guide as they write.
- To help students with the language they will need, have them go back to Exercises 3 and 4 and underline useful phrases they can use when writing their advice column. Remind them that they can also use some of the phrases listed in Part A.

B

- Have students correct their work using the Editing Checklist.

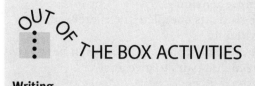

OUT OF THE BOX ACTIVITIES

Writing

- Have pairs write three simple stories (15 to 35 words) combining two or three verbs or expressions used reflexively from Appendix 3 on page A-2. Have students underline the verbs and expressions they use. Encourage students to be creative!
  Examples:
  When Sally was a child, she always <u>behaved herself</u> at school. She was at the top of the class, and she was <u>proud of herself</u>.
  Last week Sam tried to <u>teach himself</u> how to ride a horse. He fell off the horse and <u>hurt himself</u> badly. He <u>blames himself</u> for the accident.
- Have students share their stories with the class.

Reading and Speaking

- Bring in magazine interviews with famous people. Form small groups and give each group one interview.
- Have them find in the interview information about some of the items below, which you can write on the board or enlarge and photocopy.

Find:

— something the person is proud of himself/herself for
— something the person blames himself/herself for
— an occasion when the person pushed himself/herself hard
— an occasion when the person enjoyed himself/herself
— who the person is living/going out with and when/where they met each other
— who the person works with and how they get along with each other/one another

- Ask one student from each group to use reflexive and reciprocal pronouns to describe the person they read about. Challenge students to say only sentences that contain reflexive or reciprocal pronouns. *(Example: Steven Spielberg prides himself on making great movies. Spielberg and his wife, Kate Capshaw, met each other on the set of a film over 20 years ago.)*

Go to **www.myfocusongrammarlab.com** for additional listening, pronunciation, speaking, and writing practice.

Note:
- See the *Focus on Grammar Workbook* for additional in-class or homework grammar practice.

Unit 27 Review (page 390)

Have students complete the Review and check their answers on Student Book page UR-7. Review or assign additional material as needed.

Go to **www.myfocusongrammarlab.com** for the Unit Achievement Test.

UNIT 28 OVERVIEW

Grammar: PHRASAL VERBS

Unit 28 focuses on the meanings of phrasal verbs.

- Phrasal verbs consist of a verb and a particle, which often changes the meaning of the verb.
- Many phrasal verbs have the same meaning as one-word verbs. Phrasal verbs are informal and more commonly used in everyday speech.
- Phrasal verbs can be transitive or intransitive. Many transitive phrasal verbs are separable.

Theme: ANIMAL INTELLIGENCE

Unit 28 focuses on language used to talk about animals and their intelligence. Topics include Cesar Millan (the dog whisperer) and service dogs.

Step 1: Grammar in Context (pages 391–392)

See the general suggestions for Grammar in Context on page 1.

Before You Read

- Write the word *whisper* on the board and elicit or explain its meaning. *(to speak or say something very quietly)*
- Have students look at the picture and the title of the article. Then have them answer the questions in pairs, writing notes about their answers to each question.

- Call on pairs to share their answers to the questions with the class. As you get feedback from students, write a list of kinds of pets on the board.

Read

- To encourage students to read with a purpose, write these questions on the board:
  1. What is Millan famous for? *(helping out celebrities and ordinary people who have problems with their pets)*
  2. What does he do on his TV show? *(He goes to people's homes and straightens out their dogs.)*
  3. Does everybody admire him? *(no, some people don't believe in his ideas)*
- Have students read the text. (OR: Play the audio and have students follow along in their books.) Then call on students to share their answers to the questions on the board.
- To get students to share their ideas on the reading, form pairs or small groups. Have them discuss one or both of the following questions:
  1. Do you believe in Millan's talent for training dogs? Do you think change is possible in one hour? Support your answer.
  2. Do you (or someone you know) own a pet? Does the pet sometimes attack other pets, get lazy, or disobey? What do you (or the person you know) do to get the pet to behave? Give examples.

After You Read

A. Vocabulary

- Have students complete the exercise individually. Encourage them to use context clues to help.
- Have students compare answers in pairs. Then call on pairs to give answers.
- (🕐) To reinforce the vocabulary, write the following sentence halves on the board and have students match them. Go over the answers as a class. (Answers: *1. f, 2. d, 3. c, 4. a, 5. b, 6. e)*
  1. You can figure out
  2. You can straighten out
  3. You can keep on
  4. You can turn on
  5. You may give up
  6. If you take over something

  a. a computer.
  b. if you lose hope.
  c. doing something.
  d. someone who behaves badly.
  e. you take control of it.
  f. a problem.

B. Comprehension

- Have students complete the exercise individually.
- Have students compare answers in pairs. Then call on pairs to give answers.

Go to **www.myfocusongrammarlab.com** for an additional reading, and for reading and vocabulary practice.

Step 2: Grammar Presentation (pages 393–394)

See the general suggestions for Grammar Presentation on page 2.

Grammar Charts

- To explain phrasal verbs, write on the board:

Verbs	Phrasal Verb
He <u>turned</u> his head.	He <u>turned on</u> the TV.
	He <u>turned off</u> his computer.

  — Have students look at the underlined phrasal verbs. Then ask: "How many words are necessary to form a phrasal verb?" *(two)*
  — Point out that the two words are a verb and a particle. Write on the board: phrasal verb = verb + particle
  — Have students identify the verbs in the examples on the board. *(turned)*
  — Have students identify the particles. *(on, off)*
  — Point out that phrasal verbs have a meaning of their own, which is different from the meaning of the verb or the particle on its own.
  — To illustrate your point, write on the board:

turn	stop a machine
turn on	change the position
turn off	start a machine

  — Have students match the verb and phrasal verbs with their meanings.
- To explain transitive and intransitive phrasal verbs, write on the board:

Transitive Phrasal Verb	Intransitive Phrasal Verb
He took off his sunglasses.	The plane took off.
He took them off.	

  — Be sure students understand the meanings of *take off* in the examples. As a transitive phrasal verb it means remove; as an intransitive phrasal verb it means leave the ground.

— Draw attention to the examples of a transitive phrasal verb. Point out that a transitive phrasal verb is a phrasal verb that takes a direct object (noun or pronoun). Have students say the objects. *(his sunglasses, them)*

— Point to the example of an intransitive phrasal verb. Ask students why this phrasal verb is intransitive. *(because it doesn't take an object)*

Grammar Notes

Note 1

• To explain the difference between prepositions and particles, write on the board:
His office window looks over the park.
  (= faces)
He looks over the department report every morning. (= reviews)

• Have students study the examples. Then ask: "Which example contains a phrasal verb?" *(the second)* "Is *over* in the first example a particle or a preposition?" *(a preposition)* "What is *over* in the second example?" *(a particle)*

Note 2

• To explain phrasal verbs and their formal equivalents, give two examples in context. Say: "'You should *return* this book on Friday,' the librarian told a student." "'*Give* her *back* her doll,' the mother told her daughter." Write them on the board if necessary.

Note 3

• To review transitive phrasal verbs, write on the board:
He figured out the problem.

• Have students name the phrasal verb. *(figured out)* Ask: "Is it transitive or intransitive?" *(transitive)* "Why?" *(because it has an object: the problem)*

• Draw attention to the *Be Careful!* note. To explain separable transitive phrasal verbs, write on the board:
Separable transitive phrasal verbs
The object is a ——→ verb + particle + object
  noun: ——→ verb + object + particle

The object is a ——→ verb + object + particle
  pronoun:

• Make the following points:
— The summary on the board covers *separable* transitive phrasal verbs. (Point to the title.)
— When the object is a noun, it has two possible positions. (Read the section about nouns aloud.)

— When the object is a pronoun, it has only one position. (Read the section about pronouns aloud.)

• To review intransitive phrasal verbs, write on the board:
My dog wakes up at 9:00.
He sits down next to my bed.

• Have students name the phrasal verbs in the examples. *(wakes up, sits down)* Ask: "Are they transitive or intransitive?" *(intransitive)* "Why?" *(because they don't have an object)*

• Point out that intransitive verbs are always inseparable.

Identify the Grammar: Have students identify the grammar in the opening reading on page 391. For example:
. . . your dog **takes over** the dog park . . .
. . . pet owners are ready to **give up** . . .
He usually goes into their homes to **figure out** the problem.
His training **turns** their lives **around**.

Go to **www.myfocusongrammarlab.com** for grammar charts and notes.

Step 3: Focused Practice (pages 394–398)

See the general suggestions for Focused Practice on page 4.

Exercise 1: Discover the Grammar

A

• Go over the example with the class. Remind students that objects can appear between the verb and the particle or immediately after the phrasal verb.

• Have students complete the exercise individually.

• Have students compare answers in pairs. Then call on pairs to give answers.

B

• Go over the example with the class.

• Have students complete the exercise individually. Have students refer back to the text if necessary.

• Call on students to read the text aloud, replacing the underlined words with the phrasal verbs.

Exercise 2: Particles

• Go over the example with the class.

• Have students complete the exercise in pairs. Then call on a pair to read the conversation aloud.

- (⏱) For further practice, ask questions about the conversation. Have students give full answers using phrasal verbs. Ask: "Where does Vicky sit down?" *(She sits down next to Mitzi.)* "What has Mitzi taken over?" *(She's taken over the couch.)* "Does Mitzi always get along with other dogs?" *(No, she sometimes doesn't get along with them.)* "Does Carla walk Mitzi when she gets up in the morning and when she gets back from work?" *(She always walks her when she gets up in the morning, but she doesn't always walk her when she gets back from work.)* "What does Vicky think will happen at the picnic tomorrow?" *(Mitzi will probably fit in very well.)*

Exercise 3: Transitive Phrasal Verbs and Pronouns

- Go over the example with the class. Ask: "What does *it* replace?" *(picnic)* Remind students that pronouns go between the verb and the particle.
- Have students complete the exercise in pairs.
- Call on pairs to read the conversations aloud.

Exercise 4: Transitive and Intransitive Phrasal Verbs: Word Order

- Go over the example with the class. Remind students that objects that are nouns can go after the phrasal verb or between the verb and the particle.
- Have students complete the exercise individually.
- Have students compare answers in pairs. Go over the answers as a class.

Exercise 5: Meaning of Phrasal Verbs

- Go over the meanings of the phrasal verbs in the box. If needed, refer students to Appendix 4 on page A-3 and Appendix 5 on page A-4.
- Have students complete the exercise individually. Then go over the answers as a class.
- (⏱) To extend the activity, have students cover the text and look at the phrasal verbs in the box. In pairs, have students take turns using the phrasal verbs in sentences about the text. Have students write as many sentences as possible. Call on pairs to read their sentences aloud.

Exercise 6: Editing

- Have students read the website entry quickly for meaning. Then ask: "Why did the person choose Barnie as a service dog?" *(because he sat down next to him as soon as he saw him)* "What intelligent things does Barnie do?" *(picks up his owner's keys, wakes up before his owner, knows his owner's schedule, opens his owner's school bag, takes out things from his owner's bag)*
- Go over the example with the class.
- Have students find and correct the mistakes individually. Then call on students to explain why the incorrect structures are wrong.
- (⏱) Have students point out examples of correct usages of reflexive and reciprocal pronouns.

Go to **www.myfocusongrammarlab.com** for additional grammar practice.

Step 4: Communication Practice

(pages 399–401)

See the general suggestions for Communication Practice on page 5.

Exercise 7: Listening

A
- Have students read the conversations quickly for meaning.
- Go over the example with the class. Point out that both phrasal verbs are possible in each context and that students must listen carefully to distinguish the correct verb.
- Play the audio. Have students listen and complete the exercise individually.

B
- Play the audio. Have students listen and complete the exercise individually.
- Have students compare answers in pairs. Then call on pairs to give answers.
- (⏱) Have students interpret the meaning of the phrasal verbs they didn't select in Part A. If necessary, refer students to Appendices 4 and 5 on pages A-3 and A-4, or have them use a dictionary.

Exercise 8: Pronunciation

A
- Play the audio. Have students read along as they listen to the Pronunciation Note.
- To check comprehension, write on the board:
  1. Put your jacket on.
  2. Put it on.

- Ask: "In the first example, which words are stressed?" *(put, jacket, on)* "Do all the words receive the same stress?" *(yes)* "In the second example, which words are stressed?" *(put, on)* "Do both words receive the same stress?" *(no, the particle* on *receives stronger stress)*

B
- Have students read the statements and anticipate the words that they will hear stressed.
- Play the audio. Have students listen and write dots to show stress as appropriate.

C
- Play the audio. Have students listen and repeat the responses.
- Have students practice the conversations with a partner. Be sure students play both roles.

Exercise 9: Making Plans
- Draw on students' prior experience by asking them if they ever went on a field trip and have them briefly describe their experience.
- Go over the example with the class.
- Form small groups. Have students complete the discussion in groups. If necessary, refer students to Appendices 4 and 5 on pages A-3 and A-4 for help. Then call on students to share their lists with the class.

Exercise 10: For or Against
- As a class, use the phrasal verbs in the box and brainstorm sentences about pets. (Example: *A pet can cheer you up. A pet can wake you up in the morning. It's nice to see a pet playing around. Some pets don't want to get off the couch.*)
- Form small groups. Have students complete the exercise in groups. Have them make notes of reasons for and against owning a pet. Encourage students to come to a conclusion. Do the advantages outweigh the disadvantages, or vice versa?
- Call on students to share their views with the class.

Exercise 11: Writing

A
- Write the following questions on the board to help elicit vocabulary and generate ideas:
  Does the animal get up early in the morning?
  Does it play around?
  Does it cheer people/its owner up?
  Does it pick up things from the floor?
  Does it take out things from bags?
  Does it get along with people/other animals?
  Does it help its owner out?
  Does it calm its owner down?

Does it clean up its own mess?
Can it turn on a machine or device?
Has it taken over a bed/couch?
What does it do when its owner goes away on vacation?
Has it turned the owner's life around?
- Have students make notes for each question and then use them as a guide as they write.

B
- Have students correct their work using the Editing Checklist.

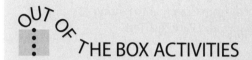

OUT OF THE BOX ACTIVITIES

Writing and Speaking
- Have each student use a phrasal verb from Appendix 4 or Appendix 5 to write one sentence.
- Have each student copy the corrected sentence onto slips of paper, separating the phrasal verb between the verb and its particle, for example:

| The students took | off their lab coats. |

- Have students put their two slips in a pile. Shuffle the pile and redistribute the slips of paper. Then have students circulate around the room, looking for the matching half of their sentence. Be sure students don't read each other's sentences but rather speak and listen to each other.

Reading
- Bring in any kind of authentic material—brochures, instruction manuals, handbooks, Internet printouts, magazines, novels, short stories, and so on. Form small groups and hand out the material.
- Have students scan the texts for phrasal verbs. Have them choose five phrasal verbs, write down the sentences they appear in, and figure out their meaning.
- Have students use a dictionary and/or Appendices 4 and 5 on pages A-3 and A-4 to check their guesses.

Go to **www.myfocusongrammarlab.com** for additional listening, pronunciation, speaking, and writing practice.

Note:
- See the *Focus on Grammar Workbook* for additional in-class or homework grammar practice.

Unit 28 Review (page 402)

Have students complete the Review and check their answers on Student Book page UR-7. Review or assign additional material as needed.

Go to **www.myfocusongrammarlab.com** for the Unit Achievement Test.

From Grammar to Writing (pages 403–405)

See the general suggestions for From Grammar to Writing on page 9.

Go to **www.myfocusongrammarlab.com** for an additional From Grammar to Writing Assignment, Part Review, and Part Post-Test.

PART IX OVERVIEW

MORE MODALS AND SIMILAR EXPRESSIONS

UNIT	GRAMMAR FOCUS	THEME
29	Necessity: *Have (got) to, Must, Don't have to, Must not, Can't*	Transportation
30	Expectations: *Be supposed to*	Wedding Customs
31	Future Possibility: *May, Might, Could*	Weather
32	Conclusions: *Must, Have (got) to, May, Might, Could, Can't*	Mysteries

Go to **www.myfocusongrammarlab.com** for the Part and Unit Tests.

Note: PowerPoint® grammar presentations, test-generating software, and reproducible Part and Unit Tests are on the *Teacher's Resource Disc.*

UNIT 29 OVERVIEW

Grammar: NECESSITY: *Have (got) to, Must, Don't have to, Must not, Can't*

Unit 29 focuses on the uses of *have (got) to, must, don't have to, must not,* and *can't* to express different degrees of necessity.

- The affirmative forms *have, have got to,* and *must* express that something is necessary.
- The negative form *don't have to* expresses that something is not necessary.
- The negative forms *must not* and *can't* express that something is against the rules.

Theme: TRANSPORTATION

Unit 29 focuses on language used to talk about rules and regulations as related to transportation. Topics include rules for international travel and street signs.

Step 1: Grammar in Context (pages 408–409)

See the general suggestions for Grammar in Context on page 1.

Before You Read

- Have students look at the title and the illustration and discuss the questions in pairs. For questions 2 and 3, have students think about things to pack, information to find out, and documents to get ready.
- Call on pairs to share their examples with the class. As you get feedback from students, write on the board a list of destinations and what travelers need to know for each of them.

Read

- To encourage students to read with a purpose, write these questions on the board:
  Why does the columnist recommend . . .
  1. renewing your passport if it will expire in three months? *(because for many countries your passport must be valid for at least six months after you enter the country)*
  2. not bringing fresh food into foreign countries? *(because many countries have strict rules about bringing in food)*
  3. getting an IDP for an around-the-world tour? *(because it is required in many countries)*
  4. moving around and drinking plenty of water on long flights? *(because otherwise you won't stay healthy)*
- Have students read the text. (OR: Play the audio and have students follow along in their books.) Then call on students to share their answers to the questions on the board.

- To get students to share their ideas on the reading, form pairs or small groups. Have them discuss one or both of the following questions:
  1. Share other rules an international traveler should know. Explain why it is important to know them.
  2. Talk about your personal experience with the topics covered in the article. How often do you travel abroad? Do you have your camera or laptop inspected by hand or do you put them through the X-ray machine? What kind of things do you usually bring back into your country? Have you ever had a problem at Customs? Have you ever rented a car abroad? If you have, did you use your local driving license or an IDP? What do you usually take—nonstop flights or connecting flights? Why?

After You Read

A. Vocabulary

- Have students complete the exercise individually. Encourage them to use context clues to help.
- Have students compare answers in pairs. Then call on pairs to give answers.
- ⏱ To reinforce the vocabulary, have students make up sentences using the words in blue and the words they did not cross out. (Example: *You need a valid passport to enter a foreign country.*)

B. Comprehension

- Have students complete the exercise individually.
- Have students compare answers in pairs. Then call on pairs to give answers.

Go to **www.myfocusongrammarlab.com** for an additional reading, and for reading and vocabulary practice.

Step 2: Grammar Presentation (pages 410–412)

See the general suggestions for Grammar Presentation on page 2.

Grammar Charts

- To explain necessity with *have to*, write on the board:
  He has to renew his passport.
  They have to board from Gate 10.
  Do they have to carry their passport?
  Does she have to make connecting flights?
  What time do they have to be at the airport?

— Ask: "Does *have to* change when the pronoun changes?" *(yes)* "How do you express necessity with *have to*?" *(form of* have to + *base form of verb)* "Do *have to* and *has to* have short forms?" *(no)* "How do you form *yes/no* questions with *have to*?" (do/does + *subject* + have to + *base form*) "How do you form *wh-* questions with *have to*?" (wh- *word* + do/does + *subject* + have to + *base form*)

— Call on a student to provide the two possible short answers for each *yes/no* question on the board. *(Yes, they do. / No, they don't. Yes, she does. / No, she doesn't.)*

— Do not erase the examples on the board.

- To explain necessity with *have got to*, write on the board:
  He has got to renew his passport.
  He's got to renew his passport.
  They have got to board from Gate 10.
  They've got to board from Gate 10.

— Ask: "Does *have got to* change when the pronoun changes?" *(yes)* "How do you express necessity with *have got to*?" *(form of* have + got to + *base form of verb)* "Do *have got to* and *has got to* have short forms?" *(yes)*

— Ask: "Do the examples with *have got to* have the same meaning as the ones with *have to*?" *(yes)*

— Point out that we do not use *have got to* in questions.

— Do not erase the examples on the board.

- To explain necessity with *must*, write on the board:
  He must renew his passport.
  They must board from Gate 10.

— Ask: "Does *must* change when the pronoun changes?" *(no)* "How do you express necessity with *must*?" (must + *base form of verb*)

— Ask: "Do the examples with *must* have the same meaning as the ones with *have to* and *have got to*?" *(yes)*

— Point out that we almost never use *must* in questions.

- To compare *don't have to* and *must not*, write on the board:
  You don't have to have an IDP in Canada.
  He doesn't have to get an IDP.
  You must not drive without an IDP in Germany.
  He must not forget his passport.

— Ask: "What are the negative forms of *have to*?" (*don't have to* and *doesn't have to*) "What does *don't have to* express?" (*that something is not necessary*) "What is the negative form of *must*?" (*must not*) "What does *must not* express—that something is not necessary or that something is not permitted?" (*that something is not permitted*)

- To compare *can't* and *must not*, write on the board:
  He can't park here.
  He must not park here.
  — Ask: "Do both examples mean the same?" (*yes*) Emphasize that both *must not* and *can't* express prohibition.

Grammar Notes

Note 1

- To compare *have to*, *have got to*, and *must*, write on the board:
  You <u>have to be</u> at the airport at 6:00.
  You'<u>ve got to be</u> at the airport at 6:00.
  You <u>must be</u> at the airport at 6:00.
  Passengers <u>must be</u> at the airport at 6:00.
- Ask: "Do all the sentences have the same meaning?" (*yes*) "Do they express that something is necessary, not necessary, or against the rules?" (*that something is necessary*)
- Explain when we use each modal. Add the following to each example on the board:
  You <u>have to be</u> at the airport at 6:00.
    (everyday speaking and writing)
  You'<u>ve got to be</u> at the airport at 6:00.
    (everyday speaking and informal writing)
  You <u>must be</u> at the airport at 6:00. (everyday speaking, but meaning is strong)
  Passengers <u>must be</u> at the airport at 6:00.
    (formal writing)

Note 2

- To explain that *have to* can be used in different tenses, write on the board:
  <u>Simple Present</u>: She has to check in now.
  <u>Future</u>: They will have to declare the new camera.
  <u>Simple Past</u>: He had to be at the airport at 4:00.
  <u>Present Perfect</u>: She has had to travel ever since she got that job.
- Point out that *have to* can be used in all tenses.
- To explain that *have got to* and *must* are only used for the present or future, write on the board:
  1. I've got to leave earlier today.
  2. I've got to make a phone call.

3. Passengers must board from Gate 4 at 5:00.
4. Business class passengers must board the flight now.
- Ask: "Which sentences refer to the present?" (*2 and 4*) "Which sentences refer to the future?" (*1 and 3*)
- Point out that that *have got to* and *must* are used only for the present or future.

Note 3

- To review questions with *have to*, write on the board:
  She has to check in now.
  They will have to declare the new camera.
  He had to be at the airport at 4:00.
  She has had to travel ever since she got that job.
- Have pairs write a *yes/no* question and a *wh-* question for each item. Go over the answers as a class. (Example: *Does she have to check in now? When does she have to check in? Will they have to declare the new camera? What will they have to declare? Did he have to be at the airport at 4:00? What time did he have to be at the airport? Has she had to travel since she got that job? How long has she had to travel?*)
- Remind students that *have got to* is never used in questions and that *must* is not normally used in questions.

Note 4

- Draw attention to the *Be Careful!* note. Point out that while *have got to* and *must* have similar meanings, *don't have to* and *must not* have very different meanings.
- To review the meanings of *don't have to* and *must not*, write on the board:
  1. You must not check in yet.
  2. You don't have to check in yet.
- Have students explain the difference in meaning between the two sentences. (*1. It is not allowed to check in yet, so the person can't check in. 2. It is not necessary to check in right now, but the person can do so if he/she wants to.*)
- Point out that *have got to* has no negative form. If necessary, write ~~You haven't got to check in yet~~ below the examples on the board.
- To review the meaning of *can't*, write on the board:
  You don't have to renew your passport.
  Passengers must not check in before 6:00.
  He doesn't have to get an IDP.
  You must not bring fresh food into the country.
- Have pairs restate the sentences with *can't* whenever possible.

Note 5

- Point out that in informal speech *have to* is often pronounced "hafta," *has to* is often pronounced "hasta," and *got to* is often pronounced "gotta." "Hafta," "hasta," and "gotta" are also used in very informal written messages.

🕐 **Identify the Grammar:** Have students identify the grammar in the opening reading on page 408. For example:

... international travelers **have to know** ...

Do I **have to put** my computer and digital camera through the X-ray machine ...

... you **don't have to put** them through the X-ray equipment.

... your passport **must be** valid ...

Go to **www.myfocusongrammarlab.com** for grammar charts and notes.

Step 3: Focused Practice (pages 413–417)

See the general suggestions for Focused Practice on page 4.

Exercise 1: Discover the Grammar

A

- Go over the example with the class. Ask: "What does *have to* express?" *(that something is necessary)* "What other words can we use to express that something is necessary?" *(have got to, must)* "What can we use to express that something is not necessary?" *(don't have to)* "And that something is against the rules?" *(must not, can't)*
- Have students complete the exercise individually.
- Have students compare answers in pairs. Then call on students to give answers.

B

- Go over the example with the class. Ask: "Why isn't it necessary to get a visa for a two-week visit?" *(because you need a visa when you stay longer than 90 days)*
- Have students complete the exercise individually.
- Have students compare answers in pairs. Then call on students to give answers. Have students support their answers.

Exercise 2: Affirmative and Negative Statements: *Have to*

- Go over the example with the class.
- Have students complete the exercise in pairs. Then call on pairs to give answers.

- 🕐 For further practice, have students use the information in the exercise to write four or five sentences about what they normally have to do or don't have to do when they go on vacation. (Example: *When I go on vacation, I don't have to worry about pets because I don't have a pet. I don't have to buy batteries for my camera because I use rechargeable batteries. I have to remember to pack my battery charger.*)

Exercise 3: Questions and Statements: *Have (got) to* and *Can't*

- Go over the example with the class. Then have students read the conversations quickly for meaning.
- Have students complete the exercise individually. Then call on pairs to read the conversations aloud.
- 🕐 Have pairs role-play the conversations.

Exercise 4: Affirmative and Negative Statements: *Must*

- Go over the example with the class.
- Have students complete the exercise individually. Then go over the answers as a class.
- 🕐 To extend the activity, have students share other rules they may know for airline travel, using *must* and *must not*. (Example: *You must take off your shoes when you go through security. You must not smoke in the cabin.*)

Exercise 5: Negative Statements: *Must not* or *Don't have to*

- Go over the example with the class.
- Have students complete the exercise in pairs. Then go over the answers as a class.

Exercise 6: Editing

- Have students read the email quickly for meaning. Then ask: "Where is Sean flying?" *(back to Australia)* "How long is the flight?" *(14 hours)* "What does his mother say he has to do during the flight?" *(walk around every three hours and drink water every hour)* "Where did he put his camping knife?" *(in his checked suitcase)* "Why?" *(because you can't bring knives in carry-on bags)*
- Go over the example with the class.
- Have students find and correct the mistakes individually. Then go over the answers as a class, having students explain why the incorrect structures are wrong.
- 🕐 Have students point out examples of correct usages of words expressing necessity.

Go to **www.myfocusongrammarlab.com** for additional grammar practice.

Step 4: Communication Practice

(pages 417–420)

See the general suggestions for Communication Practice on page 5.

Exercise 7: Listening

A

- Have students read the statements quickly for meaning.
- Play the audio. Have students listen and complete the exercise individually. Stop after each conversation to allow students time to correct the errors.
- Have students complete the exercise in pairs. Then go over the answers as a class.

B

- Have students look at the signs and discuss in pairs what they think they mean. Do not provide the correct answers at this stage. Students will find out if they were right or wrong after doing the exercise.
- Play the audio. Have students listen and complete the exercise individually. Stop after each conversation to allow students time to write their answers.
- Have students explain what the signs mean using *have to, must,* or *can't.* (a. You have to/ must stop. b. You can't stop. c. You can't drive more slowly than 30 miles per hour. d. You can't pass another car. e. You can't drive faster than 80 miles per hour. f. You have to/must turn left. You can't turn right.)

Exercise 8: Pronunciation

A

- Play the audio. Have students read along as they listen to the Pronunciation Note.
- Write on the board:
  hafta
  hasta
  gotta
- Read the items on the board aloud and have students repeat after you. Be sure they stress the first syllable and pronounce the second syllable /tæ/.

B

- Play the audio. Be sure students notice the pronunciation of the reductions.

C

- Play the audio. Have students listen.
- Have students practice the conversations with a partner. Be sure students play both roles.

Exercise 9: Picture Discussion

- Give the class a time limit of 10 minutes to discuss the signs.
- Call on students to share their ideas with the class.
- ⏱ Have students choose a sign and write a short paragraph about it. Point out that as a guide students should use the questions that prompted the discussion.

Exercise 10: Game: Invent a Sign

- Bring in colored pens and pencils and different-colored and textured paper to class.
- Give students a time limit of 10 minutes to draw the sign and write a few sentences about its meaning. Encourage students to be creative. Point out that they can make signs for their cars, their homes, the classroom, their bedroom door, or anywhere else.
- Have students show their signs to their classmates, discuss their meaning, and decide where the signs belong.

Exercise 11: What About You?

A

- Go over the example with the class.
- Have students write their lists individually. Emphasize that they should include things that they have already done this week and things that they haven't done yet.
- Form small groups. Have students discuss their lists with their classmates. Encourage them to take notes of the things their classmates have to do and don't have to do.

B

- Go over the example with the class.
- Call on students to use their notes as a guide to report to the class on what their classmates have to do and don't have to do this week.

Exercise 12: Discussion: Rules and Regulations

A

- Go over the example with the class.
- Have students complete the exercise in small groups. Encourage students to write sentences about what they have to do, what they don't have to do, and what they can't do for each of the topics.

B

• Copy the chart from the book onto the board. Call on students from different groups to come to the front of the class, share their sentences, and then write them in the chart.

Exercise 13: Writing

A

• Write these questions on the board to help elicit vocabulary and generate ideas:
  1. What application procedure will you write about?
  2. Have you ever applied for that? If so, when? Why?
  3. What must you do? (Think about what the law/the rules say/s.)
  4. What do you have to do? (Think about what is necessary to do.)
  5. What don't you have to do? (Think about what is not really necessary to do.)
  6. What is a "must not"? (Think about what is not permitted or what you are strongly recommended not to do.)
• Have students make notes for each question and then use them as a guide as they write.

B

• Have students correct their work using the Editing Checklist.

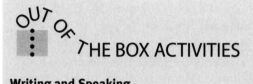

Writing and Speaking

• Have students form small groups. Ask each group to choose a place—for example, a zoo, a museum, or a train station—and write a list of 10 useful rules for that place. Point out that each rule should use one of the ways to express necessity, lack of necessity, or prohibition that students learned in this unit.
• Call on students to read the rules aloud to the class, withholding the name of the place. The class guesses the place.

Listening

• Have students play Sign Bingo as a class. Do a search on the Internet and print out 15 to 20 traffic signs that are used in the United States. (Print out several copies of the signs or make several copies of the signs you selected.)

• Cut out a colored card for each pair or group of three. Paste nine signs in a 3 × 3 grid on each colored card. Each colored card should have at least one sign that is different from the ones on the other cards. The following are three examples of cards:

• Give pairs or groups of three a card each and play bingo: Say the rules one by one as students check if they have the corresponding sign on their card. Whenever possible, use the ways to express necessity that students learned in this unit to describe the signs. (Example: *This sign indicates that you can't park in this place.*)

Go to **www.myfocusongrammarlab.com** for additional listening, pronunciation, speaking, and writing practice.

Note:

• See the *Focus on Grammar Workbook* for additional in-class or homework grammar practice.

Unit 29 Review (page 421)

Have students complete the Review and check their answers on Student Book page UR-7. Review or assign additional material as needed.

Go to **www.myfocusongrammarlab.com** for the Unit Achievement Test.

Grammar: EXPECTATIONS: *Be supposed to*

Unit 30 focuses on the use of *be supposed to* to express expectations.

- *Be supposed to* is used to express expectations that have their origin in rules, customs, predictions, hearsay, and plans or arrangements.

- It is used in the simple present to express present or future expectations and in the simple past to express past expectations.

Theme: WEDDING CUSTOMS

Unit 30 focuses on language used to talk about weddings and other important events.

There are several popular books on etiquette. A traditional favorite was written by Emily Post. Judith Martin, known as Miss Manners, has written several more recent ones. She also writes a newspaper column, answering questions about etiquette (or manners). Ms. Etiquette in this unit is a fictional character.

Step 1: Grammar in Context (pages 422–423)

See the general suggestions for Grammar in Context on page 1.

Before You Read

- Have students look at the photo, read the title of the article, and discuss the questions in pairs. Be sure students know the meaning of *wedding* (a ceremony in which two people get married) and *etiquette* (formal rules for polite behavior).

- To review question 1, call on students to say what they think the letter is about. Write students' ideas on the board. (Example: *what to do during a wedding reception, what to do before the wedding, what kind of gifts to give, what kinds of clothes to wear*)

- To review question 2, ask students who have been to a wedding or been part of one to say whose wedding it was and where and when it took place. Then to review question 3, call on students to give their answers to the question. As you get feedback from students, write two lists on the board:

  Special Clothing   Special Customs

Read

- To encourage students to read with a purpose, write these questions on the board:
  1. What has the reader been invited to do? *(to be the maid of honor at her best friend's wedding)*

2. Why does the columnist think the reader should feel proud? *(her friend's invitation means that she values their friendship)*

3. What is the maid of honor supposed to do? *(help the bride choose the bridesmaids' dresses, help the bride send the invitations, hold the bride's flowers during the ceremony, and sign the marriage certificate)*

4. What is the best man supposed to do? *(drive the groom to the ceremony and sign the marriage certificate)*

- Have students read the text. (OR: Play the audio and have students follow along in their books.) Then call on students to share their answers to the questions on the board.

- To get students to share their ideas on the reading, form pairs or small groups. Have them discuss one or both of the following questions:
  1. Compare the wedding customs in the United States with the ones in your own country. Also share what you know about wedding customs in other countries.
  2. Discuss your views on customs and traditions. Why do different countries usually have different customs and traditions? Are customs and traditions important? Is it important to respect traditions? Is it important to keep them alive?

After You Read

A. Vocabulary

- Have students complete the exercise individually. Encourage them to use context clues to help.

- Have students compare answers in pairs. Then call on pairs to give answers.

B. Comprehension

- Have students complete the exercise individually.

- Have students compare answers in pairs. Then call on pairs to give answers.

- ⏱ To reinforce the vocabulary, write the following paragraph on the board and have students complete it with the words in this section. (Answers: *etiquette, role, assistant, ceremony, select, certificate*)

  In a book about _____, I found a lot of information about the _____ of the maid of honor. She's the bride's _____. Before the _____, she helps the bride _____ the bridesmaids' dresses. After the ceremony, she signs the marriage _____.

Go to **www.myfocusongrammarlab.com** for an additional reading, and for reading and vocabulary practice.

Step 2: Grammar Presentation (pages 424–425)

See the general suggestions for Grammar Presentation on page 2.

Grammar Charts

- To explain statements with *be supposed to* with future and present meaning, write on the board:

  The bride is supposed to be arriving soon.
  We are supposed to sign the marriage certificate after the wedding.

  — Ask: "Does the first example express an expectation about the present or the future?" *(the present)* "Does the second example express an expectation about the present or the future?" *(the future)* "How do you know?" *(because the example says* after the wedding) "How do you express present or future expectations?" *(present form of* be [am, is, are] + supposed to + *base form of verb)*

- To explain statements with *be supposed to* with past meaning, write on the board:

  In the past the groom's brother was supposed to be the best man.
  The bride was supposed to be there at 6:00.

  — Ask: "Do these examples express expectations about the present, the past, or the future?" *(the past)* "How do you express past expectations?" *(past form of* be [was, were] + supposed to + *base form of verb)*

- To explain *yes/no* and *wh-* questions with *be supposed to*, write on the board:

  Is she supposed to sign the marriage certificate?
  Was he supposed to drive the groom to the ceremony?
  Were the bridesmaids supposed to arrive at 5:00?

  — Ask: "How do you form questions with *be supposed to*?" *(present or past form of* be + *subject* + supposed to + *base form)*

  — Call on students to provide the two possible short answers for each question. Have them come to the front and write the answers on the board. *(Yes, she is. / No, she isn't. Yes, he was. / No, he wasn't. Yes, they were. / No, they weren't.)*

  — Have students turn the *yes/no* questions on the board into *wh-* questions starting with *what, where,* and *what time,* respectively. *(What was she supposed to sign? Where was he supposed to drive the groom? What time were the bridesmaids supposed to arrive?)*

Grammar Notes

Note 1

- To explain the uses of *be supposed to*, write on the board:

1. It's supposed to be sunny tomorrow.	a. hearsay
2. We're supposed to leave at 8:00.	b. rule
3. The maid of honor is supposed to help the bride.	c. prediction
4. You're not supposed to drive without a license.	d. custom
5. The Argentineans are supposed to be friendly to foreigners.	e. plan or arrangement

- Go over the words in the second column and answer any questions about meaning. If necessary, explain the meaning of *hearsay* (something that you have heard about from other people but do not know to be true).

- Have students match the examples in the left column with the different kinds of expectations in the right column. Go over the answers as a class. *(1. c, 2. e, 3. d, 4. b, 5. a)*

- If necessary, point out that *be supposed to* is an idiomatic phrase and is distinct from the regular verb *to suppose,* which means to consider as probable or to believe. *(Example: I suppose I should go home. It's late.)*

Note 2

- Point out that when we use *be supposed to* for present or future expectations, what we expect may or may not happen.

- Point out that *be supposed to* in the past describes something that was expected to happen but didn't. Write examples on the board:

  We were supposed to get married this June, but we changed the date to August.
  He was supposed to pick the bride up at her house, but he went directly to the church instead!

- Point out that *was/were going to* has the same meaning as *was/were supposed to.*

(!) **Identify the Grammar:** Have students identify the grammar in the opening reading on page 422. For example:

What **is** the maid of honor **supposed to do** in a wedding ceremony?

. . . the bride **is supposed to select** my dress.

. . . the bride's sister **was supposed to serve** as her maid of honor . . .

. . . the groom's brother **was supposed to be** his best man.

Go to **www.myfocusongrammarlab.com** for grammar charts and notes.

Step 3: Focused Practice (pages 426–429)

See the general suggestions for Focused Practice on page 4.

Exercise 1: Discover the Grammar

A

- Go over the example with the class. Point out that students should underline the form of *be* + *be supposed to* + the main verb.
- Have students complete the exercise individually.
- Have students compare answers in pairs. Then call on students to give answers.

B

- Go over the example with the class.
- Have students complete the exercise individually.
- Have students compare answers in pairs. Then call on students to give answers. Have students support their answers with information from the text.

Exercise 2: Questions and Statements

- Go over the example with the class. Then have students read the conversations quickly for meaning.
- Have students complete the exercise individually. Then call on pairs to read the conversations aloud.
- (!) Have pairs role-play the conversations.

Exercise 3: *Was or Were going to*

- Remind students that we use *was/were going to* when something we expected to happen did not happen.
- Go over the example with the class. Ask: "What was the plan?" *(that Netta would select the bridesmaids' dresses)* "Who selected them in the end?" *(Sophie)* Point out the use of *instead* in the example, to indicate what happened instead of the original plan.

- Have students complete the exercise individually. Then call on students to read the sentences aloud.

Exercise 4: Editing

- Have students read the email quickly for meaning. Then ask: "Who's writing the email?" *(Jack)* "What has his friend Gary invited him to be?" *(his best man)* "What is Jack supposed to do before the ceremony?" *(drive him to the ceremony/make sure Gary gets to the ceremony on time)* "What is he supposed to do during the ceremony?" *(hold the wedding rings)* "And at the end of the ceremony?" *(help the bride and the groom leave quickly for their honeymoon and hold the plane tickets for them)*
- Go over the example with the class.
- Have students find and correct the mistakes individually. Then call on students to explain why the incorrect structures are wrong.
- (!) Have students point out examples of correct usages of *be supposed to* and *was/were going to.*

Go to **www.myfocusongrammarlab.com** for additional grammar practice.

Step 4: Communication Practice

(pages 430–432)

See the general suggestions for Communication Practice on page 5.

Exercise 5: Listening

A

- Point out that students will listen to separate conversations that take place the day of a wedding.
- Play the audio. Have students listen and complete the exercise individually. If necessary, stop the recording after each conversation to allow students time to write their answers.
- Have students compare answers in pairs. Then call on pairs to read the conversations aloud.

B

- Play the audio. Have students listen and complete the exercise individually.
- Call on students to say the customs that are mentioned in the conversations. List them on the board:

The bride's family is supposed to sit on the left during the ceremony.

The maid of honor isn't supposed to walk behind the bride.

Guests are supposed to tell the bride that she looks beautiful.

They are supposed to say "Congratulations" to the groom.

Guests are supposed to throw rice at the bride and the groom, but they don't do it anymore because it can hurt birds.

- ⏱ Follow up by asking students which of these customs are also seen in other cultures.

Exercise 6: Pronunciation

A

- Play the audio. Have students read along as they listen to the Pronunciation Note.
- Write on the board:

  sup<u>po</u>sta

  <u>gon</u>na

- Read the items on the board aloud and have students repeat after you. Be sure students stress the underlined syllable in each word and produce a final schwa sound. The first syllable in *supposta* is also pronounced with a schwa.

B

- Play the audio. Have students listen. Be sure they notice the pronunciation of the reductions.

C

- Play the audio. Have students listen and repeat.
- Have students practice the conversations in pairs. Be sure students play both roles.

Exercise 7: Discussion

- Go over the example with the class and point out the use of *be going to*. Have students restate the first sentence in the example using *be supposed to. (We were supposed to get married . . .)*
- Have students complete the exercise in pairs. Point out that students can discuss plans about studies, jobs, vacations, moving to a different town or country, getting married, or their own ideas. They should also ask follow-up questions.
- Call on students to report on how their partner's plans changed.

Exercise 8: Cross-Cultural Comparison

- Have students look at the picture and describe it. Then go over the example with the class.
- Form small groups. Encourage students to write notes about customs for each event on the list.
- Then have groups discuss the events.

Exercise 9: Writing

A

- Write these questions on the board to help elicit vocabulary and generate ideas:
  1. What are the people supposed to wear?
  2. What are they supposed to do?
  3. What are they supposed to say?
  4. What kind of gifts are they supposed to give?
  5. Is there any special food that is prepared/served?
  6. If there is a ceremony, where is it supposed to take place?
  7. Are the people supposed to do anything in particular after the event?
- Have students make notes for each question and then use them as a guide as they write.

B

- Have students correct their work using the Editing Checklist.

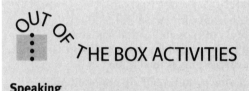

OUT OF THE BOX ACTIVITIES

Speaking

- Have students think about things that they were supposed to do last week but they didn't do in the end, or things that they expected to happen but did not happen in the end.
- In pairs, have students take turns sharing their expectations and the things that actually happened.

Writing and Reading

- Bring in questions and replies posted to an Internet column about table manners. Form small groups. Give each group at least one question.
- Have students write an answer to the question as if they were the columnist. Point out that some of their sentences should use *be supposed to*.
- Hand out the columnist's replies to the questions for students to compare with their own answer.

Go to **www.myfocusongrammarlab.com** for additional listening, pronunciation, speaking, and writing practice.

Note:

• See the *Focus on Grammar Workbook* for additional in-class or homework grammar practice.

Unit 30 Review (page 433)

Have students complete the Review and check their answers on Student Book page UR-8. Review or assign additional material as needed.

Go to **www.myfocusongrammarlab.com** for the Unit Achievement Test.

UNIT 31 OVERVIEW

Grammar: FUTURE POSSIBILITY: *May, Might, Could*

Unit 31 focuses on the uses of *may, might,* and *could* to express expectations.

• The affirmative forms *may, might,* and *could* express the possibility that something will happen.

• The negative forms *may not* and *might not* express the possibility that something will not happen. *Couldn't,* however, expresses that something is impossible.

• *May, might,* and *could* are not often used in questions about possibility. The future (*will, be going to,* the present progressive) is used instead. Phrases such as *Do you think . . . ?* or *Is it possible that . . . ?* are also used. Answers to these questions often use *may, might,* or *could.*

Theme: WEATHER

Unit 31 focuses on language used to talk about the weather and how it affects people's daily lives.

This unit talks about temperature in both Celsius and Fahrenheit measurements. The following is a conversion table:

Celsius degrees	Fahrenheit degrees
0	32
10	50
20	68
30	86
40	104

Step 1: Grammar in Context (pages 434–435)

See the general suggestions for Grammar in Context on page 1.

Before You Read

• Have students look at the weather icons on the map and say what kind of weather they symbolize. *(sunny, partly sunny, cloudy, partly cloudy, rain, snow)* Then have students look at the temperatures on the map and say if they think they are summer or winter temperatures. *(winter temperatures)*

• Have students discuss the questions in pairs.

• Call on pairs to share their answers with the class.

Read

• To encourage students to read with a purpose, write these questions on the board:
  1. Where is there a chance of snow? *(London)*
  2. Where is there a chance of rain? *(Paris)*
  3. Where will it probably be sunny? *(Rome)*
  4. Where are you likely to need an umbrella if you go out? *(Paris)*
  5. Where will you probably not need a coat if you go out? *(Rome)*
  6. Where will you need warm clothes to go out? *(London)*

• Have students read the text. (OR: Play the audio and have students follow along in their books.) Then call on students to share their answers to the questions on the board.

• To get students to share their ideas on the reading, form pairs or small groups. Have them discuss one or both of the following questions:
  1. Discuss the importance of weather forecasts. Why are they useful? Do you sometimes check the weather forecast? When? What for? Where do you usually get information about the weather—in the newspaper, on the Internet, on the radio, on TV? Why?
  2. Talk about your favorite season and the type of weather you prefer. Which country or region has the ideal climate for you? Why?

After You Read

A. Vocabulary

• Have students complete the exercise individually. Encourage them to use context clues to help.

• Have students compare answers in pairs. Then call on pairs to give answers.

- ⏱ To reinforce the vocabulary, write the following sentence halves on the board. Have students match them. Go over the answers as a class. *(1. e, 2. f, 3. d, 4. a, 5. b, 6. c)*
  1. Before going out, he checked
  2. You shouldn't exceed
  3. I'm interested
  4. You should bundle up
  5. The changes will not
  6. If this trend continues,

  a. when it is very cold.
  b. affect us.
  c. it will get hotter and hotter.
  d. in both local and international news.
  e. the weather forecast.
  f. the speed limit.

B. Comprehension
- Have students complete the exercise individually.
- Have students compare answers in pairs. Then call on pairs to give answers.

Go to **www.myfocusongrammarlab.com** for an additional reading, and for reading and vocabulary practice.

Step 2: Grammar Presentation (pages 436–437)

See the general suggestions for Grammar Presentation on page 2.

Grammar Charts
- To explain affirmative statements with *may, might,* and *could,* write on the board:
  Temperatures may drop.
  We might see some snow.
  Winds could reach 40 miles per hour.
  — Ask: "Do the examples express a possibility or a fact?" *(a possibility)* "Do they refer to the future or the past?" *(the future)* "How do you express future possibility?" (may/might/could + *base form of verb*)
- To explain negative statements with *may, might,* and *could,* write on the board:
  Temperatures may not drop.
  We might not see snow.
  — Ask: "Do these sentences express a possibility that something will happen or a possibility that something will not happen?" *(a possibility that something will not happen)* "How can you express a possibility that something will not happen?" (may/might + *not* + *base form of verb*)

— Point out that *could not* is *not* used to express a possibility that something will not happen. *Could not* has a different meaning: impossibility. If necessary, write on the board:
I could not go out because of the storm. = I was not able to go out.
- To explain *yes/no* and *wh-* questions and short answers about future possibility, write on the board:
  1. Will it snow in Paris?
  2. Is it going to rain in London on Sunday?
  3. Are you taking the 5:00 P.M. flight?
     — Ask: "Do we use *may, might,* or *could* to ask about future possibility?" *(no)* "What do we use instead?" *(a way to express the future:* will, be going to, *or the present progressive)*
     — Add possible short answers next to each question:
       1. It may. / It might. / It could.
       2. It may not. / It might not.
       3. I may. / I might. / I could.
     — Point to the first and third questions and answers and say, "*May, might,* and *could* are used for affirmative short answers."
     — Point to the second question and its answers and say, "*May* and *might* (NOT *could*) are used for negative short answers."
     — Write a new question on the board:
  4. Will it be hot tomorrow? It may be. / It might be. / It could be.
     — Point to question 4 on the board and ask: "What is the main verb in this question?" *(be)*
     — Point to the short answers and say: "*May, might,* and *could* are often followed by *be* if the question uses *be* as a main verb."
     — Do not erase questions 1 through 4.
- Have students come to the front and turn *yes/no* questions 1 through 3 into *wh-* questions starting with *where, when,* and *which,* respectively. *(Where will it snow? When is it going to rain in London? Which flight are you taking?)*
  — Add possible answers next to each question:
    1. It may snow in Paris.
    2. It might rain on Sunday.
    3. I could take the 5:00 P.M. flight.
  — Point out that it is possible to use *may, might,* and *could* in answers to questions that use future forms.

Grammar Notes

Note 1

- To review the use of *may*, *might*, and *could* to express possibility, write on the board:
  1. It may snow tonight.
  2. It might snow tonight.
  3. It could snow tonight.
- Have students study the sentences. Say: "It is possible that something will happen tonight. What is it?" *(It may/might/could snow.)* "Do the three sentences have the same meaning?" *(yes)*
- Point out that the three sentences express future possibility.
- To compare *may*, *might*, and *could* with a future form, write below the examples on the board:
  4. It's going to snow tonight.
- Ask: "Does sentence 4 have the same meaning as sentences 1 through 3?" *(no)* "Why not?" *(because it doesn't express a possibility; it expresses a fact)*
- Emphasize that we use the future (*will*, *be going to*, or the present progressive) when something is certain and *may*, *might*, or *could* when something is possible.
- Draw attention to the *Be Careful!* note. To compare *may be* and *maybe*, write on the board:
  It <u>may</u> <u>be</u> sunny tomorrow.
  <u>Maybe</u> it will be sunny tomorrow.
- Direct attention to the first example. Point out that *may* is a modal that expresses future possibility.
- Ask students what other modals could replace *may* in the first example. *(might, could)*
- Direct attention to the second example. Point out that *maybe* is not a modal but an adverb that expresses possibility. It comes at the beginning of the sentence. Point out the use of *maybe* + *will* to express the same meaning as the first sentence (future possibility).

Note 2

- To explain *may not* and *might not* and compare them with *could not*, write on the board:
  a. I may not travel with my aunt. She's too bossy!
  b. I might not travel with my aunt. She's too bossy!
  c. I couldn't travel with my aunt. She's too bossy!

- To check comprehension, ask: "Which sentences express a possibility that the person will not travel with his/her aunt?" (a *and* b) "What does the last sentence express?" *(that the person doesn't even consider traveling with his/her aunt because she is so bossy; it is impossible)*
- Draw attention to the *Be Careful!* note. Point out that we do not normally contract *might not* and that we never contract *may not*.
- To compare *may not* and *might not* with future forms, write on the board:
  1. I may not go.
  2. I might not go.
  3. I won't go.
  4. I'm not going to go.
  5. I'm not going.
- Ask: "In which sentences is the person *not certain* whether something will happen?" *(1 and 2)* "In which sentences is the person *certain* that something will not happen?" *(3 through 5)*

Note 3

- Remind students that *may*, *might*, and *could* are not normally used in questions about possibility. However, *may*, *might*, and *could* are normally used in answers.
- To clarify this point, write on the board:
  Will it rain tomorrow?
  Is it going to rain tomorrow?
  Do you think it will rain tomorrow?

  Well, the forecast says it | may / might / could | rain in the evening.

⏱ **Identify the Grammar:** Have students identify the grammar in the opening reading on page 434. For example:
  Temperatures **may drop** . . .
  We **might** even **see** some snow flurries . . .
  . . . winds **could exceed** 40 miles per hour.
  You **may not need** your coat at all . . .

Go to **www.myfocusongrammarlab.com** for grammar charts and notes.

Step 3: Focused Practice (pages 438–440)

See the general suggestions for Focused Practice on page 4.

Exercise 1: Discover the Grammar

A

- Go over the example with the class. Ask: "What does *might take the car* express?" *(that she will probably drive to work tomorrow)* "Why doesn't she know for sure?" *(because it depends on the weather)* "What other words express future possibility?" *(the modals* may *and* could *and the adverb* maybe*)*
- Have students complete the exercise individually. Point out that students should underline modals and the main verb that follows them.
- Have students compare answers in pairs. Then go over the answers as a class.

B

- Have students complete the exercise individually.
- Have students compare answers in pairs. Then call on pairs to give answers, ensuring that they say complete sentences for each item. Encourage them to use ways to express future possibility for things that are possible and future forms for things that are certain. (Example: *Cody may/might/could work until 8:00 P.M. Maybe Cody works until 8:00 P.M. Anna is taking/is going to take the 6:30 train home.*)

Exercise 2: Affirmative and Negative Statements

- Go over the example with the class. Ask: "Why is the future form with *going to* the correct answer?" *(because it is certain that she is going to graduate—she got the notice from her school)*
- Have students read the paragraph quickly for meaning. Then have students complete the exercise individually.
- ⏱ For further practice, ask: "What things is Anna sure about?" *(her graduation and her career: she is going to graduate in June and she is going to forecast the weather)* "What is she uncertain about?" *(what she will do immediately after her graduation—she might apply for a job or apply to a graduate school to get a master's degree)*

Exercise 3: Statements: *May, Might, Be going to*

- Go over the example with the class.
- Have students complete the exercise individually. Remind them that *may* and *might* have the same meaning.

- ⏱ To personalize, have students use Anna's schedule for Monday as a model to write their own schedule for tomorrow. Encourage students to write four to five items. Then have pairs use their schedule as a guide to tell each other about their plans for tomorrow.

Exercise 4: Short Answers

- Go over the example with the class.
- Remind students that we use *be* in the short answers when *be* is the main verb in the question.
- Have students complete the exercise individually. Then call on students to give answers.

Exercise 5: Editing

- Have students read the report quickly for meaning. Then ask: "What happens near Peru every few years?" *(the ocean becomes warmer)* "What may El Niño cause on the west coast?" *(rain)* "What may it cause on the east coast?" *(dry weather)* "Where may the weather become warmer?" *(in the north)* "And where may it become colder?" *(in the south)* "How do these changes affect fish?" *(They may die or swim to colder places.)* "How do these changes affect plants?" *(They might die because of lack of rain.)*
- Go over the example with the class.
- Have students find and correct the mistakes individually. Then call on students to explain why the incorrect structures are wrong.
- ⏱ Have students point out examples of correct usages of *may, might,* and *could.*

Go to **www.myfocusongrammarlab.com** for additional grammar practice.

Step 4: Communication Practice
(pages 441–444)

See the general suggestions for Communication Practice on page 5.

Exercise 6: Listening

A

- Have students read the statements.
- Play the audio. Have students listen.
- Play the audio again. Have students listen and complete the exercise individually.

B

- Have students look at the charts. Point out that all the weather conditions in the charts are mentioned in the forecast.

- Play the audio. Have students listen and complete the exercise individually. Have students listen carefully to find out if the items mentioned are *certain* or *possible*. Point out that temperatures are given in the Fahrenheit scale.
- Call on students to give answers, having them say complete sentences using future tenses or modals of possibility, as appropriate. (Example: *It might be sunny on Friday. It will be sunny on Saturday.*)

Exercise 7: Pronunciation

A
- Play the audio. Have students read along as they listen to the Pronunciation Note.
- To check comprehension, write on the board: Will you come?
  1. I may.
  2. I may not.
- Direct attention to the short answers. Ask: "In sentence 1, which word is stressed?" *(may)* "In sentence 2, which word is stressed?" *(not)* Underline the stressed words as students say them.

B
- Have students read the conversations and anticipate which words they will hear stressed.
- Play the audio. Have students listen and put dots over the appropriate words.

C
- Play the audio. Have students listen and repeat the answers.
- Have students practice the conversations with a partner. Be sure students play both roles.

Exercise 8: Conversation
- Ask students what they have heard about the forecast for this weekend. Write a forecast for Saturday and Sunday on the board, for example:

Saturday	Sunday
Cloudy	Partly sunny
Rain	High 15
High 10	Low 6
Low 3	

- Give students a few minutes to think about their plans for both days. Encourage them to make notes and decide which activities are possible and which things they will do for certain.

- Have students complete the exercise in pairs. Encourage them to ask follow-up questions to keep the conversation going.

Exercise 9: Problem Solving

A
- Have students read the profiles and the future possibilities in the box. Answer any questions.
- Go over the example and point out the modals.
- Form small groups. Have students in each group discuss the students' future possibilities.

B
- Have students individually write about their own possibilities using the listed categories of occupations, hobbies, and achievements.
- Have students share their writing in groups and then submit it to you for correction.

Exercise 10: Writing

A
- Write the following questions on the board to elicit vocabulary and help generate ideas:
  What are you going to do this weekend?
  What may/might/could you do?
  What may/might you not do?
- Have students also use the notes they wrote to prepare for Exercise 8.
- Have students make notes for each question and then use them as a guide as they write.

B
- Have students correct their work using the Editing Checklist.

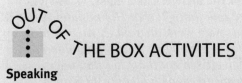

OUT OF THE BOX ACTIVITIES

Speaking

- Form small groups. Have students write a list of 10 goals that people may be interested in achieving. (Example: *break a record, become a millionaire, travel around the world*)
- Have students interview another group by asking "Do you think you will . . . ?" (Example: *Do you think you will ever break a record?*) Have students use modals expressing future possibility to answer the questions about their future. Point out that they can give serious or amusing answers. (Example: *Yes, I may break a record one day—longest sleep in history!*)
- Follow up by having students report to the class on their partners' answers.

Reading and Speaking

- Bring in magazine or newspaper articles about the environment, global warming, and how the weather is changing. Bring material from both serious and sensational newspapers.
- Have students compare how bad news seems more certain in sensational news stories than in serious ones. You may want to write two headlines as examples on the board:
  Ice Cap to Melt Soon
  Scientists Study Possible Effects of
    Global Warming
- Point out how the first headline states a fact: that the ice cap will definitely melt soon. The second headline, however, states that scientists still don't know what might happen.

Go to **www.myfocusongrammarlab.com** for additional listening, pronunciation, speaking, and writing practice.

Note:

- See the *Focus on Grammar Workbook* for additional in-class or homework grammar practice.

Unit 31 Review (page 445)

Have students complete the Review and check their answers on Student Book page UR-8. Review or assign additional material as needed.

Go to **www.myfocusongrammarlab.com** for the Unit Achievement Test.

UNIT 32 OVERVIEW

Grammar: CONCLUSIONS: *Must, Have (got) to, May, Might, Could, Can't*

Unit 32 focuses on the uses of *must, have (got) to, may, might, could,* and *can't* to express conclusions.

- The affirmative forms *must, have to,* and *have got to* express that we are almost 100 percent certain that something is possible. *May, might,* and *could* express that something is possible, but we are less certain about it.
- The negative forms *can't* and *couldn't* express that we are almost 100 percent certain that something is impossible. The negative form *must not* expresses that we are slightly less certain, and *may not* and *might not* express that we are even less certain.
- Only *can* and *could* are used in questions about guesses.

Theme: MYSTERIES

Unit 32 focuses on language used to talk about mystery stories.

Sir Arthur Conan Doyle wrote the Sherlock Holmes stories at the end of the 19th century. Holmes, a fictional character, was one of the first storybook detectives. He used his powers of observation to make deductions that helped him solve crimes. He was often accompanied by his friend Dr. Watson, who was not as brilliant as Holmes. Usually Holmes had to explain his conclusions to Dr. Watson in great detail.

Step 1: Grammar in Context (pages 446–447)

See the general suggestions for Grammar in Context on page 1.

Before You Read

- Have students look at the photograph, read the title, and discuss the questions in pairs.
- Call on pairs to share their answers to the questions with the class.

Read

- To encourage students to read with a purpose, write these questions on the board:
  1. Why is Wilson visiting Holmes? *(because he wants Holmes to solve a case)*
  2. Where did Wilson work for two months? *(at the Red-Headed League)*
  3. What did Wilson do at work? *(he copied the encyclopedia by hand)*
  4. Will Wilson continue to do this work? *(no)*
- Have students read the text. (OR: Play the audio and have students follow along in their books.) Then call on students to share their answers to the questions on the board.
- To get students to share their ideas on the reading, form pairs or small groups. Have them discuss one or both of the following questions:
  1. Share your views on the story so far: Does the Red-Headed League sound like a serious organization to you? Does Wilson's work at the League seem like useful work? Do you think Wilson was cheated? What do you think will happen next?
  2. Tell your partners about the best mystery novel or suspense movie you have read or watched. Why did you like it?

After You Read

A. Vocabulary

- Have students complete the exercise individually. Encourage them to use context clues to help.
- Have students compare answers in pairs. Then call on pairs to give answers.

B. Comprehension

- Have students complete the exercise individually.
- Have students compare answers in pairs. Then call on pairs to give answers, supporting their answers with information from the text.
- 🕐 To reinforce the vocabulary, have students use the words in parentheses to answer these questions about the story:
  1. What was Wilson's reaction when Watson discovered that he wrote a lot? *(amazed, methods)*
  2. What is the Red-Headed League? *(millionaire)*
  3. What did Wilson read in the newspaper? *(advertisement, position, salary, encyclopedia)*

- Go over the answers as a class. *(1. He was amazed and thought that Holmes and Watson's methods may work after all. 2. An organization that was started by an American millionaire. 3. An advertisement that said that the Red-Headed League had a position open. The salary was good and the job was to copy an encyclopedia by hand.)*

Go to **www.myfocusongrammarlab.com** for an additional reading, and for reading and vocabulary practice.

Step 2: Grammar Presentation (pages 448–450)

See the general suggestions for Grammar Presentation on page 2.

Grammar Charts

- To explain affirmative statements with *must, may, might*, and *could*, write on the board:
  Wilson must write a lot.
  He may be in danger.
  He might be in trouble.
  He could be a liar.
  — Ask: "What do all the examples express—facts or conclusions?" *(conclusions)* "How do you express affirmative conclusions?" *(must/may/might/could + base form of verb)*
- To explain negative statements with *must not, may not, might not, couldn't*, and *can't*, write on the board:
  Wilson must not be very smart.
  He may not have a shop.
  He might not know his clerk very well.
  They couldn't pay him for copying an encyclopedia.
  Vincent can't be an honest man.
  — Ask: "Do these examples also express conclusions?" *(yes)* "How do you express negative conclusions?" *(must/may/might/could/can + not + base form of verb)* "Which modals can be contracted in sentences expressing conclusions?" *(couldn't, can't)* "Which modals are not often contracted in sentences expressing conclusions?" *(must not, may not, and might not)*
- To explain affirmative statements with *have got* and *have got to*, write on the board:
  Wilson has (got) to be worried.
  Watson and Holmes have (got) to suspect Vincent.

— Ask: "Do these examples also express conclusions?" *(yes)* "How do you express conclusions with *have to* or *have got to*?" *(form of* have to *or* have got to *+ base form of verb)* "Are *have to* and *have got to* used in affirmative or negative conclusions?" *(affirmative conclusions)*

• To explain *yes/no* and *wh-* questions, write on the board:
Could they pay Wilson for having red hair?
Can Wilson be a liar?

— Ask: "What modals do we use for questions about guesses?" (can *and* could)

— Write possible short answers next to each question:
Could they pay Wilson for having red hair? They could. / They couldn't. / They may not.
Can Wilson be a liar? He might be. / He has got to be. / He can't be.

— Point out that in short answers all the modals can be negative, except for *have (got) to.*

— Also point out that modals are often followed by *be* if the question uses *be* as a main verb.

• Erase *Could, Can,* and *be* from the questions and replace the modals with *Do* and *Is*:
Do they pay Wilson for having red hair? They could. / They couldn't. / They may not.
Is Wilson a liar? He might be. / He has got to be. / He can't be.

— Point out that questions that don't use modals can also be answered with modals to express that we are unsure of the answer.

Grammar Notes

Note 1

• Direct students' attention to the continuum that illustrates the degree of certainty expressed by each modal.

• Explain that in sentences expressing conclusions, some modals are used only in the affirmative and others are used only in the negative. (*Have to* and *have got to* are used only in the affirmative, and both *can't* and *couldn't* are used only in the negative.)

• Explain that the affirmative and negative form of the same modal might not express the same degree of certainty. (The affirmative form *must* and the negative form *must not* do not express the same degree of certainty.)

Note 2

• To explain *must, have to,* and *have got to* for affirmative conclusions, write on the board:
Holmes solves many mysteries.

• Read the fact aloud and draw a conclusion: *He must be very intelligent.* Write the conclusion on the board and add other possible modals:

He	must be has to be has got to be	very intelligent.

• Ask: "Am I very certain about my conclusion?" *(yes)*

• Point out that we use *must, have to,* and *have got to* when we are very certain about our conclusions.

• To explain *may, might,* and *could* for affirmative conclusions, write on the board:
Holmes solves many mysteries.

• Read the first fact aloud and draw a conclusion about which you are not too certain: *He might ask the police for help.* Write the conclusion on the board and add other possible modals:

He	may might could	ask the police for help.

• Point out how these conclusions do not necessarily spring from the fact. You're less certain about it, so you use *may, might,* or *could.*

Note 3

• To explain negative conclusions with *can't* and *couldn't*, write on the board:
Copying an encyclopedia is not a serious job. You can't be paid for that.
Wilson sounded honest when he talked to Holmes. He couldn't be a liar.

• Point out that we use *can't* and *couldn't* for negative conclusions when we are almost 100 percent certain.

• To explain negative conclusions with *must not, may not,* and *might not*, write on the board:
Alexandra never cooks.
She must not like cooking.
She may not have time.
She might not know how to cook.

• Point out that we use *must not, may not,* and *might not* for negative conclusions when we are not 100 percent certain. *May not* and *might not* express less certainty than *must not.*

• Draw attention to the *Be Careful!* note.

Note 4

- To explain questions with *can* and *could* and short answers, write on the board:
  Could Holmes have a plan? He might.
  Can Wilson be a liar? He could be.
- Ask: "Which modals can we use in questions? (*can* and *could*)
- Direct attention to the first example. Remind students that we use *be* in short answers to questions with *be*.
- Direct attention to the second example. Remind students that in short answers we use the modal alone.
- Draw attention to the *Be Careful!* note. Remind students that questions that don't use modals can also be answered with modals to express that we are unsure of the answer.

🕐 **Identify the Grammar:** Have students identify the grammar in the opening reading on page 446. For example:
  Mr. Wilson **must write** a lot . . .
  You **could be** right.
  Your methods **may be** useful after all.
  They **couldn't pay** someone just for having red hair . . .

Go to **www.myfocusongrammarlab.com** for grammar charts and notes.

Step 3: Focused Practice (pages 450–455)

See the general suggestions for Focused Practice on page 4.

Exercise 1: Discover the Grammar

A
- Go over the example with the class.
- Have students complete the exercise individually.
- Have students compare answers in pairs. Then call on pairs to give answers.

B
- Have students complete the exercise individually. Have them underline the sentences in the text that support their choices.
- Have students compare answers in pairs. Then call on pairs to give answers, having them support their answers with information from the text.
- 🕐 Based on what they have read, have students draw their own conclusions about the mystery. Have students discuss them with a partner. Follow up by having students share their conclusions with the class.

Exercise 2: Affirmative and Negative Statements
- Go over the example with the class. Ask: "Why is *must* the correct answer?" *(because it is dark; we are very certain about the conclusion)*
- Have students complete the exercise in pairs.
- Call on pairs to give answers.

Exercise 3: *Must* and *Must Not*
- As a class, have students describe the map of Mr. Wilson's neighborhood.
- Go over the example with the class.
- Have students complete the exercise individually. Then call on students to read the sentences aloud.

Exercise 4: *Have got to* and *Can't*
- Go over the example with the class. Then have students read the conversation quickly for meaning.
- Have students complete the exercise individually. Then call on a pair to read the conversation aloud. Have students read their rewrites of the underlined sentences.
- 🕐 Have pairs role-play the conversations.

Exercise 5: Short Answers: *Might (not)* or *Must (not)*
- Go over the example with the class. Ask: "Why is *must be* the correct answer?" *(because Holmes has a headache and his throat is starting to hurt—he is very certain that he is sick)*
- Have students read the conversations for meaning. Then have students complete the exercise individually. Remind them that we use the modal alone in short answers, but we use *be* in short answers to questions that use *be* as the main verb. Encourage them to find information to decide how certain the speaker is.
- Have students compare answers in pairs. Call on a pair to read the conversation aloud.

Exercise 6: Questions and Statements With *Be*
- Go over the example with the class.
- Have students read the conversation quickly for meaning. Then have students complete the exercise individually.
- Have students compare answers in pairs. Then call on a pair to read the conversation aloud.

Exercise 7: Editing

- Have students read the reading journal quickly for meaning. Then ask: "What is Molly Smith trying to find?" *(her dead grandparents' first home in the United States)* "What could the townspeople be scared of?" *(they could have a secret or just hate strangers)* "What did Molly find in an encyclopedia?" *(some letters)* "Who could the bad guy be?" *(the newspaper editor)*
- Go over the example with the class.
- Have students find and correct the mistakes individually. Then have students explain why the incorrect structures are wrong.
- ⏱ Have students point out examples of correct usages of *must, have (got) to, may, might, could,* and *can't.*

Go to **www.myfocusongrammarlab.com** for additional grammar practice.

Step 4: Communication Practice
(pages 455–459)

See the general suggestions for Communication Practice on page 5.

Exercise 8: Listening

A
- Tell students that they will listen to a conversation that provides the conclusion to the mystery "The Red-Headed League."
- Have students read the sentences quickly for meaning. Have them predict the order of the events.
- Play the audio. Have students listen.
- Play the audio again. Have students listen and complete the exercise individually.

B
- Have students read the statements quickly for meaning.
- Play the audio. Have students listen and complete the exercise individually. Encourage them to take notes to support (some of) their choices as they listen.
- ⏱ Call on a student to summarize the end of the story.

Exercise 9: Pronunciation

A
- Play the audio. Have students read along as they listen to the Pronunciation Note.
- To check comprehension, write on the board:
  1. He must be a robber.
  2. He has to be a robber.
  3. He's got to be a robber.

- Ask: "In sentence 1, which word receives the main stress?" *(must)* "In sentence 2, which word receives the main stress?" *(has)* "In sentence 3, which word receives the main stress?" *(got)* Underline the words as students say them.

B
- Have students read the conversations and anticipate which words they will hear stressed. Then have students write the modals they hear.

C
- Have students practice the conversations with a partner. Be sure students play both roles.

Exercise 10: Picture Discussion

- As a class, have students describe the pictures.
- Go over the example with the class.
- Form small groups. Have students in each group discuss the pictures. Point out that if they feel the evidence is solid, they should use *must* or *have (got) to.* If the evidence is not so sound, they should use *may, might,* or *could.*

Exercise 11: Problem Solving

- Go over the example with the class and point out the modals.
- Have students complete the exercise in pairs. Encourage them to be creative.
- Have each pair come to a conclusion about each situation and then share their ideas with the class.

Exercise 12: Writing

A
- Have students read the story outline individually.

B
- Go over the example with the class.
- Write the following questions on the board and have students think of their answers individually. Have students make notes of their answers:
  Is the murder suspect a man or a woman?
  Why does he/she talk to the exercise instructor?
  Who is Dr. Lorenzo? Is he a friend?
  Do you think the suspect is ill? Or does he/she want to find out information about a drug?
  Is the hairdresser a friend?
  What does the suspect pick up at the pharmacy? What is it for?
  Why does the suspect need $10,000?

The suspect has quite a lot of money in the bank. Is he/she a robber?

Who is Mr. Jordan? What is his relationship with the suspect?

Why does the suspect call the travel agency? Is he/she planning a trip?

Why does the suspect ask for a vegetarian meal?

• Form small groups. Have students complete the exercise in groups.

C

• Go over the example with the class.
• Have students write a paragraph expressing their conclusions.

D

• Have students correct their work using the Editing Checklist.

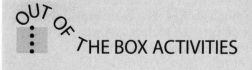

OUT OF THE BOX ACTIVITIES

Speaking

• Individually, have students write three true statements about themselves. *(Example: I never go cycling. I'm planning a vacation to Italy. I will move to a new city soon.)*
• In pairs, have students take turns sharing information about themselves with a partner and making relevant guesses. Write two examples on the board:
  A: I never go cycling.
  B: You might not have a bicycle then.
  A: Well, I have one, but I never use it!

  B: I'm planning a vacation to Italy.
  A: You must like historical places.
  B: I do!

Listening and Speaking

• Play the first scenes of a movie about a mystery or bring in the beginning of a mystery story.

• Have students watch the scenes or read the first part of the story.
• Form small groups. Have students draw conclusions about the characters or what might happen next.
• Follow up by having students share their conclusions with the class.
  Note: If some of the students have already watched the movie you selected, have them get together and write questions to ask their classmates.

Go to **www.myfocusongrammarlab.com** for additional listening, pronunciation, speaking, and writing practice.

Note:
• See the *Focus on Grammar Workbook* for additional in-class or homework grammar practice.

Unit 32 Review (page 460)

Have students complete the Review and check their answers on Student Book page UR-8. Review or assign additional material as needed.

Go to **www.myfocusongrammarlab.com** for the Unit Achievement Test.

From Grammar to Writing (pages 461–462)

See the general suggestions for From Grammar to Writing on page 9.

Go to **www.myfocusongrammarlab.com** for an additional From Grammar to Writing Assignment, Part Review, and Part Post-Test.

STUDENT BOOK AUDIOSCRIPT

EXERCISE 8 (page 11)

1. INTERVIEWER: Today's the end of your first week of classes here, Ana. How are you feeling?

ANA: Pretty good. Things are going really well. Everyone's friendly, and I'm learning a lot.

INTERVIEWER: You're living in a new country, and experiencing a new culture. What's the most difficult part?

ANA: The language. At home I speak my native language, Spanish, all the time. Right now I'm speaking English, of course.

2. INTERVIEWER: What about you, Mehmet? How are you doing?

MEHMET: Well, living here is a big change for me. In Turkey, I live in a very small town, but now I'm living in New York. New York is huge!

INTERVIEWER: Yes. New York IS a big city.

MEHMET: And it's also very exciting. Living abroad is a great opportunity.

3. INTERVIEWER: How do *you* like life in the big city, Eva? Are you experiencing culture shock?

EVA: Yes. Life here is very different. Especially the pace of life.

INTERVIEWER: The pace of life? What do you mean?

EVA: Well, I usually walk slowly, but here everyone moves very quickly.

INTERVIEWER: And what about you?

EVA: Well, now, I'm moving quickly too!

4. INTERVIEWER: What differences are you finding here, Paulo?

PAULO: Well, for one thing, I'm wearing a watch.

INTERVIEWER: You don't usually wear a watch? How do you know the time?

PAULO: Well, at home, I just ask other people. But people here expect you to arrive exactly on time. If you arrive late, they think you aren't polite. I don't want to have any misunderstandings, so, as you see, I'm wearing a watch. And I look at it all the time!

INTERVIEWER: What's the matter? You look upset.

PAULO: I just looked at my watch. It's 3:00. I'm going to be late!

5. INTERVIEWER: How do you like your classes here, Olga?

OLGA: Oh, I like them a lot. At home I study English literature, but here I'm taking a lot of other courses, too.

INTERVIEWER: Oh? What are you studying now?

OLGA: This summer I'm studying grammar and pronunciation.

EXERCISE 8 (page 26)

JANA: Good morning. You're listening to *Literary Notes*. With us in the studio today is prizewinning poet Murat Veli. Welcome.

MURAT: Thank you, Jana. It's a pleasure to be here.

JANA: Murat, in your poetry, you often write about your memories of Turkey. Were you born there?

MURAT: Yes, I was. But I came to the U.S. in 1980, when I was 10. My parents came here in 1975, five years before me. They found jobs and bought a house. Then I joined them.

JANA: Who did you live with between 1975 and 1980?

MURAT: My grandparents. Our family farm is in Sivas, in Central Turkey. I missed my parents, of course, but my life with my grandparents was wonderful. My grandmother told stories, and she knew hundreds of riddles. Very entertaining for a little boy.

JANA: So, then in 1980 you left Turkey and joined your parents in the U.S. Where did you live when you got here?

MURAT: We lived in Baltimore. You know, Jana, I felt so many different emotions when I got here. I was happy to see my parents, but I missed my grandparents. And I hated the city at first.

JANA: Really? Why did you feel that way?

MURAT: Because I had no freedom. I was a restless 10-year-old, but I was trapped in the city. I rode a school bus instead of my grandfather's horses. I had no friends to go out with, so I read. I escaped into books.

JANA: When did you start to write poetry?

MURAT: Well, first, you know, I wrote stories in Turkish all the time, from when I was only six or seven. But I wrote my first poem when I was 12—that was 1982. I wrote poetry in English.

JANA: Did you study poetry in school?

MURAT: No, I didn't. In college, I majored in farming, agriculture. But I wrote every day.

JANA: You won an award for your poetry at a very young age. When was that?

MURAT: Let's see . . . I graduated college in 1991, and I won the award a year later . . . so that was in 1992.

JANA: And what do you do when you aren't writing poetry?

MURAT: I teach it. I became a teacher in 1994, and I've been teaching since then. When I'm not farming, that is.

JANA: We have to pause for a break. When we return, Murat Veli will read one of his poems.

EXERCISE 9 (page 26)

B and **C**
1. **A:** Where'd he live?
   B: In Japan.
2. **A:** Who'd she talk to?
   B: A famous poet.
3. **A:** Why'd she move?
   B: To be near school.
4. **A:** How'd they feel about their new home?
   B: Not great at first.
5. **A:** Why'd he study poetry?
   B: He loves it.
6. **A:** Where'd he go to school?
   B: In Mexico.

UNIT 3

EXERCISE 7 (page 40)

B and **C**

OFFICER: Did you see the accident, miss?

WITNESS: Yes, I did, officer.

OFFICER: Can you tell me what happened?

WITNESS: I'll try, but it all happened so quickly. . .

OFFICER: That's OK. Try to stay calm. Take your time, and just tell me what you saw.

WITNESS: Well, I was walking down the street when I heard this car honking its horn. The driver was driving much too fast for this area. In fact, I'm sure he was speeding. The two men were just starting to cross the street. They were talking to each other and not paying attention to traffic. When they finally saw the car, they started to move out of the way, but it was too late. The car was moving too fast and was too close to the men to stop. The driver hit one of the men.

UNIT 4

EXERCISE 6 (page 53)

A: Wow! This reunion is awesome!

B: Yeah. Do you ever think back to our high school days? We were so different then. I don't know about you, but my life was really different back then. You know what I mean? Like, I always used to get up really early, and I'd never need an alarm clock. Today without an alarm clock, forget it!

A: I know what you mean. These days I can hardly get up *with* the alarm clock.

B: No kidding! And I remember, as soon as I woke up, I would have this really big breakfast. I mean *huge*—cereal, a banana, eggs, toast . . .

A: Me too. These days I'm lucky if I have time for a quick cup of coffee and a quick look at the newspaper.

B: Really! And when we were kids, we had endless energy. I used to run from morning to night. Now, I'm exhausted after just 15 minutes of aerobics.

A: Hey, do you remember that video game, uhm. . . Pacman?

B: Pacman! It used to be *really* popular. We'd play it—and other video games—for hours!

A: Yeah. Those were fun days. Kids collected all this Pacman stuff—lunchboxes, toys, puzzles. We had a lot more free time. We used to hang out with our friends every weekend, and we'd take trips in Linda's car. Remember?

B: I sure do. Well, now we're too busy to hang out. You know, we only see each other once every five years at the school reunion. I can't even *remember* the last trip I took.

A: Well, *this* is a trip.

B: A trip? What do you mean?

A: Well, it's a trip down memory lane!

B: I guess you're right!

UNIT 5

EXERCISE 5 (page 65)

A
1. I saw . . . at the restaurant.
2. The . . . car hit the truck.
3. It happened at . . .
4. . . . mother called me.
5. I reported it to . . .
6. There were . . . loud shouts.
7. . . . saw the man.
8. I have to hang up now because . . . .

B

1. **A:** I saw . . . at the restaurant.
   B: Who did you see?
   A: I saw the teacher.
2. **A:** The . . . car hit the truck.
   B: Which car hit the truck?
   A: The black car.
3. **A:** It happened at. . . .
   B: When did it happen?
   A: At 5:00 P.M.
4. **A:** . . . mother called me.
   B: Whose mother called you?
   A: My boyfriend's mother.
5. **A:** I reported it to. . . .
   B: Who did you report it to?
   A: The police.
6. **A:** There were . . . loud shouts.
   B: How many shouts did you hear?
   A: I heard four shouts.
7. **A:** . . . saw the man.
   B: Who saw the man?
   A: I did.
8. **A:** I have to hang up now because . . .
   B: Why do you have to hang up?
   A: Because the police are here!

UNIT 6

EXERCISE 8 (page 86)

1. **A:** I'm glad it's Friday. Let's go home.
   B: What are you doing tonight?
   A: The usual. I'm just staying home and watching TV.
2. **A:** Hi Pete. What are you watching?
   B: Oh. It's a program about space travel. Want to watch with me?
   A: Wow! Those photos of space are incredible!
3. **A:** There's a phone call for Professor Starr.
   B: Oh. He's working on the schedule for the next tourist flight. Can you take a message?
4. **A:** There's a lecture at the Community Center tonight.
   B: Really? What's it on?
   A: Some professor is talking about space travel. The lecture is called "To the Edge of Space." Do you want to go?
   B: I hope it's not already sold out.
5. **A:** I wish I could go to the lecture, but my parents are flying in from Florida.
   B: Oh! Are you going to meet them at the airport?
   A: No, they're going to take a taxi to my place.

6. **A:** Excuse me, what time does the train to Boston leave?
   B: The train to Boston! It leaves at 2:05. You'd better hurry. It's 2:00.
   A: Oh. Thanks.

UNIT 7

EXERCISE 5 (page 98)

MAN: Hello, Jobs Are Us. How can I help you?

WOMAN: Hi! Do you have any jobs for people with desktop publishing skills?

MAN: Yes. Have you had any work experience?

WOMAN: A little. I just graduated from college, but I worked on our college catalogue and Web page while I was in school.

MAN: OK. Do you have a résumé?

WOMAN: Yes, I do.

MAN: Fine. Why don't you email or fax us your résumé? As soon as we receive it, we'll set up an interview for you in our office.

WOMAN: OK. And what happens after that?

MAN: Well, after we interview you, you'll take a little skills test. Then, as soon as we see your test results, you'll meet with one of our job counselors. Together, we'll find the best job for you.

WOMAN: Sounds great. Will you send me on interviews at different companies?

MAN: Yes. But before we send you to any companies, you'll probably receive more job training.

WOMAN: I see. Do you have any written information about your agency that you could send to me?

MAN: Sure. I'll send you one of our brochures as soon as I get off the phone.

WOMAN: Thank you. And I'll send you my résumé.

MAN: I look forward to getting it. Goodbye.

WOMAN: Goodbye.

UNIT 8

EXERCISE 7 (page 117)

INTERVIEWER: It's nice to meet you, Eliana. So . . . about the job. WSPR would like to hire an announcer to cover college sports.

ELIANA: Well, you know, I *love* college sports. I've been an athlete myself for 15 years. I started in middle school, and in college, I played both soccer and basketball.

INTERVIEWER: How long have you been an announcer?

ELIANA: Since 2003. That's when I started college. As a student, I supported myself as an announcer for the college TV station. I reported on men's basketball.

INTERVIEWER: Have you worked as an announcer since you graduated?

ELIANA: Oh, sure. After I graduated—that was in 2007—I got a job with WESL in Tampa. I announced college sports there too. WESL *was* a community radio station. It's closed now.

INTERVIEWER: How long have you lived here in LA?

ELIANA: Since 2010. I moved here right after WESL closed. I was sorry to leave Tampa, but I like LA a lot.

INTERVIEWER: Have you worked at all since you arrived here?

ELIANA: Well, I haven't worked full-time since I moved to LA., but I've had several part-time jobs since then.

INTERVIEWER: I see, so you've only worked part-time since you moved here? How many part-time jobs have you had since then?

ELIANA: Uh, let's see. . . . I've been an announcer for WABC for six months, and for two years, I've been a sports writer for an online newspaper called Websports.com.

INTERVIEWER: How do you like sports writing?

ELIANA: You know, writing *is* one of my interests. But I've really considered myself an announcer since I was in college. My motto is: "Be where the action is." As an announcer, I have the opportunity to share that excitement with a lot more people.

INTERVIEWER: I see . . . Well, thanks for coming in, Eliana. I've enjoyed talking with you. We'll be in touch.

UNIT 9

EXERCISE 5 (page 127)

MAN: I'm getting nervous. The party's next week and we *still* haven't found a place for it!

WOMAN: Yes, we have! Don't worry! Jason said we can have it at his place.

MAN: But is Jason's place big enough? There are going to be more than 20 people. And we've already invited everyone!

WOMAN: He says it's no problem. And he's already borrowed extra chairs from his parents.

MAN: That's great. Now, what are we going to do about food?

WOMAN: Well, I haven't figured that one out yet. I might just have things like chips and salsa. I'm not sure.

MAN: What about drinks? Has anyone bought the soda yet?

WOMAN: Not yet. But we've got time for that.

MAN: OK. I can do that on Friday. Have we found someone to help us set up?

WOMAN: Yes. Ella's available. She's coming to Jason's Friday night to help us set up.

MAN: Great. You sound pretty organized!

WOMAN: Yeah. I think things are pretty much under control.

MAN: Oh! What about music?

WOMAN: Ella has already taken care of that. Relax! It's going to be a great party!

UNIT 10

EXERCISE 7 (page 142)

OLIVIA: It's time for my annual vacation and I'm looking for something different this year.

AGENT: OK. What type of vacation are you interested in?

OLIVIA: Well, I've done a lot of adventure traveling, and I've enjoyed things like white water rafting. But this time I'm looking for something *really* unusual. Something exciting and challenging. Something I've never done before.

AGENT: Well, you've come to the right place. Here at Adventure Travel, we have lots of exciting possibilities. Here, take a look at this. . . . Have you ever gone hang gliding? We've got a great trip in Australia that includes hang gliding.

OLIVIA: Hang gliding's great, but I've done it. Quite a few times, actually.

AGENT: OK. *Travel Today's* just come out with the results of their survey. Their readers say that the number one adventure vacation this year is skydiving. I bet you haven't tried that!

OLIVIA: No, I haven't. But I think that's a little too adventurous for me. I don't want this to be my *last* vacation, after all!

AGENT: I understand. How about shark diving then? Have you ever been shark diving?

OLIVIA: Shark diving? You're kidding, right?

AGENT: No. Believe it or not, it's probably a lot safer than skydiving. You get really up close and personal with the sharks, but you're in this cage. See?

OLIVIA: I don't thinks so . . . Maybe I should stay on land.

AGENT: OK. How about snowmobiling in Canada?

OLIVIA: Been there, done that. Not my favorite form of transportation—too noisy. But, you know, all this talk about adventure's made me think. Maybe what I *really* need is a nice, quiet vacation.

AGENT: Well, then this here is the perfect vacation for you! It's a wonderful location and it's quite affordable, too. Here, take a look at the brochure. . . .

UNIT 11

EXERCISE 7 (page 154)

INTERVIEWER: As you know, we've been interviewing married faculty members. How long have the two of you been married?

MAN: For 10 years.

WOMAN: Yeah, but we lived in different cities for most of that time.

MAN: That's right. It was very hard, I should say impossible, to get a job in the same city.

WOMAN: Yes, in fact, this is the first time we've been at the same university since we were graduate students back in Boston.

INTERVIEWER: How long did you live in Boston?

MAN/WOMAN: Six years.

INTERVIEWER: And how long have you been in Madison?

WOMAN: Oh, let's see. How long has it been? A year now?

MAN: That's right. We've been here for almost a year. July will be exactly a year.

WOMAN: Yes. We *finally* managed to find jobs in the same city *and* at the same university. It's been great!

MAN: Right. And now that we don't have to pay rent for two apartments, we've been able to buy a house.

WOMAN: We've only had it for a month, and we love it.

MAN: It sure beats driving six hours every weekend to see each other!

WOMAN: You can say that again!

UNIT 12

EXERCISE 7 (page 168)

B and C

1. **A:** Isn't it great?
   B: Isn't what great?
   A: Haven't you noticed? They've planted some trees in front of the new library.
2. **A:** I haven't eaten since this morning! Is anybody else hungry?
   B: I don't think so. We've been eating this pizza. Why don't you order something for yourself?

3. **A:** Hi, Eloy. We haven't spoken in a while. How's the house going?
   B: Well, it's rained a lot since we spoke, but today we've been working on it.
4. **A:** I'm sorry I've gotten behind on schoolwork, Professor Davis. I've been working on the solar house almost every day.
   B: You must be so excited about your trip to Madrid.
   A: Yeah, I really am. We just sent the house and I've packed all my stuff!
   B: Well, good luck in the competition! The house looks beautiful!
5. **A:** Have you seen the school newspaper? Jane Owen interviewed Eloy in Madrid!
   B: I saw the article. I'm surprised she had the time. She's been so busy these days.
   A: Jane's always busy. What's she been doing lately?
   B: Well, for one thing, she's been writing a book about global warming.

EXERCISE 8 (page 169)

B and C

1. **A:** *Avatar* is playing at the college theater.
   B: Oh, I've seen it.
2. **A:** I didn't see Emma yesterday.
   B: She hasn't been working Mondays.
3. **A:** I just handed in my research paper. What about you?
   B: Well, I haven't started it.
4. **A:** There's a new student in our class.
   B: I've heard about her.
5. **A:** Did you decide on a vacation?
   B: We've been thinking about it.

UNIT 13

EXERCISE 6 (page 185)

WOMAN: Our office is very busy, Karl. As you can hear, we get a lot of phone calls.

KARL: Oh, that's no problem. I can handle phones.

WOMAN: Good. Now, many of our students are foreign. Tell me, Karl. Can you speak any other languages besides English?

KARL: Well, not really. I used to be able to speak Spanish, but I'm out of practice now.

WOMAN: That's OK. Maybe it will come back to you. Now, what about your computer skills?

KARL: Well, I can do word processing and I can use the Internet.

WOMAN: Can you do spreadsheets, too?

KARL: No. But I'm sure I can learn.

WOMAN: OK. Now, how fast can you type?

KARL: Fifty words per minute.

WOMAN: That's good. Can you do any desktop publishing? We're thinking of designing a monthly newsletter.

KARL: Well, I can't right now. But I *am* taking a course in desktop publishing, so I'm sure I'll be able to do it pretty soon.

WOMAN: Great. You also have to schedule appointments. Many of our students take private dance lessons.

KARL: That's no problem. I can do that.

WOMAN: OK. Let's see. What else? Oh yeah—can you drive?

KARL: Sure!

WOMAN: Oh, that's good. I may need you to do some errands for me from time to time.

KARL: Sure, I'll be able to do that.

WOMAN: Oh! There's the music for our swing class! Can you dance, Karl?

KARL: No, but I hope I'll be able to take some classes here if I get the job.

EXERCISE 7 (page 185)

B and **C**
1. I can't dance.
2. They can speak Chinese.
3. He can fly a plane.
4. We can't understand you.
5. She can swim, but she can't dive.
6. He can't drive.

UNIT 14

EXERCISE 5 (page 197)

1. **DRIVER:** Excuse me. May I park here?
   OFFICER: Yes. Parking's allowed after 6:00 P.M.
2. **CALLER:** Hi, Mrs. Carter? This is Jeff. Can I please speak to Linda?
   MOTHER: Hi, Jeff. I'm sorry, Linda's sleeping. Could I take a message?
3. **BOY:** Can I leave the table now? I'm finished eating, and I want to watch TV.
   MOTHER: No, honey, not yet. I want you to wait until we're all finished.
4. **EMPLOYEE:** I feel awful. I've got a headache, and I'm sick to my stomach. Do you mind if I leave work now?
   SUPERVISOR: Not at all. Go home and get some rest.
5. **STUDENT:** May I take a make-up exam, Professor O'Dell? I didn't feel well during the last test.

TEACHER: Sorry, but that won't be possible this time.
6. **STUDENT 1:** Hey, can I borrow a pen? All mine have disappeared.
   STUDENT 2: No problem. Keep it if you want. I've got plenty.
7. **AGENT:** This is Globe Travel, Mr. Sanchez. Have you decided what day you want to leave for Chicago?
   CUSTOMER: No, not yet. Could I tell you tomorrow? I need to talk to my wife first.
   AGENT: I'm sorry, but I'm afraid I have to know today. This is the last day I can book your flight.

EXERCISE 6 (page 198)

B and **C**
1. Can she come with us?
2. Could I ask a question?
3. Can he sit over there?
4. May we call you tonight?
5. Could he get a ride with you?

UNIT 15

EXERCISE 5 (page 210)

1. **ETHAN:** Hey, Mom, it's Ethan. Can you drive me to the library on Saturday morning? I have a report to do for school.
   MARCIA: Sorry, I can't. I'm taking Jody to the dentist on Saturday morning.
   ETHAN: Will you take me in the afternoon?
   MARCIA: Sure. We can all go to the library in the afternoon.
2. **KELLY:** Hello, Marcia? This is Kelly. I have to ask you a big favor. We're going to a party on Saturday night. Could you babysit for us? I'd really appreciate it.
   MARCIA: Oh, I'd like to, but I can't. We're going to the movies Saturday night. Why don't you try Ann? She babysits for us sometimes.
3. **MOTHER:** Hi, Marcia. This is Mom. Listen, we're going away for the day on Sunday. Could you come and walk the dog on Sunday morning?
   MARCIA: Sure. I'd be glad to. What time should I come?
   MOTHER: Come at about 8:00. Thanks a lot.
4. **JOHN:** Hi Marcia. This is John. Are you going to the gym on Saturday afternoon?
   MARCIA: Yes, I am.
   JOHN: Would you mind giving me a ride? My car broke down this week.
   MARCIA: Not at all. I'd be glad to.

EXERCISE 6 (page 223)

Tim: Good morning! And welcome to Computer Chat! I'm your host, Tim Tommando. Today we're talking about buying a new computer. Got a question? Give me a call at 1-800-555-ENTER. I'm here to help you. OK, we've got Amy on the line from Miami. Go ahead, Amy.

Amy: Hi Tim. I'm a first-time caller.

Tim: Welcome, Amy! How can I help you?

Amy: My computer is seven years old. It's still working, but it's beginning to do some strange things. I don't know what to do. Should I get it repaired or buy a new one?

Tim: Don't even think about getting it repaired, Amy! Seven years is very old for a computer. The normal life of a computer is around five years. You really should get a new one.

Amy: OK. But, I know there have been a lot of changes in the last seven years. How do I get information about all the features in new computers?

Tim: Good question, Amy. There are a lot of excellent websites with computer reviews. You should read them and learn what's available and what you want. And, a word of advice to *all* my listeners. You shouldn't throw away your old computer if it's still working. Keep it in case you have trouble with your new one. You won't regret it!

Amy: I guess it's time for a new computer, then. Thanks, Tim!

Tim: You're welcome. We've got Jason from Toronto. Jason, you're on the air.

Jason: Good morning, Tim. Thank you for taking my call. I'm ready to buy a new computer. Here's my question: Should I buy it from one of those big companies online, or should I get it at a local computer store?

Tim: Good question, Jason. A computer from a big online company is cheaper, but if you want to be satisfied, you should avoid deciding on price alone. Service is very, very important. For the best service, you should shop at a local computer store. And you really ought to consider paying a little extra for a service contract. That way if there's a problem, they'll repair it for you—fast and at no cost. We've got Marta on the line from Texas . . .

Marta: Hi, Tim. I'm getting a new computer. What's the most important thing to look for?

Tim: RAM. That's computer memory. You should always get as much memory as you can afford. Well, we've run out of time for today. Tune in next Friday for more computer tips on computer chat. I'm Tim Tommando. And remember: always protect your identity! Goodbye, and happy computing!

EXERCISE 5 (page 241)

A

Emily: I found this recipe for Roman Apple Cake in my grandmother's old stuff. I think it sounds kind of like the cake we had in Italy. Maybe we should try it.

James: Good idea. What are the ingredients?

Emily: Here, I'll read them to you:
one and a half cups sugar
a half cup vegetable oil
two eggs
two cups flour
one teaspoon baking powder
one teaspoon baking soda

James: Wait a minute. Baking powder *and* baking soda? Why do we need both? What's the difference?

Emily: I think you need baking soda when a recipe has fruit in it.

James: Oh, OK. What else goes in it?

Emily: one quarter teaspoon salt
one half teaspoon cinnamon
one cup milk
a half cup raisins
a half cup nuts
and
three apples

B and **C**

James: Hmmm. The recipe sounds good. Let's make it. Read the ingredients again?

Emily: OK. One and a half cups sugar.

James: Sugar. We have a lot of sugar. What's next?

Emily: A half cup vegetable oil. We don't have much vegetable oil, but we have enough for the recipe. Let's see. What's next? Eggs. We only need two.

James: Well, we don't have *any* eggs. We used them all yesterday when we made the omelets. Remember?

Emily: Yeah. What about flour? We need two cups.

James: We don't have enough flour either.

Emily: OK. Well, what about baking powder and baking soda?

James: Let's see. . . . We have some baking powder, but we don't have any baking soda. What's next?

EMILY: Salt. We always have plenty of salt. I don't know about cinnamon, though. Do we have any cinnamon?

JAMES: Yes. We still have a lot of cinnamon.

EMILY: Good. Do we have enough milk? It says one cup.

JAMES: Yeah. We have enough. What else?

EMILY: The recipe calls for a half cup nuts, but it doesn't say what kind.

JAMES: Well, we usually have lots of nuts, but we used them all last week when we baked brownies.

EMILY: OK. What about raisins? We need a half cup.

JAMES: Raisins? Hmm. We have just a few, but it's enough for this recipe.

EMILY: OK. And last, but not least, we need three apples.

JAMES: Well, we don't have *any* apples. Why don't we make a shopping list and I'll go shopping.

EMILY: Great.

UNIT 18

EXERCISE 7 (page 256)

1. **AMY:** Why are you laughing?
   BEN: I just finished the story by Nasreddin. It's very funny.
2. **AMY:** What's that?
   BEN: Oh. It's the new video game. Do you want to try it?
3. **AMY:** I'm reading the story you recommended now. Who's Angelica? I can't figure it out.
   BEN: She's the princess with magic powers.
4. **AMY:** What about Aesop? Have you read the fable?
   BEN: No. I'm going to tonight.
5. **AMY:** You know, I'd like to buy a book of fables for Ava.
   BEN: Good idea. She loves fables.
6. **AMY:** Let's go to the bookstore this weekend.
   BEN: OK. We can go on Sunday after lunch.
7. **AMY:** Speaking of lunch, I'm hungry. Were there leftovers from dinner last night?
   BEN: Yeah, but I ate them. Here. Why don't you have a sandwich?
8. **AMY:** Have you seen my coffee cup?
   BEN: I think I put it on a shelf above the sink.

UNIT 19

EXERCISE 8 (page 276)

B and **C**

A: I found four apartments in Jan's list that I think we should take a look at.

B: Good! Tell me about them.

A: Well, they're all two bedrooms, and they all cost between $650 and $850 a month.

B: Great! That sounds pretty affordable. What's the first one like?

A: Let's see. The first one is described as a small charming two-bedroom in an old building. It's also very near public transportation. It doesn't say anything else about it.

B: Hmm. Right. So let's forget about that one.

A: Now, the second one has more information. It sounds like it's sunny. It says it's just been painted and is in excellent condition. It's also located near stores and schools. Oh! And it says the apartment is on a beautiful tree-lined street.

B: That sounds better. We wanted a sunny place. What about the other two?

A: OK. The third one is described as "cute and cozy."

B: Uh-oh. You know what that usually means!

A: Yeah, it's probably very small.

B: What else does it say?

A: It says the appliances are all new. And it's in a peaceful residential area.

B: Hmmm, "peaceful residential" . . . That could mean there are no stores or anything around.

A: Right. . . . And we couldn't bring Loki . . . Hey! Look at this one. It's got a photograph. It says the apartment's in a completely renovated building with a modern kitchen and bathroom and all new appliances.

B: What's wrong with that? Sounds terrific!

A: Nothing. It's available immediately, *and* pets are welcome.

UNIT 20

EXERCISE 6 (page 290)

A: How about pizza for dinner?

B: Sounds good. Any special brand?

A: Well, here's the frozen food section. Let's see what they have.

B: OK . . . there's Di Roma's and there's Angela's. Ever hear of those?

A: No. How do they compare in price?

B: Let's see. Angela's is $5.38, and Di Roma's is $4.59.

A: Hhmm. Di Roma's is cheaper, but the pizza isn't as big as Angela's.

B: Right. Angela's is bigger. You get five and a quarter slices from a Di Roma's pizza, but you get six slices from an Angela's.

A: Hmmm.

B: What are you looking at?

A: The nutrition information. Listen to this. Angela's uses low-fat cheese, so there are fewer grams of fat.

B: Sounds like Angela's is the healthier choice. What else does the label say?

A: Well, in addition to tomatoes and water, Angela's sauce has just basil and black pepper. Di Roma's has basil, oregano, garlic, onions, salt, and pepper.

B: Di Roma's sounds a lot tastier.

A: Yeah. It's hard to choose. Let's see if there's an expiration date.

B: Di Roma's says sell by February 15 of this year.

A: That's in two weeks! The Angela's says sell by April 15 of next year.

B: Then, let's get Angela's. It's fresher, and we can always add our own spices.

A: Good idea.

UNIT 21

EXERCISE 6 (page 303)

MAY: If we're going to go to Toronto next summer, we should make reservations pretty soon.

DAN: Reservations? But it's only January!

MAY: Yes, but the guidebooks all say hotels fill up fast, so we'd better not wait.

DAN: OK, this won't be too hard. We've already gotten our choices down to three hotels—the Westin Harbour Castle, the Hôtel Le Germain, and the Delta Chelsea. They all have some nice features.

MAY: Well, the Westin Harbour Castle has the best view of all three. It's right on the lake, and a lot of the rooms have good views. Oh, and they have a restaurant with views of both the lake and the city.

DAN: Sounds beautiful, but we're going to see a lot of shows so we want to be close to the entertainment district. Unfortunately, the Westin Harbour Castle is the least convenient for that. I guess we could always take public transportation, but I prefer to walk. Also, it's really big, and we both like small hotels.

MAY: OK, um . . . let's see . . . the Hôtel Le Germain is very close to the entertainment district. From there we could walk to the theater, the sports arena, and to the CN Tower. And it has only 122 rooms. Here, look at these pictures.

DAN: Wow, it looks really comfortable. Here, it says, "We give our guests every comfort, including free high-speed internet access and DVD players."

MAY: Sounds great. It's the smallest, most comfortable, *and* the most convenient of all. How much are the rooms?

DAN: They start at $295.

MAY: Ouch! So, it's also the most expensive. And the Westin Harbour Castle is only a little cheaper.

DAN: OK. Maybe we don't need absolutely the *best* view or the *most* convenient location.

MAY: Right. Well, then I think the Delta Chelsea is probably our best choice. It's the least expensive of the three, and the guidebook says it's the best value in Toronto.

DAN: It has 1,600 rooms! Is that OK with you? It's the biggest hotel in the city.

MAY: Sure. We can afford it, and it's not too far from the entertainment district.

DAN: Great. I'll get online and make the reservation, OK? This is going to be the best vacation we've ever had!

UNIT 22

EXERCISE 6 (page 314)

LENA: Niklas and I are here in Dubai at the famous Nad al Sheba Racecourse. What a race this was, ladies and gentlemen. I think most people were expecting Wild Whirl to win, but there were a lot of surprises before the finish. Nobody fell asleep during this race, I can tell you that!

NIKLAS: You're right, Lena. It was an amazing race. At the beginning, Wild Whirl was the favorite. He's an experienced racer from Sydney, Australia, and recently he's been winning the most consistently of any horse in the race.

LENA: But in the first turn, Inspired Winner was running just as fast as Wild Whirl. That was a surprise! Those two made a fast start and were leading everybody at the beginning.

NIKLAS: And remember, Get Packin' wasn't *that* far behind. He started a little slower than Wild Whirl and Inspired Winner, but he sure made history here today. Get Packin'—a newcomer, but a name everyone will know from now on.

LENA: Another surprise in the first turn—Señor Speedy and Exuberant King! They were waaaay behind all the others.

NIKLAS: You're right, Lena. That was the slowest that Exuberant King has ever started. It looked like those two were running in a different race!

Lena: But then look at what happened in the second turn. Señor Speedy took off like lightning!

Niklas: Absolutely. And that woke up Exuberant King. Did you see Señor Speedy and Exuberant King, folks? Suddenly, in the second turn, they were moving as fast as any two horses can move.

Lena: Yes, but unfortunately not fast enough. As fast as they were going, they couldn't catch up with the leaders. Señor Speedy stayed in third place until the end and Exuberant King finished fourth.

Niklas: And what happened to Inspired Winner?

Lena: That was *very* strange. At the beginning, he was right up front with Wild Whirl. Then he started running slower and slower, and Inspired Winner actually finished last!

Niklas: So at the end, the race was between Wild Whirl, the favorite, and Get Packin', a newcomer. Were you surprised that Get Packin' was the winner today? And that Wild Whirl finished second?

Lena: Totally. But we learned today that Get Packin' is a real champion. He hasn't raced as often as the others, but I've never seen a horse compete as aggressively as Get Packin' did today. He deserved to win.

Niklas: And Wild Whirl in second place is still a great racehorse and a serious competitor.

UNIT 23

EXERCISE 6 (page 329)

Patient: So, doctor, what do you think?

Doctor: Well, first of all, you must stop smoking. That's the most important thing you can do for your health.

Patient: That'll be difficult, but I'll try.

Doctor: You should also quit drinking so much coffee.

Patient: Really? I thought coffee was OK.

Doctor: It is. In moderation, though. Eight cups a day is too much. But two cups is OK.

Patient: OK. What about my weight? I've lost about five pounds.

Doctor: Well, avoid losing any more weight. Stay at 160 pounds. That's the perfect weight for you. As for your diet, you eat enough protein, but I suggest eating more complex carbohydrates.

Patient: Complex carbohydrates?

Doctor: Yes. Things like whole grain bread and pasta. Here, I'll give you a list of foods with complex carbs.

Patient: Oh, thanks. Now, what about exercise?

Doctor: Well, exercise is very important, but avoid running every day. It's too stressful on the bones. You can injure yourself.

Patient: But I enjoy running, and I want to do *some* form of exercise every day.

Doctor: And you should. Have you considered riding a bike? Cycling is something you can do every day without harm.

Patient: OK. Any other advice?

Doctor: Yes. Keep working eight hours a day. Being active mentally and physically is the best thing for you.

Patient: Great. I'll do that, Doctor.

UNIT 24

EXERCISE 5 (page 340)

Counselor: So . . . I understand you're a blended family. Do you both have children?

Woman: No, just me. I've been married once before. I have a teenage daughter from my first marriage. For a long time, Brenda—that's my daughter's name—couldn't get along with my new husband. The two of them always used to argue. Obviously, I really wanted them to discuss their problems, but that was impossible at first.

Counselor: How's that going for you now, George? Still arguing?

Man: No—and what a relief! I guess I'm a slow learner, but I finally learned not to argue with my stepdaughter.

Counselor: It's great you managed to stop. A lot of parents can't do that. How about you, Darlene? Did the arguing upset you?

Woman: Oh, sure. I felt terrible about it. But I have friends with similar problems, so I knew that blended families always have a lot to learn. I expected to have problems with my daughter.

Man: But it was much, much worse than we thought. For a while, my stepdaughter refused to talk to me at all. To be honest, sometimes I just wanted her to leave the house for a few hours.

Woman: I know what you mean. But we always tried to understand Brenda's feelings. After all, she didn't choose to live with us. I made that choice for her.

Counselor: It's good that you attempted to understand her feelings. I always advise parents to look at things through the child's eyes. But it's very hard. So I also encourage them not to give up.

MAN: It's funny that you say that because I *almost* gave up. The situation seemed hopeless. But then one day, Brenda asked me to go on a family vacation—the three of us went to California. I couldn't believe it—*and* we had a wonderful time!

WOMAN: It's true. I was amazed. We wanted her to enjoy being together as a family, and it actually happened. That trip really changed everything. Of course, we still have problems, but we can talk about them now.

UNIT 25

EXERCISE 7 (page 352)

It's fast. It's small enough to put in your pocket. It's easy to use. It's smarter than ever. And—it's here!

Here are just a few of the thousands of things you can do with it:

Hungry? Use the E-phone to look for a nearby restaurant or to help you find the perfect recipe to make yourself.

Need help with your schoolwork? No problem! Use your E-phone to bring encyclopedias and dictionaries to class. We promise—they won't be too heavy to carry!

Trying to remember what you have to do this week? With the E-phone, it's easy to stay organized. Create To Do lists and search them by person, place, or date.

Love to shop for clothing? Tap to see the latest fashion trends. Then use a program to put together an outfit just for you.

Want to know what's going on in the world? Use it to look at headlines from hundreds of newspapers.

The new E-phone has arrived and—good news! It's affordable enough for everyone to buy. But you must act fast. Supplies are limited. To order your phone, go to www.ezphone.cam or call us at 1-800-555-5555. Call within the next 24 hours and get 10 percent off. So don't delay. Call now. This offer is too good to miss.

UNIT 26

EXERCISE 7 (page 365)

INTERVIEWER: You recently joined a support group for procrastinators. Tell me about it.

EVA: Yes. I decided to join after trying to solve the problem on my own and failing. It was really discouraging. The support group has taught me a lot of useful tips to deal with my problem.

INTERVIEWER: What have you learned?

EVA: Well, for one thing I now always clean my work area before I start working. I know this sounds simple, but in the past, I didn't do it. I thought it was a waste of time. But sitting at a messy desk is distracting, and I wasted a lot of time *that* way.

INTERVIEWER: OK. Now let's say you have an important test. When do you start studying for it?

EVA: Well, in the past, I put off studying until the night before the test. Not anymore. Now I start preparing a week before the test—at least. As a result, I feel much less anxious, and I do better on the test. I also choose to study the hardest thing first.

INTERVIEWER: The hardest thing? Why's that?

EVA: It makes the whole thing easier, and that way I'm sure I can study everything.

INTERVIEWER: Sounds like good time management! What else do you do?

EVA: I follow the experts' advice and write down all my tasks on a To Do list—along with their deadlines. Then I tape the list on my computer monitor so I always see it. That way I don't forget to do anything.

INTERVIEWER: Do you take breaks?

EVA: I used to take breaks—long breaks. It was a way of avoiding work. I stopped doing that. I mean, I still take breaks now, but they're short—just 10 minutes. During my breaks I like to do relaxation exercises. This helps me work better when I start again.

INTERVIEWER: Do you ever give yourself a reward when you finish a project?

EVA: A reward? No. Finishing the project, getting good grades, and feeling less anxious is more than enough reward for me!

UNIT 27

EXERCISE 6 (page 384)

1. **A:** The guys in Mark's department did a great job this year.
   B: I know. They should be really proud of each other.
2. **A:** What's wrong? You look upset.
   B: I just heard Ed and Jeff talking. You know Ed blames himself for everything.
   A: That's ridiculous. It's not his fault.
3. **A:** I hear you're going to Japan on vacation this year. Are you going by yourself or with a tour?
   B: Oh, with a tour.
4. **A:** Did you get your test results?
   B: Yes. The doctor herself called me this morning. Everything's fine.
5. **A:** Jennifer looks happy tonight. Did Megan finally give her the promotion?
   B: No, not yet. Megan keeps asking herself if she can do the job.

6. **A:** How do you like the new computer system?
   B: I'm not sure. In our department, we're still teaching ourselves how to use it.
7. **A:** So long, now. Thanks for coming. It was good to see you.
   B: Oh, it was a great party.
   C: Yes, it really was.
   A: I'm glad you enjoyed yourselves.

UNIT 28

EXERCISE 7 (page 399)

1. **A:** Did you see Dr. Pepperberg in class today?
   B: Yes. She brought up that DVD about Alex. Very interesting.
2. **A:** What's Terry doing?
   B: She's handing out some lab reports.
3. **A:** Are you done with your report, Rea?
   B: Almost. I just have to look up some information.
4. **A:** Hey, guys. That music is disturbing us.
   B: Sorry. We'll turn it off.
5. **A:** Jason is discouraged.
   B: I know. He says he can't keep up with the class.
6. **A:** Did you hear about Lila?
   B: Yes, we were all surprised when she dropped in yesterday.
7. **A:** OK, class. It's time to take off your lab coats.
   B: Oh, could we have a few more minutes? We're almost done.
8. **A:** Hi. Can I help you?
   B: Yes, thanks. I need to pick out a book for my biology report.

UNIT 29

EXERCISE 7 (page 417)

1. **A:** OK. What do I do now? Should I go left or right at the corner?
   B: You *have* to turn left. You can't make a right turn here.
2. **A:** Why are you driving so slowly?
   B: Because the speed limit is 30 kilometers an hour.
   A: No, it isn't. The blue sign means you have to drive *at least* 30 kilometers an hour. You can't drive more slowly than that. You're only doing 25!
3. **A:** This scenery is beautiful. Let's stop and take some pictures.
   B: You can't stop here.
   A: I can't? Not even for a few minutes?
   B: Nope. See that big red X? It means "no stopping."

4. **A:** Slow down a little. It's starting to rain.
   B: I can't slow down. Look at the sign.
   A: I know. But that's the *maximum* speed—it's the fastest you can drive. You don't *have* to drive 80 kilometers an hour!
5. **A:** You have to stop here.
   B: Why? There's no traffic.
   A: Yes. But you've got to come to a complete stop when you see that sign.
6. **A:** Gosh, that car is going awfully slow.
   B: So, why don't you pass?
   A: See that sign? I have to wait. I can't pass here. It's not allowed.

UNIT 30

EXERCISE 5 (page 430)

1. **A:** Where's Netta? It's 2:00 already.
   B: Relax. She isn't supposed to be here until 2:30.
   A: Oh, OK. I guess I am a little nervous.
2. **A:** Do you know how she's getting here?
   B: Well, she wasn't going to walk!
3. **A:** What's the photographer doing up there? He isn't supposed to take pictures during the ceremony.
   B: It's OK. He's just checking the light.
4. **A:** Let's go sit down. The ceremony's going to start soon.
   B: Where do we sit?
   A: We're with the bride's family, so we're supposed to sit on the left.
5. **A:** Here come the bridesmaids now. Oooh, don't they look beautiful.
   B: Yes! But I'm a little surprised. I thought they were going to wear pink.
   A: They were, but Netta changed her mind.
6. **A:** Where is Sophie?
   B: She'll come in later. She's the maid of honor, so she's supposed to walk behind the bride.
7. **A:** I've never been to an American wedding. What are we supposed to say to the bride and groom?
   B: Tell the bride she looks beautiful. Say "congratulations" to the groom.
8. **A:** Where are Gary and Netta? They should be at the reception by now.
   B: Don't worry. They'll be here soon. They're supposed to sign the marriage certificate after the ceremony.
9. **A:** Hey, I thought we were supposed to throw rice at the bride and groom on their way out of the church.
   B: No, not anymore. People say it can hurt the birds.
   A: Really?

EXERCISE 6 (page 441)

And now for the weekend forecast.

A lot of you are still shoveling snow from Wednesday's storm, but take heart. We are going to see a warming trend very soon. Warm, dry air is moving in from the south and will be here by Friday. We might see sunny skies and temperatures in the low 50s by Friday.

Plan to get out on Saturday—it's going to be a beautiful day. It will be bright and sunny, and temperatures may exceed 60 by Saturday afternoon. There will be some wind, though, with gusts reaching 20 miles per hour. No need to bundle up, but bring a jacket.

Unfortunately, this beautiful weather won't stay with us for the whole weekend. A new storm front is right behind this good weather. By Sunday afternoon, cold, windy weather could be here again, and there might even be some flurries Sunday evening. This could affect weekend traffic, so drive carefully if you have to be on the road.

Don't put away the snow shovel yet. Winter is still with us.

This is meteorologist Steven Storm for the Weather Channel. Have a good evening, and see you tomorrow.

UNIT 32

EXERCISE 8 (page 455)

Holmes: Dr. Watson, this is Captain Rogers from the Police Department.

Captain: How do you do, Dr. Watson? Well, we're all here now. It must be 10:00. Let's go down to the basement.

Holmes: You lead, Captain. We'll follow you.

Captain: The storeroom is in here. Please close the door.

Holmes: Let's get comfortable. We may have a long wait.

Watson: I'm going to sit on one of these boxes. Uh . . . What's in all these boxes, Captain?

Captain: Gold coins. Two months ago, the bank borrowed a large amount of gold from France. There may be 2,000 gold coins in that box, Dr. Watson.

Holmes: You look amazed, Dr. Watson. But think about it—John Clay must know about this gold. That's why he took the position at Wilson's.

Watson: Right! So there is no American millionaire. Clay invented the Red-Headed League to keep Wilson away from the shop. While Wilson was copying the encyclopedia, John Clay was digging a tunnel to the bank.

Holmes: Clay just ended the Red-Headed League. So his tunnel has to be finished.

Captain: You're right, Mr. Holmes! Listen! . . . This floor is hollow. The tunnel has got to be right here, under this floor! Once again your method has solved a mystery!

Holmes: Did you bring your gun, Watson? John Clay could be dangerous.

Watson: Yes, I did. But what is he waiting for? It's after 10:00.

Holmes: He may want Wilson to be asleep before he comes.

Captain: Shhh! I hear a noise under the floor!

Holmes: That might be Clay in the tunnel! Get ready!

Clay: Police?!

Holmes: How do you do? You must be Mr. John Clay!

Captain: You're under arrest, Mr. Clay.

EXERCISE 9 (page 456)

B

1. **A:** Look at the crowds!
   B: This must be a really popular movie.
2. **A:** Do you have the tickets?
   B: Yeah, I'm sure I put them in my pocket. They have to be here somewhere.
3. **A:** This might be the best movie I've seen this year.
   B: Me too. George Clooney is so funny.
4. **A:** He may be the thief. He's already committed a lot of crimes.
   B: He can't be. He's the star!
5. **A:** You may be right.
   B: I guess we'll know in a few minutes. It's got to be over soon.
6. **A:** That was a long movie. It has to be after 10:00 by now.
   B: You're right. It's almost 10:30.

STUDENT BOOK ANSWER KEY

In this answer key, where the contracted form is given, the full form is also correct. Where the full form is given, the contracted form is also correct.

UNIT 1 (pages 2–15)

AFTER YOU READ

A. **1.** a **3.** c **5.** b
2. b **4.** c **6.** c
B. **1.** Dan **3.** Jason **5.** Ina
2. Dan **4.** Marty **6.** Marty

EXERCISE 1

JUNE 28: I'm sitting in a seat 30,000 feet above the Earth en route to Argentina! I usually have dinner at this time, but right now I have an awful headache from all the excitement. My seatmate is eating my food. I guess it's good. She looks happy.

JUNE 30: It's 7:30 P.M. My host parents are still working. Carlos, my father, works at home. My little brother, Ricardo, is cute. He looks (and acts) a lot like Bobby. Right now, he's looking over my shoulder and trying to read my journal.

JULY 4: The weather is cold here in the summer. I usually spend the first weekend of July at the beach. Today I'm walking around in a heavy sweater.

AUGUST 6: I usually feel great in the evening, but tonight I feel really tired.

AUGUST 25: I'm feeling very comfortable here now— but it's almost time to go home! My host parents usually cook a light dinner, but tonight is a special event. They're having a party for me to say goodbye. I miss them already!

EXERCISE 2

A. **2.** 're taking **6.** don't think
3. 're standing **7.** means
4. Do you think **8.** come
5. 're dating **9.** stand
B. **1.** are you doing **5.** 's talking
2. 'm waiting **6.** 's not looking
3. seem **7.** seems
4. 'm working **8.** doesn't mean

EXERCISE 3

A. **2.** starts **4.** walks
3. has **5.** appear
B. **1.** are . . . shaking **4.** meet
2. know **5.** Do . . . shake
3. shake

EXERCISE 4

2. attends class, is going on a field trip to the museum
3. eats lunch
4. is eating lunch
5. studies with his classmates, is working on the family web page
6. works in the cafeteria
7. isn't doing homework, is playing tennis
8. isn't playing tennis, is watching a video with Eva
9. is having dinner
10. has dinner
11. writes letters, is taking a walk with the family
12. isn't taking a shower, is doing homework

EXERCISE 5

2. cause
3. Are . . . living OR traveling
4. traveling OR living
5. do . . . feel OR are . . . feeling
6. go

EXERCISE 6

2. treat **7.** 'm making
3. annoy **8.** don't understand, feel
4. 'm living, don't think OR 'm feeling
5. want
6. improve OR are improving

EXERCISE 7

           I'm sitting
It's 12:30 and ~~I sit~~ in the library right now. My classmates are eating lunch together, but I don't feel

           never eat
hungry yet. At home, we ~~eat never~~ this early. Today our journal topic is culture shock. It's a good topic for me right now because I'm ~~being~~ pretty homesick. I miss speaking my native language with my friends. And I miss my old routine. At

home we always ~~are eating~~ *eat* a big meal at 2:00 in the afternoon. Then we rest. But here in Toronto ~~I'm having~~ *I have* a 3:00 conversation class. Every day I almost fall asleep in class, and my teacher ~~ask~~ *asks* me, "Are you bored?" Of course I'm not bored. I just need my afternoon nap! This class ~~always is~~ *is always* fun. This semester, ~~we work~~ *we're working* on a project with video cameras. My team is filming groups of people from different cultures at social events. We are ~~analyze~~ *analyzing* "personal space." That means how close to each other these people stand. According to my new watch, it's 12:55, so ~~I leave~~ *I'm leaving* now for my 1:00 class. Teachers here really ~~aren't liking~~ *don't like* tardiness!

EXERCISE 8 ✓

A. 2. live
   3. like . . . culture
   4. wear . . . know
   5. 'm studying

B. Usually: 1b, 2a, 3a, 4b, 5b
   Now or These Days: 1a, 2b, 3b, 4a, 5a

EXERCISES 9–13

Answers will vary.

UNIT 2 (pages 16-30)

AFTER YOU READ

A. 1. topic
   2. admirers
   3. journey
   4. restless
   5. emotions
B. 1. flowers, animals
   2. was not an important kind of poetry
   3. studied poetry, became a teacher
   4. walked, rode horses
   5. traveled to Osaka, was famous

EXERCISE 1

As the son of a samurai, Basho <u>grew up</u> in the household of Todo Yoshitada, a young lord. After his father's death in 1656, Basho <u>stayed</u> in the Yoshitada household. He and Todo <u>wrote</u> poetry together, and in 1664 they <u>published</u> some poems. Two years later, Todo <u>died</u> suddenly. Basho <u>left</u> the area.

Basho <u>was</u> a restless young man, and he <u>moved</u> around for several years. In the 1670s, he <u>went</u> to Edo and <u>stayed</u> there. He <u>found</u> friendship and success once again. Basho <u>judged</u> poetry contests,

<u>published</u> his own poetry, and <u>taught</u> students. His students <u>built</u> him a home outside the city in 1681. They <u>planted</u> a banana tree (*basho* in Japanese) in front and <u>called</u> his home "Basho Hut." That is how the poet <u>got</u> his name: Basho.

In spite of this success, Basho <u>became</u> unhappy. He often <u>wrote</u> about loneliness. His mother <u>died</u> in 1683, and he <u>began</u> his travels a year later. His trip to the northern part of Honshu in 1689 <u>was</u> difficult, but his travel diary about this journey, *Narrow Road to the Deep North*, <u>became</u> one of Japan's greatest works of literature.

As a famous poet, Basho <u>had</u> many visitors—too many, in fact. In 1693 he <u>locked</u> his gate for a month, <u>stayed</u> alone, and <u>wrote</u>. The following year he <u>took</u> his final journey, to Osaka. He <u>died</u> there among his friends and admirers.

1664	Basho (and Todo) published poems.
1666	Todo died.
	Basho left the area.
1681	Students built the Basho Hut.
1683	Basho's mother died.
1684	Basho began his travels.
1689	Basho traveled to northern Honshu.
1693	Basho locked his gate to visitors.
1694	Basho took his final journey.
	Basho died.

EXERCISE 2

2. were
3. led
4. became
5. left
6. wore
7. allowed
8. had
9. wrote

EXERCISE 3

2. liked
3. used
4. went, knew
5. didn't write
6. sent
7. were
8. didn't address, did
9. didn't own
10. wrote
11. appeared
12. didn't know, asked

EXERCISE 4

2. didn't know
3. bit
4. ate
5. drank
6. hopped

EXERCISE 5

3. Q: Where did Dickinson live?
   A: She lived in Amherst, Massachusetts.
4. Q: Did Dickinson become famous during her lifetime?
   A: No, she didn't.
5. Q: Did Dickinson's admirers often visit her?
   A: No, they didn't.

6. Q: Did Dickinson travel a lot?
   A: No, she didn't.
7. Q: How many poems did Dickinson write?
   A: She wrote 1,700 poems.
8. Q: What did Dickinson write about?
   A: She wrote about nature, time, human emotions, and science.
9. Q: When did Dickinson die?
   A: She died in 1886.

EXERCISE 6

Answers may vary slightly.

2. That's wrong. She didn't live in Chicago until 1977. She lived there until 1985.
3. That's wrong. He wasn't very shy. He was outgoing.
4. That's right.
5. That's right.
6. That's wrong. She didn't teach Spanish. She taught English and Mexican history.
7. That's wrong. She didn't go to France for her Ph.D. She went to Germany.

EXERCISE 7

Today in class we read a poem by the American poet Robert Frost. I really ~~enjoy~~ *enjoyed* it. It was about a person who ~~choosed~~ *chose* between two roads in a forest. Many people believed the person ~~were~~ *was* Frost. He ~~thinked~~ *thought* about his choice for a long time. The two roads didn't ~~looked~~ *look* very different. Finally, he didn't ~~took~~ *take* the road most people take. He took the one less traveled on. At that time, he didn't ~~thought~~ *think* it was an important decision, but his choice ~~change~~ *changed* his life.

Sometimes I feel a little like Frost. Two years ago I ~~decide~~ *decided* to move to a new country. It was a long journey and a big change. Did I ~~made~~ *make* the right decision?

EXERCISE 8

A. 2. Turkey   **4.** English
   3. read books   **5.** farming
B.

1975	parents left Turkey
1980	moved to the U.S.
1982	began to write poetry
1991	graduated from college
1992	won a poetry award
1994	became a teacher

EXERCISE 9

Note that only the full form is correct here.

B. 1. Where did he   **4.** How did they
   2. Who did she   **5.** Why did he
   3. Why did she   **6.** Where did he

EXERCISES 10–11

Answers will vary.

EXERCISE 12

Date of Birth: October 25, 1958

Place of Birth: New York

Mini Bio:

★ lived in Argentina, Venezuela, and Denmark as a child
★ attended school in Argentina
★ spoke Spanish, Danish and English
★ returned to the U.S. in 1969
★ became a movie actor in 1985
★ first movie was *Witness*
★ played the part of Aragorn in *Lord of the Rings* (This movie made him famous.)
★ finished his first book of poems in 1993 (The title was *Ten Last Night*).
★ created the paintings for the movie *A Perfect Murder*. (He played the part of the artist.)
★ wrote music for *Lord of the Rings*

UNIT 3 (pages 31–44)

AFTER YOU READ

A. 1. e   **3.** a   **5.** c
   2. f   **4.** b   **6.** d
B. 5, 3, 4, 8, 1, 7, 2, 6

EXERCISE 1

2. b   **3.** b   **4.** a   **5.** b   **6.** a

EXERCISE 2

1. b. was having
2. a. was exercising
   b. wasn't swimming
3. a. wasn't drinking
   b. was eating
4. a. wasn't looking
   b. was listening
5. a. wasn't getting
6. a. wasn't resting
   b. was enjoying
7. a. was playing

EXERCISE 3

2. stopped
3. went
4. found
5. were playing
6. looked
7. saw
8. was
9. happened
10. decided
11. was sinking
12. was playing
13. sank OR sunk
14. was eating
15. felt
16. was sitting
17. looked
18. saw
19. noticed
20. knew
21. was coming
22. arrived
23. picked up

EXERCISE 4

2. Was your wife playing with you?
3. What was she doing while you were playing cards?
4. Did you feel the crash?
5. What did you do when you heard the noise?
6. What did you do when the lights went out?
7. What was she doing while you were looking for her?
8. What did you do when you found her?

EXERCISE 5

2. The electricity went out when the wind began to blow.
3. While he was driving home, he was listening to his car radio.
4. He pulled over to the side of the road when he couldn't see anything.
5. While he was listening to the news, he heard about a car crash near his home.
6. When it stopped raining, Mr. Taylor drove home in a hurry.

EXERCISE 6

April 15

This afternoon I ~~was going~~ _went_ to a movie at school. It was *Titanic*. They were showing it because it was the anniversary of the 1912 disaster. What a beautiful and sad film! Jack (Leonardo DiCaprio) ~~was meeting~~ _met_ Rose (Kate Winslet) while they both ~~sailed~~ _were sailing_ on the huge ship. It was the *Titanic's* first voyage.

Rose was from a very rich family; Jack was from a poor family. They fell in love, but Rose's mother wasn't happy about it. When the ship ~~was hitting~~ _hit_ the iceberg, the two lovers were together, but then they got separated. Rose ~~was finding~~ _found_ Jack while the ship was sinking. Seconds before the ship went under, they held hands and ~~were jumping~~ _jumped_ into the water. Rose survived, but Jack didn't. It was so sad. When I left the theater, I still ~~was having~~ _had_ tears in my eyes.

That wasn't my only adventure of the day. When the movie was over, I left the school auditorium. While I ~~walked~~ _was walking_ home, I saw an accident between two pedestrians and a car. I was the only one in the area, so ~~while~~ _when_ I saw the accident, I immediately called the police. When the police got there, they asked me a lot of questions—there were no other witnesses. I'm glad to say that the accident had a happier ending than the movie!

EXERCISE 7

B. Set 2

C. 1. False. The woman saw the accident.
2. False. She was walking down the street.
3. True
4. False. They were talking to each other. OR They weren't paying attention to the traffic.
5. False. It hit one of the men.

EXERCISE 8

B. 1. When the phone rang, she answered it.
2. While she was talking, I was watching TV.
3. When she saw the storm clouds, she drove home.
4. While she was driving home, she was listening to the news.
5. When she got home, she put the TV on.

EXERCISES 9–11

Answers will vary.

UNIT 4 (pages 45–57)

AFTER YOU READ

A. 1. b   **3.** b   **5.** a
  2. a   **4.** c   **6.** b

B. 1. False. Sandra watched TV on Saturdays. She watched cartoons.
  2. False. She didn't play video games. There were no video games back then.
  3. True
  4. True
  5. False. Her brother and his friends never used to study.
  6. False. Her brother's lost all his hair now.

EXERCISE 1

Underlined verb forms:
would play, used to listen, never used to bother, would listen, used to be, did . . . use to do

EXERCISE 2

  1. b. used to have
  2. a. used to be
    b. used to make
  3. a. Did . . . use to play
    b. used to practice
  4. a. never used to spend
  5. a. used to sit
    b. didn't use to wear
    c. used to be

EXERCISE 3

  2. used to
  3. used to OR would
  4. used to OR would
  5. used to OR would
  6. used to OR would
  7. used to
  8. used to

EXERCISE 4

  2. used to OR would wear   **5.** used to OR would play
  3. used to OR would drive   **6.** used to OR would visit
  4. used to be   **7.** used to love

EXERCISE 5

The high school reunion tonight was awesome!
                        talked
I ~~used to talk~~ to Eileen Edwards for a long time.
Well, she's the famous country pop singer Shania
Twain now. In high school, she ~~was~~ used to be just
one of us, and tonight we all called her Eileen. She
graduated in 1983, the same year as me. Today she

         lives
~~uses to live~~ in a chateau in Switzerland and has her
own perfume brand, but her life didn't use to be
                        used
like that at all! She ~~uses~~ to be very poor, and her
                    make
grandma used to ~~made~~ all her clothes because her
family couldn't afford to buy them. She was always
                                  earn
a good musician, though. In fact, she used to ~~earns~~
money for her family that way. On Saturday nights,
              perform
she would ~~performed~~ with a local rock band, and
my friends and I would go hear her. She could really
sing! Her new name, Shania, means "on my way" in
Ojibwa (her stepfather's Native American language).
                  used to think OR *thought*
After she left Timmins, I ~~would think~~ that Timmins
wasn't important to her anymore—but I was wrong.
Now that she's famous, she has a lot of power, and
she uses it to do good things for our community.
                                      to
And tonight she was just the way she used ˄ be in
high school—simple and friendly!

EXERCISE 6

B. 2. b   **3.** a   **4.** a   **5.** b
C. Past: 1, 3, 6, 8
  Now: 2, 4, 5, 7, 9

EXERCISES 7–10

Answers will vary.

UNIT 5 (pages 58–68)

AFTER YOU READ

A. 1. b   **2.** c   **3.** b   **4.** a   **5.** c
B. 1. False. The lawyer is questioning the witness.
  2. True
  3. False. Harry Adams didn't see the witness.
  4. True
  5. True
  6. False. The woman gave him a box.
  7. True
  8. False. She was still there when the car sped away.

EXERCISE 1

  2. a   **3.** d   **4.** b   **5.** c   **6.** e

EXERCISE 2

  2. How did you get home?
  3. Who gave you a ride?
  4. What happened next?
  5. Who (OR Whom) did you see?

6. Who is or was Deborah Collins?
7. What did you do?
8. When did the police arrive?
9. What did they ask you?
10. How many police officers came?

EXERCISE 3

2. What happened?
3. How many witnesses described the crime?
4. Who (or Whom) did the witness indicate?
5. Who indicated Harry Adams?
6. Who (or Whom) did the district attorney question?
7. How did the manager look?
8. Who spoke to the jury?
9. What was the verdict?
10. Why did the jury find Adams guilty?
11. How long did the trial last?
12. How much did Adams pay his lawyer?

EXERCISE 4

Where ~~Jones went~~ *did Jones go* on January 15?
Who went with him?
What time *did* he return home?
Who ~~he called~~ *did he call*?
How much money ~~he had~~ *did he have* with him?
~~Whom~~ *Who* saw him at the station the next day?
How did he look?
Why ~~he was~~ *was he* in a hurry?
How many suitcases did he have?
When *did* the witness call the police?
What ~~did happen~~ *happened* next?
What ~~his alibi was~~ *was his alibi*?

EXERCISE 5

A. 2. b   6. b
  3. a   7. a
  4. b   8. a
  5. a
B. 2. The black car.
  3. At 5:00 P.M.
  4. My boyfriend's mother.
  5. The police.
  6. I heard four shouts.
  7. I did.
  8. Because the police are here!

EXERCISE 6

B. **Information:** 2, 3, 6
  Repetition: 1, 4, 5, 7, 8

EXERCISES 7–9

Answers will vary.

PART I From Grammar to Writing
(pages 69–71)

1

    I always exchange holiday presents with my girlfriend, Shao Fen. Last year, while I was shopping for her, I saw an umbrella in her favorite color. As soon as I saw it, I thought of her. I bought the umbrella and a scarf in the same color. When Shao Fen opened the present, she looked really upset. She didn't say anything, and she didn't look at me. I felt hurt and confused by her reaction. Later she explained that in Chinese the word for "umbrella" sounds like the word for "separation." When she saw the umbrella she misunderstood. She thought I wanted to end the relationship. After I heard that, I was very upset! When we both felt calmer, we talked about our misunderstanding. At the end, we laughed about it, and I think we're better friends because of it. I discovered something new about Shao Fen's culture. Now I want to learn more about cross-cultural communication.

2

Answers may vary.
Two weeks ago, while I was walking on a crowded street, I felt something.
As soon as I got home, I noticed that my wallet was missing.
While I was thinking about the situation, my brother came home.
When I called the police, they weren't very encouraging.
Before I go to out, I put my wallet in my front pocket.

3–6

Answers will vary.

AFTER YOU READ

A. 1. sold out
2. edge
3. incredible
4. experience
5. takeoff
6. float
B. **Now:** 1, 2, 5
In the future: 3, 4, 6

EXERCISE 1

A. **Circled Verb Forms:**
2. are you taking
3. leaves
4. won't be
5. 'll be
6. 'll be
7. 'll buy
8. 'll be
9. 'm going to love
10. 'll want
11. won't make
12. 's going to study
13. 'll send
B. 2. are you taking: Plans
3. leaves: Schedule
4. won't be: Facts
5. 'll be: Predictions
6. 'll be: Predictions
7. 'll buy: Quick decision
8. 'll be: Facts
9. 'm going to love: Predictions
10. 'll want: Predictions
11. won't make: Offers and Promises
12. 's going to study: Plans
13. 'll send: Offers and Promises

EXERCISE 2

3. 'll feel
4. 'll become
5. Will . . . feel
6. won't last
7. will . . . keep
8. 'll need
9. 'll get
10. Will . . . look
11. won't look
12. will get
13. won't recognize
14. Will . . . float
15. 'll bump
16. 'll . . . have
17. 'll use
18. 'll be

EXERCISE 3

2. He isn't going to drive. OR He's not going to drive.
3. It's going to rain.
4. He isn't going to get very wet. OR He's not going to get very wet.
5. He's going to give a speech.

6. He's going to answer the phone.
7. He's going to have dinner.
8. He isn't going to watch TV. OR He's not going to watch TV.
9. He isn't going to go to sleep. OR He's not going to go to sleep.
10. He's going to get out of bed.

EXERCISE 4

2. he's taking the train to Tokyo.
3. he's meeting friends from England for dinner.
4. he's doing the interview for *The Space Show*.
5. he's answering questions from the online chat.
6. he's working on the Space Future website.
7. he's going to an exercise class.
8. he's flying to New York for the Space Transportation Conference.
9. he's answering emails from the Space Future website.
10. he's writing a speech for the next space travel conference.

EXERCISE 5

2. **A:** How many shuttle flights leave this fall?
B: Six shuttle flights leave this fall.
3. **A:** How often does the shuttle depart for the Moon each month?
B: The shuttle departs for the Moon twice each month.
4. **A:** When does the earliest morning flight leave Earth?
B: The October 15 flight leaves at 4 A.M.
5. **A:** (At) what time does the latest shuttle leave Earth?
B: The November 19 flight leaves Earth at 6 P.M.

EXERCISE 6

2. We'll take
3. leaves
4. I'll make
5. are we going to do
6. We'll think
7. I'll bring
8. 's going to fall
9. I'll go
10. I'll see you

EXERCISE 7

Both astronauts and space tourists will ~~traveling~~ _travel_ in space, but tourists ^ _are_ going to have a much different experience. Space tourists ~~is~~ _are_ going to travel for fun, not for work. So, they ~~willn't~~ _won't_ have to

worry about many of the technical problems that
astronauts worry about. For example, space tourists

won't need
~~will need not~~ to figure out how to use tools without

aren't
gravity. And they ~~isn't~~ going to go outside the space
ship to make repairs. For the most part, space

will just OR *are just going to*
tourists ~~will just going to~~ see the sights and have a
good time.

will OR *are going to*
Still, there will be similarities. Regular activities ^
be the same for astronauts and space tourists. For

turn
example, eating, washing, and sleeping will ~~turned~~
into exciting challenges for everyone in space. And

do
on long trips, everyone is going to ~~doing~~ exercises to
stay fit in zero gravity. And both astronauts

will OR *are going to*
and space tourists ~~will going to~~ have many new
adventures!

EXERCISE 8

A. Now: 2, 3,
   Future: 4, 5, 6
B. 2. False. She thinks they're great.
   3. True
   4. False. It's about space travel.
   5. True
   6. False. It's going to leave in five minutes.

EXERCISES 9–12

Answers will vary.

UNIT 7 (pages 91–102)

AFTER YOU READ

A. 1. b   **3.** b   **5.** b
   2. c   **4.** a   **6.** a
B. 1. a   **2.** a   **3.** b

EXERCISE 1

2. a   **7.** b
3. b   **8.** a
4. a   **9.** b
5. b   **10.** b
6. b

EXERCISE 2

3. get
4. 'll have / 'm going to have
5. save

6. 'll buy / 'm going to buy
7. 'll feel / 'm going to feel
8. 'm
9. 'll learn / 'm going to learn
10. work / 'm working
11. get up
12. 'll check / 'm going to check
13. talk
14. 'll ask / 'm going to ask
15. 'll download / 'm going to download
16. write
17. 'm trying / try
18. 'll improve / 'm going to improve
19. go
20. 'll know / 'm going to know
21. do
22. 'll write / 'm going to write
23. contact
24. 'll work / 'm going to work

EXERCISE 3

2. They are going to move to a larger
   apartment as soon as Jeff gets a raise.
3. After they move to a larger apartment,
   they're going to have a baby.
4. Sandy will get a part-time job after they
   have their first child.
5. Sandy will work part-time until their child
   is two years old.
6. Sandy will work full-time while Jeff goes
   to school. OR Jeff will go to school while Sandy
   works full-time.
7. When Jeff and Sandy achieve their goals,
   they'll feel very proud.

EXERCISE 4

Graduation is next month! I need to make some

start
plans now because when exams ~~will start~~, I

won't OR *'m not going to*
~~don't~~ have any free time. What am I going to do when

I finish
~~I'll finish~~ school? My roommate is going to take a

looks
vacation before she~~'ll look~~ for a job. I can't do that
because I need to earn some money soon. I think

that after I~~'ll~~ graduate, I'm going to take a desktop

publishing class. As soon as I learn the software,

I'll look OR *I'm going to look*
~~I look~~ for a job with a business publisher. It's hard to
find full-time jobs, though. Part-time jobs are easier

before
to find. Maybe I'll take a part-time job ~~after~~ I find a
good full-time one. Or maybe I'll take a workshop in
making decisions~~x~~ before I do anything!

EXERCISE 5

A. a. 4   **c.** 1   **e.** 6
   b. 2   **d.** 5   **f.** 3
B. 2. a company
   3. a college degree
   4. training
   5. a brochure

EXERCISES 7–9

Answers will vary.

PART II   From Grammar to Writing
(pages 103–105)

1

It's Sunday night, and once again, I'm wondering, *Where did the weekend go?* So from now on, before the weekend arrives, I'm going to make a plan. My goal: have some fun *and* get the chores done. Here's how I'll achieve that goal next weekend. First, after I finish this blog post, I'm going to buy movie tickets for Saturday night online. Next, no more sleeping late on Saturday! As soon as the alarm clock rings, I'm going to jump out of bed. Then I'll clean the apartment. (And this time, I'll keep working until I finish.) Finally, coffee! While I have my first cup, I'll talk to my friends about the film festival that night. After coffee, it'll be time do the grocery shopping. This will be incredible—I'll actually get to the farmer's market before the good stuff is sold out. After that, I'll just relax until it's time to go out. On Sunday, my sister and her family are coming to lunch. No problem! By the time they get here, I'll be ready. In fact, I probably won't even start cooking until I finish my workout at the gym. Is this a plan or an impossible dream? When next Sunday night rolls around, I'll let you know!

2

b. 1, 2   **d.** 1, 2   **f.** 2, 1
c. 1, 1   **e.** 2, 1   **g.** 1, 2

3–6

Answers will vary.

UNIT 8 (pages 108–120)

AFTER YOU READ

A. 1. c   **3.** c   **5.** a
   2. b   **4.** b   **6.** b
B. 1. False. Bob Burnquist still skates.
   2. False. Since 1995, he has taken home many first-place prizes and gold medals.
   3. True

---

4. False. He is a citizen of Brazil and the United States.
   5. True

EXERCISE 1

2. a   **3.** b   **4.** b   **5.** a   **6.** a

EXERCISE 2

2. for   **5.** since
3. Since   **6.** for
4. for   **7.** since

EXERCISE 3

2. hasn't stopped   **7.** have gone
3. has been   **8.** has skated
4. have lived   **9.** has won
5. have had   **10.** has wanted
6. haven't taken   **11.** 've considered

EXERCISE 4

3. have been   **10.** have opened
4. since   **11.** Since
5. have changed   **12.** have gone
6. since   **13.** Since
7. Since   **14.** has become
8. have taken   **15.** hasn't competed
9. Since   **16.** for

EXERCISE 5

B. 2. How long have you had your M.A. degree?
   3. Have you had any more training since you got your M.A.?
   4. How long have you been a physical education teacher?
   5. How long have you worked as a sports trainer?
   6. How long have you had a black belt in tae kwon do?
   7. Have you won any awards since then?
   8. How long have you been a member of NEA?
C. 2. I've had my M.A. degree since 2000 OR for 11 years.
   3. Yes, I have.
   4. I've been a physical education teacher since 2002 OR for nine years.
   5. I've been a sports trainer since 2000 OR for 11 years.
   6. I've had a black belt for two months.
   7. No, I haven't.
   8. I've been a member of NEA since 2003 OR for eight years.

EXERCISE 6

I've had
~~I have~~ my skateboard for two years. For me,
it's much more than just a sport. It's a form of
transportation. It's much faster than walking!
Jennifer, USA

for
I've been a skater ~~since~~ five years. Since December
I've won
~~I won~~ two contests. I'd love to go pro one day and
support myself skating.
Paulo, Brazil

since
Help! I've broken three boards ~~for~~ January!!! Is this
have you
normal? How long ~~you have~~ had your board?
Sang-Ook, Korea

broken
Broken boards?! That's nothing! I've ~~break~~ my wrist
twice since I started skating!
Marta, Mexico

Last year, my board hit a rock while I was skating in
the street. I fell and hit my head and had to go to the
've
emergency room. I ⌃ always worn a helmet since
then!
Megan, Australia

've lived
I ~~live~~ in California since 2006. My first love is
surfing, but when there aren't any waves, I jump on
my skateboard and take to the streets! My motto is
"Make the best of what you have."
Ming, USA

Wow! Yesterday, my friend gave me a copy of the
watched
video "OP King of Skate." I've ~~watch~~ it three times
since then. The Burnquist part is awesome!
Todd, Canada

At last! A skate park opened near my home last week.
've
Since then I ⌃ gone every day. It's a lot more fun than
skating in the streets!
Sylvie, France

EXERCISE 7

A. 2. radio station
   3. LA
   4. part time
   5. sports
   6. a sports announcer

B. 2. since 2003
   3. since 2010
   4. for six months
   5. for two years OR since 2009
   6. since she was in college

EXERCISE 8

B. 1. How long have you been a student? ↓

   2. Have you worked since you moved here? ↑

   3. How many jobs have you had since then? ↓

   4. Have you been at your job for a long time? ↑

   5. How long have you lived here? ↓

EXERCISES 9–10

Answers will vary.

UNIT 9 (pages 121–132)

AFTER YOU READ

A. 1. organized
   2. available
   3. successful
   4. specific
   5. professional
B. Items Checked: 1, 3, 4, 5

EXERCISE 1

2. T	**5.** T	**8.** F	**11.** F
3. F	**6.** T	**9.** T	**12.** F
4. T	**7.** F	**10.** T	

EXERCISE 2

2. 've already met
3. 've already had ✔
4. A: Has . . . left already
   B: No . . . hasn't
5. A: Have . . . seen . . . yet
   B: Yes . . . have
   A: haven't seen . . . yet
6. 've already planned

EXERCISE 3

3. He's already found a location.
4. He's already written a guest list.
5. He's already bought invitations.
6. He hasn't sent invitations yet. OR He still
   hasn't sent invitations.
7. He hasn't asked friends to help yet. OR He
   still hasn't asked friends to help.

8. He hasn't planned the menu yet. OR He still hasn't planned the menu.

9. He's already picked out music.

10. He hasn't shopped for food yet. OR He still hasn't shopped for food.

11. He hasn't cleaned the house yet. OR He still hasn't cleaned the house.

12. He's already borrowed some chairs.

EXERCISE 4

Doug asked: Help! My party is next week and I ~~already~~ *still* haven't figured out the food! I'm not at all organized. I've ~~yet~~ *already* wasted three days worrying, and I still don't have any ideas. What should I do?

The Party Planner's Advice is: Don't panic!

Your guests haven't started arriving ~~already~~ *yet*, so there's still time. Ask everyone to bring something! (You've already ~~invite~~ *invited* people, right?) Or order pizza. I haven't met anyone ~~already~~ *yet* who doesn't like pizza.

Rosa asked: I'd like to find a "theme" for my next birthday party. I've already ~~have~~ *had* a pasta party (10 kinds of pasta!), and I've already ~~gave~~ *given* a movie party (everyone dressed up as a movie character). Both were very successful, but I ~~haven't still~~ *haven't yet* OR *still haven't* decided what to do this time. Any ideas?

The Party Planner's Advice is: Sure. ~~Has~~ *Have* you tried this one yet? Ask each guest to bring a baby photo of himself or herself. Collect the photos. People try to match the photos with the guests! Your guests will love it!

EXERCISE 5

A. Items Checked: 1, 2, 3, 4, 7, 8

B. **2.** the man and the woman

3. Jason

4. Jason

5. the man

6. the woman

7. the man

8. Ella

9. the woman

10. Ella

EXERCISE 7

To Do—Helmut

~~buy memory card for camera~~

~~bake the cake~~

put the turkey in the oven

~~mop the floor~~

wash the dishes

cut up the vegetables

To Do—Gisela

vacuum the carpet

~~buy flowers~~

~~wash the windows~~

set the table

~~hang the balloons~~

wrap the gift

EXERCISES 8–9

Answers will vary.

UNIT 10 (pages 133–145)

AFTER YOU READ

A. **1.** adventure

2. more affordable

3. annual

4. survey

5. ancient

6. transportation

B. **Items Checked:** 1, 4, 5

EXERCISE 1

2. ? **5.** F **8.** ?

3. F **6.** F

4. T **7.** T

EXERCISE 2

2. 've been

3. has been (OR 's been)

4. 've had

5. 've swum

6. 've eaten

7. 've slept

8. has become (OR 's become)

9. Have . . . found

10. 've thought

11. 've . . . kept

12. 've . . . written

13. have . . . been

14. 've . . . returned

15. 've . . . been

16. 've . . . wanted

EXERCISE 3

3. He hasn't ridden a camel. OR He's never ridden a camel.

4. He's gone up in a hot-air balloon.

5. He's had some really unusual food.

6. He hasn't seen ancient pyramids. OR He's never seen ancient pyramids.

7. He's sailed a boat on the Nile River.

8. He's swum with dolphins in the ocean.

9. He hasn't been on a safari. OR He's never been on a safari.

10. He hasn't flown around the world. OR He's never flown around the world.

EXERCISE 4

2. I've gone up a few times
3. I haven't done it lately
4. Have you traveled a lot
5. I have
6. Have you ever been
7. I haven't
8. I've always wanted to go
9. I've been to Africa several times
10. I've just gotten
11. I've never been
12. They've just finished

EXERCISE 5

Answers will vary.

2. She's ridden (on) a camel.
3. She's traveled (a lot). OR She's seen a lot of countries.
4. She's stayed at the Hotel Roma.
5. She's written a book.
6. She's seen *Cats* three times.

EXERCISE 6

We ~~has~~ *have* received many comments from our clients. We'd like to share some with you.

Comments

I have always ~~be~~ *been* afraid of heights. But after I saw the beautiful photos on your website, I knew I had to go hot-air ballooning! This ~~have~~ *has* been one of the best experiences of my life. Thank you!
Britta Kessler, Germany

We've ~~returned just~~ *just returned* from a fantastic vacation. I've told all my friends about your company.
James Hudson, Canada

I've always wanted to go up in a hot-air balloon. I was not disappointed!
Antonio Vega, Mexico

I ~~just seen~~ *'ve just seen* OR *just saw* some photos posted on the website! Awesome!
Bill Hampton, USA

I've never ~~went~~ *gone* hot-air ballooning, but after visiting your wonderful website I've decided to sign up!
Amalia Lopes, Brazil

We gave our parents a balloon trip as an anniversary gift. They've just ~~wrote~~ *written* to say it was fantastic.
They've ~~ever~~ *never* been very adventurous, but now they want to go rafting!
Pat Calahan, Ireland

~~You have~~ *Have you* ever seen the face of a kid on a hot-air balloon ride? The cost of the ride: a lot. That look on her face: priceless!
Lydia Hassan, New Zealand

I ~~broken~~ *broke* my leg last month, so I haven't ~~lately~~ been able to do sports ^*lately*—boring! Your mountain balloon trip has just ~~gave~~ *given* me a lift—in more than one way!
May Roa, Philippines

EXERCISE 7

A. 2. once
3. has
4. hasn't
5. dangerous
6. is not
B. **Items Checked:** 1, 3, 5
Item Circled: 4

EXERCISES 9–10

Answers will vary.

UNIT 11 (pages 146–158)

AFTER YOU READ

A. 1. b 3. a 5. a
2. a 4. c 6. b
B. 1. False. They are already married.
2. False. He's living in Korea. She's living in Canada.
3. True
4. False. They can't afford many trips.
5. True

EXERCISE 1

2. a 4. a 6. b 8. a
3. b 5. b 7. a 9. b

EXERCISE 2

2. Have you tried	**10.** had to
3. began	**11.** 've learned
4. wrote	**12.** tried
5. 've written	**13.** was
6. lost	**14.** called
7. had	**15.** stayed
8. bought	**16.** felt
9. have been	**17.** 've been

EXERCISE 3

2. posted	**7.** 've worked
3. 's been	**8.** didn't get
4. began	**9.** saw
5. 've learned	**10.** 've lived
6. has been	

EXERCISE 4

2. In 2005, he wore a beard and moustache. Since then, he's been clean-shaven.

3. In 2005, he was thin. Since then, he's gained weight.

4. In 2005, he wore blue glasses. Since then, he's had contact lenses.

5. In 2005, he was a student. Since then, he's become an engineer.

6. In 2005, he lived with his parents. Since then, he's bought an apartment.

7. In 2005, he was single. Since then, he's gotten married.

EXERCISE 5

2. When did you get married?

3. When did your wife lose her job?

4. When did she get a new job offer?

5. How long have you lived apart?

6. How often did you see each other last year?

7. How often have you seen each other this year?

8. How have you managed to stay close?

EXERCISE 6

I've just finished reading an interesting article about Felicia Mabuza-Suttle. Actually, I ~~read~~ *'ve read* several articles about her this year. She's a well-known international businesswoman, and up until 2004 she ~~has been~~ *was* a talk-show host in South Africa. Guess what! We have something in common! Although they now live together, she and her husband ~~have had~~ *had* a "long-distance marriage" for more than 15 years! She lived in Johannesburg, South Africa; he lived in Atlanta, Georgia. Just like me and my husband, that's a whole ocean apart! They ~~have met~~ *met* in the 1970s. In the first 10 years of their marriage, they ~~have lived~~ *lived* in more than 10 cities. Then, in the early 1990s she ~~has returned~~ *returned* to South Africa to help her country. In 2003 she ~~has gone~~ *went* back to the States, and she and her husband ^*have* lived there together since then. So, it looks like things have worked out for them! That's encouraging! She still makes several trips back to South Africa every year—this year she ~~was~~ *has been* there twice so far. Here's a photo of her:

I love Vancouver and my job, but I really miss my husband. We ~~didn't manage~~ *haven't managed* to see each other that much since I left Seoul. I ~~have been~~ *was* much happier when we ~~have~~ lived together. I know the situation is temporary, but I hope, like Mabuza-Suttle and her husband, we can find a way to be together again soon.

EXERCISE 7

A. Items Checked: 1, 3, 5, 6

B. 2. a job
3. university
4. lived
5. have lived
6. house
7. drive

EXERCISE 8

B. 1. /Id/   **3.** /d/   **5.** /t/
2. /d/   **4.** /Id/   **6.** /t/

EXERCISES 9–11

Answers will vary.

UNIT 12 (pages 159–172)

AFTER YOU READ

A. 1. c   **3.** f   **5.** b
2. d   **4.** a   **6.** e
B. 1. c   **2.** b   **3.** a   **4.** c   **5.** b

EXERCISE 1

Finished activities: 2, 3, 8, 10
Unfinished activities: 4, 5, 6, 7, 9

EXERCISE 2

2. has published
3. has discussed
4. has spoken
5. has created
6. have studied OR have been studying
7. 've been waiting
8. has lived OR has been living
9. has worked OR has been working
10. have planted

EXERCISE 3

2. hasn't been talking
3. 's been writing
4. hasn't been reading
5. 's been drinking
6. hasn't been drinking
7. hasn't been eating
8. hasn't been watching
9. 's been working
10. 's been raining

EXERCISE 4

2. have brought
3. have been participating OR have participated
4. have designed
5. have built
6. have been getting OR have gotten
7. have found
8. has designed
9. have developed
10. have entered
11. 've been visiting
12. 've . . . been talking OR 've . . . talked

EXERCISE 5

Answers may vary slightly.

2. —How much money has the team spent on the house?
   —They've spent $250,000.
3. —How long have you been leading tours today?
   —I've been leading them all afternoon.
4. —How many people have visited this week?
   —So far about 30,000 have visited.
5. —How long have you been interested in solar energy?
   —I've been interested in solar energy for three years.
6. —How much energy has the house produced today?
   —It's produced more than it needs.
7. —How many competitions has your team entered?
   —We've entered three competitions.

8. —How many prizes has your team won?
   —We've won one prize.

EXERCISE 6

Sorry I haven't ~~wrote~~ *written* sooner. I haven't ~~been having~~ *had* any free time since we arrived in Madrid for the solar house competition. (Our house got here before us!) I'm really excited and also really tired. Since we arrived, we've been ~~lived~~ *living* on pizza and coffee. I haven't ~~sleeping~~ *slept* more than a few hours since . . . well, I can't remember when. Our team has been working day and night for the last two weeks, and today the house looks wonderful. I'm so proud— we've designed a home that's beautiful AND reduces pollution. We're finally ready for the judges, so I've spent most of the day looking at other teams' houses. I've ~~been visiting~~ *visited* ten houses today. They are so interesting and creative! For the last hour, I've just been hanging out in a café with some people from the other teams. I've already ~~been drinking~~ *drunk* three cups of coffee—it's delicious, but really strong! We *'ve* been practicing our Spanish with the Madrid team. I still don't understand too much, but our teammate Eloy Ruiz is from Puerto Rico, and he's ~~been helped~~ *been helping* OR *helped* me out a lot. Wish us luck and check your email for photos of the house.

EXERCISE 7

A. *Answers will vary.*
B. 2. a   3. b   4. a   5. a
C. 2. 've been eating   4. 've packed
   3. 's rained; 've been working   5. 's been writing

EXERCISE 8

B. 1. 've seen
   2. hasn't been working
   3. haven't started
   4. 've heard
   5. 've been thinking

EXERCISES 9–12

Answers will vary.

1

A. While I was in high school, I worked as a server at Darby's during the summer and on weekends. ~~Summers here are very hot and humid~~. I worked with many different kinds of customers, and I learned to be polite even with difficult people. ~~They serve excellent food at Darby's~~. Because I was successful as a server, I received a promotion after one year. Since high school, I have been working for Steak Hut as the night manager. I have developed management skills because I supervise six employees. ~~One of them is a good friend of mine~~. I have also learned to order supplies and to plan menus. ~~Sometimes I am very tired after a night's work~~.

B. My restaurant experience has prepared me for a position with your company.

2

Possible answers:

3–4

Answers will vary.

AFTER YOU READ

A. **1.** b   **3.** b   **5.** a
   2. c   **4.** b   **6.** c

B. **1.** can
   2. "sit down"
   3. Dancing Wheels
   4. inside
   5. loved
   6. difficult

EXERCISE 1

2. F	**5.** T	**8.** T
3. F	**6.** ?	**9.** ?
4. ?	**7.** T	**10.** F

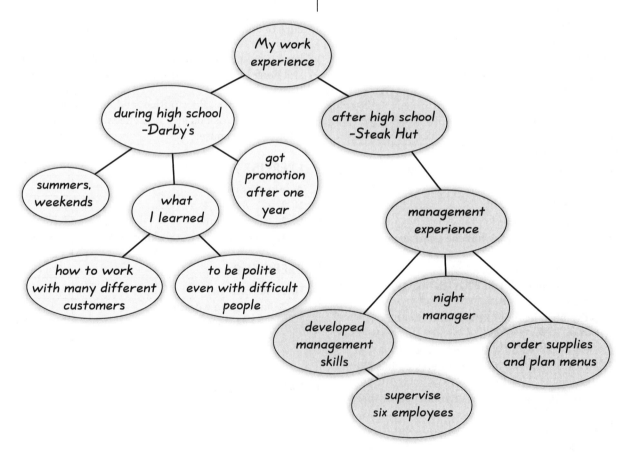

EXERCISE 2

1. **b.** can't
   c. can
   d. can
2. **a.** couldn't
   b. can

3. **a.** couldn't
   b. can
   c. can
4. **a.** couldn't
   b. could OR can
   c. can
   d. can't

EXERCISE 3

1. **b.** isn't able OR 's not able to do
2. **a.** Were . . . able to find
   b. 'll be able to compete
   c. was able to change
3. **a.** Were . . . able to speak
   b. was able to speak
   c. were . . . able to become OR have . . . been able to become
4. **a.** wasn't able to practice
   b. Will . . . be able to practice

EXERCISE 4

1. **b.** can see
   c. can't see
   d. 'll be able to see
2. **a.** can . . . dance
   b. could get
   c. couldn't get
   d. can pronounce

3. **a.** can't get
   b. can lend
   c. can pay
4. **a.** Can . . . do
   b. 'll be able to do

EXERCISE 5

Can They
How ~~They Can~~ Do That?

Last night was the first time I saw the group Pilobolus perform. And what a performance it
can't
was! I ~~no can~~ tell you that I fully understood the performance. I *can* ~~to~~ say, however, that the experience was completely wonderful.

Pilobolus is a very unusual group. The performers have no background in dance. When they began,
dance
they thought, "Maybe we can't ~~dancing~~, so why try?" So they just made interesting shapes with their
can
bodies. Well, this group certainly ~~cans~~ dance, and they are able to do much more. The six dancers in the group are athletic, artistic, and very talented.
to
They are able ∧ do amazing things with their bodies. In many dances, they move together as a single unit.

My theater companion and I had great seats.
see
We could ~~saw~~ the entire stage (not always true in some theaters). The sound system, though, had a
weren't
few problems, and we ~~didn't~~ able to hear the music clearly all the time.

Some people in the audience asked: "Is it dance or is it gymnastics?" You can decide for yourself. Many
get
people weren't able to ~~got~~ tickets for the first two performances of this series, but you can still buy tickets for next week. This is the type of dance
enjoy
performance everyone can ~~enjoys~~.

EXERCISE 6

A. 2. foreign
   3. computer
   4. monthly newsletter
   5. dance
   6. drive
B. Items Checked: 1, 4, 6, 7

EXERCISE 7

B. 1. can't   3. can   5. can, can't
   2. can   4. can't   6. can't

EXERCISE 8

Dances	March	April	May
Argentine tango			✓
Cha-cha	✓		
Fox-trot		✓	
Hip-hop		✓	
Hustle			✓
Mambo		✓	
Merengue	✓		
Salsa			✓
Swing	✓		
Tango		✓	
Waltz	✓		

EXERCISES 9–10

Answers will vary.

UNIT 14 (pages 190–201)

AFTER YOU READ

A. **1.** a **3.** c **5.** a
   2. b **4.** b **6.** a
B. **1.** Tara
   2. Heather
   3. Heather, Tara
   4. Counselor

EXERCISE 1

Underlined Phrases:
  2. c. Do you mind if I have
  3. c. Can I wash
  4. a. Could my best friend stay
    b. Sure she can!
  5. a. Could I borrow
  6. a. Could I hang

EXERCISE 2

  2. a. Can . . . do   **c.** Can . . . borrow
    b. Yes they can.
  3. a. May . . . ride
    b. Sure. OR Certainly. OR Of course. OR No
      problem.
  4. a. Could . . . bring
    b. No, you can't.
  5. a. May . . . use
    b. Sorry, but you can't.

EXERCISE 3

  2. HEATHER: Can I borrow your black sweater?
    TARA: Sorry.
  3. TARA: Do you mind if my sister stays in
      our room?
    HEATHER: No, not at all. OR No, I don't.
  4. HEATHER: May we (please) have the party in
      the dormitory lounge?
    COUNSELOR: Sure. OR Certainly. OR Of course. OR
      No problem.
  5. HEATHER: Could we (please) hang decorations
      from the ceiling of the lounge?
    COUNSELOR: Sorry, you can't.
  6. HEATHER: Could the party go until midnight?
    COUNSELOR: Sorry. It can't.
  7. TARA: Could we play some of your CDs at
      the party?
    ERICA: Sure. OR Certainly. OR Of course. OR
      No problem.
  8. STUDENT: Can I study here (OR in the lounge)?
    HEATHER: I'm sorry, you can't.

EXERCISE 4

  1. A: May we board the train now?
    B: No, you ~~couldn't~~ *can't* board until 12:30.
  2. A: Can he ~~comes~~ *come* on the train with me?
    B: Sorry. Only passengers can board.
  3. A: Do you mind if ~~I'm sitting~~ *I sit* here?
    B: ~~No, I don't~~. *Sorry.* My friend is sitting here.
  4. A: Could I ~~looked~~ *look* at your newspaper?
    B: Yes, of course you ~~could~~ *can*.
  5. A: Do you mind if my son ~~play~~ *plays* his computer
      game?
    B: No, not at all. It won't disturb me.
    A: Thanks.

EXERCISE 5

A. **2.** e **4.** f **6.** a
   3. b **5.** g **7.** c
B. **Permission Given:** 1, 4, 6
   Permission Refused: 2, 3, 5, 7

EXERCISE 6

B. **1.** she
   2. Could
   3. he
   4. we
   5. he

EXERCISES 7–9

Answers will vary.

UNIT 15 (pages 202–213)

AFTER YOU READ

A. **1.** b **2.** c **3.** b **4.** a **5.** c
B. **1.** False. She sent Marcia an email.
   2. True
   3. False. Marcia is going to distribute them.
   4. False. Ann is going to make the copies.
   5. True
   6. True

EXERCISE 1

Underlined phrases:
  2. Would you mind lending me five dollars?
  3. Can you lend me your laptop for a minute?
  4. Could you lock the door on your way out?
  5. Can you tell Ethan to come to the phone?

6. Will you pick up some milk on the way home this afternoon?

7. Would you explain this text message from Jody?

Responses:

2. a	**4.** b	**6.** b
3. a	**5.** a	**7.** a

EXERCISE 2

A. 2. e	**6.** i
3. g	**7.** b
4. f	**8.** c
5. h	**9.** a

B.

(Position of please *can vary.)*

2. Would you please shut the door?

3. Will you please buy some cereal

4. Can you close the window, please?

5. Would you mind waiting for a few minutes, please?

6. Would you mind washing your cups and dishes, please?

7. Could you please call back later?

8. Can you get that book, please?

9. Could you please repair the photocopier?

EXERCISE 3

Responses and position of please *can vary.*

1.

c. Can / Could / Will / Would you (please) keep your conversation short (please) OR Would you mind keeping your conversation short

d. Answers to questions with a modal: Sure. OR Certainly OR No problem. OR Of course. OR I'd be glad to.
Answers to questions with *Would you mind*: Not at all. OR I'd be glad to. OR No Problem. OR Of course not.

2.

a. Can / Could / Will / Would you (please) explain reflexive pronouns (please) OR Would you mind explaining reflexive pronouns

b. I'm sorry, but I can't OR I'm afraid I can't

c. Can / Could / Would you (please) come back in twenty minutes (please) OR Would you mind coming back in twenty minutes

3.

a. Can / Could / Will / Would you (please) move your car (please) OR Would you mind moving your car

b. Answers to questions with a modal: Sure. OR Certainly OR No problem. OR Of course. OR I'd be glad to.
Answers to questions with *Would you mind*: Not at all. OR I'd be glad to. OR No Problem. OR Of course not.

4.

a. Can / Could / Will / Would you (please) distribute this report (please) OR Would you mind distributing this report

b. I'm sorry, but I can't OR I'm afraid I can't

EXERCISE 4

For responses, two possible answers are shown, but other answers are possible. Please see the grammar charts.

The meetings are going well but they have been extended a day. Could you ~~call please~~ *please call* Doug Rogers to try to reschedule our sales meeting?

Sure. OR *No problem.*
~~Not at all~~. I'll do it right away.

We'll need three extra copies of the monthly sales report. Would you ask Ann to take care of that?

Sure. OR *I'd be glad to.*
~~Yes, I would~~. (Ann—could you do this?)

I won't have time to return Emma Lopes's call this week. Would you mind ~~to call~~ *calling* her and telling her I'll call her back next week?

No problem. Could you email me her phone number?

I hate to ask, but ~~will~~ *would* you mind working on Saturday? We'll need the extra time to go over the new information I've gotten.

Sorry, but I ~~couldn't~~ *can't*. My in-laws are coming for a visit. But Rob Lin says he can come into the office to help out.

One last thing. I was going to pick up those new business cards, but I won't be back in time. Would you mind asking the printer to deliver them to the office? I'd really appreciate that.

No problem OR *Of course not*
~~Yes, I would~~. I'll call and ask him to do it right away.

And this will cheer you up—It looks like our office will receive the award for Communication Excellence this year!

Great! Can I ~~told~~ *tell* everyone or is it a secret?

EXERCISE 5

A. Items Checked: 1, 2, 5, 6, 8

B. 1. f Ethan

2. a Kelly
c Marcia
g Ann

3. b Marcia's mother

4. e John

EXERCISES 7–8

Answers will vary.

AFTER YOU READ

A. 1. identity
   2. normal
   3. Avoid
   4. communication
   5. behavior
   6. Protect
B. OK: 1, 4, 6, 9
   Not OK: 2, 3, 5, 7, 8

EXERCISE 1

Underlined Phrases:
'd better not forget, shouldn't . . . be
should stop, ought to ask
'd better not do
should get
shouldn't fight

EXERCISE 2

2. 'd better not rent   **7.** should listen
3. 'd better keep   **8.** ought to read
4. ought to see   **9.** ought to watch
5. should turn on   **10.** 'd better not give
6. shouldn't use

EXERCISE 3

2. You'd better not OR You shouldn't give out
   any personal information.
3. You'd better not OR You shouldn't give it to anyone.
4. You ought to OR You'd better OR You should
   get virus protection and use it.
5. You should OR You'd better OR You ought to
   keep your virus protection up-to-date.
6. You'd better not OR You shouldn't believe
   any "get rich quick" offers.
7. You shouldn't OR You'd better not open any
   email attachments from strangers.
8. You should OR You ought to OR You'd better
   be careful.

EXERCISE 4

2. should I start posting
3. Q: Should I forward the email
   A: No, you shouldn't
4. Q: Should I buy one online
   A: Yes, you should
5. Q: Should I check the spelling
   A: Yes, you should
6. What should I say to make them stop
7. Q: Should I use my birthday
   A: No, you shouldn't
8. Q: Should I flame him
   A: No, you shouldn't
9. Q: Should I use emoticons

EXERCISE 5

JUSTME: My friend asked me to dinner and she told
me I should ~~ɪ~~ bring some food! What
kind of an invitation is that? What ~~I should~~ *should I*
bring to this strange dinner party?

SASHA: LOL! The invitation is totally normal. Your
friend is having a potluck—a dinner party
where everybody brings something. It's
really a lot of fun. You ought ˄*to* bring a dish
from your country. People will enjoy that.

TOBY: HELP! My first day of class, and I lost my
wallet! What ~~ought~~ *should* I do first? My student
ID, credit card, and cash are all gone.

R2D2: First of all, you'd ~~not better~~ *better not* panic because
you need to be calm so you can speak
clearly. You should ~~ɪ~~ call your credit card
company right away. Did you lose your
wallet at school? Then you ought to ~~going~~ *go*
to the Lost and Found Department at your
school.

SMILEY: What should an international student ~~does~~ *do*
to make friends? At my college, people
always smile and say, "Hi, how are you?"
but they don't wait for an answer!

4GUD: New students should ~~joining~~ *join* some clubs
and international student organizations.
They also ought to find a student in each
class to study with and ask about homework
assignments.

NEWGUY: Hi. I'm new to this board. I'm from
Vietnam, and I'm going to school in
Canada next year. How should I ~~will~~ get
ready?

SMILEY: Welcome Newguy! I'm at school in
Montreal, and you won't believe how cold
it gets here. ~~You're~~ *You'd* better bring a lot of
warm clothes.

SASHA: You ought ˄*to* check the school's website.
They might have a Vietnam Students'
Association. If they do, you should email
the association with your questions. Good
luck!

EXERCISE 6

A. 2. Amy   **4.** Tim   **6.** Tim
   3. Amy   **5.** Amy, Jason, Marta
B. Items Checked: 2, 6, 7, 8

EXERCISES 8–11

Answers will vary.

1

Answers may vary.

Chen,—Here is a draft of our presentation for the next sales meeting. <u>Read it.</u> I really think it's much too long. What do you think? <u>Tell me whether to shorten it.</u> <u>We will meet tomorrow to discuss it.</u> <u>My advice is that we finish the draft by Friday.</u> By the way, Nadia is in town. <u>I want to invite her to our meeting.</u>—Ed

2

Possible answers.

   Chen,—Here is a draft of our presentation for the

next sales meeting. <u>_Would you mind_</u> reading
                          (make a request)
it? I really think it's much too long. What do you

think? <u>_Should_</u> I shorten it? I hope we
         (ask advice)
<u>_can_</u> meet tomorrow to discuss it. We
(express ability)
<u>_should_</u> finish the final draft by Friday. By
   (give advice)
the way, Nadia is in town. <u>_Could_</u> I invite
                             (ask permission)
her to our meeting?—Ed

3

Possible answers.

   I think you should shorten it. The guidelines say no more than fifteen minutes. I won't be able to meet you today because of another meeting. Could we meet tomorrow instead? Also, could you please reserve the conference room for the meeting? Of course Nadia can come. I hope we can all have lunch together after the meeting.

4–5

Answers will vary.

UNIT 17 (pages 232–245)

AFTER YOU READ

A. 1. c   **3.** b   **5.** c
   2. c   **4.** a   **6.** b
B. 1. False. They contain everyday items.
   2. True
   3. False. It's in the United States OR New York City.
   4. True

5. True
6. False. People won't see it until 6939 OR for 5,000 years.

EXERCISE 1

B. Proper Nouns:
   2. Naples
   3. Rome
   4. Romans
   5. August
   6. Vesuvius

Count Nouns: *(students choose sixteen):*

2. city	**18.** archeologists
3. bay	**19.** objects
4. summer	**20.** civilization
5. villas	**21.** lives
6. volcano	**22.** century
7. feet	**23.** couch
8. people	**24.** bracelets
9. buildings	**25.** rings
10. houses	**26.** bowls
11. roads	**27.** cups
12. theaters	**28.** vegetables
13. statues	**29.** eggs
14. ruins	**30.** olives
15. years	**31.** meals
16. day	**32.** tourists
17. engineer	**33.** capsule

Non-Count Nouns:

2. ash	**8.** food
3. art	**9.** wood
4. time	**10.** glass
5. furniture	**11.** fruit
6. jewelry	**12.** bread
7. money	**13.** life

EXERCISE 2

2. shoes are	**11.** hat
3. hours	**12.** things help
4. ruins	**13.** pictures
5. streets are	**14.** batteries are
6. years	**15.** clothing makes
7. Water is	**16.** gets
8. bottles	**17.** time flies
9. sun is	**18.** people spend
10. sun block is	**19.** ruins are

EXERCISE 3

1. **b.** many	5. **a.** some
2. **a.** a lot of	**b.** a lot of
b. many	**c.** enough
c. a lot of	**d.** a few
3. **a.** some	**e.** much
b. a lot	**f.** any
c. a great deal of	**g.** some
d. any	**h.** many
4. **a.** a few	**i.** many
b. a little	**j.** some
c. few	6. **a.** a lot of
	b. some
	c. a little

EXERCISE 4

Hi Everyone!

James and I got back from Pompeii $\overset{a}{\wedge}$ few days

$\overset{few}{}$
ago. We bought a ~~little~~ souvenirs, which I'll mail to
you all very soon. We're still unpacking and looking

$\overset{photographs}{}$
over the many, many ~~photograph~~ (hundreds!) we

$\overset{guidebook}{}$
took of this amazing place. Our ~~Guidebook~~ calls ~~the~~
Pompeii a "time capsule" and I truly felt that we
were somehow communicating with this rich and

$\overset{culture}{}$ $\overset{is}{}$ $\overset{time}{}$
vibrant ~~cultures~~. There ~~are~~ never enough ~~times~~ for
everything on vacation, but that's especially true of
Pompeii. Really, there are few places in the world
this amazing. You should all try to go. I was so
impressed!

I plan to do ~~X~~ several blog posts and put up a lot
$\overset{of}{\wedge}$
$\wedge$ photos to show you what I mean. Speaking of time

$\overset{some}{}$
capsules, I was just in the attic putting away ~~any~~

$\overset{a\ lot\ of}{}$
suitcases, and I discovered a trunk with ~~much~~ old

$\overset{was}{}$
stuff. The old clothing ~~were~~ still in great shape—I
might wear some of the skirts and blouses. Oh, and

$\overset{lot}{}$
I found a ~~great deal~~ of letters that Grandpa wrote

$\overset{Grandma}{}$
to ~~grandma~~ when he was working in Italy on an
archeological dig. A few of them made me cry, and
one of them had a recipe for Roman Apple Cake! I

think we'll try to make it$\overset{}{\wedge}$and we'll let you know how
it turns out.
Love,
Emily

EXERCISE 5

A. the whole recipe filled in:

Roman Apple Cake
✓ 1 ½ cups _____sugar_____
½ cup vegetable _____oil_____
2 _____eggs_____
2 _____cups_____ flour
1 teaspoon baking powder
1 _____teaspoon_____ baking soda
¼ teaspoon _____salt_____
½ teaspoon cinnamon
1 cup _____milk_____
½ cup _____raisins_____
½ cup _____nuts_____
3 _____apples_____

B. Items checked on the recipe: sugar, vegetable oil, baking powder, salt, cinnamon, milk, raisins
C. Shopping List: eggs, flour, baking soda, nuts, apples

EXERCISE 6

B. Crossed out vowels:
  2. We saw sev~~e~~ral wall paintings.
  3. Don't forget your cam~~e~~ra!
  4. It makes a big diff~~e~~rence.
  5. I'm studying hist~~o~~ry.
  6. We ate at my fav~~o~~rite restaurant.
  7. The veg~~e~~tables are delicious.
  8. I bought some jew~~e~~lry for my family.

EXERCISES 7–9

Answers will vary.

UNIT 18 (pages 246–261)

AFTER YOU READ

A. 1. struggled
  2. enormous
  3. immediately
  4. famous
  5. wonderful
B. "The Ant and the Dove": 5, 3, 2, 1, 4
  "The Town Mouse and the Country Mouse":
  3, 4, 2, 5, 1

EXERCISE 1

  2. a   **3.** b   **4.** b   **5.** b   **6.** a

EXERCISE 2

3. (blank) 9. (blank) 15. the
4. the 10. the 16. the
5. the 11. the 17. (blank)
6. (blank) 12. (blank) 18. (blank)
7. the 13. the 19. the
8. (blank) 14. the

EXERCISE 3

2. the 12. a 22. The
3. a 13. The 23. a
4. a 14. the 24. The
5. a 15. the 25. an
6. a 16. a 26. the
7. a 17. a 27. a
8. a 18. The 28. the
9. a 19. the 29. the
10. the 20. an 30. the
11. the 21. The

EXERCISE 4

2. the 9. a 16. the
3. the 10. the 17. the
4. a 11. the 18. the
5. an 12. Ø 19. The
6. the 13. the 20. a
7. a 14. Ø 21. the
8. Ø 15. the 22. the

EXERCISE 5

1. b. an 4. a. (blank)
   c. the b. The
   d. a c. (blank)
2. a. the d. (blank)
   b. the e. the
   c. An 5. a. an
   d. A b. the
3. a. the c. the
   b. (blank) 6. a. the
   c. (blank) b. (blank)
   c. (blank)

EXERCISE 6

Once there was a plumber named Mario. ~~Plumber~~ *The plumber*
had _a_ beautiful girlfriend. One day, ~~a~~ *an* ape fell in love
with the girlfriend and kidnapped her. The plumber
chased _the_ ape to rescue his girlfriend. This simple tale
became *Donkey Kong*, ~~a~~ *the* first video game with a story.
It was invented by Shigeru Miyamoto, an artist with
Nintendo, Inc. Miyamoto loved ~~the~~ video games, but
he wanted to make them more interesting. He liked

fairy tales, so he invented _a_ story similar to a famous
fairy tale. ~~Story~~ *The story* was an immediate success, and
Nintendo followed it with *The Mario Brothers* and
then with *Super Mario*. The third game became
popular all over ~~a~~ *the* world, and it is still _the_ most famous
game in video history. Nintendo has continued to
add ~~the~~ new adventures and new ways to play _the_ game.
Now players can follow Mario to outer space and
play the game on their Wii. But success and space
travel do not change Mario. He is still _the_ brave little
plumber in a red hat.

EXERCISE 7

A. 2. the 6. the
   3. the 7. a
   4. the 8. a
   5. a
B. 2. a 6. a
   3. a 7. b
   4. a 8. b
   5. b

EXERCISE 8

B. **Pronounced /ði/:** 3, 5, 6, 7
   Pronounced /ðə/: 1, 2, 4, 8

EXERCISE 9

Answers will vary.

EXERCISE 10

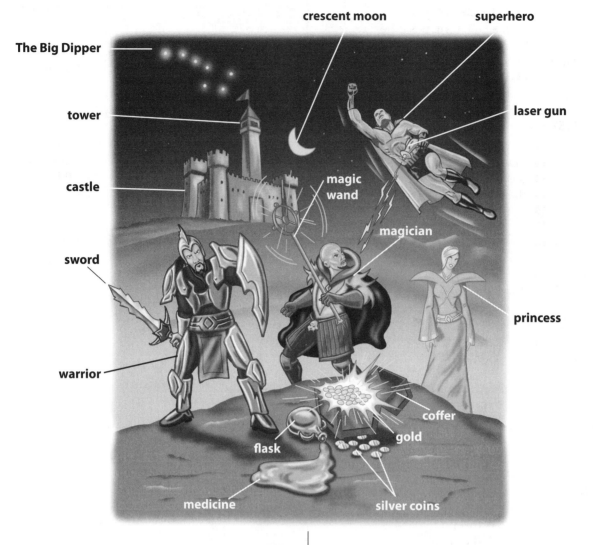

The Big Dipper

crescent moon

superhero

tower

laser gun

castle

magic wand

sword

magician

princess

warrior

coffer

flask

gold

medicine

silver coins

EXERCISES 11–12

Answers will vary.

PART V From Grammar to Writing
(pages 262–263)

1

2. We also create an altar and put candy skulls on it
3. For my sister, we offer toys.
4. My family always hires a mariachi band

2

1. *Los Días de los Muertos*, November 1 and 2
2. To remember our relatives who have died
3. **a.** food, loaves of bread called "souls," candy skulls
   b. special gifts for the dead, a new hat for my grandfather, toys for my sister
   c. music, we hire a mariachi band, we all sing

3–6

Answers will vary.

UNIT 19 (pages 266–281)

AFTER YOU READ

A. **1.** a   **3.** c   **5.** b
   2. b   **4.** c   **6.** a
B. **1.** False. It's in a safe neighborhood.
      OR It isn't in a dangerous neighborhood.
   2. True
   3. False. It's in a peaceful area of the city.
      OR It isn't in an exciting area of the city.
   4. True
   5. False. There are two apartments for rent now.
   6. True

EXERCISE 1

Are you looking for a place to live? This <u>charming</u> apartment is in a <u>new</u> building and has two <u>large</u> <u>comfortable</u> bedrooms and a <u>small</u> <u>sunny</u> kitchen. The building is ⟨very⟩ <u>quiet</u>—⟨absolutely⟩ <u>perfect</u> for two <u>serious</u> students. It's <u>near</u> the campus on a <u>peaceful</u> street. There's <u>convenient</u> transportation. The bus stop is an <u>easy</u>, <u>pleasant</u> walk, and the <u>express</u> bus goes ⟨directly⟩ into town. You can run or ride your bike ⟨safely⟩ in <u>nearby</u> parks. The rent is ⟨very⟩ <u>affordable</u>. <u>Small</u> pets are <u>welcome</u>. The apartment is <u>available</u> on June 1. <u>Interested</u> students should call Megan at 555-5050. We're sure you'll be <u>satisfied</u>. Don't wait! This apartment will rent ⟨fast⟩. Nonsmokers, please.

EXERCISE 2

2. really	**7.** gorgeous	**12.** shy
3. new	**8.** lucky	**13.** good
4. beautiful	**9.** great	**14.** quickly
5. hard	**10.** totally	**15.** exciting
6. happily	**11.** nice	**16.** terribly

EXERCISE 3

2. terribly disappointed	**6.** awfully loud
3. surprisingly convenient	**7.** pretty accurately
4. incredibly fast	**8.** absolutely perfect
5. very clearly	**9.** really upset

EXERCISE 4

2. pretty upsetting things	**7.** absolutely charming apartment
3. arrived really late	**8.** think about it very carefully
4. awfully important meeting	**9.** it happened so quickly
5. reacted quite well	**10.** take it immediately OR immediately take it
6. didn't seem angry at all OR at all angry	

EXERCISE 5

2. charming	**6.** exhausting	**10.** fascinated
3. annoyed	**7.** exhausted	**11.** confusing
4. charmed	**8.** relaxing	**12.** amazing
5. disgusted	**9.** fascinating	

EXERCISE 6

2. charming old house
3. peaceful residential neighborhood
4. enormous old tree
5. wide bedroom window
6. Japanese stone bench
7. beautiful large OR large beautiful antique German table
8. friendly, helpful man
9. young Polish woman
10. nice Italian neighborhood restaurant

EXERCISE 7

RATE YOUR DORM

★★★☆☆ **Jeff W.** The Northwood dorms are pretty ~~awesomely~~ *awesome*. They're clean and modern, and they're a convenient walk to class and the dining hall. The halls get ~~noisy terribly~~ *terribly noisy* sometimes, though. When I'm studying ~~hardly~~ *hard* for exams, I have to go to the library.

★★★★☆ **Sheryl** Miller Hall is the ideal dorm for freshmen. It's quite small, so I was able to make friends ~~fastly~~ *fast* there. Also, the floor counselors are great. Ours explained ~~clearly the rules~~ *the rules clearly*. She was a ~~young French nice~~ *nice young French* woman, and she was always available when you needed to talk. I was ~~extreme~~ *extremely* satisfied. I would absolutely recommend this ~~dorm amazing~~ *amazing dorm* to anyone.

☆☆☆☆☆ **Tania** Warning! Keep away! Wyeth Hall is totally ~~disgusted~~ *disgusting*. The lounges are ~~incredible~~ *incredibly* dirty. The toilets don't work ~~good~~ *well*, and the halls smell ~~badly~~ *bad*. I had a small brown ~~depressing~~ *depressing OR depressing* room on the ground floor. My parents were ~~shocking~~ *shocked* when they saw the place.

EXERCISE 8

A. *Answers will vary*

B. **2.** old   **7.** peaceful
    3. near   **8.** modern
    4. excellent   **9.** new
    5. located   **10.** immediately
    6. new

C. Apt. 2   sunny
    Apt. 3   awfully small, not near stores, can't
               bring Loki
    Apt. 4   sounds terrific

EXERCISE 9

B.

1. A: This is a **nice apartment**.

   B: And it's such a **sunny place** too!

2. A: Alice seems like a **friendly neighbor**.

   B: Yes, and she's a **helpful neighbor**, too.

3. A: It's got a **small kitchen**.

   B: No, it doesn't! It's the **perfect kitchen** for you.

4. A: Did the landlord give you **new appliances**?

   B: No. But these aren't **bad appliances**.

5. A: Do you have a **helpful landlord**?

   B: Yes, but he's a **nosy landlord**, too!

6. A: Well, I hope you like your **new home**.

   B: Thanks. I'm going to like it more than my **old home**.

EXERCISES 10–14

Answers will vary.

UNIT 20 (pages 282–295)

AFTER YOU READ

A. **1.** b   **3.** a   **5.** a
    2. b   **4.** c   **6.** c

B. **1.** crowded, new, popular
    2. young
    3. delicious, fresh, good

EXERCISE 1

2. T   **5.** T   **8.** T
3. T   **6.** T   **9.** F
4. F   **7.** T   **10.** T

EXERCISE 2

2. is not as expensive as
3. tastes as good as
4. doesn't taste as good as
5. doesn't smell as delicious as
6. smells as delicious as

EXERCISE 3

2. hotter than   **8.** sweeter than
3. less expensive than   **9.** shorter than
4. spicier than   **10.** less varied than
5. less salty than   **11.** less expensive than
6. healthier than   **12.** sweeter than
7. cheaper than

EXERCISE 4

2. better and better, the better . . . the higher
3. less and less crowded; heavier and heavier
4. more and more interesting; more and more difficult
5. more and more popular; The harder . . . the more popular
6. worse and worse; the spicier . . . the better
7. faster and faster; The faster . . . the shorter

EXERCISE 5

When I was a teenager in the Philippines, I was an expert on snacks and fast foods. I was growing fast, so the more I ate, the ~~hungry~~ *hungrier* I felt. The street vendors in our town had ~~the~~ better snacks than anyone else. In the morning, I used to buy rice muffins on the way to school. They are ~~more~~ *much* sweeter ~~than that~~ American muffins. After school, I ate fish balls on a stick or *adidas* (chicken feet). Snacks on a stick are ~~small~~ *smaller* than American hot dogs and burgers, but they are much *more* ^ varied. My friend thought *banana-cue* (banana on a stick) was really great. However, they weren't as sweet ~~from~~ *as* *kamote-cue* (fried sweet potatoes and brown sugar), my favorite snack.

When I came to the United States, I didn't like American fast food at first. To me, it was ^ *less* interesting than my native food and less ~~tastier~~ *tasty* too. Now I'm getting used to it, and it seems ~~deliciouser and deliciouser~~ *more and more delicious*. Does anyone want to go out for a pizza?

EXERCISE 6

A. 2. frozen   **5.** woman
   3. two   **6.** buy
   4. price   **7.** Angela's
B. Di Roma's: 1, 4
   Angela's: 2, 3, 5

EXERCISES 8–10

Answers will vary.

UNIT 21 (pages 296–306)

AFTER YOU READ

A. 1. a   **2.** c   **3.** c   **4.** b   **5.** c
B. 1. False. Toronto is the largest Canadian city. OR No Canadian city is larger than Toronto.
   2. False. Toronto is the most important financial city. OR No Canadian city is more important financially.
   3. True
   4. True
   5. False. Toronto is the safest city in North America. OR No city in North America is safer than Toronto.

EXERCISE 1

- **Go to the CN Tower.** It's one of <u>the tallest</u> buildings in the world. From there you can get <u>the best</u> view of the city and countryside.
- **Drive along Yonge Street.** At 1,200 miles (1,800 km) it's <u>the longest</u> street in the world. For one weekend in July it's one of <u>the liveliest</u> too. Come and join 1 million others for the exciting Yonge Street Festival.
- **Visit PATH,** <u>the</u> world's <u>largest</u> underground shopping complex.
- **Explore the Old Town of York.** It has <u>the most historic</u> buildings in the whole city.
- **Take the Yuk Yuk Comedy Tour** of the Entertainment District—you'll have a good time on <u>the funniest</u> bus ride in town.
- **Visit the Toronto Zoo.** There's always something new and fascinating going on. Local people call it <u>the best</u> family outing in Toronto.

EXERCISE 2

1. the biggest
2. the smallest
3. the smallest
4. the coldest
5. the hottest
6. the coolest, the warmest, the most comfortable
7. The rainiest, The driest
8. the cheapest, the most expensive
9. the cheapest, the most expensive

EXERCISE 3

2. the most famous   **5.** the clearest
3. the heaviest   **6.** the fastest
4. the most popular   **7.** the longest

EXERCISE 4

Answers will vary.
   1. X is the most multicultural city I've ever visited.
      Y is the least multicultural city I've ever visited.
   2. X is the most comfortable place I've ever stayed.
      Y is the least comfortable place I've ever stayed.
   3. X has the friendliest (OR the most friendly) people I've ever met.
      Y has the least friendly people I've ever met.
   4. X is the most expensive trip I've ever taken.
      Y is the least expensive trip I've ever taken.
   5. X is the most attractive place I've ever seen.
      Y is the least attractive place I've ever seen.
   6. X is the most exciting team I've ever watched.
      Y is the least exciting team I've ever watched

EXERCISE 5

    Greetings from Toronto—the ~~beautifulest~~ *most beautiful* city I've ever visited. Yesterday we went to the CN Tower—the ~~more~~ *most* recognizable structure in all of Canada. From there you get the best view of the city—the different neighborhoods, the harbor, the fast traffic—it made my head spin! This is one of ^*the* most dynamic places I've ever visited! The restaurant was the most ~~expensivest~~ *expensive* I've ever seen, so we just enjoyed the view and then went to Kensington Market to eat. This place has the ~~baddest~~ *worst* crowds but the cheapest and the ~~goodest~~ *best* food we've had so far. We're staying in East Toronto. It's not the ~~closer~~ *closest* place to downtown, but it has some of ^*the* most historic buildings. In fact, our bed-and-breakfast is called 1871 Historic House. John Lennon slept here!
Love, Marissa

EXERCISE 6

A. 2. three
   3. restaurant . . . city
   4. district
   5. $295
   6. the least expensive OR 1600
   7. best

B. the most convenient: Hôtel Le Germain
the least convenient: Westin Harbour Castle
the most comfortable: Hôtel Le Germain
the most expensive: Hôtel Le Germain
the least expensive: Delta Chelsea
the biggest: Delta Chelsea
the smallest: Hôtel Le Germain

EXERCISE 7

B. 1. be~~st~~ view
   2. most expensive
   3. most interesting
   4. safe~~st~~ city
   5. least expensive
   6. nice~~st~~ places

EXERCISES 8–10

Answers will vary.

UNIT 22 (pages 307–318)

AFTER YOU READ

A. 1. d   **2.** e   **3.** b   **4.** c   **5.** a
B. 1. Thailand
   2. Australia
   3. a lower score than
   4. has scored a lot
   5. almost as good as
   6. nobody

EXERCISE 1

In the first basketball game of the season, the Comets beat the Lions, 90 to 83. The Lions played a truly fantastic game, but their defense is still weak. The Comets defended the ball much <u>more aggressively than</u> the Lions did.

Of course, Ace Hernandez certainly helped win the game for the Comets. The Comets' star player was back on the court today to the delight of his many fans. He was hurt badly at the end of last season, but he has recovered quickly. Although he did<u>n't</u> play <u>as well as</u> people expected, he still handled the ball like the old Ace. He certainly handled it <u>the most skillfully</u> of anyone on the team. He controlled the ball <u>the best</u>, shot the ball <u>the most accurately</u>, and scored <u>the most consistently</u> of any of the players on either team. He played hard and helped the Comets look good. In fact, <u>the harder</u> he played, <u>the better</u> the Comets performed. Watch Ace this season.

And watch the Lions. They have a new coach, and they're training <u>more seriously</u> this year. I think we'll see them play <u>better and better</u> as the season progresses.

EXERCISE 2

   2. doesn't fit as comfortably as
   3. supports the ankles as well as
   4. don't support the ankles as well as
   5. doesn't protect the feet as effectively as
   6. protects the feet as effectively as
   7. lasts as long as
   8. doesn't last as long as
   9. don't cost as much as

EXERCISE 3

   2. less aggressively than
   3. as aggressively
   4. as hard as
   5. the most effectively
   6. more consistently than
   7. more cooperatively than
   8. better
   9. longer
   10. less than
   11. the faster
   12. the faster

EXERCISE 4

   3. the slowest OR the most slowly
   4. slower than OR more slowly than
   5. the farthest
   6. faster than
   7. higher than
   8. the best
   9. the worst

EXERCISE 5

Last night was the last game of the season, and the Lions played the ~~goodest~~ *best* they've played for months. Both the Cubs and Lions play a great offensive game, but this time the Lions really played defense much more effectively ~~as~~ *than* the Cubs. Hernandez, the Cubs' star player, has been shooting more ~~aggressively and more~~ *and more* aggressively all season. But in last night's game, the more ~~aggressive~~ *aggressively* he played, the ~~most~~ *more* closely the Lions guarded him. Then, in the last two minutes, "Tiny Tim" O'Connell made the winning shot for the Lions. "He's less than six feet tall, but he runs ~~more fastly~~ *faster* than anyone else on the court," the Cubs' coach said. "O'Connell doesn't shoot as often ʌ *as* other players, but he's a lot more ~~accurately~~ *accurate* than the bigger guys." The Cubs played a great game last night too, but they just didn't play as ~~good~~ *well* as the Lions. Can the Lions play like this consistently? If so, they may be this season's new champion.

EXERCISE 6

A.
_4_ Exuberant King   _3_ Señor Speedy
_1_ Get Packin'   _2_ Wild Whirl
_5_ Inspired Winner

B. 2. Wild Whirl
   3. faster
   4. slowest
   5. faster
   6. slower and slower
   7. most

EXERCISES 8–10

Answers will vary.

PART VI From Grammar to Writing
(pages 319–320)

1

   I live in a (small) (comfortable) (one-bedroom) apartment with a (convenient) location (close) to school. The living room is my (favorite) room. It's (sunny), (warm), and (peaceful). Its (best) feature is the (old) (brick) fireplace, which I frequently use on (cold) (winter) nights. In the corner there's a (large) (soft) (green) couch. I like to sit there and read. Next to it is a (small) (wood) table with a (charming) (modern) lamp that I bought in town. It's a (cozy) living room, and I enjoy spending time there. It's an (ideal) room for a student.

2

See figure below.

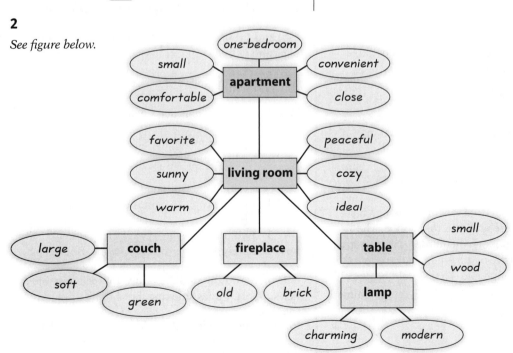

3

Words in parentheses fit into more than one category.

a. things that are big: large, enormous, huge

b. things that are small: little, tiny, (cozy), (cute)

c. things that look good: attractive, (cute), gorgeous, lovely, (cozy)

d. things that look bad: run-down, hideous, ugly

e. things that feel good: soft, comfortable, (cozy)

f. things that feel bad: hard, coarse, rough

4–6

Answers will vary.

AFTER YOU READ

A. OK: approve of, in favor of, permit
   Not OK: ban, illegal, prohibit
B. 1. Japan
   2. Austria
   3. Canada
   4. Zambia
   5. Austria
   6. Mexico
   7. The United Arab Emirates

EXERCISE 1

Re: Can't Stand <u>Seeing</u> Those Signs!

Posted by Grofumeur on February 16, 2011 at 15:30:03
I can't stand <u>seeing</u> all the new No <u>Smoking</u> signs. It's getting harder and harder to have a good time. Next thing you know, they'll ban <u>laughing</u>! <u>Eating</u> in a restaurant or <u>having</u> an espresso in a café is just no fun anymore! Junk food is worse than <u>smoking</u>. But I bet the government won't prohibit people from <u>ordering</u> burgers and fries for lunch!

Reply posted by Nuffsed on February 17, 12:15:22
Hey, Grofumeur—I'm against <u>smoking</u> in public places. I'm even in favor of <u>banning</u> smoking in apartment buildings. I don't get sick when my boyfriend has a Big Mac, but <u>sitting</u> in a room full of his cigarette smoke makes my hair and clothing stink. I'm really <u>enjoying</u> the new regulations.

Reply posted by Swissfriend on February 17, 20:53:11
Hi, Smokers! I am a member of Freunde der Tabak, a Swiss group of smokers and non-smokers. We always suggest <u>practicing</u> courtesy to non-smokers and tolerance of smokers. I enjoy <u>smoking</u>, but I dislike <u>inhaling</u> secondhand smoke. I don't see a problem with people <u>smoking</u> outside, and I'm against <u>banning</u> it.

Reply posted by Cleanaire on February 18, 9:53:11
Friend—Have you ever tried to stop <u>smoking</u>? If so, then you know you are addicted to nicotine. The younger you start <u>smoking</u>, the harder it is to quit. I definitely don't approve of <u>advertising</u> cigarettes or <u>selling</u> them to young people. That should be illegal!

EXERCISE 2

2. Staying
3. smoking
4. Exercising
5. starting
6. Not eating
7. eating
8. increasing
9. Not going
10. joining

EXERCISE 3

2. denied eating
3. enjoy running
4. go swimming
5. admitted (OR admits) being
6. avoids eating
7. mind exercising
8. are considering taking

EXERCISE 4

2. You can improve your health by quitting smoking.
3. I'm very happy about starting an exercise program.
4. This program gives you great ideas for solving health issues.
5. Now I'm proud of myself for swimming a mile every day.
6. They can help by listening to your concerns.
7. I ran my first 10K race without stopping.
8. You should ask a doctor before starting an exercise program.

EXERCISE 5

Day 1   I quit to ~~smoke~~ *smoking*! This was the first day of the rest of my life as a non-smoker. ~~Get~~ *Getting* through the day wasn't too difficult. I quit drinking coffee today too, and I think that helped. I used to enjoy ~~had~~ *having* a cigarette with a cup of coffee in the morning. But now I'm looking forward to ~~get~~ *getting* healthier.

Day 3   Today was harder. I called Dinah and admitted ~~wanted~~ *wanting* to smoke. She advised ~~takeing~~ *taking* deep breaths and staying busy. That worked. I have to resist ~~eat~~ *eating* too much. Gaining five pounds ~~aren't~~ *isn't* a big deal, but I don't want to gain more than that.

Day 5   I got through the workweek smoke-free. My boss definitely approves of the new me. She keeps ~~tells~~ *telling* me, "You can do it." I really appreciate ~~to have~~ *having* her support. I miss smoking, but I <u>don't</u> miss ~~to standing~~ *standing* outside in the cold just to smoke. I also don't mind ~~don't~~ *not* burning holes in my clothes!

Day 7 Dinah suggested ~~to go~~ *going* out to dinner, but I can't risk ~~be~~ *being* around smokers. Instead, we went ~~shoping~~ *shopping* and I bought a shirt with the money I saved during my first week as a non-smoker. Also, I'm happy about ~~have~~ *having* clothes that smell fresh! Not smoking has advantages.

EXERCISE 6

A. OK to Do: 2, 4, 6, 7
   Not OK to Do: 1, 3, 5
B. 2. stay the same   **4.** running
   3. complex carbohydrates   **5.** working

EXERCISE 7

B. 1. Smoking is bad for your health.
   2. Smoking causes health problems.
   3. Quitting is very difficult.
   4. He's opposed to smoking near other people.
   5. He's even opposed to **smoking outside**.
   6. She doesn't like seeing those signs.
   7. She used to enjoy **lighting up** after dinner.
   8. She plans on **quitting in** April.

EXERCISES 8–10

Answers will vary.

UNIT 24 (pages 334–343)

AFTER YOU READ

A. 1. c   **2.** d   **3.** a   **4.** e   **5.** b
B. 1. False. Lonely hasn't been successful in meeting people.
   2. True
   3. True
   4. False. Annie says that friendships take time to develop.
   5. True

EXERCISE 1

Annie advised me to join a club or take a class, and I finally did it! I decided to join the school's Outdoor Adventure Club, and I went to my first meeting last night. I'm really excited about this. The club is planning a hiking trip next weekend. I can't wait to go. I hope it won't be too hard for my first adventure. Last night they also decided to go rafting in the spring. At first I didn't want to sign up, but the leader was so nice. He urged me not to miss this trip, so I put my name on the list. After the meeting, a group of people asked me to go out with them. We went to a coffee shop and talked for hours. Well, I hoped to make some new friends when I joined this club, but I didn't expect everyone to be so friendly. I'm glad Annie persuaded me not to give up.

EXERCISE 2

   2. attempt to find
   3. warns single people not to leave
   4. urges them to use
   5. fail to plan
   6. plan to fail
   7. like to meet
   8. Ask two friends to read
   9. Tell them not to worry
  10. Begin to participate
  11. Ask friends to arrange
  12. advises people not to feel
  13. wants to be

EXERCISE 3

Answers may vary slightly.
   2. reminded Lily to get stamps.
   3. invited Mary to join them for coffee.
   4. agreed to come home by 10:30.
   5. forgot to go to the staff meeting.
   6. encouraged Lisa (OR her) to try once more.
   7. needs to use the car.

EXERCISE 4

You'd like to ~~making~~ *make* some new friends. Maybe you're at a new school or job, or, possibly, you have changed and the "new you" wants ^*to* meet new people. First, I strongly advise ^*you* to turn off your computer and TV. "Friending" people on Facebook just isn't the same as making real friends. And those people on that old show "Friends" aren't YOUR friends. You need ^*to* go out and interact with real people. Decide right now ~~to don't~~ *not to* refuse invitations. When a classmate or co-worker invites you for coffee, just say "Yes." Join a club and volunteer to ~~doing~~ *do* something. That responsibility will force you to attend the meetings. By doing these things, you will manage ~~meeting~~ *to meet* a lot of new people. But don't rush to become close friends with someone right away. Learn to listen. Encourage the person to ~~talks~~ *talk* by asking questions. Allow each relationship ~~develops~~ *to develop* naturally, and soon you'll have a group of people you're really comfortable with.

EXERCISE 5

A. 2. True

   3. False. She expected to have problems with her daughter. OR She wasn't surprised to have problems with her daughter.

   4. True

   5. False. They tried to understand her feelings. OR They were interested in her feelings.

   6. False. The girl OR the stepdaugher invited the man to go on a family vacation.

   7. True

B. 2. b   **3.** a   **4.** b   **5.** a   **6.** b   **7.** b

EXERCISE 6

B. 1. She **advised me to stay**.

   2. They **prefer to study** at home.

   3. Would you **like to leave**?

   4. We **encouraged her to join** a club.

   5. My parents **expect me to call** them tonight.

   6. He **said to park** here.

EXERCISES 7–9

Answers will vary.

UNIT 25 (pages 344–356)

AFTER YOU READ

A. 1. b   **3.** a   **5.** b
   2. b   **4.** c   **6.** c

B. 1. True

   2. False. People use them for many things.

   3. False. People of all ages use them.

   4. True

   5. False. She uses one to translate words.

   6. False. She uses it to look up book reviews.

   7. True

   8. True

   9. False. They are still expensive because of the monthly service charge.

  10. False. A lot of people don't like that people expect you to work and be available all the time.

EXERCISE 1

The telephone has really changed a lot in less than a century. From the 1920s through the 1950s, there was the good old-fashioned rotary phone. It had just one function, but it wasn't that convenient to use. Callers had to turn a dial to make a call. And it was too big and heavy to move from place to place. (Besides there was that annoying cord connecting it to the wall!). The 1960s introduced the touch-tone phone. It was much faster to place a call with it. You just pushed buttons in order to dial. With cordless phones, introduced in the 1970s, callers were free to move around their homes or offices while talking. Then came a really major change—hand-held cell phones. These were small enough to carry with you and you didn't even have to be inside to talk to your friends. But it wasn't until the invention of the camera phone that people began to use the phone to do more than just talk. And, that was nothing compared to today's multipurpose smart phones. People use them to do almost everything. What will the newest technology bring to the phone? It's hard to predict. But one thing is certain: It will be faster and smaller. And, as always, people will find uses for it that are difficult to imagine today.

EXERCISE 2

A. 2. d   **3.** a   **4.** e   **5.** c

B. 2. He took the bus in order not to be late.

   3. We turned off the phone in order not to get calls.

   4. She recorded her favorite TV show in order not to miss it.

   5. She went to the electronics store (in order) to buy a new phone.

EXERCISE 3

   2. to drive to Montreal

   3. to pass it

   4. to get more gas

   5. to exchange money

   6. to buy fruit and vegetables

   7. to have coffee

   8. to communicate with her

EXERCISE 4

   2. to use

   3. to spend

   4. to carry

   5. to watch

   6. to find out

   7. to own

EXERCISE 5

   2. early enough to call (her)

   3. too quickly for me to understand (her)

   4. well enough to pass.

   5. cheap enough for him (to get)

   6. I'm too busy to go (tonight)

EXERCISE 6

> to tell
> Click here ~~for telling~~ us how you've used your smart phone recently.
>
> I was riding my bike when I saw an accident. A car hit a truck, but it didn't stop. I used my
>   to
> smart phone ⌃ take a picture of the car and the license plate number. Then I used it to call the
>   use
> police. It was so fast and convenient to ~~using~~!   **Jason Harvey, England**
>
> I was at a great concert in Mexico City. I wanted to share the experience with my best friend
>   send
> back home. I picked up my smart phone and used it to make a video and ~~sending~~ it to my
>
> friend. Instantly my friend was "there" with me. Awesome!   **Emilia Leale, Italy**
>   not to
> I sell houses. I always use my phone in order ~~no~~ waste my customers' time. When I see an
>
> interesting house, I immediately send a photo. Then, if they are interested, I make an
>   too
> appointment for them. Without a smart phone, my job would be ~~to~~ hard to do.
>
>   **Andrea Cook, U.S.**
>   help
> Last night I used it to ~~helping~~ me make dinner. First, I searched online for a recipe. It was in
>   convert
> grams so I used a program to ~~converts~~ it to ounces. Then I used another program to create a
>   remind
> shopping list. When I returned home from shopping, I set the phone's timer to ~~reminded~~ me
>
> when to take the food out of the oven. While dinner was baking, I used the phone to listen to
>
> my favorite songs. I love this thing! It combines functions for work and play, and it's
> smart enough
> ~~enough smart~~ to do almost everything. Too bad it can't do the dishes, too!
>
>   **Kim Soo-Min, South Korea**

EXERCISE 7

A. 2. easy **4.** affordable
  3. thousands **5.** online
B. Items checked: 2, 3, 7, 8, 9

EXERCISE 8

B.

1. It's easy to use.

2. It's good to know.

3. It's cheap enough to buy.

4. It's light enough to carry.

5. She's available to work.

6. It's too hard to understand.

EXERCISES 9–13

Answers will vary.

AFTER YOU READ

A. 1. project
  2. universal
  3. anxious
  4. put off
  5. task
  6. discouraging
B. Items Checked: 2, 4, 5, 8

EXERCISE 1

A.

Like many students, Eva is a procrastinator. She keeps (putting off) her schoolwork. When she studies, she often stops <u>to go</u> for a walk in the park. She wants <u>to improve</u> her study habits, but she isn't sure how. Eva decided <u>to make</u> a list of things she needs <u>to do</u> every day. She always remembers <u>to make</u> her list, but she often forgets <u>to read</u> it. It's very discouraging, and Eva is worried about (getting) bad grades. Last night Eva remembered (reading) an article in the school newspaper about a support group for procrastinators. She thinks (being) in a group is a good idea. She likes (sharing) ideas with other students. Maybe it will help.

B. 2. False. She often goes for walks.
  3. True
  4. True
  5. False. She often forgets to read it.
  6. True
  7. True
  8. True

EXERCISE 2

2. starting
3. to study OR studying
4. finishing
5. making
6. doing
7. working
8. to do OR doing
9. to work
10. to do
11. making
12. being
13. to do
14. to improve
15. putting

EXERCISE 3

2. doing
3. starting
4. to do
5. to spend
6. doing
7. working
8. to take
9. to give
10. finishing
11. doing
12. joining

EXERCISE 4

3. Working on a long project is difficult.
4. It feels great to complete a job on time.

5. It's a good idea to reward yourself for finishing a project.
6. It's very helpful to be in a support group.
7. Meeting people with the same problem is good.

EXERCISE 5

2. meeting Todd
3. to come later. OR to be there tonight
4. taking too many breaks
5. listening to music
6. to go home
7. to give Eva a ride home
  to stay a little longer
8. to drive carefully

EXERCISE 6

For months I was thinking about ~~to go~~ *going* to a support group for procrastinators, but I kept putting it off! Last night I finally decided ~~going~~ *to go*, and I'm glad I did. I'm not alone! There were a lot of people there with the same problem as me. I expected them ~~being~~ *to be* boring, but they were really quite interesting—and helpful. I even knew some of the other students there. I remembered ~~to meet~~ *meeting* a few of them at a school party last year. I really enjoyed ~~to talk~~ *talking* to Todd, and before I left I promised ~~coming~~ *to come* again.

I have a math test tomorrow, so I really should stop ~~to write~~ *writing* now and start studying. See, I've already learned something from ~~to be~~ *being* in this group! I have to stop making excuses and start my work! NOW!

EXERCISE 7

A. 2. True
  3. True
  4. False. She now feels less anxious before tests.
  5. True
  6. True
B. Things Eva Does: 1, 3, 4, 6
  Things Eva Doesn't Do: 2, 5, 7

EXERCISE 9

Answers will vary.

EXERCISE 10

EVA: I remember meeting you.
TODD: I hope to see you here again.
PAT: I quit making excuses.

LEE: I decided to join the group.
UTA: I keep trying to change.
KAY: I can't afford to fail.
LEV: I finished writing my paper!
JEFF: I learned to start projects early.

EXERCISES 11–13

Answers will vary.

PART VII From Grammar to Writing
(pages 372–373)

1

2. but	**5.** but	**8.** or
3. and	**6.** and	**9.** and
4. but	**7.** and	**10.** so

2

2. or   **3.** but   **4.** so

3–6

Answers will vary.

UNIT 27 (pages 376–390)

AFTER YOU READ

A. 1. finally   **4.** maintain
2. reaction   **5.** fault
3. realize   **6.** impact
B. Tom: 2, 4
Sara: 1, 3
Tom and Sara: 5

EXERCISE 1

Positive self-talk can affect our thoughts, feelings, and actions. It can even make the difference between winning and losing. Top athletes not only compete against <u>one another</u>, they also compete against <u>themselves</u> when they try to improve their performances. Many athletes use self-talk to maintain their self-confidence and help <u>themselves</u> reach new goals. If you've asked <u>yourself</u> how Korean Olympic gold winner Kim Yu-Na can do those perfect jumps under so much stress, now you know it's probably because she's telling <u>herself</u>, "I can, I will, I am."

One sports psychologist believes that Olympic athletes are not very different from <u>one another</u>—they are all the best in their sports. When two top athletes compete against <u>each other</u>, the winner is the one with the most powerful positive "mental movies."

According to psychologists, ordinary people <u>themselves</u> can use these techniques too. We can create "mental movies" to help <u>ourselves</u> succeed in difficult situations.

EXERCISE 2

2. ourselves	**6.** herself
3. A: myself **B:** yourself	**7.** themselves
4. each other, myself	**8.** ourselves
5. ourselves	

EXERCISE 3

2. myself	**6.** itself
3. one another OR each other	**7.** themselves
	8. himself
4. yourselves	**9.** myself
5. one another OR each other	**10.** myself

EXERCISE 4

2. Tom cut himself (while he was shaving).
3. Sara smiled at herself (in the mirror).
4. Tom talked to himself.
5. Tom and Sara talked to each other (OR one another) (on the phone).
6. Sara drove herself (to the party).
7. Tom and Sara greeted each other (OR one another) (at the party).
8. Tom and Sara introduced themselves (to a woman at the party).

EXERCISE 5

Jan's birthday was Wednesday, and I forgot to
call him. I reminded ~~me~~ *myself* all day, and then I forgot
anyway! I felt terrible. My sister Anna said, "Don't be
so hard on ~~yourselves~~ *yourself*," but I, myself, didn't believe
her. She prides herself on remembering everything.
Then I finally remembered the article on self-talk. It
said that people can change the way they explain
problems to ~~theirselves~~ *themselves*. Well, I listened to the way
I talked to ~~me~~ *myself*, and I realized it sounded really
insulting—like the way our high school math teacher
used to talk to us. I thought, Jan and I are good
friends, and we treat each ~~other's~~ *other* well. One mistake
shouldn't impact our friendship that much. In fact,
he forgave ~~myself~~ *me* for my mistake right away. And I
forgave him for forgetting our dinner date two weeks
ago. Friends can forgive ~~themselves~~ *each other* OR *one another*, so I guess I can
forgive myself.

EXERCISE 6

A. 2. himself   **5.** herself
   3. yourself   **6.** ourselves
   4. herself   **7.** yourselves

B. 2. a   **4.** b   **6.** b
   3. b   **5.** a   **7.** b

EXERCISE 7

B.

   1. Sara looked at herself in the mirror.

   2. They felt proud of themselves.

   3. The job itself wasn't important to him.

   4. They met each other at work.

   5. We all told one another about our jobs.

   6. Tom helped himself to the food.

EXERCISES 8–12

Answers will vary.

UNIT 28 (pages 391–402)

AFTER YOU READ

A. 1. c   **3.** b   **5.** a
   2. e   **4.** f   **6.** d

B. 1. attack other dogs, get lazy
   2. of celebrities, with serious problems

   3. in their homes, on his ranch, on his TV program
   4. frightened dogs, the dogs' owners
   5. dog psychology is complicated, change takes time

EXERCISE 1

A.

Cesar Millan puts his running shoes on as soon as
he gets up in the morning. Then he wakes his dogs
up, and they all set out on their daily four-hour walk.
The exercise is part of Millan's dog therapy. Most of
these dogs were once dangerous, but now they are a
"family" that teaches problem dogs how to fit in and
get along in a group.

Millan's dream began on the farm in Mexico
where he grew up. There, he found out he had a
special ability with animals (his family called him
"El Perrero"). When Millan was thirteen, he told his
mother, "I'm going to be the best dog trainer in the
world." A few years later, Millan went to the U.S.
He was homeless for a while, but he never gave up
his dream. Finally, he found a job as a dog groomer.
On the job, Millan showed owners some ways to
calm their dogs down. Jada Pinkett (wife of actor
Will Smith) hired him and also paid for his English
lessons. After that, he was able to set up his own
business. Today the Dog Whisperer lives and works
on a 40-acre ranch with his pack of around 50 dogs
and many other kinds of animals.

B. 2. e   **3.** c   **4.** a   **5.** b   **6.** d

EXERCISE 2

   2. down   **10.** out
   3. on   **11.** out
   4. down   **12.** up
   5. ahead   **13.** back
   6. over   **14.** out
   7. out   **15.** out
   8. along   **16.** in
   9. out

EXERCISE 3

   2. put it on   **5.** pick her up
   3. turn it on   **6.** wake them up
   4. take it off

EXERCISE 4

   2. Set up the experiment. OR Set the experiment up.
   3. Carry it out.
   4. Sit down when you're done.
   5. Go on to page 26.
   6. Write up your reports. OR Write your reports up.
   7. Hand them in.

8. Take off your lab coats. OR Take your lab coats off.

9. Put them away.

10. Clean up the lab. OR Clean the lab up.

EXERCISE 5

2. got along
3. turned on
4. looked up
5. found out
6. carried out
7. calm down
8. made up
9. go away
10. passed away
11. keeps on
12. passing on

EXERCISE 6

For a long time, I looked ^for the right service dog
~~for~~. I almost gave ^up ~~on~~, but as soon as I met Barnie, I knew he was the one. The trainer had four puppies, and I picked out Barnie right away. Actually, he
^picked me out ~~picked out me~~. He walked over to my wheelchair and sat down next to me. After that, I didn't have to think it ^over ~~down~~ at all. I just said, "Come ^on ~~by~~, Barnie, let's go home."

When I started to train him, I was surprised at how fast he caught ^on ~~back~~. He learned to pick my keys up from the floor when he was only nine weeks old. Once I fell out of bed, so he started to wake ^up ~~on~~ before me. Now he stands next to me while I get up and get into my chair.

When we started school, he figured my schedule ^out ~~through~~ right away. After the first week, he would go to the right classroom and lie down. He stands up just before the bell rings. (How does he know how to do that?) When I need a book, he opens my book bag and ^takes it out ~~takes out it~~ for me! He really loves to take care of me.

Today, the famous Dr. Pepperberg dropped into my animal behavior class and brought an African gray parrot. At first, Barnie looked a little excited, but he calmed ^down ~~back~~ right away. I know I can always count on him.

EXERCISE 7

A. 2. handing out
3. look up
4. turn it off
5. keep up
6. dropped in
7. take off
8. pick out

B. 2. False. Terry is giving some reports to the students.
3. True
4. False. They're going to turn the music off.
5. True
6. True
7. False. It's time to take off the lab coats.
8. True

EXERCISE 8

B.

1. My service dog **picks them up.**
2. I'm **cleaning the lab up**.
3. I can't **figure it out**.
4. I'll **write it down** for you.
5. I'll **pick the music out**.
6. It always **calms me down**.

EXERCISES 9–11

Answers will vary.

PART VIII From Grammar to Writing (pages 403–405)

1

Dear Felicia,

Thanks for staying in my apartment next weekend and taking care of the dog. Help (yourself)[Felicia] to the food in the fridge—(you)[Felicia] can use (it)[food] all up if (you)[Felicia] want. (I)[Ted] rented some DVDs for (you)[Felicia]. (They're)[DVDs] on top of the TV. (I)[Ted] picked out some action movies. (I)[Ted] hope you like (them)[action movies]. The DVD player is easy to figure out. Just turn (it)[the DVD player] on with the remote control. But please remember to turn (it)[the DVD player] down at 11:00 P.M. My upstairs neighbor is very touchy about noise. There are just a few other things to remember. Red's friendly, but please keep (her)[Red] away from my neighbor's poodle. (They)[Red + poodle] don't like each other *(Red + poodle)* Her bowl is on the kitchen counter.

Fill it *(bowl)* up once a day with dry food. Please walk her *(Red)*

twice a day. When you *(Felicia)* go out, remember to turn on

the answering machine. It's *(answering machine)* in the living room. The

Sunday newspaper arrives at about 8:00 A.M. Pick it *(newspaper)*

up early—sometimes it *(newspaper)* disappears! Finally, when

you *(Felicia)* leave for work Monday, just leave the keys with

Mrs. Delgado next door. I'll *(Ted)* get them *(keys)* from her *(Mrs. D.)* when

I *(Ted)* get back.

Thanks again!

Ted

2

Dear Dara,

Welcome! I hope you enjoy staying here this week.
Here are a few things to keep in mind:

• The mail is delivered every day around noon.

You'll find ~~the mail~~ *it* in the mailbox in front of the

building. Please pick ~~up the mail~~ *it up* and put ~~the mail~~ *it*
on the dining room table.

• Feel free to use the air conditioner, but please turn

~~off the air conditioner~~ *it off* when you leave the house.

• There's plenty of food in the refrigerator! Please

feel free to use ~~up the food~~ *it up*.

• I'm expecting a few phone calls. If you're home,
could you please take a message? Just write

~~down the message~~ *it down* on the yellow pad in the top left
desk drawer.

I think you'll find that the apartment is pretty

comfortable. Enjoy ~~the apartment~~ *it* and make yourself
at home!

See you in a week

Rachel

3–6

Answers will vary.

AFTER YOU READ

A. 1. computers   **4.** sleeping
  2. teeth   **5.** books
  3. movies   **6.** bottles

B. 1. False. Passengers don't have to put
     computers and cameras through security
     X-ray equipment.
  2. False. A passport isn't always valid. OR A
     passport can expire.
  3. True
  4. False. You can't bring most types of cheese
     into the U.S. without a permit.
  5. True
  6. False. You don't have to have one, but it's
     recommended.
  7. False. To stay healthy on long flights,
     passengers must get up and move around.

EXERCISE 1

A.

BEN: Hello. I'm Australian, and I'm planning to
spend several weeks in Europe with my
family. I have some questions. First, <u>do we
have to get</u> visas to visit Italy?

CLERK: Not for a short visit. But you <u>can't stay</u>
for longer than 90 days without a visa.
Australians also <u>have to have</u> a Permit to
Stay for visits in Italy longer than eight
days. You <u>must apply</u> for the permit at a
local police station within eight days of your
arrival. It's a hassle, but you<u>'ve got to do it</u>.

BEN: Can my wife and I use our Australian driver's
licenses in Italy?

CLERK: You <u>have to carry</u> your Australian license,
but you <u>must</u> also <u>have</u> a valid International
Driver's Permit. And you<u>'ve got to be</u> at least
18 years old.

BEN: When <u>do we have to get</u> the IDPs? Is it
possible to apply for them when we get to
Europe?

CLERK: No, you <u>must apply</u> before you leave. The
Australian Automobile Association can help
you. You<u>'ll</u> also <u>have to get</u> an International
Insurance Certificate to show you have
insurance. They're very strict about this,
but you'll be able to get one at the car rental
agency.

BEN: We'll be in Italy in January. We don't have a
set schedule, so we haven't made any hotel
reservations. Is that going to be a problem?

CLERK: Yes, you<u>'ve got to have</u> reservations, even
in January—especially in major cities like
Rome, Florence, or Venice.

BEN: OK. Thanks a lot. You've been very helpful.

B. Necessary: 2, 7
  Not Necessary: 1, 4
  Against the Rules: 3, 5, 6

EXERCISE 2

Answers may vary slightly.

. . . and he has to give the house keys to Nora.

Ann has to buy phone cards online, and she has to buy batteries for the digital camera.

She doesn't have to call Pet Care or stop the mail for two weeks.

Sean and Maya don't have to pack clothes.

They have to choose DVDs and CDs for the trip, and they have to say good-bye to friends.

EXERCISE 3

1. **b.** can't start
   c. have to (OR have got to) check in
   d. Do . . . have to get
   e. we do
   f. have to (OR 've got to) do
   g. has to (OR has got to) park
2. **a.** can't weigh
   b. 'll (OR 're going to) have to pay
   c. Do . . . have to bring
   d. I do
   e. 've got to (OR have to) have
   f. 've got to (OR have to) go
3. **a.** 've . . . had to wait
   b. won't OR don't have to wait
4. **a.** 've got to (OR have to) call
   b. can't use
5. **a.** 've got to (OR have to) walk
   b. do . . . have to get
   c. can't sit
6. **a.** won't OR don't have to be

EXERCISE 4

2. must	7. must not
3. must not	8. must
4. must	9. must
5. must not	10. must not
6. must	11. must not

EXERCISE 5

2. don't have to bring	6. must not enter
3. must not play	7. don't have to leave
4. must not dive	8. must not stay
5. don't have to swim	

EXERCISE 6

We're on our way back to Australia. We ~~have~~ *had* to leave the hotel at 5:30 this morning, and then we had ~~got~~ to wait in line at the airport for hours. What a hassle! This flight is great, though. There are computers and TVs at every seat and hundreds of movies to watch. But Mom says we can't sit for more than three hours at a time because it's unhealthy, and we must ~~X~~ drink water every hour when we're not sleeping. This flight is 14 hours long, so we have to ~~taking~~ *take* care of ourselves. Thanks for the camping knife. I used it a lot in Italy, but before we left, I ~~has~~ *had* to put it in my checked suitcase because of the safety regulations. You ~~don't have to~~ *can't* OR *must not* bring knives in carry-on bags. Well, I *'ve* ^ got to get up and walk around again. Email me. We'll be on this plane for 10 more hours!

EXERCISE 7

A. **2.** False. She must drive faster.
   3. False. She must not OR can't stop.
   4. True
   5. True
   6. False. She has to wait. OR She can't pass.
B. **a.** 5   **d.** 6
   b. 3   **e.** 4
   c. 2   **f.** 1

EXERCISES 9–13

Answers will vary.

UNIT 30 (pages 422–433)

AFTER YOU READ

A. **1.** a   **2.** b   **3.** c   **4.** a   **5.** b   **6.** a
B. Items Checked: 2, 5, 6

EXERCISE 1

A.

It <u>wasn't supposed to be</u> a big wedding.
The Stricklands wanted a small, quiet wedding—that's why they eloped to Block Island, off the Atlantic Coast of the United States.

The ferry they took to their wedding site doesn't carry cars, so the Stricklands packed their bikes for the trip.

The couple found a lonely hill overlooking the ocean. The weather <u>was supposed to be</u> beautiful, so they asked the town mayor to marry them on the hill the next afternoon. They <u>were going to have</u> a small private ceremony in this romantic setting.

"When we got there, we found a crowd of cyclists admiring the view," laughed Beth Strickland.

When Bill kissed his bride, the audience burst into loud applause and rang their bicycle bells. "We <u>weren't supposed to have</u> 50 wedding guests, but we love biking, and we're not sorry," Bill said.

When they packed to leave the island the next day, Beth left her wedding bouquet at the hotel. She remembered it minutes before the ferry <u>was going to leave</u>. Bill jumped on his bike, recovered the flowers, and made it back to the ferry before it left.

"Cyclists <u>are supposed to stay</u> fast and fit," he said. "Now I know why."

B. 2. False. The weather was supposed to be beautiful.
   3. True
   4. True
   5. False. She remembered it before the ferry left.
   6. True

EXERCISE 2

   2. a. Were . . . supposed to do
       b. were supposed to deliver
   3. a. is supposed to start
       b. are . . . supposed to stand
   4. a. 're not (OR aren't) supposed to be
       b. isn't supposed to see
   5. a. 'm supposed to wear
       b. 's supposed to rain
   6. a. 's supposed to be
   7. a. were supposed to stay

EXERCISE 3

Answers may vary.

   2. Netta's parents were going to mail 180 invitations, but instead, they mailed 210 invitations.
   3. Netta was going to order a vanilla cake, but instead, she ordered a chocolate cake.
   4. Gary's parents were going to hire a rock band, but instead, they ordered a jazz band.
   5. Sophie was going to give the bridal shower on May 10, but instead, she gave it on May 20.
   6. Gary was going to plan the rehearsal dinner, but instead, Gary's parents planned it.
   7. Netta was going to find a photographer, but instead, Jack found a photographer.
   8. Jack was going to rent a limo, but instead, he rented a red sports car.
   9. Sophie was going to order flowers by April 1, but instead, she ordered them by April 15.
   10. Netta's parents were going to buy candles as bridesmaid's gifts, but instead, they bought clocks.

   11. Gary was going to send the wedding announcement to the newspaper, but instead, Jack sent it.

EXERCISE 4

Remember my old college roommate Gary? He's getting married tomorrow, and I'm the best man! He and his fiancée ˄*were* supposed to have a small wedding, but they ended up inviting more than 200 people! As best man, my role is mostly to be Gary's assistant.

For one thing, I'm ~~supposing~~ *supposed* to make sure Gary gets to the wedding ceremony on time—not an easy job for me. At first we ~~was~~ *were* going to hire a limousine and driver, but I decided to drive him there myself in a rented red sports car. I'm also supposed to hold the wedding rings during the ceremony. Then, at the end of the reception party, I'm supposed to ~~helping~~ *help* the newlyweds leave quickly for their honeymoon. They're going straight to the airport (I'm also ~~suppose~~ *supposed* to hold the plane tickets for them). They ~~are~~ *were* going to go to Hawaii, but they changed their minds and are going to Aruba instead. Oh! I just looked at the clock. I'd better sign off now, or I'll be late for the rehearsal dinner. I ˄*was* going to leave five minutes ago! By the way, Sophie, the maid of honor, will be there too. I've never met her, but she ~~supposes~~ *'s* (OR *is*) *supposed* to be very nice. I'll let you know how it goes!

EXERCISE 5

A. 2. False. She wasn't going to walk.
   3. True
   4. True
   5. True
   6. False. She walks behind the bride.
   7. False. They say "congratulations" to the groom. OR They tell the bride she looks beautiful.
   8. True
   9. True

B. 2. wasn't   **6.** is
   3. isn't   **7.** are
   4. aren't   **8.** are
   5. were   **9.** aren't

EXERCISES 7–9

Answers will vary.

UNIT 31 (pages 434–445)

AFTER YOU READ

A. 1. c   **3.** c   **5.** b
   2. a   **4.** a   **6.** c

B. 1. False. Temperatures might (OR may OR could OR will possibly) drop 11 degrees in Great Britain.
   2. True
   3. False. There might (OR may OR could OR will possibly) be stormy weather in France.
   4. True
   5. False. Western Europe is going to get warmer.
   6. False. Temperatures might (OR may OR could OR will possibly) be above 20 degrees Celsius in Rome.

EXERCISE 1

A.
ANNA: Are you going to drive to work tomorrow?
CODY: I don't know. I <u>might take</u> the car. Why?
ANNA: I just heard the local weather report. It <u>may snow</u> tonight.
CODY: Oh, then I <u>may have to</u> <u>shovel</u> snow before I leave. You know, I <u>might</u> just <u>take</u> the 7:30 train instead of driving. I have a 9:00 meeting, and I don't want to miss it. Do you have a class tomorrow morning?
ANNA: No, but I'm going to the library to work on my paper. <u>Maybe I'll bundle up</u> and <u>take</u> the train with you in the morning. And, let's try to go home together, too. <u>Maybe</u> <u>we could</u> <u>meet</u> at the train station at 6:00, OK? I'm taking the 6:30 train home.
CODY: I <u>might not be able to</u> <u>catch</u> the 6:30 train. My boss said something about working late tomorrow. I <u>may be stuck</u> here until 8:00. I'll call you tomorrow afternoon and let you know what I'm doing.
ANNA: OK. I'll get some takeout on the way home. Do you mind eating late?
CODY: No. I definitely want to have dinner together.
ANNA: Me too. Definitely.

B. CODY:
   Certain: 4, 6, 7
   Possible: 1, 2, 3, 5
   ANNA:
   Certain: 1, 2, 5, 6, 7
   Possible: 3, 4

EXERCISE 2

2. could   **5.** 'm going to
3. might   **6.** may
4. may not   **7.** might

EXERCISE 3

2. She may (OR might) buy some notebooks before class.
3. She's going to go to a meeting with Mrs. Humphrey at 11:00.
4. She may (OR might) have coffee with Sue after class.
5. She's going to go to work at 1:00.
6. She may (OR might) go shopping after work.
7. She may (OR might) take the 7:00 train.

EXERCISE 4

2. they won't   **5.** It could be
3. It could be   **6.** It could be
4. It could

EXERCISE 5

Every few years, the ocean near Peru becomes warmer. This change is called El Niño. An El Niño ~~maybe~~ *may* cause big weather changes all over the world. The west coasts of North and South America might have very heavy rains. On the other side of the Pacific, New Guinea might ~~becomes~~ *become* very dry. Northern areas could have warmer, wetter winters, and southern areas ~~maybe~~ *may* become much colder. These weather changes affect plants and animals. Some fish ~~mayn't~~ *may not* survive in warmer waters. They may die or swim to colder places. In addition, dry conditions could ~~causing~~ *cause* crops to die. When that happens, food may get very expensive. El Niño does not happen regularly. It may happen every two years, or it might not come for seven years. Will El Niños get worse in the future? They could ~~be~~. *may OR might OR could* Pollution ~~will~~ increase the effects of El Niño, but no one is sure yet.

EXERCISE 6

A. 2. local   **5.** driving
   3. warmer   **6.** Saturday
   4. bring a jacket

B.
Friday
     Possible: Sunny, Low 50s
Saturday
     Certain: Sunny, Windy
     Possible: 62°
Sunday
     Possible: Cold, Windy, Snow flurries

EXERCISE 7

B.

1. B: It could.

2. B: They could be.

3. B: I might not.

4. B: They may not.

5. B: I might be.

6. B: It could be.

EXERCISES 8–10

Answers will vary.

UNIT 32 (pages 446–460)

AFTER YOU READ

A. 1. A: amazed **B:** method
   2. A: position **B:** salary **A:** advertisement
   3. A: millionaire **B:** encyclopedia

B. 1. c   **3.** a   **5.** b
   2. b   **4.** b   **6.** c

EXERCISE 1

A.

Sherlock Holmes studied the note: *The Red-Headed League does not exist anymore.*

"This <u>could be</u> serious," Holmes told Wilson. "What can you tell us about your clerk, Vincent?"

"Vincent <u>couldn't be</u> dishonest," replied Wilson. "In fact, he took this job for half the usual salary because he wanted to learn the business. His only fault is photography."

"Photography?" Holmes and Watson asked together.

"Yes," replied Wilson. "He's always running down to the basement to work with his cameras."

Wilson left soon after that.

"Wilson's clerk <u>might be</u> the key to this mystery," Holmes told Watson. "Let's go see him." An hour later, Holmes and Watson walked into Wilson's shop. The clerk was a man of about 30, with a scar on his forehead. Holmes asked him for directions. Then he and Watson left the shop.

"My dear Watson," Holmes began. "It's very unusual for a 30-year-old man to work for half-pay. This clerk <u>has to have</u> a very special reason for working here."

"Something to do with the Red-Headed League?" Watson asked.

"Yes. Perhaps the clerk placed that ad in the newspaper. He <u>may want</u> to be alone in the shop. Did you look at his legs?"

"No, I didn't."

"He has holes in his trouser knees. He <u>must spend</u> his time digging a tunnel from Wilson's basement. But where is it?"

Holmes hit the ground sharply with his walking stick. "The ground isn't hollow, so the tunnel <u>must not be</u> here in front of the shop. Let's walk to the street in back of Wilson's shop."

B. Possible: 2, 4
   Almost Certain: 3, 5, 6

EXERCISE 2

2. must not   **6.** could
3. might   **7.** might not
4. might   **8.** may
5. could

EXERCISE 3

2. Vincent must not be the clerk's real name.
3. He must not know about the poster.
4. He must be very clever.
5. Number 27 Carlisle Street must be City Bank.
6. Vincent's tunnel must not lead to those shops.
7. Vincent's tunnel must lead to the bank.
8. The tunnel must be almost finished.

EXERCISE 4

2. That's got to be wrong.
3. It's got to cost less than $50.
4. It can't be after 11:00.
5. It's got to be nearby.
6. You can't be tired.

EXERCISE 5

2. might not   **5.** must be
3. might   **6.** might not
4. might   **7.** must OR might

EXERCISE 6

2. could be   **7.** could be
3. couldn't be OR can't be   **8.** Could . . . be
4. couldn't be OR can't be   **9.** couldn't be OR can't be
5. Could . . . be   **10.** could . . . be
6. couldn't be OR can't be   **11.** could be

EXERCISE 7

The main character, Molly Smith, is a college ESL teacher. She is trying to find her dead grandparents' first home in the United States. It may ~~being~~ *be* in a nearby town. The townspeople there seem scared. They could ~~be~~ have a secret, or they ~~must~~ *might* OR *may* OR *could* just hate strangers. Molly has found some letters hidden in an old encyclopedia that might lead her to the place. They are in Armenian, but one of her students ~~mights~~ *might* translate them for her. They ~~got to~~ *'ve got to* OR *have to* be important because the author mentions them right away. The letters must contain family secrets. I'm sure of it. Who is the bad guy? It couldn't be the student because he wants to help. It ~~must~~ *might* OR *may* OR *could* be the newspaper editor in the town. That's a possibility.

EXERCISE 8

A. a. 5   **c.** 6   **e.** 4
  b. 1   **d.** 3   **f.** 2
B. Possible: 3, 9, 10
  Almost Certain: 2, 4, 7, 8
  Fact: 1, 5, 6

EXERCISE 9

B. 1. must be   **4.** may, can't
  2. have to   **5.** may, 's got to
  3. might   **6.** has to

EXERCISES 10–12

Answers will vary.

PART IX From Grammar to Writing
(pages 461–462)

1

I am writing this letter of complaint (because) one of your cashiers treated me rudely. (Even though) I was sure I paid her with a $20 bill, I only received change for $10. I told her that there was a mistake. She said "You're wrong" and slammed the cash drawer shut. I reported the incident. Later the manager called. He said the cashier was right (because) the money in the cashier drawer was correct.

(Even though) the mistake was mine, I believe the cashier behaved extremely rudely. (Although) I like Hardy's, I also value polite service. I hope I won't have to change restaurants (because) I can't get it there.

2

  2. contrasting idea
  3. comma
  4. must also
  5. doesn't have to
  6. sender's
  7. before
  8. colon

3–6

Answers will vary.

Single-User License Agreement

System Requirements

WINDOWS®	MACINTOSH®	BOTH
• Windows XP/Vista/7	• Mac OS X (10.4 & 10.5)	• 256 MB RAM minimum (512+ MB recommended)
• Intel Pentium processor 1GHz or higher	• PowerPC & Intel processor 1GHz or higher	• Monitor resolution of 1024 x 768 or higher
• Internet Explorer® 7.0 or higher OR Firefox® 2.0 or higher	• Safari® 2.0 or higher OR Firefox® 2.0 or higher	• Sound card and speakers or headphones
		• 500 MB hard disk space
		• 10X CD-ROM drive or higher
		• Adobe Flash 8 plug-in or higher
		• Internet Connection: DSL, Cable/Broadband, T1, or other high-speed connection
		• Microsoft® PowerPoint Viewer

Installation Instructions

WINDOWS®

• Insert the CD-ROM into the CD-ROM drive of your computer. On most computers, the program will begin automatically.

If the program does not begin automatically:

• Open "My Computer."

• Right-click on the CD-ROM icon.

• Click on Open.

• Double-click on the "Start" file. Leave the CD-ROM in the computer while using the program.

MACINTOSH®

• Insert the CD-ROM into the CD-ROM drive of your computer.

• Double-click on the CD-ROM icon on your desktop.

• Double click on the "Start" file. Leave the CD-ROM in the computer while using the program.

Note: The original CD-ROM must be in the CD-ROM drive when you use the program.

TECHNICAL SUPPORT

For Technical Product Support, please visit our support website at www.PearsonLongmanSupport.com. You can search our **Knowledgebase** for frequently asked questions, instantly **Chat** with an available support representative, or **Submit a Ticket/Request** for assistance.